# What others are sa

"With striking detail an[...] is nothing if not compelling. Every bit [...] and shocking as can be imagined, *Cherries: A Vietnam War Novel* is a refreshingly honest account of a life few of us would ever choose to live - and, thus, should feel fortunate that we don't have to. A highly recommended read."
**- Karynda Lewis, <u>Apex Review</u>**

"As an avid reader of many historical memoirs, both fiction and autobiographical, rarely have I found one as in depth and revealing as Mr. Podlaski's work....undoubtedly this scene is occurring today with veterans returning from the Middle East. By reading Cherries, you will get the knowledge and feel of what it was like in Vietnam, stories that many memoirs of this war collectively failed to mention! *Cherries* is a highly recommended read!"
**- Bernie Weisz, Vietnam War historian**

"The author is a terrific storyteller. This book flows so well, you will not be able to go to sleep without reading the next chapter. Podlaski has you in the palm of his hand."
**- William E. Peterson, <u>Missions of Fire and Mercy</u>**

"Once I started reading John's *Cherries,* I could not put it down - intense, provocative, mesmerizing, emotional, and heartfelt. You will feel as if you are right there in the platoon with the grunts as they live through the terrors, the dangers, the trials and tribulations, and sometimes the joys and humor of being at and in war. One 'read' will not be enough. You will want to pass through the pages of `Cherries' more than once just to savor the up close and personal story again."
**- Jerry Kunnath, author**

"I could never have written this amazing book. When I told my story, I had to fill it full of the emotion I felt but never expressed in Vietnam. Podlaski, on the other hand, managed to stay true to the original experience by telling his story with little or no emotion. The effect is that Cherries is an excellent primer for students of the

Vietnam War that are interested in the grunt experience. The last chapter alone is well worth the price of this book."
- **Terry P. Rizzuti, <u>The Second Tour</u>**

"Podlaski takes readers on a gritty, visceral tour of 'Nam through the eyes and lives of the men who fought the war and who, at any given moment could be thrust into harm's way. We are right there with his characters on patrol, setting up claymores, walking point, and above all trying to stay alive. This is the day-to-day life story of the men who started out as "cherries" and tried to stay alive."
- **Jeffrey Miller, <u>War Remains</u>**

"I am not a person who generally reads war novels, but I really could not put this book down. I read it twice! The author takes you along on the journey where you get to watch the main character grow from a scared young kid just out of high school into a savvy, skilled leader in the span of a year, and he helps you to understand how it happens."
- **Janet Shupe**

"I just finished reading *Cherries*. I could so relate to many things in this well written novel. I know what it is like to see so many lose their life. I helped carry them out onto the choppers. My 3rd week over in the "Nam" we were choppered in on helicopters to be a blocking force. Four hours later, we went from 250 or so to only 79. The rest were killed or wounded. It was hard for me to get through this book due to the tears that brought back so many similar episodes."
- **Joel Lee Russell, <u>Escaping Death's Sting</u>**

"*Cherries* weds a matchless sense of dramatics with the ability to tell a marvelous story. You have staged excellent, realistic action with convincing effect. You paint your main characters and supporting characters with passionate realism. *Cherries* has a compelling magnetic quality. Parts of it are unforgettably conceived and written."
- **Manuscripts International, 1987**

# CHERRIES
A Vietnam War Novel

# CHERRIES
## A Vietnam War Novel

By

John Podlaski

Copyright 2010 John Podlaski
All rights reserved.
Revised Edition

EAN-13: 978-1-4528-7981-9
ISBN: 1452879818

Cover design @ 2010
http://Digitaldonna.com

Barbara Battestilli, Copy / Content Editor
Interior design by Nicole A. Podlaski
Editorial Coordination by Janice J. Podlaski

Printed in the United States of America

Without limiting the rights under the copyright reserved above, no part of this publication may be reproduced, stored in or introduced into a retrieval system, or transmitted in any form or by any means (electronic, mechanical, by photocopying, recording or otherwise) without the prior written consent of the copyright owner and the publisher of the book.

The scanning, uploading, and distribution of this book via the Internet or by any other means without the permission of the author is illegal and punishable by law. Please purchase only authorized printed or electronic editions and do not participate in or encourage electronic piracy of copyrighted materials. Your support of the author's rights is appreciated.

While *Cherries* is largely a work of fiction, many of the events and anecdotes described in the novel are based upon the actual experiences of the author. The places and units mentioned were real and did exist. All characters portrayed are fictional, and any resemblance to actual persons, living or dead, organizations, events, and locales, are entirely coincidental.

## Acknowledgements:

I would like to thank all who have encouraged me to complete this novel, your persistence, and faith in me kept my spirit alive. A special thanks to *Cherries* Editor, Barbara Battestilli, and cover designer, Donna Casey - their hard work, attention to detail, and patience has made *Cherries* what it is today. I am also deeply indebted to my daughter, Nicole, who spent hundreds of hours typing and laying out the interior of this book. Finally, and most importantly, thanks to my wife, Janice - without her love, sacrifices, and support over the years, this work would not exist.

For Janice and Nicole – Thank you for making my dream come true! *Cherries* is dedicated to you both.

"There's many a boy here today that looks on war as all glory, but boys, it is all hell."

-**General William T. Sherman, Address, 1880**

God Bless America's soldiers – Past, Present, and Future

# CHAPTER ONE

Many U.S. Army personnel began their journey to South Vietnam from the Overseas Processing Terminal in Oakland, California. It was 1970, and just outside the compound, hundreds of hippies and former soldiers picketed and protested against the war. They targeted those soldiers who were dropped off by cabs and heading toward the main gate. Dozens of Military Police officers (MP's) were holding the protesters at bay and created a clear path through the mob. The crowd tossed flowers at the passing soldiers and chanted loudly for peace. Some in the group pleaded with the new arrivals, trying to convince them to quit the military and refuse to fight in the war. Most soldiers passed through the gates without hesitation; however, a few did stop on occasion to seriously reconsider their options.

John Kowalski had passed through the main gate earlier in the day and was wandering through the massive facility, a converted airplane hangar, in search of friends from his Advanced Infantry Training (AIT) Platoon at Fort Polk, Louisiana. The entire training company had received orders for Vietnam, and each person was to report there after a thirty-day leave.

The PFC was maneuvering his six-foot frame through a maze of cubicles. The rubber soles of his newly acquired combat boots squeaked loudly as he crossed through these quiet sections. An earlier coat of wax on the red tile floor also made it appear wet and slippery; John stepped along cautiously as if walking on ice.

The twenty-foot-by-twenty-foot cubicles comprised of eight-foot high pieces of plywood and two-by-fours rose up toward the thirty-foot ceiling. Each of these enclosures held a dozen bunk beds; sleeping youths occupied many while awaiting their turn to fly off to war.

His efforts to find a familiar face within the maze were unsuccessful, so he began a quarter-mile hike to the other side of the building, which was set aside for recreation.

He found the area to be quite active and noisy compared to the morgue-like atmosphere he had just left. Here, there were hundreds of highly enthused soldiers, all dressed in jungle fatigues – the green machine! Rows of pool and Ping-Pong tables cluttered the area, but were barely visible through the crowd. It was obvious that many of the players were having difficulty with their games, the close proximity of the many spectators inhibiting their movements.

John stood on the outskirts looking in. He removed his olive green baseball cap and ran his hand over the light brown stubble length of hair. Satisfied that it was again growing, he replaced the cap and traced a line across the rough four-inch long scar on the left side of his neck - the consequence of a confrontation with some escaped felons during Basic Training. His hazel eyes continued to scan the many faces, hoping to spot someone he knew.

Suddenly, a player on a nearby Ping-Pong table backed up quickly to return a hard serve from his opponent. He tripped over a spectator, creating a domino effect on the group standing behind him. A young soldier, who looked fifteen at most, found himself sprawled out on top of the adjacent pool table. The remaining balls were scattered, some falling to the floor along with a stack of ten-dollar bills. All of this happened as an African-American soldier, twice the kid's size, was preparing to take an advantageous shot.

He became enraged. "You dumb motherfucker! I had this game in the bag."

"It wasn't my fault," the kid cried out in a shaky voice, "I got pushed up here by those other guys," he pointed to those soldiers standing around the Ping-Ping table.

"Pushed, my ass," the black soldier challenged, "you just cost me a hundred bucks. So pay me what I lost, and I'll let you slide."

"I don't have that kind of money," the skinny kid replied, climbing down from the table.

"Let me see your wallet, and I'll take what I think is fair," the behemoth threatened, reaching behind the kid to snatch the wallet from his back pocket.

The kid pushed back into the crowd, attempting to escape the reach of the thoroughly pissed off Army private.

"It was an accident!" he hollered. You're not taking my wallet!"

The crowd tightened, everyone shifting to find the best-unobstructed view of the altercation. Trapped, the kid had no place to go.

"Come on brothers, are you with me?" The soldier called out to a group of black comrades standing nearby. "This white boy owes me some money!"

His supporters wielded cue sticks and pool balls and moved toward the petrified youth.

A group of white soldiers took a step forward, ushering the young kid behind the pack and quickly engulfing him. One of them stated in a southern drawl, "Why don't you boys pick on somebody your own size?"

Hearing this, the leader of the black group turned to his followers and said giddily, "I guess we have to kick a whole lot of white ass to get my money."

"Yeah, let's do it. We're with you!" his followers chanted.

Individuals within the black group were now beating the palms of their hands with the thick end of the cue sticks and lofting pool balls lightly into the air. Two of them broke ranks and moved toward the white group.

Suddenly, a dozen MP's forced their way through the crowd before either of the two groups could strike a blow.

"Let's break this shit up!" The MP Sergeant ordered, separating soldiers, and shoving them out of his way. He stopped, facing the leader of the black group. "What is this all about?" He asked.

"That skinny white boy owes me a hundred bucks!" The black private protested, pointing out the alleged culprit. "All I want is to get my money back and these white boys want to come over and start some shit with us."

"That's bullshit, sarge," the southern soldier responded. "There was an accident. The kid fell on the pool table and fucked up their game. He doesn't owe him shit."

"Is that correct, private?" The sergeant fixed a deep, piercing stare at the kid.

"Yes, sergeant," he replied in a trembling voice, "there was a lot of shuffling and pushing behind me. I found myself sprawled out on top of the pool table. I couldn't help myself."

"That's a damn lie!" The black soldier protested. "I couldn't give a fuck about the game; I'm pissed because he pocketed my money during all the commotion."

"I don't think he has the balls to do something like that," the sergeant replied after sizing him up. "I'd be willing to forget this incident if everybody would just walk away and return to what they were doing."

"What are you going to do if we don't? Send us to Vietnam?" a voice called out from the crowd.

The taunt was enough to change the atmosphere of the group and some began to laugh and snicker.

"Yeah, you'll still go to Vietnam, but you may spend a few weeks in our stockade first," the sergeant growled.

The crowd started to disperse, and soldiers moved away, resuming their activities from before the interruption.

The black soldier shifted back and forth from one foot to the other, his expression changing as he tried to compose himself.

The MP Sergeant looked at him. "Well, what's it going to be?"

"I'll let it go, man. I don't need any bad time on my record. I want to serve my year and get back home."

"Then, do I have your word that you won't bother these guys anymore?"

"Yeah, man, you got my word." He turned and walked back to the pool table and his waiting friends. The kid had vanished.

Once everything was back to normal, John turned and moved toward yet another undiscovered part of the large building. After a few minutes, he heard a familiar voice call out, "Hey, Polack!"

He stopped and looked around for the source.

"Hey, Polack, over here," a tall, lanky soldier with red hair, freckles, and a broad, toothy grin called out again. He was pushing through the crowd and waving frantically.

John's face lit up in recognition, returning the man's wave with a wild one of his own.

"Bill," he called loudly after seeing his close friend from training.

They embraced warmly like long-lost relatives.

"Polack, you son of a bitch, am I ever glad to see you." Bill, as gaunt as a scarecrow, slapped John's back a few times.

"I am too, Bill. How the hell are you?"

"I'm good. When did you get here?"

"About four hours ago. What about you?"

"I got here yesterday."

"Why did you come so early, Bill? Didn't they have a flight available when you needed it?"

"I didn't fly. I took a train instead."

"You rode a train all the way here from Tennessee? Are you shitting me?"

"Nope, I've never been on a plane in my whole life, Bill admitted sheepishly. I was so afraid of the thought of flying that I checked into the train schedule and found that I had to leave a couple of days earlier to get here on time."

"How did you get home from Fort Polk?"

"I rode in by bus."

"Damn Bill, you missed out on three days of your leave just because you're afraid of flying?"

"Yeah, I know, I know. Don't remind me."

"Now you don't have a choice. There aren't any trains or buses that go to Vietnam."

"I know and thought hard about that on the way here. I've got a perfect solution – I'll get drunk and pass out. That way, somebody could carry me on board."

"Maybe they can just give you a shot or something to relax."

"No thanks. I've had enough shots for now! Once I got here, they gave me a worse physical than the one I had to take when the Army first called me up. Here, they move you along like an assembly line."

"I know what you mean. And that paper work was really a bummer - there must have been twenty-five forms to fill out!"

Bill produced a wide smile, "Yeah. That part took me almost an hour."

5

The two young men commiserated about the humiliating experience of having to strip down to their underwear and stand in long lines of strangers from all over the country–herded along like cattle.

"What did you think when you saw the ten doctors on each side of the line giving everyone shots with those air-powered guns?"

"I didn't have time to think. I just blindly followed everyone else and hoped for the best."

"A guy in front of me moved his arm just as the doctor pulled the trigger," Bill commented. "When the blood squirted out, I almost shit myself."

"The shots weren't too bad - kind of felt like a punch in the arm. But, as I'm standing here now, they're starting to ache pretty damn bad," John said.

"It'll feel better in a few hours. I feel fine today," Bill volunteered.

"The thing I didn't like was having to ship all our own clothes and stuff home. What a hassle! And these new jungle fatigues and boots we're in are just like those in basic training."

"Yeah, but it was all worth it. Don't we look good?" Bill asked, striking a pose.

John would not have been more surprised if Bill's ball cap came off his head and twirled in the air by itself. Bill flexed his arms and posed like a body builder in the final pose of a competition. His head quivered as he strained his muscles. Bill's face was stern and solemn as he concentrated on this show of strength.

John suddenly burst out laughing "Damn Bill, what was all that about? It looked like an advertisement for Scarecrows Incorporated." He stopped chuckling before continuing, "All you needed was a bit of hay sticking out in the right places, and you'd have nailed it." John pointed to Bill's face, "I especially like how you managed to cover your front teeth with your lower lip. You did look scary, but it also seemed like you had a mouth full of snuff."

"Okay. Okay. You've had your fun for the day, Polack." Bill looked more hurt than embarrassed.

Bill Sayers, raised in the back woods of Tennessee, spoke with a heavy southern drawl. He was the third eldest of nine children who shared everything from chores to clothes while growing up on the family farm. He had never experienced the feeling of receiving new clothes–all he had ever worn were hand-me-downs from his older brothers. When the Army issued him the first five sets of new fatigues, he treated them as if they were made of gold.

"C'mon Bill. I'm just giving you a hard time and didn't mean anything by it." John wrapped his arm over his buddy's shoulder and pulled him tightly. "You have to admit - it was funny as hell!"

Both men shared a hearty laugh.

"Have you found a bunk yet?" Bill asked.

"Not yet."

"Great, then come with me, I have a cubicle all to myself."

"Lead the way."

John followed Bill to the other side of the building and then through the maze of cubicles for another ten minutes before reaching the smaller room with six bunk beds.

"Looks like it'll be nice and quiet here."

"Shit, it is now. Yesterday, you couldn't hear yourself think."

"And why was that?" John inquired.

"I had to share this cube with ten other guys who have been together since Basic Training. All they did was party the whole night."

"What happened to them?"

"They left on the first flight this morning. So I guess it's just you and me until new neighbors move in."

"I'm okay with that. Have you seen anyone else from our AIT Platoon yet?"

"Yeah, matter of fact, yesterday, I bumped into Joel McCray and Larry Nickels. Do you remember them?"

"I do. Where are they?"

"They left this morning with those other guys. And you'll never believe who else was with them."

"Who?"

"Sergeant Holmes."

"No shit? I thought he was returning to Fort Polk this week to start training a new platoon of recruits."

"That was his original plan, but he had his orders changed during his leave and volunteered for a second tour."

"Why did he do a fool thing like that?"

"He told me that he was fed up with the civilians and all the hippies. He said that while he was on leave, people spit on him and got into his face yelling that he was teaching soldiers to be baby killers and then sending them off to Vietnam. He said there was not a day gone by without somebody picking a fight with him. After the cops had jailed him for the second time for disorderly conduct, he went and signed the papers."

"The world is filled with jerks. Too bad, he had to volunteer for Nam to get away from it all. Did you know he was wounded during his first tour?" John asked.

"Yeah, I remember him telling the story about that big Tet offensive in '68. He got some shrapnel in his back from a mortar round, but also said that the fighting is not at the same level as it was in 1968 or earlier, so we all have a good chance of making it home in one piece."

"I hope that's true.

In the AIT Company, everyone liked Bill because he always had something good to say about others. Stories told about life in the big cities fascinated him to no end. It was difficult for him to imagine doing things that many city folks took for granted as part of their everyday lives. He walked everywhere, including the three miles each way to school and back. In fact, the first time Bill had ever ridden a bike was in the Army.

Bill and John became very close while serving together in the Army. They had developed a friendship that made it easy to confide in one another on sensitive issues. John had promised to visit Bill in the hills of Tennessee one day, but only if Bill agreed to visit him in Detroit. Bill was ecstatic and could not wait; he continued to remind John periodically of this agreement.

All the excitement of the day was beginning to take its toll. Both were tired and struggling to stay awake.

"I had it rough last night." John began, "My mother gave me a going away party yesterday. All of my close friends and relatives were there. After dinner, we all sat in the living room and talked while the news was on TV. Everyone quieted down when a bulletin came on from Vietnam. It seems some outfit ran into an ambush. They showed helicopters burning. Dead and wounded soldiers were carried past the camera, and the commentator sounded so nervous. The women looked over at me and started crying. They all ran over and hugged me."

"Damn," Bill said with a sympathetic look upon his face.

"Well you know me." John continued, "I put on the brave act and told them that nothing was going to happen to me while I was in Vietnam. I told them that we'd all be back in this same living room in a year to laugh off those worries."

"What happened then?"

"Everyone started to leave for home before it got too emotional. When everyone left, I went up to my bedroom and tried to sleep, but just couldn't. I kept thinking about that news story and got all shaky and nervous."

"Polack, you aren't alone in that feeling. I'm scared too."

Both sat quietly for a few moments.

John lay back on his bunk and glanced to his watch. It was 3:30 in the morning. He thought about everything that had happened since leaving Detroit only fifteen hours earlier. Everything seemed to be "hurry-up-and-wait."

On the flight to California, he had been the only military passenger. The flight attendants and fellow passengers had made him feel special. When they heard he was en route to Vietnam, they bought him drinks, offered him magazines and candy, and wished him luck on his tour. He was very proud and felt honored by the way he was treated. His fellow passengers respected him, and not one person had treated him as Sergeant Holmes had been treated.

"Hey Polack, get your lazy ass out of that bunk!" Bill shook him a few times.

Startled, John jumped up from the bed quickly, bumping his head on the frame of the upper bunk.

"Damn you, Bill, you scared the shit out of me," he grumbled, rubbing the top of his head. John looked at his watch and noted that it was 1330 hours.

"Jesus, Bill, its one-thirty. When did you get up?"

Bill looked at his watch, "about six hours ago."

"Why didn't you get me up sooner?"

"Hell, I'd have been wasting my time. I know you city boys like your sleep. You would sleep all day long if somebody let you. Besides, it wasn't necessary for both of us to check the shipping manifest for today."

"What did you find out?"

"Both of our names are listed, and we're leaving for Vietnam at ten o'clock tonight."

## CHAPTER TWO

"This is your captain speaking," the voice announced on the public address system within the Pan American jet, "we will be landing in Bien Hoa, South Vietnam, in about forty minutes. They are reporting sunny skies, temperatures of 97 degrees and 100% humidity."

Whoops and cheers erupted from the military passengers. "Welcome to Hell," someone called out.

The captain continued, "As you know, we've passed through several time zones since leaving California, so let me take this opportunity to get you all up to date. First, there is a time difference of thirty-one hours between Vietnam and the west coast of the United States. For example, in Oakland where many of you started your journey, it is 8:30 on Friday morning. And right now in Vietnam, it's Saturday, August seventh, and 4:30 in the afternoon."

Again, some comments referring to a time machine and blasting into the future echoed from the rear seats.

"After we touch down, we're asking everyone to remain in their seats until the plane comes to a complete stop. There will be no need to panic and rush for the doors as this airport is in one of the more secure areas of South Vietnam. It is very safe where we are landing and nobody is in danger. So sit back, relax, and enjoy the scenery.

"On behalf of the crew, we hope you have enjoyed your flight. We do wish you the best of luck while you are here in Vietnam, and God's speed for a safe return home. Thank you for flying Pan American Airlines."

"Yeah right, like we had a choice," one of the soldiers uttered loudly to his companion across the aisle.

John was looking at his watch and trying to do the math in his head. "Bill, do you know it took us almost twenty-six hours to get here?"

"Hard to believe isn't it? You may also want to think about us being on the other side of the world from Tennessee. It just blows my mind."

"I thought China was on the other side. Didn't you ever hear people say that if you dug straight down in your backyard, you'd end up in China?"

"Who is going to do a damn fool thing like that?"

"Nobody is. It's just a saying that I grew up with."

"You city folk have some strange notions about things!" Bill returned to watch the scenery passing below the cabin window, hoping to see something more than just clouds and ocean.

Prior to leaving Oakland, an Army Doctor had given Bill some tranquilizers to take prior to departure. On the first leg to Hawaii, he sat in a half-comatose state in the window seat next to John. The effects had worn off an hour before landing in Hawaii, and after fully regaining his senses, Bill found flying to be rather enjoyable. He would tell everyone that his favorite part of flying was the takeoff, and how he enjoyed the same sensation as the astronauts must have felt when they left for the moon.

During this long flight, he had spent most of the time looking out the window, enchanted by the view from that height. It was a new world to him, and he savored every minute.

Bill grabbed John by the arm and pulled him toward the window. "Look, Polack, you can see land," he said excitedly.

John leaned over Bill's legs to see for himself. The word spread quickly and everyone started crowding the windows for their first look at their destination. After flying over water most of the time, it was a pleasure to see land below.

From fifteen-thousand feet, Vietnam appeared as a vat of shimmering colors. Bright blue threads snaked through shades of green, brown, and yellow-colored earth. A large mountain chain was visible in the distant northwest and seemed to cut the country in half. It became quiet throughout the cabin as the laughter, talking and singing suddenly ended. The steady roar of four jet engines continued but was unnoticed as every passenger fixated on the scenery unfolding below.

As the altitude of the plane gradually dropped, the vistas below changed in shape, color, and became more recognizable. Soon, the sprawling city of Saigon and its neighboring villages took shape and grew in size as the jet approached and flew overhead. Cars and trucks appeared as they inched along the roads. On the final approach for landing, the tiny, ant-like moving dots took the shape of thousands of people moving about.

The plane landed smoothly and taxied toward the terminal. A few moments later, it stopped abruptly and the engines began their dying throes. There was an absolute hush on the plane, and the rapid heartbeats of two-hundred new arrivals hammered in unison.

Suddenly, a loud noise erupted in the front of the plane when the cabin door slid open. Everyone on board was fidgeting about, trying to get a better look at the doorway.

An Air Force Major walked through the opening; he was dressed in his best Class-A uniform with several rows of battle ribbons proudly displayed over his left breast. Following him inside were two Army Captains, dressed in green jungle fatigues and baseball caps. The trio walked up the aisle, stopping at the forward flight attendant station.

They stood for a moment, surveying the new arrivals. The major stepped to the side, lifting the microphone from the mounting plate on the wall.

"My name is Major Brown and joining me are Captains Willis and Sharkey. We welcome you to Bien Hoa Air Force Base in the Republic of South Vietnam." All eyes fixed upon the major as they listened intently.

"Our job today is to get you men off this plane, through Customs, and finally loaded onto buses that will transport you to the Reception Center. We want to complete this portion of your in-county training safely and in an orderly manner. After disembarking this aircraft, I expect to see everyone joined up and standing in four perfect ranks out on the tarmac. When we are certain that everyone is present, we will then proceed to the baggage area inside the civilian terminal. There, you will secure your duffel bags and proceed directly to the area marked 'Customs'. The officials will have you empty the contents of your bags onto counters and perform a search of your body. The MP's will be looking for drugs and any other illegal contraband that you may be trying to smuggle into the country."

At that moment, many soldiers exhibited some nervousness. Some frowned and rolled their eyes. Others stirred anxiously in their seats with a panicked look upon their faces.

The major continued, "If anyone is concealing contraband, then I strongly suggest you drop it in your seats as you leave this aircraft. There will be no questions and nobody will come looking for you afterwards. This is also your only warning. Once outside, there are no second chances. If arrested, we will take you to LBJ – which is Long Binh Jail for you Cherries. There, I can guarantee you will serve some hard time for your foolishness.

"When you clear through Customs, you will then exit the terminal and board the awaiting buses. They will transport you to the 90th Replacement Center in Long Binh, which is about a three-mile drive. There, you will begin final in- processing and assigned to your new in-country unit.

"At this time, I would ask that all officers aboard, please stand up and begin to disembark at the front door."

As they moved up the aisle way, John and Bill noticed a few items left behind on the seats. Bags of weed, pills, and other unidentifiable items lay openly or tucked between cushions.

Bill and John shuffled down the aisle toward the front of the plane. "Look at this stuff. Do you think these people carried it with them all the way from Oakland? I seem to recall that some of us were searched before getting on the plane."

"No, I don't think so, Bill. It would have been too risky in Oakland. The guys must've bought this stuff during our three stops along the way. There were a lot of shady characters in those terminals, and I remember seeing a lot of money flashed around."

"You're right, now that you mentioned it. I can remember overhearing some people talking on our stopover in Guam. They were talking about having a big party once they settled into their new digs, but I didn't think it would be with grass and drugs."

"Shit, Bill, dope users are on the rise. This stuff is getting really popular back home and more people than we know are turning to it. Just give me a beer or a mixed drink and my cigarettes and I'll be happy."

"I'm with you there, partner. I wonder if anybody is going to try and smuggle some dope into the country."

"Your guess is as good as mine."

Each person walked out of the air-conditioned plane, hesitating briefly on the top step of the boarding ramp as the full impact of hot and humid air engulfed him. For a moment, it was difficult to breathe. Some made a feeble attempt to re-enter the plane, but the rush of exiting personnel pushed them back out.

There was a green hue outside as rays of silvery sunlight reflected from everything colored olive drab green: helicopters, planes, gun emplacements, and buildings with sandbagged walls surrounding them.

Dozens of helicopters were lifting off and landing in areas next to the runway. Small green, single-seat Piper Cub airplanes and larger Phantom Fighter jets were also moving about and taxiing toward different areas of the airport to wait in lines for their takeoff.

Bill and John cleared Customs easily and walked out to the waiting buses. The vehicles were identical to those used during training on the American bases and were painted olive green like everything else around, with one distinct difference - there were no glass windows. Instead, bars and chicken wire covered each framed opening.

The two close friends took a seat in the first row behind the driver.

"Why is all this shit covering the windows instead of having glass?" John asked the driver.

"It's there to protect the passengers from grenades or any other foreign objects that might be thrown in from the side of the road," he answered.

"Protect the occupants? It gives me the feeling of being a criminal on the way to prison."

"We are in prison, my man," the person behind John said with a smile. "Think about it. We're all locked up in this country for the next year and there's nothing we can do about it but serve our time."

"Yeah, you right!" Some of the other passengers agreed.

Once the buses loaded, the drivers closed the door and started the engine.

Two MP jeeps pulled alongside, stopping next to the lead bus. Each had long fifteen-foot whip antennas swinging from the two rear corners and dual M-60 machine guns mounted to a cross bar behind the front seats. The soldier standing behind the guns was busy loading them and ensuring they were in proper working order while the other guy talked casually into the handset of the radio.

"Look at the Rat Patrol jeeps!" John exclaimed.

"What's a Rat Patrol jeep?" Bill asked.

"Don't you remember seeing them on TV when we were young? They were always kicking the shit out of the Germans in Africa during the Second World War."

"You know I never had a TV," Bill said quietly.

"Oh yeah, I forgot. Just take my word for it, Bill - they were a bad ass outfit."

The procession of five buses began to move, and both gun jeeps raced to the head of the line and fell in. As the convoy picked up speed, red dust from the road swirled through the air, making it difficult to breathe - the horrible residue immediately coating everything. As if on cue, the new arrivals began choking and gasping for clean air. The passengers quickly pulled out handkerchiefs or used shirts to cover noses and mouths in an attempt to filter some breathable air from the thick red fog.

The convoy appeared to be traveling through a corridor. Both sides of the road had a ten-foot high barbed wire fence running alongside. Hundreds of small, straw-roofed huts, about the size of a single room lakeside cabin in the states, stood as far back as they could see. The barbed wire fences made it appear as if the area was either a prison or a refugee center.

Every person they passed appeared to be very old. Some were in front of their huts, sitting on the ground or cooking over open fires. Others simply stood near the fence and watched the parade of buses pass; every one of them was chewing something and spitting a brown liquid onto the ground.

"Those people are all chewing tobacco!" Bill exclaimed.

"That's not tobacco," the driver volunteered, "it's the juice from betel and nuts."

"What the hell are betel and nuts?" John asked.

"The Areca nut grows wild in the husks of some trees around the country. These people cure the nut and slice it into sections. For chewing, they wrap a few slices in betel leaf and add a lime, cloves or anything else to improve the bitter taste. When taken like that, the stimulant causes a hot sensation in the body and heightened alertness, although the effects vary from person to person. However, most of them mix other shit with it to get high, too."

"You mean like dope?" Bill asked the driver.

"Yeah, exactly like dope. Most of these people are high all the time. They wouldn't be able to stand it otherwise."

"Just look at all those folks by the wire. They remind me of the cows back home, all of them standing along the fence and chewing their cud. Their heads turn as you pass and they keep watching you until you are long gone."

The driver laughed, "That's original."

The convoy approached a tight right turn, and each bus slowed to complete the maneuver. Several groups of villagers were standing at the corner waiting for the traffic to clear. Just then, John grabbed Bill by the arm and pointed out the window. "Bill, take a look at that!"

Speechless, they continued to stare at the sight greeting them.

A group of seven women, each appearing to be close to a hundred years old, was standing on a corner, waving to the buses as they passed. Their wrinkles were deep and wide, their skin dark and shriveled like prunes. It appeared that most were heading home after working in the fields, since they were carrying rakes, hoes, and shovels. Two of them balanced long poles on their shoulders with large bamboo baskets attached to each end. They are wore black nylon pants and oversized shirts, covered with dried mud and stains. All of them wore straw conical hats that helped to shield their faces from the strong rays of the sun, and they were all smiling broadly.

Many were toothless or had only a few teeth left in their mouths. All looked as if they had mouths filled with black licorice. Their lips, gums, teeth, and insides of their mouth looked like posters from the Cancer Foundation, warning against the dangers of smoking.

"That's what happens when you chew those betel nuts all your life," the driver explained.

Bill and John could only look at each other and shake their heads in disbelief.

"Daaaaaaaaaaaamnnnnn!" John finally said in one long drawn out breath.

Further up the road, young children were everywhere. Most were small boys of pre-school age.

"Hey GI, you souvenir me cigarettes, candy, you numba one," they called, running along the side of the road to keep up with the buses.

Some of the people on the bus felt sorry for them and began flicking cigarettes through the chicken wire windows. This resulted in several scuffles as each group began to zero in on the tossed tobacco sticks, fighting each other to claim the prizes.

In the background, behind the packs of fighting boys, stood the little girls, not any older than eight years or so. Some held half-naked babies in their arms and others shouted at the fighting youths. A few of them even entered the fracas and began to pull the boys apart, appearing to scold them.

"Why are all the little girls holding babies?" John asked the driver.

"Those little girls help raise the family, cook, and clean around the hut while their parents work in the fields."

"That's so sad," both responded together.

Every human being passed so far on the convoy was either old or very young. There were no teenage boys hanging around on the corners, no young or middle-aged men walking around in the villages.

At another turn, the buses slowed down again. One corner had a small outpost shaped like a triangle. Large bunkers were at each corner of the complex; machine gun barrels poked through several of the gun slits. A twenty-foot high tower and spotlight stood guard in the center of the compound. Loops of barbed wire and walls of sandbags encircled the small base. Overall, about twenty Vietnamese soldiers moved about the compound. It was unlikely that any of them weighed more than a hundred pounds.

"Look at those guys; they're only kids."

"Shit, Bill, we're not much older ourselves."

"Yeah, but we can put in our year and go home. These poor guys probably live up the road apiece and will have to continue fighting this war long after we're gone."

"I guess you're right, Bill. I just can't imagine having to fight a war in my own neighborhood back home. It's got to be hard keeping focused on a day-to-day basis when you don't know if your property will still be there, or if your family is okay after a firefight. What a life of hell!"

Five minutes later, the bus made a left turn and slowed to a crawl as it approached a gate straddling the road. It reminded the young soldiers of Fort Apache, as portrayed in old western movies. A sign over the gate read, "Welcome to the 90th Replacement Battalion - Long Binh".

# CHAPTER THREE

As the buses unloaded, a trim and muscular Army Captain stood on a platform, patiently waiting for the group to get into some type of military formation. His folded arms rested against his chest, allowing his bulging biceps to inflate the end of his rolled up fatigue jacket sleeves. He continued to shift his two-hundred pound, rock solid frame from one foot to the other, appearing both impatient and nervous. His deep tan and unblemished complexion accented his straw- colored hair and blue eyes. His green jungle fatigues were heavily starched and sharply creased, fitting like an outer skin – a real candidate for a U.S. Army recruiting poster! After five minutes, he turned on the microphone and began to speak.

"Good evening, gentlemen," he began. "I'm Captain Richards, and I'd like to welcome all of you to the 90th Replacement Battalion. As I call out your name, fall out into the building behind me. There, you will exchange your greenbacks for Military Payment Certificates (MPC), which is the currency used by Americans in this country. Greenbacks are illegal in Vietnam, and possession of any after you clear this area is a court martial offense. After completing your money transfer, find an empty bunk in one of these six barracks." He pointed out the buildings across the street and behind the formation.

"Tomorrow there will be shipping formations at 0800, noon and 1600 hours. These readings are mandatory and everyone must attend. Those of you called out tomorrow will move on to your new units. The rest of you staying behind will work on projects around the center. Until that time, you will be on your own and free to use all the facilities available to you. Are there any questions?"

Scanning the formation, there are no hands raised. "Okay, now listen up for your name."

The 90th Replacement Battalion was a large camp, measuring two miles long by one-half mile wide. Bunkers alternated with towers on the perimeter. To their front were varied configurations of razor sharp barbed wire, stretching out for at least five-hundred feet. The six-foot high protective barrier resembled tangled spools of lethal thread. The small flares interspaced throughout awaited combustion when the engaged trip wire pins were pulled from the device, illuminating the immediate area in the dark of the night. Deadly claymore mines, positioned randomly around the perimeter served as a first line of defense. Controlled remotely, detonators are accessible within each bunker; two quick squeezes on the "clacker" will blow the mines. Small metal cans full of loose stones bobbed in the wind; a sudden pull on the wire caused the cans to clang out a warning to the bunker guards.

The barracks were single-story, green buildings and closely resembled their cousin buildings in the states. There was, however, one exception – no glass windows - just like in the buses. Instead, mosquito netting covered each opening. In the event of a rocket or mortar attack, these openings would provide additional exits for quickly vacating the building. The roof overhung sufficiently to keep rain from coming through the net windows.

John stood waiting for Bill in the shade of a palm tree, just outside the money-changing building. The late afternoon sun hung low in the royal blue sky but was still strong enough to make standing outside of a shaded area uncomfortable. When Bill finally exited, the two of them proceeded through the ninety-five degree heat toward the first barracks.

They entered and luckily located two beds, side by side, at the far end near the back door. The two friends tossed their duffel bags onto the bare mattresses and flopped down beside them.

"Well, John, what are we going to do now?"

"You feel up for a walk to scout this place out?"

"Lead the way." Bill worked his way out of the bed and onto the dirty plywood floor.

They exited the building and walked down the four steps leading to the road, stopping briefly to look over the lay of the land.

"Let's find out why all those people are hanging around in the street." John suggested, pointing in that direction.

They walked up the road and came upon a large purple building - the sign on the door read, 'Alice's Restaurant'- a reference to singer Arlo Guthrie's 1967 hit folk song.

"Will you take a look at this?" John asked excitedly. Latching onto Bill's arm, he pulled him toward the building. "It's a goddamn restaurant, right here in the middle of a war zone. Let's go inside and check this out."

"Okay, I've got your back."

Once inside, they found the restaurant divided into three sections: a dining room, a game room, and a bar. They hesitated for a moment in the doorway taking it all in.

"How about getting something to eat?" Bill asked. Patting his stomach, he continued, "I'm starved!"

"Cool. I'm kind of hungry too."

They sat at a table in the middle of the dining room; a young Vietnamese girl quickly offered them menus. She was about four and a half feet tall, with long, flowing, silky black hair. She wore black silk pajama bottoms under a knee-length powder blue dress; slits extended on both sides from her hips down. She was so tiny that she couldn't have weighed more than eighty pounds. She stood by the table with an order pad and pencil in hand, smiling politely, awaiting their order.

Both quickly scanned over the single page menu framed in black leather and covered with clear plastic. Items listed were hamburgers, hot dogs, fries, barbecued chicken, coleslaw, ice-cold soda, and beer.

It only took a few seconds before they were ready to order.

"I'll have a hamburger and fries." John said, handing the menu back to the server.

"I'll have the same," Bill chimed in.

"What do you want on your burgers? We have tomato, onion, ketchup, and mustard."

"Everything for me, please."

"Me too," Bill added.

"What would you like to drink?"

"What kind of beer do you have?"

"Falstaff and Black Label is all we have."

"Ewww!" The men responded with sour expressions on their faces.

The server saw that neither of them was happy with the selections. "I'm sorry, but this is all we have," she apologized

John pondered over the choices. "I never tried Falstaff beer, so I guess I'll try one of them."

"A beer is a beer, and I guess we shouldn't be fussy. Make it two of them there Falstaff's." Bill raised two fingers into the air.

"Okay, I'll be back in a minute with your beer, but the food will take a little longer." She left to take the order to the kitchen. Her waist-length hair waved at them with each step, swinging gently from side to side.

"You should be ashamed of yourself, Bill."

"What did I do now?" Bill frowned, looking confused.

"Did you hear that chick talk? You were born and raised in the states, and this Vietnamese girl speaks better American than you do."

"Shit, you call that American? I speak excellent American and her accent isn't anything close to mine." They both laughed.

The atmosphere in the restaurant was a refreshing change. It was so peaceful; a person would find it difficult to believe a war was even going on outside the perimeter.

As they might have expected, the décor inside of Alice's Restaurant catered to the peace-loving hippie movement. Posters of rock stars and the concert at Woodstock hung from the dirty white pine walls. Black neon lights helped to enhance the psychedelic posters and made the bright colors stand out. Gold - colored beads hung in the doorways and crackled like pebbles dropping onto the cement floor when someone passed through them. A strong smell of incense permeated the air; several chimneys of smoke climbed lazily to the dimly-lit ceiling at various locations throughout the building. The aroma was somewhat pleasant, and did an excellent job of covering the stench of cigarette smoke, and spilled beer. A jukebox played a variety of music, changing periodically from hard rock to soul music and even an occasional country western song.

Suddenly, something interesting caught John's eye. "Bill, there are slot machines in the next room!"

"Wow, I've never played one before."

"Neither have I. Let's go and try one of them before the food gets here."

They jumped up and hurried over to the bank of nickel machines. Once there, neither of them had an idea of how to load their paper money into the machines because there was only a coin slot available. The new military payment certificates were all in paper, including the denominations less than a dollar.

A nearby player observed their dilemma and volunteered, "Go over to the cashier window. They'll change your monopoly money for tokens."

"Thanks!" Both soldiers replied in unison and crossed the floor toward the cashier window.

They exchanged a five-dollar MPC note for one-hundred nickel tokens and walked up to one of the ten machines. Playing three tokens a pull and winning a few here and there, they were only able to play on the machine seven minutes before losing all their coins. Disappointed, they returned to the restaurant table to find their food and beers waiting.

It was twilight outside when they exited the restaurant. Dim lights, hanging from the front of each building enabled them to see in the fast-approaching darkness.

Further up the road, the sound of music, cheering, and loud whistling made them curious enough to investigate. After pressing through the crowd, to their amazement, they found a seven-member band performing on a stage. Three female dancers were half-naked and slowly removing the rest of their outfits. The surrounding bleachers overflowed with cheering soldiers; most were on their feet and roaring their approval.

"Oh my God," Bill hollered above the noise. His mouth opened wide and his jaw dropped to his chest, exposing rows of pearl white filling-free teeth. His mouth moved up and down, trying to speak words, but nothing came out. He closed his mouth again and swallowed hard. "Come on, Polack, let's go find us a seat," Bill finally managed to spit out in between his heavy breathing.

There were no seats available anywhere so the two of them migrated to an area between the stage and bleachers, joining other excited youths that were tightly packed into the small, crowded space.

"Do you believe this?" Bill asked. "This sure is the first time I've ever seen anything like this."

"You mean seeing the half naked strippers or the live band?" John joked.

"I've never seen a naked lady in person before."

"So what's the big deal? These Asian girls aren't shit. I've seen guys in Basic Training with bigger tits."

"I did too, but they didn't affect me the same way. How often will we be able to see something like this?"

"Now, how in the fuck am I supposed to know that?"

Bill was unable to respond. He stood rock-solid, hypnotized by the strip tease taking place upon the stage. The crowd in front of the stage tightened up and pulsated forward as more men arrived and tried to force their way in for a better view of the show.

Pandemonium broke out when one of the girls was completely naked. The audience erupted in catcalls, whistling, waving fists into the air, clapping hands, and whooping it up, the bleachers sounding as if they were going to collapse from the impact of hundreds of feet stomping loudly on the wood boards.

When the other two girls were also naked, the three of them began to dance wildly, gyrating in different directions and moving from one side of the stage to the other. Each of them made obscene gestures and teased the audience. After a full minute of individual flaunting, they all returned to center stage, slowly arching backwards and pumping their hips to the beat of the wild song. There was nothing left to the imagination now and many in the audience were freaking out; some soldiers had to restrain their friends in order to prevent them from rushing the stage and grappling the girls.

The band had written this wild song; none of the Americans had ever heard it before. The rhythm was contagious and sounded like something out of a King Kong movie, inducing the girls to gyrate and work themselves into a sexual frenzy. Most of the men in the audience enjoyed this new sound, finding it difficult to watch the show without gyrating to the beat themselves.

When the number finally ended, the girls quickly dashed off stage, and entered a portable dressing room. The musicians set their instruments to the side and joined the women in the small room. The audience was still in a high state of excitement and now realizing that the concert was over, began to clap their hands and chant for an encore. Several minutes elapsed and not one person had left the area; the chanting and clapping continued in hopes of convincing the band to return for one last song.

The dressing room door finally opened, and the musicians burst out, running across the stage to their instruments. Seconds later, the three girls reappeared, dressed now in different colored silk robes; all using towels to wipe away sweat. The audience roared its appreciation.

The lead guitarist began plucking out soft notes to quiet the crowd. The center dancer of the three picked up a microphone and smiled at the crowd. "We are 'The Crescent' from the Philippine Islands, and we want to thank all of you for attending our concert. This will be the final song of the evening and is dedicated to all of you. Be safe and good luck!"

Suddenly, the guitar tempo changed and the band joined in, the dancers swaying from side to side. This song was heard many more times in various in-country concerts during the many months to come. The crowd quieted and the girls began singing 'The Green, Green Grass of Home'. The sad song stimulated memories of home and of those left behind. The rowdiness had ceased and the atmosphere changed drastically to one of calm and sentiment. Many in the audience were singing along and swaying sideways to mimic the singers on stage.

Bill and John left before the end of the song in order to beat the rush back to the barracks.

When arriving, they found most everybody asleep, except for six people down on the far end of the building. Two of them were sitting on John's bunk. When approaching the group, they stopped talking and looked up to the new arrivals.

"How are you guys doing? My name's John and this is Bill. Seeing as you're sitting on my bunk, do you mind if we join you?"

One of them, appearing to be the leader of the group, spoke up, "Hell no, we don't mind. Come on and have a seat. This is Dan, Billy, Paul, Mike, Joe, and I'm Steve," he said, pointing them out when saying their name. "We're just shooting the shit."

This was the group's second night in the Replacement Center, and therefore, they knew their way around the basecamp. It was an opportunity for John and Bill to learn more about their temporary home. When interrupted, Paul had been in the middle of a story about the massage parlor on the next block. For the benefit of their new acquaintances, he started over from the beginning.

"It was a real bitch, man. They had twelve tables in this room. You strip in this little back closet, hang your clothes on a hook, and walk out with a towel wrapped around your waist. I got on the nearest table where this forever-smiling chick was waiting for me. There were at least nine other guys getting massages at the time. Man, that chick had magic fingers. In the fifteen minutes, she worked on me; it felt so good that I almost fell asleep. She was just about finished working on my legs when, get this, she asks me if I wanted a hand job."

Everyone laughed.

"Go on, Paul, don't stop now," said one of the guys on the bunk.

"Well you know that sounded pretty good to me." Paul continued, "I never had a chick do that to me before, so I asked her how much, and she tells me twelve bucks."

"Twelve bucks," Joe blurted out. "Shit, I'll beat you for twelve bucks."

The laughter was so intense that it was difficult for the men to hold back the tears in their eyes.

"Come on, guys," Paul pleaded. "Let me finish."

It took a few minutes for the group to regain their composure. Finally Dan volunteered, "Go on, Paul. We'll try to control ourselves."

"Okay, well I told her that I only had five bucks in my wallet, so I'd come back another day. Then she says, 'No sweat, GI, I do for five dorrers'. Shit, I thought that was a bargain, so I told her okay. Now, instead of taking me somewhere else that was more private, she pulled my towel off right then and there and grabbed hold of me."

Dan and Billy elbowed each other in the ribs; Joe slapped his knee and started chuckling. Paul looked at them incredulously and continued, "That was the last thing in the world I expected. Man, I jumped right off that table, embarrassed as all hell, and snatched back my towel, wrapping it around my waist. She looked hurt and some of the other people were looking over at us. I caught my breath, leaned over, my mouth inches from her ear, and told her calmly that I did not want her to do this right here in front of everyone. She smiled – looked straight into my eyes and asks me if I was a Cherry boy."

The small group could not take anymore and began to howl and roll around on the two cots. The racket began waking some sleeping soldiers; they scowled at the group and told them to keep it down. Nobody wanted to start any trouble so the group apologized and continued to converse in a lower tone.

"I don't believe it. Our own Paul chickened out - poor thing couldn't handle the pressure," Dan said sarcastically.

Paul shot back coldly, "If you think you're such a bad ass, then why don't you go try it tomorrow. Show everybody what you have?"

"That'll be the day I pay some chick five bucks to beat my meat." Dan stated, nodding his head affirmatively and looking at the rest of the group for support.

"Yeah, you probably do it every night too, don't you?" Paul retorted.

Joe interceded, "Goddamnit, Paul. Don't get bent out of shape. You know we're just fucking with you."

Paul sat there and fumed. It would take him a few moments to compose himself and allow the angry color to drain from his face.

The group quickly changed the subject and began talking about other topics for the next couple of hours. As they were conversing,

John could not help but notice the diverse regional accents and slang terms he was encountering for the first time in his life. It both fascinated him and made him feel a long way away from his home in Detroit.

During one of the discussions, Dan informed Bill and John of the radiophone in a building next to the PX. The MARS station allowed a person to call home for a small fee. It was not a telephone, and both parties had to use proper radio procedures and military etiquette, such as saying "over" when one party finished talking, before opening the channel for the other to reply. Bill and John agreed to look into it the following day.

In the morning, the first manifest included the names of those six soldiers from the late night muster. Assigned to the 101st Airborne Division, they would be traveling north to a place called Phu Bai. Somebody in the crowd stated that the 101st was in dire need of replacements as the North Vietnamese Army (NVA) regulars were kicking their asses in a valley called the A Shau. Rumor had it that entire platoons were lost during those hard-core firefights.

After all the names on the manifest are read, Bill and John left quickly to avoid any work details and headed straight for the MARS station, anxious to place a call home. Instead, they found a long line of prospective callers and observed several pages of names posted on the door - a waiting list. Neither had any idea how long it would take to rotate through the list, but added their names to it, just in case they were still at the Replacement Center when it was their turn.

With nothing else to do until the next reading in a couple of hours, both decided to walk around the center. They found an outdoor movie theater, another restaurant, a swimming pool, post office, two basketball courts, baseball diamond, and the notorious massage parlor. It was like visiting a recreation center or youth camp, with the only sign of war being the bunker line and barbed wire.

After the noon manifest reading, those remaining soldiers filled in the holes and tightened up the formation. Several Non-Commissioned Officers (NCO's) weaved through the formation, grabbing personnel for various details. A young buck sergeant, looking younger than most of the men standing on the street, strolled through the formation and chose Bill, John and a dozen other soldiers for a painting detail. This time nobody could escape.

John and Bill's group painted in the hot sun all afternoon. Ironically, they were painting the fence enclosing the Reception Center's swimming pool. The water teased and beckoned to them all day. Finally, unable to control himself any longer, Bill dropped his brush, rushed through the gate, and jumped fully clothed into the refreshing and cool water.

The rest of the men in the paint detail exchanged glances in stunned silence. Then, as if on cue, everybody dropped their brushes and followed Bill's lead. They splashed around in the water, unchallenged for several minutes, like a group of grade school children on a field trip. All at once, two service club attendants emerged and ordered them from the pool. Reluctantly, one by one, they emerged from the water and returned to their tedious detail.

Clothes dried quickly in the hot, blaring sunshine, and soon they were all sweating again, contemplating a second dip in the pool. At five in the afternoon, the project only required another hour to finish, but they were all relieved of their duty and told to go to the mess hall for dinner.

After John and Bill ate dinner and cleaned up, they returned to Alice's Restaurant. This time, their attempt to win on the slot machine was successful when Bill hit the jackpot with the first three tokens.

Bill stood there dumbfounded and watched the hundreds of coins dropping into the tray below. Bells and sirens were sounding from the machine and a red strobe light above signaled that somebody had just hit the jackpot.

"Glory be - this sure is my lucky day! Just look at all these here coins," he cried out joyfully.

The noise and strobe light quickly attracted other soldiers who began to gather around the two winners. Everyone watched the payout window; numbers continued to climb and approached one-thousand - falling tokens already filling most of the tray below. Those standing around showed mixed support; some congratulated Bill and were happy for him, others simply looked on, saying nothing. One person, in particular, appeared to be quite upset, complaining loudly to his friend, "Damn! I just left that machine. Had I stayed and played another coin that jackpot would have been mine!"

Someone turned and responded to him loudly, "Yeah, but you didn't, and now it isn't. So get over it and give the guy a break!"

"Fuck it, don't mean nothin'," he mumbled and walked away.

Meanwhile, Bill frantically raked the tokens into old coffee cans and found it difficult to keep up with the machine payout. The counter was still rolling and had passed fourteen-hundred. It stopped suddenly at fifteen-hundred and was quiet again.

Someone yelled out, "Way to go man. You just hit for seventy-five! Don't spend it in one place."

It took several more minutes for the two of them to transfer all the coins from the machine tray into empty coffee cans. When they finished, they muscled the five filled cans over to the cashier cage. The woman behind the counter congratulated them and paid Bill in military certificates.

"Come on, Polack, it's time for us to drink a few beers and celebrate." Bill said proudly, guiding John to a nearby table.

After a few hours of drinking beer, both were surprised to find that neither of them could stand without support.

"Oh shit, I can't see things clearly anymore," John stated, holding on tightly to the back of his chair.

"I can see okay, but everything is spinning like I'm on a merry-go-round," Bill slurred.

"Are you gonna puke?"

"I don't think so right now, but we need to find the way back to our bunks."

"I do remember that we have to turn left and go to the last row of barracks on top of the hill."

"Let's get started before we pass out."

The two of them leaned onto one another, shuffling through the door and then down the steps to the road. Some of the by-standers watched them closely, amused by their inebriated state. Once they reached the road and turned left, the two soldiers started singing marching tunes from Basic Training while weaving across the road. Both were off-key and very loud, one trying to sing louder than the other. Angry voices echoed in the darkness from every building they passed:

"Hey, ass holes pipe down!"

"Shut the fuck up out there!

"Sing another note and I'll personally come out and kick your ass!"

They disregarded the threats and warnings, not stopping until they reached their destination. Once inside, they collapsed.

At 0300, the loud blast of air raid sirens abruptly awakened the inhabitants of the 90th Replacement Battalion.

Those drunk or stoned sobered up immediately. Chaos reigned! Cherries spilled out from the barracks, most escaping through open doorways, others choosing speed instead, dove through the openings in the sidewalls. In doing so, the mosquito netting pulled from the walls and encapsulated many of the fleeing youths in a nylon cocoon; this further enhanced their panic. Outside, the men bump into one another, confused and unsure of what to do next.

A voice on the public address system began yelling barely audible instructions above the shrill sirens. "Yellow alert! Yellow alert! Head for the nearest bunker and take cover immediately!"

Thankful for the directive, everyone raced toward the available bunkers. Once inside, the men sat nervously on the ground. All were trying to control their breathing, gasping, as if just completing a ten-mile race. Voices rang out from the total darkness within:

"My heart is pounding so fast, it's going to explode."

"What in the hell is happening?"

"Are we getting hit?"

"Where are our weapons?"

"Yeah, how are we going to protect ourselves?"

"What in the fuck does a yellow alert mean?"

The sight within the bunker was also bizarre, with twenty soldiers all in different levels of dress. Some were barefoot, wearing nothing else except green boxer shorts – one of them even wore a helmet. Others wore just a pair of trousers and boots, another bunch only a shirt and shorts, and three men stood in complete uniform with helmets. One of the Cherries stood next to the entrance of the bunker holding a broom – the handle facing outward like a bayonet on a rifle.

Just then, a heavyset person wearing a cook's hat and apron, leisurely strolled into the bunker and took a double glance at the person standing guard with the broom.

Shaking his head side to side, he took in the curious picture. Of course, since he had been at the Replacement Center for almost four months, similar scenes had played out repeatedly.

"Relax, guys, it's only a test," he said in a reassuring voice.

"What do you mean "a test"?" a voice snapped in the darkness.

"The camp officers fuck with us every other night and run this alert at different hours. It's supposed to remind us that we are still at war. It doesn't bother me any because I'm in the kitchen all night long cooking. The sirens should stop and they'll give the 'all clear' in another minute or so."

"What a bunch of lifer mother-fuckers," someone mumbled.

"At least they could have given us some warning. Now I've got to clean the shit out of my pants," said another.

Five minutes later, the "All Clear" sounded. Everyone began to file out of the bunker, returning to the barracks – thankful, but pissed off about the inconvenience. Almost everyone dropped onto their bunks, but were unable to return to their dreams, still too shaken to sleep. Most just lay in bed awake until dawn.

Bill Sayers and John Kowalski heard their names called during the first shipping formation of the day. Both men got orders for the 25th Infantry Division; the division basecamp was near the city of Cu Chi, which is twenty miles northwest of Saigon. Their convoy was leaving at 1000 hours.

"Thank you, sweet Jesus!" Bill said solemnly, "thank you for not sending us up to the 101st."

"Amen," John added.

Those called for the morning transport began arriving at the pickup point, duffel bags in hand, dropping them in the area designated for the 25th Division. With an hour remaining before departure, Bill and John rushed over to the PX to purchase 'boony hats'. They are very similar to those worn by amateur anglers. The soft, green, cloth-like material enabled a person to shape it into any configuration necessary to protect their eyes and back of the neck from the blazing sun. They were lighter and more practical than the traditional baseball caps worn by new recruits. While both waited for a tailor to embroider their names on the hats, John scanned the showcase filled with division patches.

"Bill, let's get us a patch for the 25th Division and have it sewn onto the hat too," John suggested.

They were not sure what the patch looked like, but thankfully, located a display board that identified these unit patches. The patch for the 25th Division looked like a red strawberry, two inches wide by four inches long, with a yellow lightning bolt piercing it diagonally. Each purchased one and had them sewn in place.

John moved to the next counter. Noticing a large Bowie knife among the many knives in this showcase, he immediately purchased it.

"Check this out," he called over to Bill.

John had already threaded his belt through the leather scabbard. With the knife now hanging from his right hip, he was tying the bottom leather lace around his thigh.

"That knife looks cool as hell!" Bill said, admiring the new item.

"Makes me look kind of bad ass, doesn't it?" John asked proudly.

"Yes, it does. I think I'll buy one for myself," Bill said, then placed his order with the salesperson.

Neither of them thought of the knife as being much more than a decoration. However, they would both find out later that it was the most valuable tool used while patrolling through the jungle.

At 0930 hours, five two-and-a-half ton trucks, commonly called "Deuce -and-a-Half" trucks, arrived. A layer of sandbags were piled upon the bed of each truck to protect the riders if the truck should hit a mine in the road; a soldier stood behind the cab working on the tripod-mounted M-60 machine gun on the roof. The Rat Patrol jeeps arrived to escort the Cherries to their next destination.

Bill and John were among the first twenty to board the trucks and fortunate enough to get a seat on one of the two pull-down benches running the length of the truck bed on both sides of the vehicle. The other fifteen had to sit in discomfort on the hard sandbag-covered floor.

The convoy moved out precisely at 1000 hours. Once leaving the security of the 90th Replacement Battalion, a lone helicopter gunship joined the convoy and circled lazily overhead, providing additional security for the parade of five trucks.

They passed endless rice paddies where the Vietnamese people worked painstakingly to harvest their crops in knee-deep water. Young boys rode on top of huge water buffaloes whacking the big brown animals on their rump with a bamboo stick.

Whenever a convoy passed from the opposite direction, everyone raised their arms and flashed peace signs to one another. Every now and again, the passengers saw the front of an Armored Personnel Carrier (APC) poking out from a stand of bushes on the side of the road. Their gunners acknowledged the fellow Americans, waving enthusiastically to the convoy from behind 50-caliber machine guns.

Traveling at speeds in excess of 40 mph, it took no time at all for the convoy to reach Cu Chi – home of the 25th Infantry Division.

## CHAPTER FOUR

The Rat Patrol jeeps concluded their mission after leading the convoy deep inside of Cu Chi Base Camp. All 126 Cherries stood in the trucks, trying in vain to rid themselves of the clinging red dust.

Bill laughed when John removed his sunglasses.

"What's so funny?"

"You have white rings around your eyes."

"And what, that's supposed to be funny?"

"Yeah, with all that red shit on your face you look like a fucking raccoon."

"At least you can see my eyes. Your whole head looks like it was dipped in shit."

"Go ahead and have your fun," Bill grumbled. He brushed himself feverishly in an attempt to get all the dust removed from his clothes. "Give me a hand wiping my back, and I'll brush you off."

"Okay, just don't play with my ass when I turn around," John replied.

"You're all ass and I won't be able to avoid it."

"What - are you a comedian now?"

As they finished brushing each other's back, loud voices on the side of the trucks were barking commands to the group.

"All right, Cherries, un-ass my trucks right now!"

"Come on, come on, move it!"

"I mean now! Let's go, everyone!"

"I want four ranks starting right here," bellowed an impatient Puerto Rican sergeant. He stood forty feet away and drew a long line across the ground with a large stick. "Let's go! Get on the line, I don't have all day!" He barked.

The Cherries leapt from the trucks and moved quickly to form four ranks, unsure if punishment was forthcoming for not being on line fast enough.

"What the fuck, are we in basic training again?" John mumbled to Bill.

"I hope not. We're supposed to be all done with that. This is Vietnam, isn't it?"

The sergeant paraded back and forth in front of the formation. He wore a black baseball cap with the word 'Cadre' stenciled on the front in large white letters. It was impossible to see the look in his eyes, as mirrored aviator sunglasses covered them. His beer belly looked unnatural for a man with a thirty-four inch waist and it bounced with every step he took.

"Listen up, Cherries!" He shouted in an attempt to get the ranks to settle down. "You are here for a mandatory week-long course of in-country training. During this time, we will review your past training and teach you all about your enemy. Our first class will begin in fifteen minutes. When I give the word, grab your gear and store it in the hooches behind me, then return to the exact spot you are standing in right now.

"You'll all have plenty of time later to unpack and get squared away. You have ten minutes, starting now. Move out!"

The ranks collapsed as men rushed to find their duffel bags in the large pile. Once in hand they raced to the various hooches. Bill and John could not find two adjacent cots in either of the first two hooches, but were successful in the third one. They threw the gear on top and moved back outside.

"What do you 'spose this is gonna be like?" Bill asked.

"Most likely a lot of classroom training, just like we did in Basic."

"Hell, I thought there's a war going on here. Why are we going to sit around in classrooms?" Bill complained.

"You heard the guy. He said that we were going to learn all about the enemy."

"What more do we have to learn? A little guy out there has a gun and wants to kill me. I have to kill him first – it's that simple. We don't need to learn anything more."

The Puerto Rican sergeant led the formation to a large shaded area not too far from the hooches. This was the first classroom of the day.

"Have a seat on the ground, gentlemen. If you have any smokes, feel free to light up."

He stood in front of the group, next to a large six-foot wide green chalkboard mounted between two trees. "Sgt. Ramone," printed in large, white chalky letters across the top, let everybody know who he was.

"Don't be afraid to sit on the ground," he stated after observing the reluctance of some to do so. "You'll be mighty lucky if this is the dirtiest you get in this country. You ground pounders (infantry) will be living on the ground. So get used to it now while there's no pressure on you."

He waited for the entire group to take a seat before continuing, "This area is where you will come for most of the classes during this course. My name is Sergeant Ramone," he enunciated both syllables and then used the stick to point out his name on the board.

"I will be one of your instructors during this next week. Today, we will review military maneuvers, different attack and defensive formations, the military alphabet, coding, map reading, and the proper use of the PRC-25 field radio. Are there any questions before we begin?"

No hands went up.

"Good, let's get started."

Later that day, John and Bill unpacked their belongings in the single-story screened building.

"Those classes we just finished were not all that bad," John admitted.

"Now I beg to differ with you. It was boring as hell to go over all that shit again. We've had enough of it shoved down our throats in the last six months."

"It may be boring, but look at it this way. It's one less day that we'll have to spend in the field."

Bill thought about that statement for a second, and then replied, "I guess you're right."

John looked at his watch, surprised. "Damn, it's already 10:30. We better get some sleep. I have a feeling it's going to be another long day tomorrow."

Both flopped down on the hard, olive-colored canvas cots and quickly fell asleep.

The following morning, everyone drew out an M-16 rifle from the armory before heading out for the first class of the day.

"Good morning, gentlemen," the instructor began, after everyone was seated in the outdoor classroom. "We will spend the morning taking these weapons apart, cleaning them, and then putting them back together again."

Moans and objections echoed from the crowd.

"Aw, fuck!"

"We did all this shit hundreds of times already."

"What a fucking waste!"

The instructor, having heard enough, got everyone's undivided attention when he struck the chalkboard with a stick; it sounded like the sharp crack of a rifle.

"Knock off the bullshit!" He ordered. "This part of the class is so important that it may very well save your lives!" He pushed both hands into his pants pockets and walked among the group. "It's true that you've done this a hundred times already, but how many of you can do it blindfolded? Do you know that most attacks and firefights occur in the dead of the night? It is pitch black and you cannot see your hand in front of your face. Now just suppose your weapon fails during one of these firefights, and the VC are rushing over the wire to kill you. Are you able to take your M16 apart and fix it in the dark, so you can protect yourself?"

He hesitated for a few seconds and then continued, "Before this class is over today, each of you will learn to do just that. The circumstances will be different - it won't be dark and enemy soldiers will not be trying to kill you, but you will successfully demonstrate this ability while blindfolded."

Again, protests and moaning sounded from the group.

"This is bullshit!"

"Fuck this shit! I'm a cook and probably won't handle a rifle the whole time I'm here."

The infantry guys took the advice to heart and began to disassemble and assemble their weapons. Each time, they were more proficient and confident. There was no need for blindfolds; they were all able to demonstrate this task with their eyes closed.

After lunch, the group returned to the classroom with weapons in hand.

"I sure feel more confident being here with a rifle now," Bill said.

"I know what you mean! We've been in-country almost a week and this is the first time I've actually held one in my hands."

"Isn't that odd, too, with everything we've heard about Vietnam during our training in the states?"

"You're right, Bill. I was expecting to get shot at or at least mortared when we walked off that plane."

"I was thinking the same thing. Now, if you think about the replacement center and now this place - aside from the convoys - I haven't seen anyone carrying a weapon or heard shots fired since our arrival."

"I don't know what to think. Maybe all that shit in training was just a bunch of brainwashing."

"Maybe, maybe not," Bill responded. "This is, supposedly, a secure rear area, and maybe they already killed all the enemy soldiers around here. I heard some of the guys talking earlier about firebases out in the boonies. That's where the real shit hits the fan."

"I wish we could just stay here," John said sincerely.

"Me too, old buddy."

The class spent the afternoon on the firing range, where each soldier could test-fire his weapon. They hit many of the targets; bits and pieces of cardboard sailed through the air and fell onto the already littered ground. Puffs of dirt rose into the air around each target, as the bullets burrowed deep into the dry, hard earth.

After each person had fired thirty rounds, they gathered and began walking back to the outdoor training classroom.

Sgt. Ramone was waiting there for everyone to complete the short walk back from the firing range. "Gentlemen, everybody enjoy target practice?"

"Yeah, it was great!"

"It's about time!"

"Good, I'm glad you enjoyed yourselves. We're all done for the day, except for the cleaning of these weapons." The men groaned one more time. "Nobody leaves for chow until each piece of equipment is spotless and returned to the armory. I will look them over later this evening and God help the poor slob who did not do a good enough job. After chow, you are on your own until the morning formation. Have a good evening!" Sergeant Ramone left the Cherries and headed toward the mess hall.

"Well, so much for our sense of security!" John spat.

"I know the feeling."

The following morning, the class returned to the firing range, where they found various weapons displayed, both on a table and at different intervals across the range firing positions. Five additional Cadres were also present to help with this class.

Sgt. Ramone split the men into five groups so each person would have an opportunity to fire many of them. The arsenal consisted of M-79 grenade launchers, 50 caliber, and M-60 machine guns, one sniper rifle with attached scope, smoke grenades and a 60mm mortar tube and base plate. The Cadre put on a mortar demonstration and fired three rounds: white phosphorus, a night flare, and high explosive, for those soldiers seeing them for the first time. One lucky person in each group would also have an opportunity to fire the LAW, a two-piece plastic disposable rocket launcher. When opened fully, it measured thirty inches long and looked similar to a shortened World War II bazooka.

After lunch, work details picked up spent brass shell casings from the ground, rebuilt the destroyed practice bunker, and cleaned the arsenal of fired weapons.

It was late in the evening when the last detail returned to the barracks.

On the fourth morning, John and Bill walked to the range with the rest of the class.

"What do you think they have in store for us today?" Bill asked.

"I don't have a clue, but it does seem odd that we're going without weapons."

"It sure does," Bill agreed.

Upon their arrival, the Cherries took a seat on the ground; this was now an automatic reflex and nobody hesitated or complained.

A large, black staff sergeant, who could pass for a professional football player, was their instructor for the day. He was holding a short rifle in one hand; wood covered most of the barrel and stock. A half circle, twelve-inch long black magazine protruded from the housing, an inch in front of the trigger guard. Perhaps it was possible for the shooter to hold on to the magazine and fire it like the Tommy Guns of old. Under the barrel, a pointed, two-foot long, finger-thick piece of silver metal lies horizontally, secured to the weapon by a hinge.

"What kind of gun do you suppose that is?" Bill asked and motioned toward the instructor with his head.

"I've never seen anything like it before. Maybe it's a VC gun or something new we have to learn how to fire."

Bill simply shrugged, "Makes sense to me."

The 6 foot, 8 inch, and 260 pound instructor removed his black cap with his free hand, using the sleeve to wipe the sweat from his forehead. Moisture on his freshly shaven head glistened in the sunlight. After returning his cap, he smiled brightly to the class, exposing a gold cap on one front tooth.

"Gentlemen," he began, "I am Staff Sergeant Jones, and now let me introduce you to the Russian-made AK-47 Assault Rifle. This little beauty is the primary weapon of your enemy."

He held the rifle high in the air for all to see.

"At times, it is more accurate, deadly, and dependable than your M-16. This banana clip holds thirty rounds instead of the twenty in our magazines," he said, ejecting the magazine and holding it high in the air.

"You should also note that the enemy's bullets are larger." The instructor set the rifle on a table and then pushed out one of the rounds from the magazine. After placing the magazine on the table next to the weapon, he reached into a pants pocket and withdrew an M-16 bullet. With a bullet in each hand, he lifted them both high into the air so the audience could see the difference.

"This 7.62mm round is identical to those we use in our M-60 machine gun. It is larger and has a lot of power, definitely doing some damage when hit. As you can see, the M-16 rounds are smaller, but their design allows them to tumble when hitting something. So a hit to the stomach may exit from the hip or upper back, tearing up everything in between."

He placed the two rounds in a pocket and picked up the rifle from the table. "And this is the bayonet," he continued, grabbing the silver steel appendage and unfolding it until it clicked and locked in a fully extended position.

"It is permanently fixed to the rifle and folds down when not in use. If Charlie sticks you with this, you'll be in a world of hurt."

He replaced the weapon on the table, then looked up to scan the many faces in the class; most showed concern.

"During the last six months of training, each of you has become accustomed to the sound of your own rifles. Today, I will fire this rifle and some other enemy weapons to demonstrate the distinct sound each one makes. It is very important that you recognize these different sounds because not all rifles are the same. The war in Vietnam is a guerrilla war, where you will hear the enemy more than see him. When ambushed in the dense jungle, with a weapon firing next to you, the sound of the weapon will determine immediately if it is a friend or foe. Your very lives - and the lives of your fellow soldiers - depend on you knowing the difference.

"I'm quite certain all of you were always on the sending end of a bullet since joining the military. How many of you know that every weapon makes a different sound when the bullet is flying toward you or overhead?"

The class shifted about nervously, nobody daring to raise their hand in acknowledgement to his question.

"Is this fucker going to shoot at us?" Bill whispered.

"Would it surprise you?"

The sergeant continued, "Before this day is over, I will guarantee that each of you will be able to distinguish between the pop of this AK-47 and the sharp crack of your own M-16. So, let's get started." He reinserted the magazine and chambered a round in the Russian weapon. "Listen closely!" He fired ten single shots downrange, spaced about three seconds apart, and then switched to automatic, emptying the magazine in two short bursts. "Gentlemen, what you just heard were the sounds of your enemy's weapon when firing away from you. Now you get an opportunity to hear the same weapon when the firing is directed toward you."

He moved the class up range, half way to the targets, and then returned to the firing line. The Cherries were sitting on the ground, facing the targets. Some panicked after the sergeant fired a short burst over their heads. They jumped to their feet and bolted toward the firing line, like fullbacks running all out to score a touchdown. Yet others crawled toward a nearby dried stream bed and lay prone in the depression.

Upon seeing this, the staff sergeant roared with laughter.

"Damn, you Cherries never cease to amaze me! Listen up!"

He was not trying to embarrass anyone, but by this point could barely contain his laughter. "Nobody is going to get shot on this range. I'm firing twenty feet over your goddamn heads, which is an extremely safe distance."

He turned and addressed the half-dozen soldiers standing on the firing line with him. "Get your asses back out on that range with the others."

The men hung back, stalling. One of them even turned around and kicked at the dirt, hoping to create a dust cloud large enough so the sergeant could not see him. Finally, after some coaxing and encouragement, they all walked back to mid-range and lay in the dried creek bed with everyone else.

"Okay, let's try this again," the sergeant yelled when they were all safely in place.

The group remained in that prone position for almost an hour as Staff Sergeant Jones fired the different enemy weapons. Aside from the AK-47, his arsenal also included an RPD Machine Gun, SKS Rifle, and a Chicom Pistol. When he was confident that his class had learned the lesson for the day, he called out, "The demonstration is over; everyone come back to the firing line."

The Cherries stood up, brushing themselves off before walking toward the awaiting staff sergeant.

Once they were clear of the firing range, he gathered them together. "Okay men, are there any questions regarding the sounds you've heard today?"

Not seeing any hands, he continued.

"That's good, I must have been real convincing. Before we break for the day, I have one final demonstration for you." Staff Sergeant Jones walked over to his Jeep and emerged with yet another strange weapon.

"Gentlemen, this is a Rocket Propelled Grenade and launcher, called an RPG for short. It is very deadly and feared most by the mechanized and aviation units, although, the enemy uses them in routine fire fights too. It is just like our LAW and can penetrate seven inches of armor before exploding. This weapon is responsible for shooting down helicopters and destroying or disabling APC's and tanks as well. Unlike the LAW, it has no back blast so the shooter does not have to worry about a clear field of fire behind him. Now keep your eye on the practice bunker to your front."

The RPG resembled a four-foot green pipe with a long, orange, pineapple-shaped missile sticking out from the front. There were a couple of extra rounds lying on the ground, each resembling a pineapple attached to a stick.

Jones leveled the weapon, aimed through the sight, and fired. The men could clearly see the speeding missile and its trailing exhaust; they watched it all the way to its target. When the round hit, the impact created a cloud of dust a microsecond before the entire structure exploded outward. The results were much more devastating than that of the LAW demonstration the day before. Debris scattered further away; rebuilding would take twice as long.

"Holy shit," Bill exclaimed, "look at what that thing did."

"Wow, that is some awesome weapon," John added.

"How do you stop something like that?"

"By shooting the fucker before he fires that damn thing!"

"What if you don't see him first?"

"Then when you see it bearing down on you, either jump the fuck out of the way or take a second to kiss your ass goodbye."

The next few classes were the most intriguing of the entire week – dealing with enemy booby traps and their deployment.
Sergeants Jones and Ramone were the primary instructors.
"Most of the time, booby traps are very cleverly concealed and remain undetected until it's too late," the black sergeant began. "In these classes, we will make you aware of the many different types of booby traps and how to avoid them. You must also take precautions against supplying Charlie in the field."
This statement baffled the Cherries, "Who in their right mind would do that?" Bill questioned.
"Shhhh, listen, and he'll probably tell us." A person, sitting behind Bill, whispered, poking him playfully in the center of his back.
"Use extreme caution when using trails and roads, entering village huts and tunnels, uncovering caches, moving around on rice paddy dikes, and on frequently used landing zones. These are all coveted locations for booby traps.
"Most of their booby traps are intended to maim and not kill. Charlie uses them for two reasons: the first is to slow down a unit, and the second is the probability of shooting down the unarmed helicopter when it arrives to evacuate the wounded." Staff Sergeant Jones finished the introduction and stepped to the side.
A few minutes passed and then Sergeant Ramone walked before the class. "Many booby traps used by the enemy are armed with pressure release devices. A person is safe when standing on one, but the second he steps off, the sudden drop in pressure will explode the charge. You could lose a foot, leg, or even die from shock.
"One of the most feared of all booby traps is the Bouncing Betty." The infantry soldiers perked up at this revelation, leaning forward, anxious to hear more.
"Buried, it has a tripping device sticking out of the ground. This mine has two charges: one will propel a balloon-shaped explosive charge upward, and the second will explode at waist level – throwing shrapnel into the stomach and groin areas. If you survive, chances

are excellent that you'll be left without your manhood to start a family."

Many of the men reached down and checked their genitals, as if they were doing so for the very last time. Each looked at his neighbor with pursed lips and wide eyes, shaking their heads incredulously.

"Some of Charlie's booby traps include American-issued items. At times, the infantry soldier is hot, tired, and gets lazy. The long patrols in this climate will force many to discard items to lighten the unbearable loads. They may throw away belts of ammunition, grenades, claymore mines, and M-79 rounds into the jungle.

"However, some of these items can also be left behind quite by accident. After a break on the side of a trail, you may get up and unknowingly have an item fall off or out of your rucksack. Charlie makes it a point to search those trails thoroughly.

"He loves to find grenades, as they are the easiest to convert into a booby trap. All he has to do is to tie them to a tree, attach one end of a trip wire to the pin, and run it across the trail. The thin fishing line is hard to see, but is strong enough to pull the pin from the grenade when somebody walks into it.

"Favorite scrounging areas for Charlie are those locations where Americans get resupplied and those of a former night defensive position. GI's always have an abundance of supplies and seldom use all they get. Unwanted C-Rations, detonation cord, and personal effects lay discarded throughout these areas. Some are buried, but most are not."

Sergeant Ramone broke in to continue, "A claymore mine is an anti-personnel plastic mine, eight inches wide by five inches high, and one inch thick. It contains hundreds of one-quarter inch steel balls embedded into the cover, and when detonated, they blow outward, covering an arc of 130 degrees; the killing zone is within thirty feet. Every soldier in the field carries at least two of them, which are set up during the night around defensive perimeters. Sometimes, the soldiers are rushing and forget about them, leaving them behind.

"Heat tabs, used for heating water and food, are another simple luxury a soldier can't live without in the field. Most of us hate C-Rations as it is, and eating them cold is out of the question. After running out of heat tabs, some soldiers have cracked open the claymore mines and removed the plastic C-4 explosive to heat their food. If it is not compressed, it burns like gasoline. Then, no longer needing the casing with the embedded steel projectiles, the grunts have thrown them away into the jungle. Now what do you suppose Charlie does with them when finding such a prize?"

The class responded in unison, "He makes booby traps!"

"Correct! The United States Armed Forces has fired millions of artillery and mortar rounds since their arrival in this county, and occasionally, some are duds and do not explode. Charlie is very resourceful in finding them and converting them into booby traps as well. He will hang them in trees or lay them on the side of a trail, arming them in one of two ways: by a trip wire or command detonation device. This kind of booby trap can waste an entire platoon."

Jones cut back in, "We're all creatures of habit, and many soldiers are injured because of it. At least one of every five soldiers will either pick up or kick a can if it is seen lying on a trail. Charlie knows about this strange American habit. He will booby-trap anything that may appeal to the curiosity of young soldiers or to the fortune hunters looking for souvenirs.

"The punji pit is another type of booby trap. They vary in size from one foot to six feet deep. Pointed stakes as round as pencils line the bottom of the pit. Their tips, dipped in shit, can be fatal if they break the skin. These pits look very natural in the middle of a path once twigs and leaves cover them.

"However, many of them were dug during the 1950's when the French fought here, and over time, they have long since rotted. If a soldier were to step into one of these older pits, the stakes would crumble and the most he would end up with is a sprained ankle or knee. These pits are rare and again, primarily used earlier in the war.

"Do not accept bottles of whiskey or soda from the villagers, as many of them are VC sympathizers. They grind up glass and put it into the sealed bottles. The shards are so fine it is difficult to see them with the naked eye. If you drink from these bottles, the slivers of glass will tear up your insides.

"For those of you heading out to the bush, let me leave you with a final thought. Burn or bury what you do not use. Never leave it behind for your enemy to find, because they will find some way to use it against you.

"This concludes your in-country training. If you learned anything in the course that will save your life, then we have succeeded in our goals. At this time, we are asking that you return to your hooches, retrieve your gear, and fall out into the assembly area for the last formation. Once everyone is there, you will receive orders and transportation to your new units. Good luck everyone!"

"What outfit are you going to, Bill?" John asked.
"Alpha Company, 1st Battalion, 27th Infantry."
"All right, so am I!"
"Talk about luck, this is great! We've been together this long; it would be a shame to break us up now."
"Yeah, pretty cool, huh?"
They picked up their gear and moved toward one of the trucks.
"Where are you guys headed?" The driver called down from his cab.
"1st Battalion, 27th Infantry," they replied.
"Hey, that's the Wolfhounds, you guys really lucked out."
"Why is that?" John asked.
"Shit, you haven't heard? The Wolfhounds are the most ass-kicking outfit in this division. They're so bad the VC post 'WANTED' posters with huge rewards throughout their area of operations."
"No shit!" Bill and John responded together. Excitement lit their faces.
The driver announced, "Throw your shit in the back and jump on board, I'll run you guys up the road to their area."
"Thanks!" The two men climbed on board and joined twenty other Cherries.

When they arrived in the new area, the First Sergeant had been expecting them. He was waiting outside the orderly room; a gray building with a large blue board mounted to the front. On top, it read 'Company "A" Body Count' in tall white letters. Just below the heading, two eighteen - inch white painted bones formed an oblong "X"; a human skull hung over the center of the crossed bones. If the board were black, it would have looked like a pirate flag. In any case, it was apparent that the purpose of the board represented death.

Beneath the skull and crossbones, the left column listed each of the platoons, and to their right, a column with four rows of numbers. First Platoon had the highest number of kills with thirty-seven. Fourth Platoon only had twelve.

After the First Sergeant was certain that all the Cherries had enough time to scrutinize the tote board, he introduced himself. "Gentlemen, my name's First Sergeant Michaels, but you can call me Top. I would like to welcome you all to Alpha Company, 1st Battalion Wolfhounds. As you can see by the number of combined kills, we are kicking ass out in the bush."

"How often do the numbers go back to zero?" someone asked.

"We go back to zero each quarter, so what you see listed today is from July first until now. If there are no more questions," he hesitated for a moment, and not seeing any hands raised, he continued, "When I call out your name, raise your hand, so I can see you, and I'll assign you to one of the four platoons."

Top called four names before calling Bill and then John immediately after him. Bill was going to the Third Platoon and John to the First.

"Way to go, buddy," John consoled.

"It was bound to happen sooner or later."

"Let's talk to Top after the formation and see if he'll put us together in the same platoon."

"It's worth a try and we don't have anything to lose if he turns us down," Bill agreed.

"Tomorrow," Top continued after completing the list of names, "you eight men will fly out to our forward Fire Support Base Kien. You will draw out weapons and all the other supplies needed just before leaving in the morning. When this meeting is over, you can

John Podlaski

head over to the platoon barracks and find an empty cot for the night. Signs on each building will let you know if you are in the right one or not. I want everybody back here in formation again at 0800 hours. Until that time, you are all on your own and welcome to visit the Service Club or PX down the road. You're dismissed!"

Bill and John struck out with the First Sergeant, who quickly shot down their request to be together. Disappointed, they departed in different directions, but agreed to meet again in front of the orderly room in fifteen minutes.

"Are you cool with checking out the sights in this camp?" John asked.

"I've been dying to see this place. Between those classes, eating, and sleeping, we haven't been able to do shit in the last week, Bill drawled."

"Well, we better get started. We only have a half day to sight see."

Cu Chi was the main base camp for all units of the 25th Division, and it would take the rest of the day for them to tour the enormous base.

"These rear echelon troops really have it made here. It's like living in a big city," John stated matter-of-factly while observing the surroundings.

They found the PX similar to a large department store in the states. A person could buy anything from newspapers to television sets; it even boasted a catalog department.

The Service Club included a library, writing rooms, a TV room, a small cafeteria, and individual recording rooms under one roof.

The recording rooms were a little larger than telephone booths, but inside, a person could listen to his favorite record or cassette tape and relax in private. Many of the soldiers in Vietnam recorded letters to their families on cassette tapes and then mailed them home. Upon receiving a cassette, he could return and play it back on the recorders.

Every night, the Red Cross female volunteers (Donut Dollies) conducted bingo games in the cafeteria. Since it was free, there was usually a large turnout. The prizes were small: normally, a wallet or a transistor radio, but the games were not important. Soldiers only

Cherries – A Vietnam War Novel

went there to see these American female volunteers. Outside of the hospitals, this was the next best place to see "round-eyed" women.

Just down the street from the Service Club, they found an Olympic-sized swimming pool with both one and three-meter diving boards. Bathing suits were available for anyone wishing to take a dip. It too, was crowded during this late afternoon.

Further down the road, they discovered an authentic Chinese restaurant. Rumors had it that the food was delicious and a welcome change from the Army chow or Service Club hamburgers.

During the tour, someone mentioned that the forward infantry companies came out of the field periodically and would spend three days in Cu Chi to rest and recuperate (R&R). He said that resting in the security of the base camp was a great way of relieving the built-up stress after grueling weeks or even months in the bush.

John lay wide-awake on his cot. Thoughts of leaving for the firebase in the morning rambled through his head. He had no idea what it would be like and the uncertainty continued to feed his anxiety. He flashed back to an earlier conversation with Bill just prior to calling it a night. Bill was nervous too, and expressed how sad it was that they would not have each other for close support any longer. However, Top assured them that their paths would cross on numerous occasions, not only in the field or in the firebase, but also during R&R in Cu Chi. He said that they should not take the separation, as though they would never see each other again.

John was a pessimist and worried that every time something was going to change, it would not be in his best interest. However, he did realize that, in reality, nothing bad had happened to date. On the contrary, every change had turned out to be a good experience. Perhaps the odds would continue in his favor and tomorrow would be uneventful. He felt somewhat relieved and eventually dozed off, alone in the First Platoon barracks.

The next morning, Top instructed the eight infantry Cherries to empty out the contents of their duffel bags onto the ground, telling them to toss all military clothing forward, one pile for fatigue tops and the other for pants. It was unnecessary for them to take fatigues out to the firebase; clean uniforms were usually available during each resupply. Of those remaining personal items, the First Sergeant cautioned the men to take only what they were willing to carry on their backs. After choosing the most treasured of keepsakes, the remaining items went back into their duffel bags for storage in the company supply building - accessible to the men whenever in Cu Chi.

The company clerk, PFC Jimmy Ray, led the line of men to the supply building. First, they dropped off their duffel bags, then received weapons and a limited amount of gear. Each man signed for an M-16 rifle, a bandolier of two-hundred rounds of ammunition, ten empty magazines, a steel helmet with liner, two canteens, a canteen cup and web gear, which resembled a wide canvas belt, and a set of suspenders.

Top gave them an hour to get everything squared away. Each of them loaded their ten magazines with ammo - placing five into pouches on the web gear belt and the rest back into the green cotton bandolier which hung from the shoulder. After packing and inspecting their weapons, the Cherries moved to the portable water tank (water buffalo) to fill canteens. The water was still cool from the lower night temperatures, but would soon be warm and difficult to drink. Top wished them well and sent them on their way.

The company clerk escorted the group to the landing pad near Battalion HQ, where three Huey Helicopters waited. Each helicopter had the insignia of the 25th Infantry painted on its nose. Two were completely full of clothing, mail, ammunition, and cases of C-Rations, beer, and ice. The clerk instructed the eight Cherries to load up on the remaining chopper.

John and Bill teamed up and headed toward their transportation.

"These are some bad-ass looking guys," John observed, looking over the crews.

The two door gunners wore flak jackets and sat on each side of the helicopter. Both were busy checking their M-60 Machine Guns mounted on a swivel to their front, the barrels pointing down and outward from each side. Opening a can and extracting a belt of ammunition, the gunners placed one end into the loading mechanism and then closed the cover to lock the belt of ammo in place. The belt of three-hundred rounds would allow the gunner to fire controlled bursts for up to three minutes if fired upon by the enemy.

The entire crew was dressed in olive drab flight suits with dozens of zippered pockets, and olive green flight helmets with black sun shields. The helmets had internal speakers - a small microphone on a flexible metallic arm attached to the side of the helmet for communication. A cord extended from the helmet to a jack in the wall. When plugged in, the crew could communicate with each other through the internal intercom, as well as broadcast over the radio on many available frequencies. Both pilots wore shoulder holsters with 9mm pistols.

"They look cool as hell," John commented, taking a seat on the floor just behind the pilot. His legs stuck out of the helicopter and dangled toward the landing skids. Bill took a position in the doorway between John and the door gunner.

"Yep, sure do!" Bill agreed, looking for a way to hold on tight.

When the grunts were all aboard, both door gunners leaned out to check the area around the aircraft. Announcing over the intercom that the rotor was clear, a loud whining noise alerted everyone that the turbine engines were starting. The overhead rotor blades began turning slowly, gaining momentum with each rotation. The helicopter started to vibrate and shake wildly as if trying to break away from invisible bonds securing it to the ground.

It lifted from the ground a few feet, slowly at first, throwing dirt and stones in every direction. When at a height of six feet, the chopper turned 180 degrees, dipped its nose slightly, and then raced forward. The three-helicopter formation climbed into the sky, heading west and away from Cu Chi.

As the airships gained speed and altitude, the wind rushed in through the open side bay doors, catching the unsuspecting Cherries in a mini-tornado or vortex inside.

"Hey, Polack, hold on to me!" Bill hollered in a panic above the noise of the engines and wind.

"Shit, you hold me! My ass is sliding toward the door and I don't know if I'm being sucked out or blown out." John yelled, hoping his voice carried over the loud noise level.

"Come on, Polack, I'm not kidding!" Bill screamed, "I can't stop myself from sliding out the door."

"Use your right hand to hold onto the door gunner seat and then loop your other arm in mine. I'll use my left arm to push away on the wall next to the door."

That seemed to work, stopping their sliding sensation. However, their faces paled and their eyes were wide with terror.

"Keep doing this; it seems to be working." John shouted, "Neither of us is leaving this ship until it lands."

Once the flight left the populated areas around Cu Chi, the sights below were mostly thick jungle and small villages with surrounding rice paddies. Dirt trails snaked everywhere, extending in many different directions. Suddenly, a large clearing came into view. Bunkers, and barbed wire surrounded an area the size of a football field; artillery guns and mortar pits were visible near the center of the compound. There was movement below, and many individuals were walking about shirtless and gathering near the main gate.

The sliding sensation finally subsided as the helicopter slowed and dropped altitude. Bill and John puffed their cheeks out and breathed slowly from pursed lips in an effort to catch their breath.

The flight took twenty minutes. The copter was now preparing to land in an area by the front gate, just outside of Fire Support Base Kien.

# CHAPTER FIVE

As the choppers hovered above the landing zone (LZ), the tremendous back-blast of wind from the horizontal blades sent those items not secured sailing through the air.

Several soldiers were waiting nearby; each faced in the opposite direction, covering his eyes for protection against the flying debris.

When the three choppers finally touched down, the rotors continued turning at a high RPM. One of the nearby soldiers ran toward the lead helicopter with the new arrivals, the rest converging upon the other two supply-filled helicopters.

"Okay, Cherries, it's safe to get off," yelled the lone soldier. "Put your shit over there by the first hooch inside of the gate," he instructed, pointing to a dilapidated square block of boxes and sandbags. "Then give us a hand unloading those two resupply ships," he added before rushing back to the next bird in line.

A single long line of soldiers led away from each of the two helicopters; crates and bags moved quickly along the human conveyor belt, passing from one pair of hands to another. After placing their gear near the hooch, the Cherries split up and joined their hosts at the end of each line, which by then extended through the gate twenty feet. In five minutes, both birds were unloaded and the contents stacked into piles almost two-hundred feet away.

When the two lines of soldiers dissolved and moved away, the RPM on the choppers increased significantly. In turn, each of them lifted a couple of feet from the ground and then launched into the cloudless blue sky. In less than a minute, the windstorm and loud whooping noises were gone.

John Podlaski

Bill and John bumped into one another en route to retrieve their equipment. "Bill, that was tough as hell, I tried everything humanly possible to keep up and not drop anything."

"In my line, somebody did drop a box, but the line never stopped and stuff continued coming as if nothing happened. The guy wiped himself off and jumped back in without missing a beat."

"I never did anything like that before," John admitted. "Things were moving so fast that when I turned back around, the guy in front of me was already dropping his package; I caught a lot of them in midair."

The other six Cherries rejoined Bill and John near their stored equipment, "I think those other guys are trying to size us up," one in their group stated.

They all glanced at the group from the firebase and found them to be watching the Cherries, commenting among themselves. There was pointing, snickering, and some giving each other a high-five.

There was a distinct difference between the two groups. The Cherries, dressed in brand new fatigues with creases, looked particularly out of place. Their shirt sleeves were neatly rolled up above the elbow; all but the upper most button secured, tops of T-shirts peeking through from underneath. Hair was short, faces cleanly shaven, and the green canvas sides and black leather boots sparkled in the glaring sun.

The other group, however, was just the opposite and offered the Cherries a preview of how they would soon look. Shaggy-haired and browned from the sun, many were shirtless. Their uniforms were severely wrinkled, bleached by the sun and a thousand laundry washes. Some sleeves were cut off, and all fatigues appeared two sizes larger than needed. None wore belts, their boots were muddy brown and yellow, some not even laced.

Three black soldiers stood out from the firebase crowd; each adorned with jewelry fashioned from black shoelaces. Braided necklaces hung from their necks, with four-inch wide bracelets covering their wrists. One of the soldiers had a braided cross hanging from his necklace. This form of 'braiding' was the same taught in arts and crafts at summer youth camps. The square and round versions were always popular when making lanyards or whips with the thin, flat, different colored lengths of vinyl strips. In this case, shoelaces offered a much thicker and larger version. This "jewelry" made a statement, signifying the Black Power movement, and many of the black enlisted men in country wore them.

Suddenly, two black Cherry soldiers left their group and rushed over to greet the other three. They began a ritual handshake referred to as 'DAP'; hands moved up and down each other's arms, shoulders touched, fingers snapped, chests beaten, palms slapped, fists bounced, finally ending in a traditional handshake. The last step in this process was for them to take their free hand and encapsulate the clenched hands. The greeting alone between the five of them lasted two full minutes.

One Cherry remarked to the others, "Ain't this a bitch? I bet after all that, they still don't know each other's names."

The group chuckled and some began to give each other high fives.

A black soldier, the shortest and possibly the youngest, left his group and approached the Cherries. He was lighter skinned than the rest, and he flashed deep dimples when he smiled – a distraction from his curiously missing earlobes. He walked with a slight limp, trying to support his weight on the stronger left leg.

"Are any of you Cherries from Detroit?" He asked, looking over the group.

John said excitedly, "Yeah, I am," and raised his right hand in acknowledgement.

"Where in Detroit are you from, Chuck?" He asked.

John stopped in his tracks, scrunching his face in disgust. He shook his head from side to side and replied, "First of all, my name's not Chuck. You can call me either 'John' or by my nickname, 'Polack.' It's your choice. And yes, I'm from Detroit and live in the Harper-Van Dyke area."

The short black man began to laugh, briefly grabbed his crotch, and then turned to smirk at his friends. "Don't you know that over here in the Nam all you pretty white boys are called 'Chuck'?" he asked in a singsong manner. "You've been born again and should start getting used to your new name."

"Aw, fuck off!" John responded. "I don't believe in all that extreme Black Power shit. Some of you people think you own the fucking world. I've got lots of black friends back home and none give me any shit like you're trying to do."

John backed up a few paces, so he could see both the smaller soldier and the four other black soldiers nearby. He did not want any trouble, but if something were to start, he would be ready. Looking the short soldier straight in the eye, John said, "Why don't you just go back to your 'bloods' and practice up on your DAP? You may be good at it someday! Or better yet, maybe I could teach you."

Immediately, the black soldiers in the other group started to howl and laugh. They gave each other high-fives and began swaying, leaning into each other, as if they were all going to fall over. Then their catcalls began.

"Hoowee, I know I heard that."

"Damn, blood, I guess he told you."

"Look here, we have us a white brother in the group."

The smaller soldier frowned and lowered his shaking head, not even sure that he heard John correctly; nevertheless, he had been embarrassed in front of his peers.

"Hey, brother man, all white boys from Detroit like you?" One of the black soldiers with a small pick sticking out from his Afro hairstyle asked.

"I don't exactly know what you mean, but in my neighborhood in Detroit, we all try to get along with each other. Besides, aren't all of us here on the same side?"

"Yeah, man, don't sweat it. It don't mean nothin' . . . we jus' fuckin' with ya."

The short soldier raised his head and looked to John. "That was a good one, man; I didn't expect a comeback from you. What platoon are you in?"

"I'm in the First Platoon."

"Cool. Good for you!" He said and walked over to rejoin his group.

After a few minutes, the veteran group merged with the Cherries, questioning them about news updates, hometowns, platoon assignments, football teams, and that 'free love' they heard so much about from back home. The chatter gained momentum and became more intense as the one large group split into several smaller discussion groups.

The soldier who earlier challenged John, approached him slowly. He stood about four inches shorter and leaned into his ear. "Hey man, relax," he whispered. "My name is Junior Brown. My folks live near Six Mile and Van Dyke, which isn't too far from where you live, right?"

Caught off guard, John did not answer him immediately. Instead, he continued to stare at the young man, unsure of what may come next. Suddenly, Junior took him by the arm and gently led him away from the groups to an area behind one of the mobile water tanks (water buffalos).

"Look here, John, I'm sorry about that 'Chuck' shit earlier. I'm really not like the rest of the brothers, but it's an image thing and something I have to do when not in the bush."

"What image?" John asked suspiciously.

"Well, you know, the brothers have been preaching that we are the minority over here, and we need to stand together to protect ourselves. Ever since the riots in Detroit and Newark a couple of years ago, they say it looks bad for a black man to be friendly with a white guy." Junior shuffled his feet and shoved his hands into his pants pockets. Both glanced over to the mixed groups to see everyone talking to each other and being very cordial.

"That's a bunch of shit, Junior! If that were true, then why are you here talking to me, and why are the other brothers now acting friendly with everyone else over there?"

"It's a family thing." Junior began. "See, as it turns out, all of us are in Alpha Company. This firebase supports the entire battalion; guys are here from every company, and families got to stay together."

"Aren't we all one big happy family here?"

"Yeah, in a way we really are. Consider your fellow platoon members as brothers, and then those from other platoons are your cousins. As a company, we're one happy family. The other companies are like neighbors; you'll help them out and all, but you don't really want to get into their business. We watch over our own, regardless of color, both in the bush and here on the firebase. We have to depend on one another and watch each other's back. We can't let an issue like race fuck that up. By the way, I'm also in the First Platoon."

"So you're telling me that we're brothers now?"

"Yeah, isn't it a bitch? But I will tell you, my brother, that you blew me away when you mentioned where you lived. In my four months in the Nam, every time I met someone who said they were from Detroit, they actually lived in Battle Creek, Port Huron, or Flint. When I heard you say that you were from Detroit, I thought, oh no, here we go again. Then when it finally hit me that we really were almost neighbors, it shook me up."

"We're actually three miles apart from each other, but even so, I've never met anyone in the service that lived so close to me."

"Why don't you go and get your gear and I'll show you around and help you to get squared away? Then we can rap a little about home."

"Okay, but give me a few minutes first. I want to talk to my friend and let him know what's going on. He's in the Third Platoon, so I guess he's our cousin."

Both laughed.

John walked over to where Bill and the others were listening to one of the "brothers" speak. When he was within earshot, Bill turned and acknowledged him.

"Damn, Polack, I thought you and that colored guy were going to mix it up." Bill drawled, "I did keep my eye on you just in case something developed."

"Thanks, Bill! For a while, I thought it was gonna come to that, too. As it turns out, he's not a bad guy, and I learned that he's almost a neighbor of mine back home. He's also in the First Platoon and is going to help me get squared away."

"Well, I'll be!" Bill said, somewhat surprised. "You do know that you're the only one out of this bunch not assigned to the Third Platoon? You see this guy here." Bill nodded his head toward the person talking to the group, "he's from the Third Platoon too, and told us that half of their men were lost last week."

"How did they lose half a platoon?"

"Morris - that's the guy's name - said ten of them finished their tours and went home. Four others were hurt by a booby trap."

"Did they get hurt bad?"

"He said nobody died, but assured us they won't be back any time soon."

"Shit! Booby traps . . . Oh, my god . . ."Both thought back to the final class of in-county training a few days ago.

"Bill," John said after regaining his composure, "I better get going. I'll look you up later if I get the chance."

"Take care of yourself, buddy," Bill said. They clenched hands - not in a conventional handshake, but in the gesture of youthful brotherhood - chest high with palms together and thumbs intertwined. They pulled themselves together and warmly slapped each other on the back.

John gathered his gear and returned to where Junior waited. Together, they headed for one of the hooches.

"Hey, you and that other guy seem to be really tight," Junior said. "Have you known each other very long?"

"We met on our first day in the service. We went through Basic and AIT together and then met up again in Oakland. His name's Bill."

"That's pretty cool, and now you both lucked out and got into the same company over here." Junior held open the makeshift door of the hooch and followed John inside.

"This is some weird shit," John stated, looking around. "I've never seen anything quite like this before."

"It sure beats sleeping under the stars; you'll do enough of that out in the bush."

This 'hooch' was as big as an average-sized bedroom in the modest wood-framed bungalows of John's neighborhood back home. It was constructed from wooden artillery shell crates (each measuring two-feet long by one-foot high by two-feet deep) which were filled with dirt and sand and stacked atop one another, forming the walls of a room that was twelve feet across by seven feet in height.

A picture collection, mainly comprised of Playboy centerfolds in simple wooden frames and protected by clear plastic covering, hung

John Podlaski

on the walls. This display reflected the efforts of a seasoned soldier who may have already gone home; the newest picture was over a year old.

The ceiling had a base of flat steel plating that traversed the walls and supported six layers of green sandbags. Several four-inch thick wooden beams, spaced evenly throughout the hooch supported the heavy roof. A hundred-bulb string of holiday tree lights hung overhead and provided the only source of light.

The cool dampness of the hooch was a relief from the stifling, muggy heat outside. The air was still and without circulation, but the sweet smell of burning incense emanating from a corner covered the predominantly musty odor throughout.

"Junior, just how strong is this thing?" John asked, glancing around the shelter.

"I don't know. Never seen one destroyed. I have heard that it will take a direct hit from a mortar and stop bullets, but those 122mm rockets and RPG's wreak havoc with bunkers and hooches. I wouldn't want to be in here then."

"Did this place ever get hit?"

"Yeah it did; twice at the beginning of last month. Normally, there's only an infantry platoon providing security for the firebase artillery unit. On that particular day, though, an entire company of soldiers spent the night in the firebase, making it really overcrowded. During that night, the VC put Sappers in the wire. One was careless and hit a trip flare, and it immediately lit up the whole damn area."

John listened, captivated, while Junior continued to relay the details of the assault, fascinated by Junior's knack for storytelling.

"Bunker guards began a mad minute, shooting at shadows all around the perimeter. The rest of the company joined in the firing after reaching the surrounding berm. Now, people have told me that the sight and sound of all that firepower was awesome. Only one mishap occurred when several claymores went off at the same time; the explosions created a powerful, bright light that temporarily blinded the men on that side of the perimeter. Even with their eyes closed, the outline of the explosion remained and continued to affect their vision for a solid fifteen minutes. They said it was like staring at a bright light bulb for thirty seconds, and then closing your eyes - the glow remained for a long time. Hundreds of tracer rounds, fired during the attack, added to the whole fireworks display. There were strings of moving red lights that flew across the ground and ricocheted into the sky after hitting the ground. The next morning, patrols discovered six VC bodies in the wire, and several blood trails leading away from the firebase. Then, two nights later, after the company had returned to the bush, the firebase was hit with twenty mortar rounds, but only a couple of our guys got hurt and there wasn't much damage."

"Where's the company now?" John asked at the end of Junior's account.

"They're in a place called the Hobo Woods, finding VC and booby traps all over the place. In the two weeks they've been there, they've killed twelve of the enemy and found a couple of caches. But we lost a bunch of guys too; some might be back in a week or so."

"When do you think I'll be going out?"

"They were just resupplied this morning, so you missed your chance. You'll most likely go out on the next one in a couple of days."

"Will you be going out, too?"

"Nah, not for a while. I caught some shrapnel in my leg last month." Junior lifted his pant leg to show John two raw and scabbed cuts on his calf. "I'm still restricted to light duty and pull bunker guard each night until I can walk without pain."

"Wow, how did that happen, Junior?"

"We were mortared during one of our resupplies."

"Were you really scared when you got hit?"

"Scare me? Hell yes, it scared me. Brother, I thought the bottom of my leg had been blown off." Junior hesitated for a moment as he replayed the incident in his mind. "I was happier than shit when I found out there were only two pieces of shrapnel, but they went deep into the muscle. I had to learn how to walk again - it still hurts like hell."

There was an awkward silence for a moment, John cleared his throat and started to ask another question before Junior cut him off. "I know you have a lot of questions. I did too, when I first got here, but save them for later. Okay?"

John bit his lip, took a deep breath, and conceded to Junior with an affirmative shake of the head.

"We should go and see the Executive Office (XO). He'll want to meet you and know that you're here."

Junior led the way out of the hooch. The sudden brightness stopped John in his tracks. Shielding his eyes, he stood there for a moment in the doorway until his eyes adjusted.

"That's why you got to get some shades like me," Junior quipped. "Not only do they make you look good, but they help at times like this."

Both men smiled and began moving again. Junior reached into his pocket and pulled out some dirty and crumpled military bills. "Come on, John, I'll buy you a cold pop."

"You know, that's really funny. This is the first time I've heard somebody call soft drinks 'pop' since joining the Army. It's been 'soda' from day one and people look at me like I'm crazy if I ask for 'a pop'."

"I know the feeling. I still call it 'pop', too."

The young men were suddenly aware that it was good to hear their hometown lingo across the world from Detroit.

They came upon a tent filled with cases of soda and beer. Just inside the entrance, cans of soda filled a fifty-five gallon barrel to the brim, smothering them in quickly melting ice.

"Better get them now while they're cold," said the soldier who managed the store.

"He's got that right," Junior agreed, "enjoy it while you can. There's nothing cold to drink in the bush. Everything will be either piss warm or hot."

Junior paid for the two drinks. John quickly opened his can and took several long swallows.

"Whew! This hits the spot!" John proclaimed, then wiping his mouth with an arm sleeve.

"Not bad for a dime, right?" said Junior. "After you've been in the bush for a month, you'd gladly pay ten dollars for an ice cold pop."

They finished the drinks and threw the empties into a nearby trash barrel. Junior led the way to a large bunker in the middle of the compound; it was the main communications bunker, where battalion personnel constantly monitored activity in the field. They walked down several steps and entered a room. One of the walls had several maps pieced together into one large map, representing the battalion's current area of operations. A small red 'X' marked the individual locations of each unit in the field; at least thirty of them were scattered across a single area of the map. Several PRC-25 radios lined another wall; a lone soldier looking bored sat idly on a stool and waited for one of them to come to life. He would not have long to wait, it was already late in the day and soon the patrols would begin calling in their night defensive locations. Once deciphered, the soldier could update the map with his grease pencil.

"Hey, L-T," Junior called out, "we have us a new Cherry in the First Platoon. Do you have time to meet him before I help him get squared away?"

"Just a second, Junior," a first lieutenant mumbled from behind a handful of reports. His face, disfigured slightly on the right side, looked like he had experienced a fire during childhood. "I'll be right there."

The XO stood about six feet tall, and could not have weighed more than 150 pounds. His custom-tailored uniform was starched with neat creases that could probably have cut paper. Even his boots were spit-shined and gleaming.

Until a few weeks ago, he had been the First Platoon's leader and had humped the bush with them for nine months - three months longer than normal field duty for an officer. The colonel had to force him out of the field to serve as the XO for the company. He only had six weeks remaining in country before heading home. His job at the firebase was to liaison between the grunts (infantry) in the field and the rear, making sure the troops received everything they needed. Another part of his duty was to write letters to the families of soldiers killed in the company.

He walked over to John and extended his hand. "Hi, I'm Lieutenant Dobry. Kowalski, isn't it?" John took his hand and shook it warmly.

"Yes sir," the Cherry responded.

"Welcome to Firebase Kien. While here, be sure to pick Junior's brain and gather all the information you can from him. He has been in Vietnam a while and knows many of the tricks used in the bush." Junior smiled upon receiving this recognition.

"Tonight, to get your feet wet - so to speak - I want you to accompany Junior on bunker guard. This will give you an opportunity to learn a few things and get your eyes accustomed to working in the dark of night."

"Great, at least I'll have some company for a change," Junior exclaimed.

The L-T continued, "Then, tomorrow afternoon, you'll accompany a team going on road security. Trucks will transport you about six clicks (kilometers) up the road to a knoll overlooking the main highway to Saigon. The team provides security for the passing convoys. They have been going to the same place for the last two weeks and nothing has happened thus far, so you might actually enjoy the experience. Your team leader will brief you before leaving right after lunch."

"When will I be going out to the field?" John asked.

"The day after tomorrow, when the company receives their next re-supply."

After a brief moment of silence, Lt. Dobry asked, "Do you have any more questions for me?"

"No, sir, I don't. But if I think of any, I'm certain Junior will be nearby to answer them."

"That's good enough for me. Junior, would you take John over to Supply and help him draw out the rest of the equipment he'll need for the bush?"

"No sweat, L-T."

"And be sure to give him a hand packing his ruck," the L-T added.

"Shit, sir, it was already on my list of things to do."

The Lieutenant looked at his watch and noted, "It's almost dinner time, and you two should head out and grab a quick bite first. Remember, you've only got a little more than an hour before you have to report to your bunker."

"Yeah, can't work on an empty stomach," Junior agreed, patting his stomach.

"I'll see you two later then. Have a good night."

"Catch you later, L-T," Junior responded. John waved and nodded his head slightly in response.

"Junior, the L-T appears to be a real decent officer."

"That he is, and he doesn't act like the other lifers here. You'll find all the officers in the bush to be like him. You'll see what I mean when you get out there."

After dinner, they headed to Supply and drew out the items that John would need for the field. It took the two of them to carry everything back to the hooch. Only fifteen minutes remained before they had to report for the night guard duty.

"We need to get your stuff together for tonight and head on out. It's almost that time," Junior said, noting the time on his watch.

"What do I need?"

"Just take your air mattress, poncho liner, web belt, your 16, and throw the rest of your stuff on the cot."

With those items in hand, they left the hooch two minutes later.

The perimeter is actually a four-foot high earthen berm, created by a bulldozer when constructing the firebase. It circled the many hooches, tents, and smaller bunkers of the compound. Twelve standard-sized bunkers, eight-feet cubed, were evenly spaced on the perimeter. Supplementary firing positions, nothing more than semi-circular metal culverts covered with sand bags, stood in between each bunker.

To their front, rows of spiral barbed wire extended outward for fifty feet. Single strands of wire, pulled taut at ankle length were interspersed within the other coils.

Trip flares, hanging metal cans with stones, and claymore mines completed the defensive perimeter. Hundreds of detonation wires snaked along the ground through the sharp barbed wire, connecting the claymore mines to triggering devices within each bunker.

A green rectangular box with a telephone receiver cradled on top was also standard equipment within each bunker. A wire attached to the landline phone connected each bunker to the Command Post (CP). During the night, they would contact each bunker periodically to ask for a situation report (sit rep). In turn, anyone on the perimeter could use the same phones to contact the CP for special needs or requests of illumination after seeing or hearing movement within the wire. Mortar crews were on alert all night, as it was usually the busiest time of their watch.

Junior showed John another standard piece of equipment - the Starlight Scope. It looked like a telescope, three inches in diameter and twelve inches long. An infrared light source within enabled the viewer to see in the dark, although everything appeared in a green hue.

Their bunker was number five.

Junior walked to the small opening in the front of the bunker and pointed out to the wire. "The claymores within our area of responsibility are spread out across our front and all points forward," he said, redirecting John's attention to several devices lying in a row across a sandbagged shelf under the firing ports. "These are the detonators for each mine. You'll notice that only the center ones are pointing straight ahead and those on either end are pointing in slight angles to either the right or left." Junior indicated to them to ensure John understood the difference. "These detonators point toward the mine facing in that direction. So if you see something in the wire, pick-up the right one, remove the safety and squeeze it."

John lifted one of them for a closer examination.

"Now, as you can see," Junior continued, "the clackers are similar in design to the V-shaped exercise grips a person might use to strengthen his hands and wrist, except these offer very little resistance and only a small amount of pressure will collapse the handle. We usually squeeze those two or three times in quick succession until the mine blows.

"This is your first night out here so don't panic and start blowing up the whole place just because you hear something. Wake me if you get spooked. And above all, don't fall asleep during your watch."

John consented with a nod and then looked out into the wire, trying to familiarize himself with the scenery to his front, making a mental picture of everything he saw. Of course, it would all look totally different to him when it was pitch black outside.

Meanwhile, Junior cranked the handle on the landline, waited a few seconds, then spoke into the mouthpiece, "This is number five, manned and secured for the night."

After Junior returned the handset, he looked over to John. "Another thing I forgot to tell you was not to smoke or light a match in the open. If you must have a smoke, then you have to cover up and light it like this."

Junior placed a cigarette in his mouth then covered himself with the poncho liner. When he emerged, the lit cigarette was invisible in his cupped hands.

"That's how you do it," he continued, "To smoke it, cup your hands over it with the filter sticking out between your thumbs like this."

The flaming portion of the cigarette was invisible in Junior's cupped hands; only the butt stuck out.

"You have to bend over low to the ground to take a drag. You'd be surprised how far a lit cigarette or flame can be seen at night; a sniper only has only to sight in on the glow for a perfect head shot."

John tried it.

"My man," Junior said, complimenting him after the demonstration. "You'll get better with practice." Junior looked at his watch and said, "We'll take turns at watch tonight and split it up every two hours. This way, we can both get some sleep during the night. You can have the first shift; wake me in a couple of hours. You have any questions?"

"Not that I can think of."

"Okay. Don't fuck it up now."

Junior lay on the air mattress and covered himself with his poncho liner. It was beginning to get chilly in the bunker, so John covered his back and shoulders with his own poncho liner and then moved upstairs to the top of the bunker. Sitting with his feet dangling from the roof of the bunker, he quietly looked out into the wire.

It was dark enough for the shadows to begin playing tricks on his eyes; he was nervous and jumpy. As the shadows continued to move, John slowly lifted the Starlight Scope to his eyes, hoping not to make any sudden movements that would result in a volley of bullets fired in his direction. Through the scope site, he was momentarily relieved to see that the shadows were only the leaves of a distant tree shaking - and not VC sneaking up on him.

At nine o'clock, John retreated to the inside of the bunker. As he entered, the landline buzzed. This startled him, as he had already forgotten about the phone. Taking a few deep breaths, he walked over to the buzzing phone and lifted the handset to his ear.

"Hello?" he said meekly.

"Number five, this is the CP. Give me your sit rep," ordered the voice on the other end of the line.

"This is number five, all clear," John reported.

"Roger out."

He replaced the handset onto the cradle then returned to continue his vigil in the darkness. At ten o'clock, he woke Junior and took his place on the air mattress.

"Everything go okay?" Junior asked.

"Except for that damn phone scaring the shit out of me, it wasn't too bad."

Junior smiled and moved to the front of the bunker.

"Get some rest and I'll wake you at midnight for your next shift."

A half-hour passed and John had just dozed off when the sound of a large explosion caused him to jump from the air mattress and move aimlessly through the bunker. "What's happening?" He hollered in a panic, "Are we getting hit?"

Junior reached out and grabbed John by the shoulder. "Damn, John, settle down. We're not being attacked."

John stopped, undecided about what to do next.

"Sit your white ass down and catch your breath," Junior ordered. "You just scared the fuck out of me by jumping up like that."

"I – I didn't mean to," John stammered.

"I know you didn't, but you sure got a lot to get used to before you go out into the bush."

John tried to catch his breath and heard voices from the center of the compound: "Adjust right one-five degrees, charge four, six rounds hotel echo, fire."

He suddenly realized that the destructive rounds were firing outward and were not enemy rounds coming at them. "Man, those big guns are really loud this close up. Why are they firing anyway?"

"The CP said that Charlie Company spotted flashlights about five-hundred meters from their location. They've asked to fire several 105mm rounds around the area and will send out a patrol in the morning to investigate."

A distant and deep crump, crump, crump noise interrupted Junior's train of thought when the artillery rounds landed several miles away. A buzzing sound also came from the same direction, almost like a circular saw cutting across a wood board.

"What's that new sound?" John asked.

"It's probably a Cobra Gunship. We'll know for sure in a minute."

"Now, how in the hell can you tell that from this distance, especially in the dark?"

"You're a question machine. Just keep facing in the direction that you heard the shells hit. If we're lucky... look, there, see it?" Junior asked, pointing to a long, thin red line in the sky; it extended from somewhere in the air to the ground.

"Get some Charlie Company!" Junior cheered.

After a second, the end of the red line raced to the ground, and the sky went dark again. These 'lightening strikes' continued for a few moments and then stopped for good.

Every fifth round on a belt of ammunition was a 'tracer round', chemically treated to leave a gas vapor trail. When fired from the mini-guns of the Cobra, the rate of fire was so intense those rounds appeared as a solid line to the target.

"Wow, that looks pretty," John volunteered.

"It is to us, but you can bet your ass the VC doesn't think so. They say that when a Cobra flies over a football field firing that mini-gun, you'll find a bullet in every square foot of that field."

"Damn!" Was all John could say.

After the show, things quieted down and John returned to the air mattress, wide-awake. The rest of the night continued without incident and he became accustomed to some of the nighttime sounds of war, making it easier for him to relax.

The next morning at six o'clock, they were relieved from guard duty. Both decided against breakfast, and instead, headed straight to the hooch to get some sleep.

When John awoke at eleven, Junior was already gone, so he headed toward the mess tent to get a bite of lunch. He did not have much time to spare, as the road security team was leaving at noon.

In the mess tent, John was surprised to see Bill standing behind a serving table, dishing out mashed potatoes from a green insulated container.

"Hey, Bill, got stuck with KP, eh?" He ribbed.

"Yeah, but it ain't bad. It is just like slopping the hogs back home. All I gotta do is pass out this food. The cooks do all the pot and pan washing."

"That doesn't sound all that bad. Were you able to sleep last night with all that racket going on?"

"I slept for shit, John, and lost count of how many times I bounced into the air from my cot."

"You should have seen me! I was on bunker guard last night with that black guy, Junior. Talk about jumpy. It was a real bitch for me."

"What are you doing this afternoon?" Bill asked.

"I have to go out on road security detail in forty-five minutes. I understand we'll be back by seven, so maybe we can get together then, okay?"

"Sounds good; don't do anything stupid while you're out there, Polack. I'll look for ya later."

The road security team positioned itself on the top of a small knoll, three miles from the nearest village. Using binoculars, the six men took turns at watching the road and the surrounding rice paddies. The view was so unobstructed, they could see for five miles in any direction.

Throughout the entire afternoon, at least thirty kids surrounded the soldiers at any given time. Most of them were hustlers who tried to sell them anything from soda and whiskey, to women, chickens, and dope. It was like a flea market with everybody making sales pitches. The time passed quickly.

One of the soldiers, a pimple-faced, blonde-haired teenager reading a comic book, looked up and commented to the group, "Be very glad that the kids are out here with us today."

"Why is that?" John asked.

He dropped his book and looked John in the face. "If they weren't around, then something would definitely happen out here. The villagers know when Charlie is around, and are smart enough to not let their kids be caught in the middle of a firefight," he remarked before returning to his 'Archie' comic book.

The security team returned to the firebase at 1930. It was later than expected, but the cooks held back some food for the late arriving details. The small tent was crowded so John took his tray of food back to his hooch. When he walked in, Junior was waiting for him.

"Come on, man, I've got twenty-five minutes before guard duty, and we've got a lot of packing to do before then," Junior said.

"I didn't have a chance to eat yet," John protested.

"That's too bad. I promised the L-T that I would help you get ready for the bush. You're going out tomorrow and I won't have another chance before you leave."

"Oh, alright... let's get this over with," John whined.

"First thing we have to do is fit this aluminum frame to your back. All your possessions will be carried on your back so you better make sure it's comfortable."

Junior removed the frame after adjusting it properly and then attached an empty ammo can to the bottom of the frame. "Put all your important shit it here, like your wallet, camera, radio, writing paper, and anything else that you want to keep dry and uncrushed."

Once filled and with the waterproof lid clamped into place, Junior attached John's rucksack to the top of the frame, allowing the bottom to rest on top of the ammo can.

"John, the main thing to remember is to keep this thing balanced. Everything will have its own place. You'll have to get rid of this air mattress," Junior said, tossing it to the side. "It squeaks and makes too much noise in the bush."

"What will I have to sleep on?"

"Your poncho and the ground, just like everybody else."

"Aw, that blows!"

"Hey, man, this isn't a Boy Scout outing," Junior scolded, "Now, go through this case of C-Rations and pick out the meals you want to eat for the next three days, but take just enough to get by. Don't take any breakfast meals; it will cut down on the weight. All you'll really need in the morning is coffee or cocoa, and they don't weigh shit."

John separated the meals and placed them on the bottom of the ruck. Next, they rolled up the poncho liner and stuffed it inside, covering the cans of food. There was barely enough room left to fit two claymore mines, wires, and clackers into the pack. John pulled the flap over the bulging ruck and then secured it tightly, utilizing the pouches on the rear and sides of the rucksack, stuffing them full of packets of cocoa powder, sugar, coffee, plastic utensils, heat tabs, and cigarettes.

They added four one-quart canteens next, placing two on each side of the ruck for proper balance and then tied four smoke grenades and trip flares to the straps on the back of the ruck. The handles of six grenades fit nicely into the metal rings on the front of the web harness for easy access. The last thing they did was roll up the vinyl poncho and tie it to the underside of the ammo can with two shoelaces.

"Well, it's packed. Try it out," Junior suggested.

John put on his web harness, looped the bandolier of ammunition around his neck, and then tried to pick up his rucksack. Surprised, he was unable to lift it beyond his knees.

"Goddamn!" He exclaimed, struggling with the pack while trying to swing it onto his back.

Junior laughed. "My man, there's a trick to it," he said and reached to stop John so he wouldn't hurt himself. "Put it back on the ground, and sit down with your back against the frame."

John dropped the pack and sat on the hard-packed ground. He slid backwards across the dirt, stopping when his back touched the frame.

"Place your arms through the straps and pull yourself up by grabbing hold of something. If you can't locate anything, then turn over onto your knees and try to get up that way."

John secured the frame to his back and managed to pull himself up, taking hold of a support beam next to him. Once on his feet, he weaved from side to side and almost toppled over before Junior reached out and grabbed him.

"It'll take some time to get the feel of it. Try walking around some more," Junior encouraged.

The longer he stayed on his feet, the easier it appeared. After a couple of minutes, John was certain he could manage without falling flat on his face. He flashed a wide grin to Junior.

"How does it feel?"

"Not bad now. These sixty pounds don't seem all that heavy once you get used to it."

"Get used to it?" Junior laughed loudly. "Bro, listen up, I've been humping a ruck for four months, and I still ain't used to it. Wait until you start humping that thing out in the bush. You will swear to God it weighs three-hundred pounds. It won't be long before you cut down to one meal a day and look for other ways to make the load lighter."

Junior looked at John with admiration for the way he tried to conceal his strain under the heavy load.

"Okay, now put the ruck down. Later, you can practice more. I only have a couple of minutes left to finish up."

John dropped the ruck to the ground and looked at Junior in disbelief. "I thought we were all done."

"We're done with the ruck, but now we have to get you ready. Take off your shorts, socks, and belt, and get rid of them," Junior ordered.

"Get rid of them?" John asked. "Are you joking?"

"No joke, my man. Believe me when I tell you that you do not need them in the bush. With all that humping and sweating out there, you will rub your balls raw if you wear drawers. And not wearing a belt will prevent the ticks and leeches from getting under your belt line and burrowing into your skin. Socks will only give you problems in the bush. Without them, your feet will stay drier and you will not have as many blisters. You can either take my word and do it now, or learn it the hard way."

John was not interested in arguing with Junior, so he started removing the items as Junior had suggested. When finished, he reached for his tray of now-cold food.

"Not yet, brother," Junior cautioned. "We still have one last item remaining on the checklist."

"Now what else could be left?"

"Take your shoelaces halfway out of your boots."

Without questioning him any further, John untied his first boot and looked up to Junior with a look of uncertainty. "Why am I doing this? I'm not interested in braiding my shoelaces. This silver chain around my neck is all the jewelry I need," he stated sarcastically.

"Would you just knock off the shit and do what I tell you? I'm already late for guard duty," Junior shot back.

"Okay Junior, now what?" He asked when both boots were half laced.

"Take the dog tags from the chains around your neck and attach one to each shoelace. Then, retie your boots."

"Won't they get all muddy on my boots?"

"They'll get muddy, all right. At least they won't rattle as they do now hanging from your neck. You'll find out how important noise discipline is in the bush."

John sat back and stared at Junior after tying both boots. "I'm afraid to ask, but are we finally through?"

"Yeah man, go ahead and eat your chow. Try and get some practice with that ruck tonight; it'll make it a little easier on you tomorrow."

"'Sorry I was so impatient, Junior. All bullshit aside, I really do appreciate all your help. I couldn't have done it by myself."

"That's okay, what are brothers for, anyway? Someday, you'll be able to help out a Cherry and he'll be grateful and thank you for your help and understanding. Like I told you yesterday, we have to take care of each other."

Junior gathered his gear for guard duty and was about to rush out of the door when John intercepted him. "Junior!" He called, placing his hand onto the black man's shoulder. "I'm starting to get a little uptight. Will it be really bad out there?"

Junior stopped cold. "No sweat, you'll do just fine. Respect and listen to the old timers who have been here for a while, and do exactly what they tell you. Who knows, it might be weeks before you have your first firefight, and then again, it may be tomorrow. Just don't go out there thinking you are John Wayne, because it will get you killed. Get some rest tonight and don't worry about it. I gotta go. I'll see you in the morning before you leave." Junior turned with his gear in hand, and quickly dashed out through the doorway.

In the morning, everyone struggled with their gear and stumbled out of the main gate toward the helipad. When the Cherries arrived, every one of them immediately fell to the ground, exhausted. Alpha Company was not in a position yet to accept the re-supply, so the group had to sit in the hot sun and wait for over an hour.

The engines started, thus signaling an end to the uncomfortable wait. The Cherries awkwardly got to their feet and quickly boarded the choppers to wait once again. John and Bill found themselves sitting in positions identical to those of their first helicopter flight. A look of dread and despair came over them.

"Maybe our rucksacks weigh enough to hold us in."
"Let's loop arms anyway. It seemed to work the first time."
"Okay, at least we know what to expect this time."

When looking toward the gate, John could see Junior running through the whirlwind toward his chopper.

"Thought you'd leave without me saying goodbye?" He yelled over the noise of the engines.

John could only shake his head and try to force a smile.
"Good luck, Polack! I'll see you soon."

It was the first time that Junior ever called John by his nickname. John knew at that moment that, not only was Junior his mentor, he had also become his buddy.

The door gunner motioned for Junior to back away. The RPM increased wildly and the chopper began to rise. In an instant, Junior was gone.

# CHAPTER SIX

The choppers flew at a high altitude over the deep green jungle and hills. Occasionally, they passed over clearings on the peaks of hills - prior landing zones created by soldiers with C-4 explosives or possibly the result of dropped bombs and fired rockets from past encounters with the enemy.

It was ironic how beautiful everything appeared from this height; it seemed to be a tropical paradise - like photographs seen in a National Geographic magazine. There's a war going on here? How can that be? Unfortunately, for those aboard, it was the one and only time they would think of this place as paradise.

During this sightseeing excursion, each Cherry sat nervously on the chopper with his weapon held tightly in his hands. Eyes displayed fear, and they cast frenzied glances throughout the aircraft. Most chewed gum, moving their jaws rapidly in nervous anticipation of landing in the hostile bush for the first time. The speed of the choppers seemed slow from this height, but in reality, they were traveling over one-hundred knots per hour.

After twenty minutes in the air, a chimney of yellow smoke rose from the corner of a small clearing ahead. The door gunners, alerted to the impending landing, moved into action. They raised the machine guns toward the surrounding jungle and peered over the top for any signs of the enemy.

The chopper banked slightly and began to drop toward the smoke-filled clearing.

"Nice knowing you, Bill," John said, looking into Bill's sympathetic eyes.

"Likewise, buddy" Bill responded.

Two soldiers, stood sixty feet apart in the waist-deep elephant grass, holding their rifles high overhead – the pilots bore down on the men and landed just to their front. Once down, groups of soldiers dashed into the clearing and ran toward the choppers.

"Get the fuck off the bird and hurry into the tree line," one of them hollered over the noise to the helicopter full of Cherries. He pointed toward a large bamboo thicket on the edge of the clearing.

The Cherries pulled themselves across the floor and leapt from the chopper, running as fast as they could toward the protective cover of the jungle tree line. Once there, the eight soldiers bent over at the waist, gasped for air, and awaited instructions. The new arrivals, fascinated by the group of soldiers in the clearing, watched intently as they unloaded the choppers. They pushed and threw everything out of the doors and onto growing piles on the ground, emptying the supplies in thirty seconds. The guide-on soldier, patiently waiting in front of each chopper, gave the pilot a thumbs-up sign when everyone was clear of the aircraft. Acknowledging, the pilots prepared for departure. The whining pitch of the turbines increased and the chopping sound made by the rotors intensified; on cue, the pilots jerked their birds back into the sky.

When they were gone, the unloading party picked up and began carrying boxes and sacks to different locations around the small clearing.

"Hey, guys follow me," one of them said as he passed, carrying a case of C-Rations on each shoulder.

He led them through the brush to a spot where a group of ten men sat around, some conversing in a small circle.

"This is the Company Command Platoon (CP)," the stranger informed the Cherries. "Stay right here and somebody will help you in a minute." He continued to move across the area to deliver the supplies he was carrying.

The captain was in a conference with his four lieutenants. They sat on the ground in a small circle, individual maps laid out in front of them. Two of the lieutenants were drawing symbols and sketching reference lines on their maps with grease pencils as the captain discussed his plan for the next three days - reviewing routes of travel, prospective ambush sites, and potential hot spots. The other soldiers outside of the circle, sat and lay casually on the ground in small groups. Their rucks and attached PRC-25 radios sat beside them; two of the radios had long, twenty-foot tall antennas attached. The radio operators continuously chatted on their handsets, coordinating with the firebase and Battalion HQ in Cu Chi.

When the staff meeting ended, the captain was the first to acknowledge the new group of Cherries.

"Gentlemen," he said to his officers, "it appears our new replacements have arrived."

The lieutenants turned and candidly glanced at the group. The captain, a short man appearing to be no older than the Cherries themselves, stepped out of the circle and moved toward them.

Waving to them with his shorter, modified M-16 rifle, he quipped, "Welcome to the war. I'm Captain Fowler." He stopped, turning toward the four second lieutenants, who were rising slowly from the ground, folding their maps. He motioned to the four officers and turned his head to address the Cherries.

"These men are the officers of Alpha Company," he began, "Lieutenant Ramsey is from the First Platoon." A tall, blond-haired man with wire-rimmed glasses acknowledged the group with a smile. "Lieutenant Monroe is from the Second." A light skinned, black man with the right brim of his boony hat folded up Aussie-style raised his arm in greeting.

"What's happening, blood?" one of the black Cherries asked, raising a clenched fist in the air.

"At ease, troop!" Lt. Monroe replied, his stare hard and glaring.

The captain, glancing between the two men, wondered how far this would go. Satisfied, he continued, "This is Lieutenant Carlisle from the Third." He motioned to a slightly overweight and shortest of the four men, who smiled broadly.

"Most of you are assigned to my platoon," he volunteered cheerfully.

Captain Fowler smiled in acknowledgement. "And finally, we have Lieutenant Quincy from the Fourth Platoon." The partially bald man and oldest of the four, removed a corncob pipe from his mouth and smiled, exposing a mouthful of crooked, yellow, nicotine-stained teeth.

"We work as a team in the bush," the captain continued. "Every one of us wants to get out of this alive and return to our families in one piece. So listen to your squad leaders and follow their instructions.

"The company will be leaving in two hours. You men already know your platoon assignments, so join up with your respective officer and they will show you where the rest of your platoon is camped. So let's get this resupply over with and get out of here." Captain Fowler was all business and did not give any of them a chance to ask questions.

Seeing Lt. Ramsey gathering up his gear, John quickly left the group of Cherries and moved toward him.

"Excuse me, sir, my name is John Kowalski. It appears I'm the only one going to the First Platoon."

The L-T picked up his rucksack with the left hand and swung it over his shoulder. He then offered John his right hand. "Glad to meet you, John," he said, shaking the soldier's hand warmly. "Did you join this man's Army or were you drafted like many of us?"

"I was drafted, sir."

"You can dispense with the formalities out here in the bush. There's no need to call me "sir"; L-T will be fine."

"Yes sir, I mean L-T," John replied.

Lt. Ramsey chuckled.

"Come on and follow me. I'll show you where our position is."

John followed Lt. Ramsey as he led him around the outskirts of the clearing to the other side of the LZ. En route, they passed various groups of soldiers lying about in the underbrush. They were writing letters, eating, sleeping, playing cards, or packing their rucks with new supplies. A few of them looked up as the two passed, offering a nod of encouragement. Others made comments from the shadows.

"Welcome to Hell, Cherry."

"Just look at this! Uncle Sam is robbing the cradle and sending them over right out of grade school."

"Somebody throw this boy a towel, so he can wipe behind his ears."

"Fuck him, he probably won't last the night."

There was laughter as the men congratulated each other for their ingenuity and quick wit.

"Don't pay any attention to them," the L-T offered, "it's kind of an initiation, and we all go through it."

The two-man parade continued. When they reached their destination, only a handful of grunts were sitting in the shade around twice as many rucksacks.

"Just park it right here," Lt. Ramsey instructed. "You'll be in Sixpack's Squad."

"Where are they now, L-T?"

"They're on Listening Post (LP) about two-hundred meters out, watching for Charlie in case he tries to surprise us during the resupply. I'll introduce you to them when they get back in." The L-T walked away.

John sat on the ground away from the others and waited, leaning against a thick trunk. He scanned the dense vegetation and thought about the woods on Belle Isle back home.

Belle Isle was a small island in the middle of the one-half-mile wide Detroit River, located between the shores of downtown Detroit and Windsor, Ontario, Canada. The island was notorious for many reasons, and was used as a loading point for bootleggers, ferrying alcohol from Canada during Prohibition. One obtained access to the island by crossing over a quarter-mile long bridge from the east shore of Detroit, unless, of course, he had a boat - there were several marinas with docks in which to moor any size watercraft. In 1926, it was from this very same bridge that the famed magician, Harry Houdini, attempted a dangerous water-escape trick. The trick failed and the magician was recued – a few moments longer and he would have drowned in the murky waters below.

The residents of Detroit came to the island for relaxation and to escape the heat and stresses of big city living. During a summer weekend, the beaches, picnic areas, athletic fields, zoo, aquarium, and flower gardens overflowed.

As an alternative to visiting the crowded public areas, many people simply cruised the loop around the island, driving slowly to enjoy the cool island air. The panorama of freshly manicured lawns, ornamental flowerbeds lining the road, and lovers paddling canoes through the many internal canals was enough to tranquilize the senses.

It was common to see families either sitting on blankets at the shoreline or parked in cars on the side of the road. Everyone watched in awe as the large lake freighters and pleasure boats passed in both directions.

For families of modest means - such as John's – Belle Isle offered the closest thing to a vacation they'd experience, and for many, it was their only frame of reference for the great outdoors.

At night, however, the island took on an entirely different aura. The woods on the island were always dark and mysterious. Sometimes, while driving through the shadowy forest, deer and other forms of wild life suddenly made their presence known to the people venturing into their domain. Vines and bushes surrounded the tall trees, growing wild, reaching up from the ground to choke them. The brush was so thick it was near impossible to enter beyond twenty feet of the road. Insects thrived both in the island air and on the ground.

Sometimes at night, teenagers would dare each other to make their way through the woods on foot. Tales of murderers, thieves, bums, and the ghost of The Great Houdini lurking around in the eerie shadows, compelled the jittery youths to bolt through the dark abyss.

The foreign sounds of jungle wildlife interrupted John's reverie. The sight of a weasel-like monkey swinging through the branches above further catapulting the young soldier back to reality. It was difficult to see the bright sun through the thick foliage; the jungle was filled with creeping shadows, making it appear late in the afternoon. John glanced at his watch and was stunned to find it was not yet noon.

The damp ground and musty smell made him feel uncomfortable. When he looked into the clearing of the LZ, the bright sunlight affected his eyes as it did when exiting a dark movie theater in the middle of the day.

The radio operator nearby could be heard calling out, "L-T, both LP squads are coming in."

"Thanks Bob. Notify the rest of the perimeter," the L-T ordered, "No reason at all for an accident."

As his eyes gradually adjusted to the change in light, John made out the forms of approaching men.

Even from a distance of fifty feet, he could make out the noticeable and jagged scar on Sgt. Holmes' face; it started just above his top lip - a thick black mustache concealed most of it - and then continued across the left side of his face, ending abruptly below the ear. John would find out later that it was the result of a car accident twelve years earlier, that claimed the life of his older brother. Holmes' shaggy and curly black hair appeared longer than most, a green bandanna tied securely around his head kept the hair out of his eyes. At six feet, six inches tall, he towered above the rest of the soldiers.

Larry carried an M-60 Machine Gun across his shoulder. An unbroken belt of ammunition wrapped around his body from his waist up to his chest. His build was similar to Sgt. Holmes, but stood almost a foot shorter. Somehow, he had managed to find a black beret, which covered the blond hair on his head. Larry wore a pair of oversized plastic-rimmed glasses, which, at first glance, appeared to be goggles. He was the first to spot John.

He pushed Sgt. Holmes to get his attention. "Hey, Sixpack, look, it's the Polack," he hollered out in surprise.

"I'll be damned!" Sgt. Holmes said, surprised to see John sitting there.

Both raced over to where John now stood, wrapping their sweaty arms around him.

"Polack, what a surprise," Larry exclaimed.

"Am I ever glad to see you guys!"

"So am I," Sgt. Holmes added, "it's always good to see a friendly face."

"What squad are you in?" Larry asked after releasing John from a bear hug.

"The L-T said I was going to Sixpack's Squad. I'm waiting for him to show up."

"Look no more," Sgt. Holmes said, "you're looking at him."

"No shit?"

"No shit, Polack."

"Why do they call you that?"

"I'll tell you later when there's more time."

"Hey, Sixpack," Larry interrupted, "we better get our supplies before they're all gone."

"You're right. Polack, stay right here, we'll be back in a short." Grabbing their rucksacks, both headed over to the stash of First Platoon supplies. A red nylon bag with 'U.S. MAIL' stenciled in bright white letters lay off to the side. Larry dropped two letters into the bag and picked out a pair of washed fatigues from a pile of delivered clothes. Both he and Sixpack were in dire need of new fatigues, as theirs were torn and heavily soiled with sweat. While changing, John noted neither of them were wearing underwear or a belt.

"Junior wasn't bullshitting me," John said to nobody in particular.

After the change, they quickly picked out their supplies and began packing them into the deflated rucksacks. In ten minutes, both returned to the area with bulging rucksacks.

"Polack, come with me," Larry said upon reaching John, pulling him up by the arm. "I'll introduce you to the rest of the squad."

They walked over to the only remaining people who were busy packing their own rucksacks.

"Hey, guys, we have a new member in the squad. I want you all to meet Polack. We go all the way back to Basic Training," Larry informed them, placing his arm across John's shoulders.

John smiled to each of them as Larry said their names and pointed them out. "This is Zeke, Wild Bill, Doc, Frenchie, Scout, and the Vietnamese is Nung."

They all acknowledged John, either nodding or giving him a faint wave when Larry introduced him.

"I can see you're all busy, so we'll talk to you guys later." Larry turned to leave with John in tow.

"Why is there a Vietnamese with the squad?" John asked.

"Nung is our Kit Carson scout. He used to be an enemy soldier, but changed sides after some renegade Communists killed his family. He once fought against us in this very same area, so after retraining in Saigon, he is now our scout. Nung usually knows when something is not right. The other guys have said that his intuition had saved this platoon many times already; they have a lot of respect for him."

"Can he really be trusted?" John asked.

"Hell yes, man, he's like one of the family."

After returning, they found Sixpack sitting on the ground, leaning against his rucksack and smoking a large cigar. Both sat down on the ground close to him.

"Hey Sergeant, how about telling me why they call you Sixpack now," John asked.

"I guess now is as good of a time as any," he replied after exhaling a puff of cigar smoke in John's direction. "I brought a six-pack of beer to Nam with me from Oakland. It's stored back in the rear with my belongings, and I plan to open the cans and suck them dry in a celebration during the flight home after my tour. The guys in Cu Chi were pretty amused by this and began calling me Sixpack, so the name stuck."

"Did anybody else we know make it to the 25th with you?" Larry pushed his glasses up higher on the bridge of his nose.

"Only one I know for certain is Bill Sayers. He went to the Third Platoon."

"No shit. Do you remember him, Sixpack?" Larry asked.

"Not really."

"Bill Sayers is that red-headed hillbilly who looked like Howdy Doody. We met up with him in Oakland?"

"Oh yeah, I remember him now. Everything fascinated him."

"That's the guy!"

The three of them collected their gear and then joined up with the rest of their squad.

Before they had a chance to start any conversations, the L-T walked over. "I can see you found the right squad," he said, looking directly at John. "The three of you act like old buddies. Do you know each other from back in the world?"

Sixpack responded, "Polack and Larry were both in my AIT Platoon back in Fort Polk."

"Polack - is that his new nickname?" L-T Ramsey asked.

"No, he got it in Basic. We've been calling him that since," Larry volunteered.

"That's great – Polack it is! I do hate to break up this reunion," he said, turning to address the squad as a whole. "The bird is on its way to pick up the mail and extra supplies. We will be moving out as soon as it is airborne. Third Platoon will be on point, and we will follow with the Company CP. Get your people ready, Sixpack." The L-T turned and walked back to join his RTO, Bob.

"Oh, just fucking great!" Zeke protested. "Those motherfuckers make one loud noise while they're with us, I'll shove those radios right up their asses."

"What's wrong with the CP?" Sixpack asked.

"Those guys don't know what it's like to be quiet. They're forever yakking on their radios, cussing and complaining during the humps, breaking branches, and always slowing things down."

"That's not fair, Zeke," Sixpack interrupted, "we need those guys and their radios in the bush."

"I know we need the radios, but I just don't care for the fuckers that carry them. They make me too nervous."

"Relax, Zeke, let's see how it plays out. Maybe there's been a change since you moved with them last."

"Okay, but if they . . ."Zeke stopped abruptly at the sound of a smoke grenade popping out on the LZ. The familiar whipping and chopping sound of an impending Huey helicopter echoed through the jungle, getting louder as it approached. It soon landed, picked up the unused supplies, and was airborne again within fifteen seconds.

After the sound of the chopper faded, the RTO called out, "Third Platoon is coming through, and we're starting to move out."

Within a minute, two soldiers approached and headed toward the hole in the jungle, where the two squads had come through earlier. The lead person (point man) held a machete in his right hand and carried his M-16 by the handle in his left. The person directly behind him carried a shotgun and followed the point man closely.

There was a twenty-foot gap, and then a line of soldiers began to pass.

As they went by, those knowing each other exchanged words of encouragement.

Every one of them was bending forward at a thirty-degree angle, trying desperately to manage the heavy loads they carried. They would be lighter the next day, when some of the food and water were gone.

"Okay, saddle up! We're moving out right behind these guys," the L-T ordered.

As the First Platoon members struggled to stand and help one another to their feet, the last person in the passing column, Bill Sayers, approached. His eyes were wide and a smile lit his face when he saw John, Larry, and Sixpack standing together.

"Hey there!" He called, "can I get a transfer to your platoon?"

"Not right now, but hang in there, and I'll see if I can pull some strings."

"I'll be counting on it, Sergeant Holmes."

"It's 'Sixpack' to my friends."

Bill hesitated, "Okay, Sixpack."

As he passed, members of the First Platoon fell in, joining the caravan. The heat was unbearable, feeling like an inferno. Shirts were already soaking wet from sweat and they had only been moving for ten minutes. John continuously wiped the sweat from his burning eyes with the sleeve of his shirt. Beads of sweat ran down his back, collecting in an uncomfortable puddle where the rucksack frame rested on the small of his back. He tried to relieve the itching sensation but could not do so without removing the rucksack.

Zeke's helmet bobbed up and down in front of John as they inched along. He had only thirty days left before his yearlong tour ended. He had been with the same squad the entire eleven months, and at nineteen years old, was one of the "old timers" in the platoon. The L-T occasionally called on him for advice before sending out patrols, and considered him the platoon's most valuable asset. In his time there, he had witnessed many situations requiring a cool head, and saw enough VC tactics to quickly recognize potential ambush sites. He was aggressive and did not cut any slack, which helped him get through it all without a scratch. John was to find out later that Zeke had already received the Bronze Star with a "V" device for Valor for saving two grunts who were hit during a firefight and later trapped by the enemy. He had crawled through the gunfire and pulled them both to safety.

John's steel helmet began to give him a stiff neck and the straps of the rucksack made his shoulders numb. Although he had always been fairly athletic and played football in high school, nothing he had ever experienced physically in his past even came close to this bone-deep exhaustion.

'I hope we'll be stopping soon for a breather. I can't go on any further,' he uttered to himself.

He continued to follow Zeke absentmindedly for another thousand steps. His only concern at that point was in finding a way to manage the extreme weight on his back coupled with the hellish temperature. Finally, word made its way back to the men to take a five-minute break. John let the weight of his ruck pull him to the ground. Once he slipped out of the ruck straps, the circulation returned to his numb shoulders, but the throbbing pain continued. He unhooked one of his quart canteens, drank three-quarters of the warm water, and then poured some of the contents over his head.

"Hey! Dumbass! Easy with the water," Zeke scolded in a hushed voice. "It has to last you two more days. You keep drinking like that, and you'll be out of water in an hour, get all cramped up, and fall flat on your ass."

John was embarrassed, looking around; he noticed others taking very small sips of water; nobody pouring any over themselves.

"Sorry, Zeke," John whispered back humbly. "Thanks for the advice."

Two minutes passed and John looked to Zeke, whispering, "Why does everyone have green towels hanging from their necks? Isn't it too hot for that?"

"The towel doesn't make a difference in this heat, but it is a great help when humping. It serves as a cushion under your shoulder straps, and comes in handy for wiping sweat from your eyes instead of using your shirt sleeve."

"Thanks, teach."

"Don't mention it."

John quickly pulled his towel from his rucksack and draped it over his shoulders.

Up ahead, people began to move about and help each other to their feet. The caravan was on the move once again.

This time, the towel helped to make it a little easier on John. When the next break came, he was not hurting quite as bad.

In the two hours of humping, the company had only managed to travel one click (one thousand meters or one kilometer) through the nearly impenetrable jungle. The column stopped and bunched up when the point man came upon a large, unmarked trail. It measured ten feet across and showed signs of recent activity. The Third Platoon sent out small recon patrols to investigate in both directions, the rest of the company dropped in place for a break. After a twenty-minute delay, the column began moving once again.

When Sixpack's Squad reached the trail, they crossed it one man at a time. As John moved across, he noticed a few members of the Third Platoon crouched fifty feet away on both sides of the column. They were watching for the enemy and providing security while the company traversed the open ground.

After the last man in the company had crossed the trail, the column halted once again. This time, however, it was to set up a Night Defensive Position (NDP).

Before assigning individual positions, Sixpack spoke to the other three squad leaders, coordinating the night ambush. Each squad had to give up two men. The eight soldiers would ambush the trail from two different locations. Zeke and Frenchie from the First Squad quickly volunteered.

"I want to be as far away from this CP as possible. With only thirty days left in this country, I don't want to get hit because of some noisy-assed radio operators," Zeke declared.

"I don't blame you!" Frenchie added.

As the L-T briefed the ambush teams, Sixpack assigned the remaining First Squad members to sleeping positions around their sector of the perimeter.

They shared a few machetes among themselves to dig out sleeping areas - hacking away at branches, roots, and stones until they were sure nothing protruded from the ground to poke at their sleeping bodies during the night.

When ponchos and liners were in place on the ground and gear was stored properly, only then could they prepare dinner. Everyone had his own recipe and special additives from home to make the C-Rations taste better. Heinz-57 sauce and Tabasco were two favorites; squad members shared them freely.

After dinner, Sixpack instructed his squad on the placement of claymore mines and trip flares. The guard position had to be set up in a central location to be accessible to every sleep position; a clear and unobstructed path was necessary so very little noise was made during the night when changing the guards.

It was evening and there was still a bit of light in the jungle when everyone finished their tasks to secure the NDP for the night. Each soldier took a few minutes to familiarize himself with the immediate surroundings. During the pitch black of night, when it was impossible to see, it was essential to know the routes of travel, as well as the sleeping position of your guard duty replacement.

Sixpack assigned each squad member an individual time for the night watch. John had the shift from five to six in the morning. Since it was the last watch, he also had the responsibility of waking everyone in the morning. He was ecstatic, and felt lucky to be able to get a full night's sleep on his first night in the bush.

John squeezed out some "bug juice" into the palm of his hand, wiped the repellent across his exposed skin, and lay on his makeshift bed. He was completely spent from the long hump that day.

Sixpack walked up to him. "Hey, Polack, are you all squared away for the night?"

"As good as I'll ever be."

"Good. Later when you are on watch, the CP will call you on the radio for a situation report. Our call sign is Romeo-six. If everything is all right, you do not have to say anything, just push the call switch of the handset once – we call it keying the mike. Make sure the volume is set low on the radio and then hold the handset close during the watch. The radio is our lifeline, so if called or something unexpected happens; it has to be available quickly without any stumbling around in the dark to look for it. If you get nervous, wake me, I can keep you company. I know the first night in the bush is a bitch, and I can sympathize with you."

"Romeo-six, keying the mike, keep the volume of the radio turned down, check, I think I have it," John recited.

"Hang in there," Sixpack replied, then turned to leave.

"Sixpack!" John whispered. "How about answering a question before you leave?"

"Sure, what is it?"

"The night before last, when I was on guard duty at Firebase Kien, we saw a Cobra working out. Junior, the guy with me, said that Charlie Company saw something and had requested the artillery and gunships. Did they find anything?"

"Yeah, but it doesn't sound too good. The L-T told us earlier that it was more than they had bargained for."

"What do you mean by that?"

"They sent out two squads on this routine patrol to check the area this morning and found six VC bodies. They began to celebrate and got careless, making too much noise on the return to their NDP. The VC heard them and immediately laid an ambush. When sprung, half of the men in the patrol went down. The rest took off, shooting wildly toward their ambushers to break contact. The intensity of the ambush made them believe they were greatly outnumbered. In their haste to escape, they left the dead and wounded behind. When they returned within an hour in full force, all the bodies were gone."

"What will happen now?"

"They asked for Alpha Company's help. We'll link up with Charlie Company tomorrow and make a sweep of the area to see what we can find."

"You think we'll find the missing bodies?"

"I don't know. We may run into the VC first. So we should prepare for the worst and be ready for anything."

John took a few deep breaths. "I sure hope there aren't going to be any VC around."

"I'm not too fond of a firefight either, but don't lose any sleep worrying about it - that will just make you crazy." Sixpack advised and then started to walk away. "I'll see you in the morning."

John lay back down and tried to make himself as comfortable as possible. The exotic sounds of jungle wildlife were especially loud tonight. In the twilight, he tried to spot stars in the sky through the thick overhead growth. He knew it wasn't possible to see the sun through the dense trees in the daytime, but just maybe it was different at night.

His astronomy search ended abruptly when he spotted something he hadn't noticed earlier. Just several feet above his head were two huge spiders, both as big as pancakes, and sitting in the exact center of their circular webs. A chill ran down his spine and goose bumps broke out on his arms. He was scared to death of spiders, and it was too late to move to a new area. Furthermore, by no means was he going to knock them from their webs to crawl around on the ground with him.

Now, finding himself in an uncomfortable position, there was no alternative but to keep an eye on them. He stared at them for ten minutes, just to make sure they did not move around. As he did this, he noticed swarms of flying insects above the webs. The larger dragonflies and horseflies dominated the airspace as they darted through swarms of buzzing mosquitoes. He hoped that a few of them would get caught in the webs so the spiders would be occupied for the rest of the night and wouldn't drop in on him while he slept.

John covered up with the poncho liner and tucked it in over his head. It was enough to keep out the swarms of flying insects, but the buzzing around his ears was unbearable.

"Hey, Polack, get up, it's your watch," someone whispered in his ear.

He sat upright and tried focusing his eyes in the now pitch-black darkness. It was no use, and he wondered if it was possible to have gone blind while asleep.

"Who's that?" John whispered.

"It's Scout," the same voice replied. "Take hold of my arm, and I'll guide you to the watch area."

He picked up his rifle and ammo then snatched a handful of Scout's shirt, following him like a blind man. In spite of his best efforts earlier to memorize landmarks, John was very unaware of his location, which caused a feeling of total helplessness.

"Are you going to be alright, Polack?" Scout asked, sensing something was wrong.

"Scout, I think I'm blind. I can't see shit," John whispered.

"Give it a couple of minutes. Just sit down and I'll stick around until your night vision comes to you."

John sat quietly with Scout. After a few minutes, he could finally make out the shadows of a few bushes and trees to his front. When John turned to face him, he could see the sharply defined profile of the Cherokee soldier nicknamed 'Scout' sitting next to him in the darkness.

"Okay, thanks, I can see you, so I'll be fine now."

"I'm glad. It is always a bitch when you first wake up in the bush. It happens to everyone. Oh well, at least I still have forty-five minutes to get some sleep. Here's the radio handset," he said, holding it out and tapping him on the shoulder. "I'll see you later."

He vanished into the darkness, leaving John alone at watch.

John sat perfectly still, straining to see. He held the handset to one ear and tried to listen in on the eerie jungle sounds with the other.

"Thank God it'll be light in half an hour," he said to himself.

Just then, he heard a rush of static in the radio receiver and a voice whispering, "Romeo-six, this is Alpha-one, sit-rep, over."

John squeezed the handset once, as Sgt. Holmes had instructed him earlier, which caused the noisy static to cease for an instant and then return after releasing the button.

"Sierra-six, this is Alpha-one, sit-rep, over," the voice through the handset continued. A break in the static was their response. That continued for the next couple of minutes until all the elements of the company had responded - including the ambush teams.

The jungle began to lighten up a little at a time toward the end of John's shift. He watched as a fog began materializing. The moist dew appeared to move as it saturated everything within four feet of the ground. When he felt his poncho liner and fatigues, he found they were already wet.

At six o'clock, he took his rifle and walked over to where Sixpack was sleeping. After John gave him a couple of shakes, he opened his eyes.

"Morning, Sarge," John said cheerfully. It's time to get up." Sixpack jumped to his feet and began to stretch.

"Thanks, Polack," he said. "Start waking everyone else in the squad and tell them to hurry and eat breakfast. We have to be ready to leave on a patrol at seven."

"OK, will do." John left to wake the other five men, making sure he passed on the information as Sixpack had instructed. As he was doing this, the two ambush teams had arrived at the NDP, and individual members were moving through and returning to their designated squad locations. Sixpack caught both Zeke and Frenchie when they arrived and personally informed them of the upcoming patrol.

When John returned to his sleep area to pack up his gear, he looked up and found the two spiders still centered in the webs. Had they not been there, he would have scoured the ground looking for them before sitting down.

He pulled out a heat tab and began to heat some water for cocoa. It was ironic for a person in this country to be so very hot during the day, yet so cold at the night.

John added a packet of cocoa powder to his canteen cup of boiling water, stirring the contents with a plastic spoon. Before taking a drink, he raised the cup as in a toast, and said, 'I made it through my first day in the bush, only 335 more days to go.'

# CHAPTER SEVEN

Sixpack called for a pre-patrol briefing before the squad members had a chance to eat breakfast; most of their time since waking was spent retrieving claymore mines and trip flares from their hidden positions of the night before. The men trickled over, carrying their morning meal of coffee, cocoa, or C-Rations, to consume while listening.

Sixpack and Scout extracted a brittle muffin from a vacuum-packed C-Ration tin and spread jelly over the top. Then, with painstaking care, they pecked at theirs gingerly so it would not fall apart, crumbling in their hands. Doc, Zeke, and Wild Bill took a seat on the ground, leaning against a nearby tree with a two-foot wide trunk; each brought a can of semi-solid scrambled eggs and a canteen cup of steaming cocoa. John sat across from Sixpack and appeared very nervous; his canteen cup of coffee, shook in his hand when he raised it to his lips. Larry arrived with some coffee and continued brushing his teeth. After finding a suitable place to sit, he removed the toothbrush and spat the foamy liquid onto some nearby bushes. He took a sip of coffee, swirled it around, and then swallowed the sweetened liquid. Nung sat next to Sixpack, quite content with his meal of cold spaghetti and meatballs.

"Listen up, guys." Sixpack sipped from his canteen cup of steaming coffee, holding it in both hands while speaking. "We have to check out the trail we crossed yesterday."

"How far do we have to go?" Scout asked.

"I don't know. We have to be back here in a couple of hours, so we'll play it by ear."

"What's happening in two hours?" Wild Bill asked, scratching at some mosquito bites protruding from a wild stallion tattoo on his forearm.

"We have to assist Charlie Company in a sweep of their area later to help find their missing guys."

"That's going to be fun," Zeke said sarcastically.

Ignoring the comment and flashing Zeke a look of disappointment, Sixpack continued, "Okay, when reaching the trail, we'll go west for a while and scope it out. I do not want anybody walking on the trail itself. Stay off to the side and cut bush if you have to. Something this well - used is sure to be booby-trapped and watched by the VC; the shrubbery will help us with concealment and cover. Order of march will be Nung, Scout, and Larry, me, Polack, and Doc. Frenchie, you and Zeke will bring up the rear."

"What about me?" Wild Bill asked.

"I want you on our left flank. Stay within twenty feet of the column and keep us in sight at all times."

"Who's going to carry the radio?" Zeke inquired. He was squeezing out a generous portion of white salve onto his red, swollen feet, and then rubbing them vigorously to work in the medicine. Zeke's feet were infected with jungle rot, a fungus quite common to GI's in the wet jungle. Both feet looked like prunes; some areas looked like layers of skin had already come off and had a nauseating smell. Zeke's attempt to disinfect the raw skin and wrap his feet with sterile gauze just did not seem to be enough. John wondered how he was even able to walk.

Doc glanced at Zeke's feet. "Looking much better, my man, keep up the good work."

Zeke nodded his head in agreement, continuing to rub in the ointment. John could not fathom that Zeke's feet could have looked any worse.

"Bob, the L-T's RTO, will be going with us," Sixpack said.

"What does the brass know about this trail?" Scout asked.

"Not a thing, I'm going to sketch the trail on my map as we go along. Everyone should bring a claymore. Zeke, you, and Frenchie take enough supplies to build a mechanical ambush. We'll find a good spot and set it up before heading back. If we run into an ambush, break contact as fast as you can, and work your way back down the trail to regroup. Remember, nobody leaves anyone behind if he's hit."

"How soon before we leave?" John asked.

"In thirty minutes."

At seven sharp, the First Squad left the defensive perimeter and set out for the trail, walking along the same path created the day before. Men in the column should have been spaced evenly apart, with at least ten feet separating them. However, the dense, tangled jungle did not allow for this without each man losing sight of the person to his in front.

On this patrol, rucksacks stayed within the NDP. The grunts wore only suspenders and web gear, which held a canteen of water, ammo pouches, grenades, a claymore, and smoke grenades. Without the added weight, the ten men maneuvered quickly through the tunnel of foliage, covering the two-hundred meters to the trail in less than thirty minutes.

"Look at the size of this thing!" Larry exclaimed, peering down the width of the trail. "I bet you can drive a semi-truck through here."

"They can make it wider yet by smashing down this elephant grass," Wild Bill added.

"Yeah, then it would be a three-lane highway," Zeke said, glancing up and down the trail.

"It sure didn't look this big yesterday."

"Hell, we didn't have this much time to admire it."

Nung walked through the chest-high elephant grass, then squatted near the oversized trail. The dirt was packed solid from heavy use; most likely it was a route to Cambodia.

"No wonder it isn't on the map," Wild Bill speculated, "There's no way a plane could spot it through these tall trees and heavy overhead cover."

"It's natural camouflage," Zeke added, looking upward into the canopy.

"I wonder if we're the first GI's to stumble across it," Larry remarked.

"I doubt it, but the last time had to be a while ago," Sixpack replied.

"Sergeant, come for one minute!" Nung called from a spot thirty feet up the trail.

"What do you have?" Sixpack asked when reaching him.

"Look!" Nung parted some shrouds of elephant grass and held them apart so Sixpack could see the Ho Chi Minh sandal footprints along the trail. This style of footwear was most common to the Viet Cong, who produced them from old truck tires - the tread marks on the soles plainly visible in the dirt of the trail.

"How old do you think they are?" Sixpack asked.

"They short time, maybe two hours." Nung felt along the impressions; the edges of the footprints collapsed when he pressed down with his finger. Something older would be stiff and hardened by the hot sun by now.

The two men rose to their feet and walked back toward the squad.

Sixpack whispered to the others, "Nung found some fresh prints in the elephant grass about thirty feet forward and to the side of the trail. We will keep to this side of the trail and move through the elephant grass. Do not use machetes; this way the breeze will help cover any sound of our movements. Stay within sight of the person in front of you and keep your eyes and ears open."

Sixpack then faced Nung and patted him on the shoulder. "Nung, lead the way," he ordered in a hushed tone.

Nung moved through the now head-high elephant grass with his M-16 ready to fire. He was hunched over and stalking through the jungle with the agility of a cat, head turning slowly from side to side with each step, making certain not to miss anything. Walking three feet behind him, Scout scanned the treetops and overhead cover for trail-watchers and snipers.

Larry had found two extra belts and fashioned a sling for his M-60, allowing it to hang from his shoulder. Holding the heavy weapon at hip level, he could pivot from side to side and fire instantly.

Sixpack stopped the column periodically to check his bearings, duplicating the route of the trail on his map with a grease pencil.

Bob, the RTO, followed closely on Sixpack's heels with the short whip radio antenna folded over and tucked into his ammo harness. To ensure noise discipline, Bob had the volume so low, it was necessary to hold the handset to his ear while moving.

John tried to be as quiet as possible. He fumbled along, attempting to place his feet into Bob's footsteps. His head swiveled from side to side, and his eyes darted in all directions watching for the enemy, which he suspected were hidden everywhere around him.

The squad soon arrived at the location of Zeke's night ambush site. It was there that Nung decided to stop the column for a break. Each member stopped in his tracks and put a knee on the ground. Except for a few flattened areas in the elephant grass, there were no other signs of the ambush team having been there.

John turned and looked at Doc, who was wiping sweat from his face with the towel hanging around his neck. When the medic saw him watching, he flashed a bright smile and gave a thumbs-up sign. John silently returned the gesture.

Frenchie stood ten feet beyond Doc, aiming his M-79 Grenade Launcher at the trail, watching the jungle behind the column. A beehive round - a special shell that fired pellets like a shotgun – was chambered in his weapon. Each round resembled an oversized bullet, one and a half inches in diameter and three inches long. Frenchie's special vest held a combination of beehive rounds, high explosive rounds (like grenades), and white phosphorus rounds, thirty in total.

Zeke was the last man in the column. He sat down in the high grass between the column and the main trail, a spot which offered the best view of the trail behind them. He watched the trail intently, periodically scanning the canopy above.

When the patrol resumed, the pace was slower and more cautious. Twenty minutes later the column stopped suddenly. Nung was agitated as he moved back along the column toward Sixpack.

"Sergeant, please come," he whispered upon reaching him.

Sixpack turned to John. "Stay put and pass it on," he whispered, then departed with Nung to the front of the column.

Five minutes later, they returned with Scout in tow. Sixpack circled his arm over his head, and then pointed toward the rear. The squad performed an about-face and began moving in the opposite direction the way they came. After walking three-hundred steps, Sixpack halted the men and called them together.

"There's something big back there, but we don't know exactly what. It could very likely be a base camp. Nung found another trail crossing ours; we followed it for about fifty feet and stopped after hearing Vietnamese music and people talking. We spotted a lookout on a platform in a tree; they were watching for movement on the main trail. I don't know if anyone saw us, but I know our squad wouldn't have a chance in a place like that. I'm going to call the L-T, then request some artillery. Meanwhile, Zeke and Frenchie, set up the mechanical on the trail right here. Spread out five mines along the trail and place the tripwire in the center. Polack, you can give them a hand and learn how to build one. Larry, take your gun to the side of the trail and blast anyone who comes walking this way. Scout, cover the other end of the trail. Zeke, you let us know when you're done."

As the squad deployed, Sixpack called on the radio, "Romeo-one actual, this is Romeo-one-six, over."

"This is Romeo-one actual, go," the L-T replied.

"Romeo-one actual, be advised that we may have located a major base camp along the trail and I'd like permission to call in artillery on that position."

"Wait one."

While Sixpack spoke on the radio, Bob used the daily code sheet to cipher the coordinates so Sixpack could pass them over the radio without a delay.

"Romeo-one-six, Romeo-one actual," the L-T called after a few minutes.

"Go ahead, Romeo-one actual."

"Permission granted, over."

"Roger. I will send the coordinates to Wolfpack and request the fire mission. You can listen on their net to pick up my location."

"Wilco. Do you plan on leaving a mechanical en route?"

"That's affirmative. We're working on it now."

"Roger. Keep me informed. This is Romeo-one actual, out."

John assisted in placing a claymore mine every ten feet along the trail and covered them with leaves and branches as instructed; the mechanical ambush covered seventy feet of the trail. Meanwhile, Frenchie unrolled the detonation cord, and cut off pieces at twelve-foot lengths. Zeke took them next, attaching blasting caps to both ends. After he completed two of them, he handed them to John.

"Start connecting the mines," Zeke ordered.

"How do I do that?" John asked.

"Go to the furthest mine on the left and stick the blasting cap from one end of a detonation cord into the right side hole, and then take the other end and stick it into the left hole of the fourth mine. Do the same thing with the second cord and connect number four to number three."

John connected the two mines and returned to where Zeke continued working on the blasting caps. "Okay, I think I've got it now."

"Good," Zeke said, handing him two more cords, "Now connect number three to two and two to one with these pieces. They call this 'daisy chaining'. When you finish, cover all the white cord with grass and leaves, but make it look natural."

John returned, satisfied that he had camouflaged the cord to Zeke's specifications.

"Okay, we're all set, announced Zeke. You two wait here and I'll double check everything."

Once he was sure that everything was positioned correctly, Zeke called out to Scout, who was securing the area and hidden from sight, "Scout, we're good to go. Come on, time to head back."

"I'm with ya, bud!" Scout replied. The two men hurried back through the elephant grass to Frenchie and John, who had already unrolled the fifty feet of wire to its full length behind and perpendicular to the row of mines.

Frenchie looped the end of the wire over a tree branch and the four men rejoined the rest of the squad.

"It's ready to go, Sixpack. All we have to do is hook up the battery."

"Good job, Zeke! Take Polack and Frenchie with you, connect the battery, and get back here on the double. We'll move back down the trail a ways and call in a fire mission on that base camp and get the hell out of here."

Frenchie produced a six-volt square battery and the three returned to where they had left the end of the long wire. Once there, they lay prone on the ground while Frenchie secured each of the two wires to the battery posts. Both he and Zeke breathed a sigh of relief when no detonation occurred.

"It's ready to blow," Frenchie announced with a smile.

"How does this mechanical work?" John asked.

"That's right, I forgot you're a Cherry and don't know shit yet." Zeke and Frenchie connected with a smile. "The fishing line running across the trail is pulled taut and only one end - the one with the plastic knife - will give if somebody trips through. Now the knife is keeping two pieces of metal from touching. As you know, the mines are daisy-chained so they will blow after mine number-five gets an electrical charge. To make that happen, you ran that last brown wire with a blasting cap to number-five so it will be the first to blow and the others will follow in succession. I took the two ends of that cord and attached one wire to each lid. Then we took the two ends of this cord," Zeke shook it for John to see, "and secured each wire to the same two metal lids like we did the first one. Now that Frenchie hooked these two wires to the battery, the ambush is live and deadly. With an electrical charge running to both halves of the metal lid, only that plastic knife is keeping them apart. When something trips the wire, the knife will pull out and allow the two halves of metal to touch. Then, BOOM." Zeke raises his voice enough to startle John. "The five mines explode in sequence and in three seconds, it's all over."

"We're a pretty good distance from the mines, so why did we have to lay on the ground to hook up the battery?"

"That's so a malfunction won't kill us. Some of these blasting caps can be defective, or the knife might pull out and we wouldn't know it. If the mines blow, you can still get hurt standing behind them, even from this distance."

"Has that ever happened before?"

"I've heard of it happening before, but I've never personally had it happen to me."

"Come on, guys, let's get the fuck out of here," Frenchie insisted, "We can play twenty questions later." They quickly got to their feet, allowing Frenchie to lead them back down the trail.

When joining up with the squad once again, Sixpack took the radio handset from Bob and called the artillery unit.

"Wolfpack-one, this is Romeo-one-six. I have a fire mission at coordinates x-ray, papa, mike, lima, tango, tango, alpha."

"Roger, Romeo-one-six. What is your target?"

"This is Romeo-one-six. We have a suspected enemy base camp. Fire one round Willie Pete and wait for correction."

"Roger. We'll notify you when shot is out, over."

"Romeo-one-six, standing by."

After a moment of silence, a voice called out from the radio, "Romeo-one-six, this is Wolfpack-one. Shot is out."

The sound of the 105mm artillery gun firing from Firebase Kien reached the squad a few seconds before the round whistled by overhead. They looked in the direction of the enemy base camp and watched for the White Phosphorus shell to explode in the air. If Sixpack calculated correctly, it should explode three-hundred meters away.

A bursting white cloud materialized just above the canopy a split second before the report of an explosion reached the squad. Sixpack studied his map and looked at the spreading smoke a couple more times, before getting back on the phone with the artillery crew.

"Romeo-one-six, add two-hundred feet and fire six rounds of hotel echo (high explosive)."

Seconds later, Wolfpack-one called, "Romeo-one-six shot out."

They heard the distant firing again, but this time, tremendous ear-shattering explosions shook the ground following the whistling overhead.

"This is Romeo-one-six, left two-hundred feet, and add one-hundred," Sixpack requested.

"Roger."

Fifteen seconds later, Wolfpack-one called, "Shot out."

This time the explosions triggered a secondary explosion.

"Goddamn!" Zeke exclaimed. "If it was a basecamp, it sounds like we hit their ammo dump."

"Wolfpack-one, Romeo-one-six. We heard the report of a secondary explosion. Traverse the area and fire for effect," Sixpack then tossed the handset to Bob. "Okay guys; let's get the fuck out of Dodge."

They moved just short of a full sprint. Overhead, the rounds whistled as they continued toward the target. After fifteen minutes, it suddenly quieted.

"Romeo-one-six, this is Wolfpack-one. Fire mission is complete," the voice over the radio relayed proudly. "Do you need anything else?"

"Negative, Wolfpack," Sixpack replied into the handset while running. "Nice shooting, and thanks for your help. We will let you know what we find when we check it out. Romeo-one-six, out."

When the squad arrived at the hacked out trail leading to the company NDP, the sound of a loud ripple explosion from the trail stopped them cold.

"Whoo-weee!" Zeke cried out. "That was our mechanical! I would sure like to know how many of them we killed."

"This is not the time; we'll find out as soon as we finish with Charlie Company," Sixpack replied. "But you can bet your ass we won't check it out with any less than a full company," he announced.

Bob called to the CP on the radio, "Romeo-one, this is Romeo-one-six, returning to NDP. ETA is five minutes."

"Roger, Romeo-one-six. Welcome back."

The First Squad had not been in the perimeter for more than thirty minutes before Sixpack gave the word to saddle up.

"Get your shit together," he ordered. "We have to hump to yesterday's resupply LZ and catch choppers that will take us to join up with Charlie Company."

"How about giving us a break?" Larry moaned. "We haven't even caught our breath yet."

"I know, but the captain says we have to link up and be on the move with Charlie Company by 1400 hours, so get the lead out. Let's go, let's go," he repeated.

Second Platoon had taken the point during the return procession, which took them across the same terrain they passed through the day before.

The column humped the entire distance without a break. After reaching their destination, they had to wait another twenty minutes before the birds arrived. Many of the soldiers took this time as an opportunity to eat something.

First and Second Platoons would be extracted first. Each platoon moved onto the extensive LZ, and then split into smaller elements as they moved across the large, grassy meadow. The seventy soldiers boarded the ten awaiting helicopters for the short flight to link with Charlie Company.

"ETA of the birds is three minutes," yelled a radio operator from the CP.

Upon hearing the announcement, one person from each group of seven moved to a predetermined position thirty foot away from their respective groups. When the time came, these ten men raised their rifles high overhead to signal the location for the chopper pilot to land. This protocol, used for every extraction, was the most efficient way to load a helicopter and get it airborne again.

A green smoke grenade popped in the center of the LZ, signaling, and then confirming that it was the correct location. The gaggle of helicopters was approaching in a similar formation to the men standing on the ground. During their final descent, two Cobra Gunships arrived and circled overhead like mother hawks keeping an eye on their chicks, shadowing the formation en route to the next LZ and back for the second sortie.

The flight to Charlie Company's LZ took ten minutes, saving the men of Alpha Company from humping ten hours to cover the same distance on the ground.

The new LZ was much smaller and was only large enough to accommodate two helicopters at the same time. The insertion was almost as fast, with both platoons together on the ground within one minute of the first helicopter touching down.

The men moved into the tree line and waited for the rest of the company to land. It did not take long for the comments and innuendos to begin.

"Look out, here comes bad-ass Alpha to save the day."

"Yeah, that's right! If you sorry fuckers hadn't left your wounded behind, we wouldn't have to come to bail your sorry asses out."
"Fuck you!"
"Fuck your mama."
"Leave mothers out of it."
"Why should I? It's her fault for raising an asshole."

Only a handful of individuals engaged in this banter, and it appeared to be more of a personal vendetta between those men. Different groups of Charlie Company soldiers lay in the shade of the jungle surrounding the LZ. One such bunch of men huddled together in the shadows of a large bamboo hedgerow. They were smoking cigarettes and paying little, if any, attention to what they saw or heard between the two groups. However, once the CP landed twenty minutes later, it all abruptly came to a halt.

One shirtless man wearing a green bandanna tied around his head and several necklaces of peace beads around his neck, approached the LZ, a radio operator following on his heels. He rushed out to greet Alpha Company's Captain.

"Morning, Joe, glad you've come."

"Hello, Henry, glad we're able to help." The two men shook hands and walked back into the thick vegetation.

Captain Joe must have known the Charlie Company Commander well, as he was not surprised or taken aback by the lack of professional appearance.

After reviewing the plan and coordinating the search, both companies moved out in separate columns, heading deeper into the jungle.

The chopping noise heard overhead continued as two gunships kept pace with the moving search party. They flew lazy circles nearby and stood ready to provide additional firepower in the event of an enemy attack. An officer from Battalion HQ also buzzed around in a small Loach helicopter at treetop level. From above, he directed the two companies in their every move. The search turned out to be no more than an endless hump through the jungle as they continued to move deeper into the bush.

"I can't understand how we're supposed to sneak up on the enemy while we're making this much of a racket," Larry stated.

"It doesn't make sense to me either," John added.

"At least they know we're coming. Maybe they'll run and hide."

"Don't you Cherries know anything?" Zeke spoke up. "We're going to be very lucky if Charlie doesn't ambush us."

"Give them a break," Scout complained. "Don't you remember when you were a Cherry?"

"I do, but I wasn't as fucking ignorant."

"Yeah, so you say! In reality, none of us was any different when we first came here. We were all scared and full of questions."

Zeke did not respond and instead continued forward in silence.

At 1700 hours, the gunships left and both companies split up to find a separate night defensive position.

When they were five-hundred meters apart, Captain Joe stopped Alpha Company and set up a large perimeter.

Everyone was exhausted. The men dropped their ponchos onto the jungle floor without any concern for the condition of the ground beneath.

When John applied some bug juice to his exposed skin, he winced in pain. After looking closely, he discovered dozens of razor-like cuts on his face, neck, and arms. Surprised, he called for Doc.

"How did this happen?" He asked Doc.

"You most likely got them from the elephant grass this morning. The edges are razor sharp and cut through the skin unknowingly. It stings like hell when alcohol in the bug juice washes over them."

"Don't I know it!" John added.

Doc pulled a tube of ointment from his pack and squeezed a small dab of white cream onto his finger, wiping it across several slits on John's arms and face. "That should do it," he said after administering the first aid.

"Thanks, Doc."

"No sweat, my man. I have to go now. Just about everyone else is having the same problem so it'll be awhile before I can rest."

"Take it easy, Doc," John called to the departing black medic.

Soon, Larry and Wild Bill dropped in at John's position.

"What the fuck happened to you?" Larry asked.

"Doc said I was cut from the elephant grass this morning."

"Isn't it a bitch?" Wild Bill stated. "You don't know the cuts are even there until you use bug juice. Next time we are in the high grass, keep your sleeves rolled down and your collar up. It'll be warmer, but you won't get as many cuts."

"What kind of shit do you guys think we're going to get ourselves into tomorrow?" Larry asked.

"I can't even begin to imagine," John replied.

# CHAPTER EIGHT

Alpha Company arrived in the area where the ambush took place just after 0900. There was no question a firefight took place here; brass casings from weapons of both sides littered the trail, glistening in the sunlight like dropped gems on this narrow, bloody path.

The captain halted the column and dispatched Third Platoon to recon the immediate area while everyone else took a break.

The sun blinded the men as it neared its apex in the hazy, blue sky. Most sought refuge from the hot, burning rays; John, Larry, and Wild Bill moved from the trail and took a seat in the shade of a small palm tree. A light, refreshing breeze blew steadily through the palm trees. Leaves swayed gently, allowing tiny spots of sunlight to dance on the faces of the three young men.

"I can't begin to imagine what happened here three days ago," John commented.

"I know what happened," Wild Bill began. "See those brass casings on the trail?"

"Yeah."

"Most are from AK-47s."

"So," Larry asserted, "Charlie Company was ambushed. There should be more rounds from the Russian-made weapons."

"That's not the point," Wild Bill searched for the right words. "Any time you are ambushed by the enemy, you try to break contact by returning more fire, then regroup to either attack or withdraw. I could only spot a handful of M-16 casings, which means Charlie Company did very little firing after they were hit."

"But look at all the bloodstains on the trail and leaves; they can't all belong to the missing soldiers."

"You'd be surprised at how much blood a body loses," Wild Bill continued. "Two or three guys hit in the right places could have created all this mess."

The rest of the squad, led by Sixpack, walked over to join the three men in the slowly disappearing shade.

"We're going out with a squad from Second Platoon on a patrol," Sixpack informed them.

"What's the deal?" Zeke asked.

"The entire company is splitting up to search through a specific area within a grid. Our area is two-hundred yards up this trail. Once we get there, we will fan out to the left of the trail and sweep the area on our way back. If any of you spot something, holler, and we'll check it out."

"Come on, let's get this over with," Zeke said, rising to his feet.

Fourth Platoon was staying behind to secure the equipment, remaining on alert and ready to reinforce any of the small groups if they got in trouble.

After moving up the small trail for fifteen minutes, the two-squad patrol made a turn to the left and cut their way through the vegetation. The last man in the column passed the word along when he entered onto the new footpath.

"Hold it up!" Sixpack raised his right arm to signify a halt when the word reached him. Leaving his position in the column, he moved forward toward the point man. "Close it up some," he instructed, trying to get them on line for the sweep. "Keep about ten feet between yourselves. Come on, get this line evened out." Sixpack paced back and forth in front of the row of nineteen soldiers.

That part of the jungle was not very dense and consisted of knee-high elephant grass and shoulder-high bushes. However, a hundred feet to their front, several thickets of bamboo rose up from the earth. As large as houses, the green, thorny, and leafy hollow stems were entwined tightly in the impassible clump of vegetation.

"Okay, let's move out," Sixpack ordered. The row of men began moving forward in a slow, controlled march.

As they advanced, they whipped at the grass with their legs and poked into the bushes with rifles. John was unsure of his duties as he moved forward at a leisurely pace.

"Hey Zeke!" John called to the soldier on his left.

Zeke broke formation and walked over to him. "Will you shut the fuck up?" He was pissed and his manner caught John by surprise.

"Hey, I'm sorry. I thought with the gunships and Loach flying around, the VC knew we were coming anyway. I'm not sure what to look for and I don't want to pass over anything important."

"Aw, shit man," Zeke sighed, "just look for signs of somebody having been through here. See if you can spot any broken branches, blood splotches on leaves, or loose dirt on the ground."

"Why worry about loose dirt?"

"It could be a tunnel entrance, shallow grave, or maybe a weapon cache. Just be careful not to touch anything," Zeke cautioned.

"Thanks, Zeke."

Zeke rendered an irritated expression before returning to his position in line.

Now understanding his task, John continued to search, but couldn't help being distracted by the drama down on the ground. Hordes of insects moving over everything fascinated him. Several columns of large black ants moved in the same direction, carrying leaves, pebbles, and twigs.

After following the ant caravan for thirty seconds, he came upon an area swarming with the small insects. It was not a social event for the many colonies of ants, but a war between the black ants he was following and thousands of vicious red fire ants. Reinforcements for both sides poured into the quagmire from all directions. It was a fierce battle. Fresh troops steadily arrived, joining in the fight, others departing, carrying dead or wounded comrades in their jaws or on leaf stretchers.

When John suddenly looked up, he found himself at least forty feet behind the row of soldiers. In a panic, he leapt through the battlefield like a child playing hopscotch.

He returned to the line and then heard Sixpack holler from an unseen position to his left.

"Stop where you are and work your way towards me. Somebody find the L-T."

Zeke sprinted toward the sound of Sixpack's voice. "What did you find?" He asked upon arriving.

"Looks like a cache."

Zeke and Sixpack worked carefully, gently probing for booby traps with knives before clearing away some underbrush and matted elephant grass from the side of a tree.

"There's stuff buried here!" Zeke yelled.

"Careful," Sixpack cautioned, "let's wait until the L-T gets here."

Meanwhile, the line of soldiers had collapsed and gathered around the two men. Before any of them could ask questions, Lt. Ramsey arrived with the other two squads, forcing his way through the crowd.

"What is it, Sixpack?" He asked.

"Looks like a cache, L-T."

"Okay, give us some room and back away," he said to the surrounding mob. "Bob, get the captain on the horn. Tell him we might have found a cache, and I'll get back to him as soon as possible," Lt. Ramsey ordered his RTO.

While the three men further probed the entrance, the balance of the platoon moved away to set up a small perimeter around them.

With the large hole in the ground exposed, Sixpack reached in and felt around.

"All clear, it's not booby trapped." He then lifted out a fifty-pound sack of rice from the hole.

"Shit, man, there's enough in here to supply an enemy platoon for a month," Zeke declared.

"What a find," the young lieutenant stated. "Let's empty this hole and see what it all amounts to."

"Polack, Frenchie, Scout, Wild Bill, come here!" Sixpack called.

The four men left their positions on the small perimeter and hustled over toward the sergeant.

"What's up?" Scout was the first to ask when arriving.

"We've got to empty this hole. Set up a line to my left. Zeke and I will pull everything out of the hole and pass it along; you guys stack it where the L-T tells you."

"How much is there?" Wild Bill asked.

"I don't know. We can't see the bottom," Zeke answered.

As the lieutenant supervised, the human conveyor emptied the contents of the hole.

"Bob, call the captain and ask him what he wants to do with all this shit," Lt. Ramsey ordered. "Make sure you tell him there's enough to fill a chopper," he emphasized and then watched Wild Bill walk by with another large bag of rice in his arms.

Sixpack raised his head above the rim of the crater.

"Hey L-T, seems to be another cavern down there. Do you want me to check it out?"

"Go ahead, but be careful."

The eight-foot deep by six-foot wide pit looked like a miniature silo. Grooves chiseled into the rocky brown clay wall resembled rungs of a ladder from top to bottom.

Sgt. Holmes cautiously made his descent back into the hole and upon reaching the bottom, dropped to his hands and knees. First, he removed his thirty-eight caliber automatic pistol from a shoulder holster and unclasped the flashlight from his harness belt, setting the rest of his equipment to the side. Following the beam of his flashlight, Sixpack slowly moved forward on his forearms and knees into the four-foot-by-four-foot entrance in the wall. He held the flashlight far to the side and away from him, hoping that if the enemy spotted the light and fired at it, it would thus miss him. He could return fire by aiming directly at the flash of the other weapon.

His heart pounded and sweat poured from him as he inched along the claustrophobia-inducing corridor. Twenty feet later, he came upon - what he believed to be - the end of the tunnel. Instead, he found that it continued after a ninety-degree turn. Sixpack held his breath, cautiously peering around the bend.

"Well, kiss my ass!" He uttered.

To his astonishment, there was a trap door in the wall with light emerging from its cracks. Curious, he moved slowly toward it. Once there, he placed the revolver on the ground and unsheathed his

Bowie Knife, using it as an extension of his hand to probe around the wooden doorway.

After a painstaking inspection, he found the door free of booby-traps and explosives. Sitting back on his heels, he took a few deep breaths, hoping to slow his rapid heartbeat.

After a minute, Sgt. Holmes regained his composure. Returning the large knife, he picked up the pistol and took hold of the trap door.

"Here goes nothing," he said, pulling gently on the door. It squeaked loudly, startling him enough to mutter "Holy fuck!" He quietly closed the trap door and inched his way backward several feet. He found it impossible to turn himself around in the small confines of the tunnel, quickly crawling backwards toward the cache pit.

"Zeke, there's one hell of a complex down here," Sixpack gasped, standing and brushing the red mud from his clothes while trying to gulp air.

"Hey, L-T, Sixpack found an underground complex," Zeke called from his position at the top of the pit.

"Tell him to get the fuck out of there," Lt. Ramsey ordered. "We'll call for a tunnel team." The L-T rushed over to the rim of the hole and stood with Zeke.

After Sixpack reached the top rung of the earthen ladder, both Zeke and Lt. Ramsey took hold of an arm and pulled him from the shaft. His uniform and hair were drenched with sweat and coated with red mud.

"Jesus Christ," Sixpack began, "I've never seen anything like it before." His heavy, labored breathing continued.

"Take your time, Sixpack," the L-T insisted. "After you catch your breath, you can tell us what you saw."

"Sir," he began, and then struggled to breathe deeply, quivering as a slight and sudden breeze sent a chill down his wet spine. "I found a trap door at the end of the tunnel," he continued. "And after checking it for booby traps, I pulled it open."

Sixpack stopped again to fully inhale the fresh air.

"Come on, Sixpack, the suspense is killing me," Zeke prodded.

"Don't push him, Zeke," the L-T cautioned, "he'll tell us when he can."

Sixpack smiled and continued, "When I looked through the door, there was a hallway large enough for me to walk down. Bright lights hung from the walls and lit up the entire complex. I can't believe something like that existed underground."

"Did you see anybody?"

"No, I didn't."

"Good. It will be easier for the tunnel team when they arrive. "Nice work, Sixpack!"

"'Just doing my job, sir."

"Nevertheless, it was a hell of a job," the L-T commended. "We need to comb the immediate area and look for breathing tubes in the ground, another entrance, or anything else suspicious."

"I'll get my men on that right away." He turned to Zeke, "gather everyone up and I'll join you in a few minutes."

"Will do!" Zeke walked to the perimeter, seeking out the rest of his squad members.

After the fruitless search, the platoon gathered around the various piles of supplies.

"Don't touch anything," Lt. Ramsey cautioned. "Everything is listed on this paper," he said, waving it at the group. "Here's what we have so far: six fifty-pound bags of rice, three cases of U.S. C-Rations, sixteen mortar rounds, five AK-47 assault rifles, two pistols, one RPD machine gun." The officer stopped briefly, then continued, "five crates filled with thousands of rounds of ammunition, seventeen B-40 rockets, fifteen grenades, various medical supplies, uniforms, eight pairs of Ho Chi Minh sandals, four shovels, three picks, and five empty NVA rucksacks and web gear."

"Son of a bitch!" Frenchie commented, his face showing concern. "What in the hell are NVA doing this far south?"

"I haven't the slightest idea."

"Frenchie, what do you mean by NVA?"

"There are two kinds of enemy soldiers in the Nam, Larry. The Viet Cong, or VC, generally operate in this part of the country; they either snipe at us or spring a fast ambush before running away. Most of them are nearby villagers. The North Vietnamese Army, or NVA, on the other hand, are hardcore motherfuckers who go to army training like us. They do not run like the VC. Instead, they dig in and fight your ass, even if it means fighting to the last man."

"That doesn't sound good at all. Do you think this cache belongs to them?"

"You can bet your ass on that, Larry."

"What's going to happen now?" John asked.

"I'm curious as hell to find out what else is down there," Lt. Ramsey replied. "But we just have to wait patiently for the right people to do that job."

Suddenly, a Huey helicopter appeared overhead. The Brigade Commander had received word of the find and was circling for a view from above.

"Look at that cocksucker flying around up there. Probably never humped the bush since he's been here," Zeke stated when he saw the C&C (Command & Control) Huey overhead.

"Hey, L-T," Bob called, "there's a bird on the way with a couple of teams and a tracker dog. They'll be here in ten minutes."

"Okay, people, you heard the man. Set up some kind of a perimeter. We don't want any dinks walking up on us," the L-T ordered.

When the team arrived, they went right to work. A dog handler and two other men descended into the silo, while two intelligence officers who arrived with them remained above ground. One of them took pictures of the cache from every angle as the other looked over the L-T's list of contents.

Along the hasty perimeter, the men stole glances at two officers as they sifted through the treasure, acting like a couple of kids in a toy store. Both officers were frenzied in their investigation, closely looking over each item before returning it to one of the piles.

After forty-five minutes, one of the tunnel rats emerged from the hole.

"You guys really came onto something big," he stated to Lt. Ramsey, before turning to address one of the captains from the intelligence team. "Sir, it appears to be an underground staging area and hospital. We found two operating rooms, complete with enough medical equipment to perform major surgery. The place is loaded with documents and is unbelievably spotless."

Their faces lit up at the news, jubilant at the significant discovery. The same reaction would have been exhibited by the troops around the perimeter had they suddenly been informed that the war had just ended.

A One-Star General and his entourage finally arrived at the location. After a few words with the officer holding the camera, he headed to one of the piles of captured enemy supplies. Placing a foot upon an ammo crate, he picked up one of the AK-47 rifles and held it proudly in front of him, smiling while the photographer snapped away.

"Isn't this a crock of shit?" Zeke declared. "We find the fucking thing, and it's the General who gets his picture taken, just like he stumbled upon it himself."

"Why do you let shit like this get to you, Zeke? It's not the first time this happened here, and it won't be the last. If the Division General was around, his ass would be out here taking credit and posing for pictures, too," Doc pointed out.

"Fuck those lifer motherfuckers!"

"Lieutenant," a major from the General's staff called to the First Platoon leader, "please assign a squad to go down into the tunnel with the demo team, so they won't have to watch over their shoulders while setting the charges."

"Fuck them!" Zeke blurted. "They took the credit for the find. Let them provide security and blow the bitch themselves."

Fortunately, for Zeke, the General and his staff did not hear his outburst - or if they did, they chose to ignore it. Nevertheless, Sixpack strolled over and led the upset soldier away from the tunnel entrance. "Come on, Zeke, cool it, man. You're going home in three weeks and don't need to do anything stupid to blow it for yourself now. Just let him get his nuts off."

"This is bullshit, Sixpack! It's been like this since I got here. Every time something like this happens, the brass comes in and takes all the credit. We get dirty, they get to pose and smile. What's wrong with all of us posing with them? I wouldn't have a problem with that, but they've never even asked us."

"Zeke, I saw the same thing during my last tour. I guess it depends on the individual. The colonel we had used to involve everybody in the picture and then have articles written in the Stars and Stripes newspaper. They're not all the same. Just let it go. It don't mean nothin'."

The two intelligence officers entered the hole to join the dog, his handler, and the two tunnel rats as they made their way into the complex. They needed to be thorough and to be certain not to overlook anything during their exploration.

Fifteen minutes later, the demo team touched down with the explosives. First Squad drew the shortest straw, so they would escort the demo team and provide security underground. Together, they had to move three hundred pounds of plastic explosive, dozens of blasting caps, a few hundred feet of detonation cord, and several electronic gadgets into the complex.

Sixpack led his squad of eight men down into the silo. Upon reaching the entrance, each man crawled into the tunnel, either pulling or pushing his cargo until exiting through the trap door and into the bright hallway of the underground complex. Everyone stood in awe, admiring the unbelievable sight before them.

"How in the hell does somebody create something like this underground?" John asked incredulously, taking it all in.

"These people have been fighting wars in this country for decades. Since World War 2, it's been the Japanese, then the French, and now us", reminded Doc. "There's no telling how long this place has been here."

"I remember seeing old war movies that showed the POWs building tunnels from their barracks so they could escape. It seemed like it took them months to complete them," Larry chimed in.

"Yeah, but you got to remember that those POWs had to scrounge for material. The VC, on the other hand, had supplies brought in by the truck load. Now, add a few hundred workers to the plan, and they can dig out complexes like this in no time."

Wood planking braced the six-foot high walls; packed closely together, the earth behind barely showed. As the squad proceeded along the dirt floor of the corridor, they noticed a dozen portable lights hanging from the walls at ten-foot intervals. They also found several side rooms in the complex; most were small, measuring less than one-hundred fifty square feet. Four of them must have been for recovering patients, containing cots and footlockers in each of them. Two others were larger - almost twice the size of the single rooms – and had wooden floors and bright reflective lights hanging from the seven foot ceiling. Various trays of operating instruments rested upon rolling carts in a corner near small sterilizing units. The dried blood spatter on the floor - most likely from a recent surgery - stood out among the well-scrubbed and maintained walls.

The furthest room from the entrance had a small generator and air pump supplying oxygen into the complex via bamboo tube ducting, which was why they had not found breathing tubes on the surface.

Across the aisle was an office and communication center. The two intelligence officers spent most of their time in there gathering various documents. Much of their findings consisted of patient files, medical supply request forms, and reconnaissance reports about nearby American and ARVN activity. A large map hung from the wall with arrows pointing in different directions, apparently signifying troop movements. The location of Firebase Kien and several other military compounds were circled and highlighted.

Earlier, the officers had found a PRC-25 radio, six extra batteries, and a couple of U.S. code books. The frequencies had been set to the same as Alpha Company, which might have accounted for their quick getaway. The enemy departed in such haste that they failed to take many important documents and supplies with them. Escaping with their very lives was the priority.

When Doc, Zeke, and Frenchie entered one of the rooms, they found it empty and bare, which was curious, as every other room contained either equipment or supplies. Doc leaned against a wall and suddenly lost his balance as it gave way and swiveled inward.

"What the hell?" Zeke commented when he noticed the medic sprawled on the floor. "Doc, you okay?"

"The fucking wall moved." Doc said soberly. He was slow to rise, but managed to get to his feet when helped by John and Larry.

Frenchie left to notify the others.

Zeke approached the small section of the wall and pushed it open. "Shit, this is nothing but wood and dry mud, and there's a stairway leading up."

Sixpack and the others entered the room after hearing of the new discovery.

"Wild Bill, go topside and let the L-T know we've found another exit. Tell him we're coming up, and to pass the word on to the rest of the company so they don't shoot our asses up," Sixpack ordered.

When Wild Bill returned several minutes later, Sixpack and the others observed the dog and his handler cautiously ascending the steps and approaching the camouflaged exit, which was a small trap door, barely large enough for the handler and his charge to squeeze through. He returned after a few minutes.

"You guys aren't going to believe this. Come take a look for yourself."

One by one, they climbed the stairway and exited the tunnel complex, only to find themselves standing within a twenty-foot thick clump of bamboo with a small crawlspace cut through the thicket. Scout crawled through the thorny vegetation first and succeeded in dislodging the 'bamboo plug' used to camouflage the entrance.

"Get a load of this!" he proclaimed from the other side.

Each of them had similar reactions upon exiting the thicket.

"Well, kiss my ass!"

"Holy shit!"

"Do you fucking believe this shit?"

An awkward and surprising sight greeted them. Members of the Fourth Platoon milled around the same bamboo thicket, guarding the company's rucksacks, until their owners returned. In fact, the First Squad's rucksacks were only a few feet away from the camouflaged opening to the tunnel complex.

Both groups of men simply stood there staring at each other and trying to process the fact that they had been sitting on top of the compound for the last few hours, never having a clue that it existed below.

"Now I know where Charlie took off to after their encounter with Charlie Company. They just slipped back into the ground like snakes."

"You're right, Zeke, but it doesn't look like they took the missing soldiers into the hole as we didn't see any evidence of them down below."

"They moved the bodies before Charlie Company came back to nose around the area. They needed to protect their complex and did what was necessary to prevent its discovery."

"It looks like they wasted their time, Sixpack, since we found it anyway."

"Yeah, but it looks like they expected us to find it. Otherwise they would have stuck around and put up a fight."

"If they left through this exit, wouldn't the Fourth Platoon have seen them?" Scout asked.

"Who said they left from this entrance? You saw how we stumbled upon it. Well actually, Doc did." Some laughter ensued. "There are probably more hidden exits that we didn't find and most likely that's how they escaped."

"Anything's possible, Zeke, maybe they just bugged out before we even got here," Sixpack replied.

"We'll never know the answer. It'll be buried with the rest of the complex and supplies."

It took almost two hours to set the charges in the complex. Zeke and Frenchie were the explosive experts in the platoon, so they assisted the demo team with the setting and wiring of the explosives. After they finished, everyone returned topside.

The General was getting irritated because the complex was causing such a delay. He sensed the enemy nearby, and wasting time here was depriving him of a body count.

While Alpha Company awaited word to move out, the Radio Telephone Operators (RTO's) in the CP started chattering among themselves. Bob left the group and hurried toward First Platoon.

"Charlie Company found their missing guys about a half a click away from here," he said somberly. "They were all dead and found together in a shallow grave. Two bamboo poles marked the site;

each had a severed head mounted on top. Now get this, there was a sign hanging from one of them that said, 'Wolfhounds leave Vietnam, or you will end up like your comrades'."

"Holy Jesus!" Larry was visibly shaken by the news.

"Bitch!" Zeke could only muster.

"Rotten motherfuckers," Wild Bill added.

"Wait, there's more," Bob interrupted. "They were naked and each of the bodies was missing his dick."

A highly agitated Sixpack began to pace. He seemed to be muttering to himself while kicking at the dirt. "Now, see what happens when you leave somebody behind? I would bet that only a couple of them were dead when moved from the area. The VC probably enjoyed torturing the rest of them before they finally died." He bowed his head to disguise his weeping. "If we are ever on patrol and I get hit, so help me God as my witness, I'll blow away the first of you that turns tail and runs."

"That goes double for me." Frenchie shed some tears as evidenced by the streaks running down his dirty face.

"Sixpack, I hate to interrupt, but we gotta get moving, and get as far away from here as possible before it gets dark!" Zeke exclaimed, bringing everyone back to reality. "You had better let the L-T know the complex is ready to blow. He may also want to ask the General if he wants to push down the plunger. If so, make sure he brings his cameraman", he added bitterly.

"Too late, they already bugged out. Probably got too hot for them out here in the bush," Wild Bill volunteered.

All but Sixpack laughed at the comment.

After returning from his conference with the L-T, Sixpack informed the soldiers, "The company is moving out, and we're staying back to provide security until the complex is blown. Afterwards, we'll escort the demo team to a nearby LZ where the rest of the company will be waiting for us."

"It's gonna be a loud son of a bitch and will feel like an earthquake," Frenchie stated.

"I agree," Sixpack said, "Zeke, Frenchie, Scout, and Nung, you guys stick close to the demo guys. The rest of us will take your gear and wait for you down the trail."

The two groups split up. The demolition team moved toward the silo while the remaining men headed in the opposite direction, carrying a rucksack on each shoulder. The packs, light without their full ration of food and water, were easy to carry. However, that would only last until the following day, with a resupply scheduled at the firebase.

Sixpack's group paced five-hundred feet down the trail, stopping to wait for the expected explosion.

Meanwhile, the demolition team made their final preparations. The chief demo specialist took a roll of wire, splicing both ends onto the two wires leading up from the hole.

"Come on, guys, let's unreel this and move back where it'll be safer."

Nung took the point and led the group toward the trail that they would soon be traveling. Frenchie and Zeke followed them; staying about thirty feet back to ensure that nobody would sneak up on them or cut the wire.

"I think this is far enough," the leader announced, dropping to one knee. "Give me the plunger."

He unscrewed the two nuts on the poles of the small black box and wrapped a wire around each one. After reattaching the nuts securely, he pulled the plunger up until he heard a click.

"It's ready to go."

Scout removed the metal cap from the top of a twelve-inch long by one-inch round cylinder, fitting it over the metal on the opposite end. He held the cylinder tightly in his left hand and pointed it into the air, then raised his right arm to strike the cap underneath with the heel of his hand. There was a loud popping sound as a star cluster flare shot into the sky like a Fourth of July firework.

Upon seeing the signal, RTO's relayed a warning over their radios: "Fire in the hole!"

The demo team leader counted off, "One, two, three, ready, now!" He instantly twisted the handle on the black detonator box to fire the charge.

The ground erupted with such force it lifted everyone within close proximity into the air, the tremendous explosion temporarily deafening them. Stones, dirt, and vegetation rained from the sky, and a giant dust cloud formed, soon engulfing the men.

Fifteen minutes later, the platoon was back together and moving toward the LZ with the demolition team.

"That fucking place isn't going to hide any more VC," Frenchie informed those around him. "All that's left of that complex is a huge hole in the ground."

"What happened to all the stuff we took out of that place?" John asked.

"Fourth Platoon loaded most of it onto choppers while we were wiring the place. The rest was burned," Sixpack replied.

"One of those pistols is mine," Frenchie said proudly.

"How do you figure that?" Zeke asked.

"The L-T had me tag it with my name and send it back to the rear on one of the birds."

"Shit, Frenchie, that gun is already tucked away in somebody's personal belongings back in Cu Chi. That tag is probably sitting at the bottom of a shit can in one of the latrines on the base," Zeke blurted.

"If it's not there when we get to Cu Chi, and I find out who has it, they'll learn about stealing from the wrong grunt."

"Now you're catching on," Zeke admitted. "All those rear echelon motherfuckers are the same. They give a fuck less what we have to hump on our backs, or what kind of hills we have to climb to get there. They're happy as long as they don't miss the happy hour in their favorite Saigon bar at five o'clock."

Doc looked over at John, who was trying to absorb the information. "Don't pay him any attention, Polack. Zeke was never like this before. He's just getting nervous because he's going home soon. They say that you can be as fearless as a lion after your first month in country, but then feel like a Cherry again during that last month. I'd probably feel the same way if I'd been through the shit he has in his eleven months in this hellhole."

"When are you going home, Doc?"

"I hope to board that Freedom Bird in six months."

"By that time, Larry and I will be the only ones left from this group today. We'll be the 'old men' in the squad."

"Maybe not for long, haven't you read the papers?"

"Not really."

"They're saying that Nixon wants to pull the GIs out of Nam and send them all home. You might not even have to spend a whole year in this god-awful war."

"That would be great! This whole place just scares the fuck out of me. I'm ready to go home right now."

"Aren't we all?"

At 1700 hours, the company arrived at the same LZ where they had landed the previous day. They would bush there for the night and be transported by choppers to Cu Chi in the morning.

John moved to join Larry and Wild Bill.

"I'm fucking exhausted," he said, after arriving at their position.

"Me too," Larry added.

"Look at it this way. At least we did something different today. We didn't have to hump our asses off all day long in this jungle paradise," Wild Bill offered.

"That was the good part of it, but I've been thinking about what Frenchie said about the NVA."

"Yeah, it's unusual for them for be in this part of the country."

"It's not only that. Larry, you remember during training, they were always telling us that the enemy was smart and sneaky, but as a fighting unit, they were backwards and poorly supplied?"

Larry nodded, sharing the memory with John.

"Shit, Polack, you've been listening to the wrong people," Wild Bill exclaimed. "Did you take a good look at that complex today? They have it better than we do. We hump our ass off to find them, and all they have to do is sit and wait for us. It's no different from fighting in your own neighborhood: you know where all the safe hiding places are. It's just not possible that a "backward" group of people built that place." Wild Bill said.

"That's what I mean," John agreed.

"That place showed class and ingenuity. If Sixpack hadn't stumbled across that cache, we would have walked right over them. You better change your attitude about the enemy right now. If you don't respect them - and continue to underestimate them - you'll never make it home alive."

John pondered that thought before conceding, "Yeah, I guess you're right."

"I know I'm right," Wild Bill concluded.

"Look at the bright side," Larry broke in. "Tomorrow we can get some rest and party in the rear."

"You're right! At least we can forget about this war for a couple of days."

"I can't wait to drink something cold."

"Man, you know I agree with that!"

John thought back to Junior's remark on the firebase. He was right about a person being willing to pay ten dollars for an ice-cold pop or even a piece of ice in the bush; they had been drinking lukewarm water for three days. Suddenly, it seemed worth ten bucks for the privilege of swirling ice-cold liquid around in your mouth. They could not wait until tomorrow.

# CHAPTER NINE

At daybreak, the atmosphere within the NDP was at a frenzied pitch as everyone prepared for his return to Cu Chi.
"Who wants to trade a can of fruit cocktail for some pound cake?" Frenchie asked.
"I will!" Doc replied. The two men tossed cans through the air to one another.
"Does anyone need extra water?" Wild Bill held two full canteens in the air.
"You guys can have all my shit!" Zeke emptied the contents of his rucksack onto the ground. Several eight-ounce green cans of fruit cocktail, peaches, pound cake, and some smaller tins of peanut butter, crackers, and cheese, fell in a heap.
"Why are you doing this?" Scout asked from his position a short distance away.
"I won't need them anymore."
"What do you mean?" We're only staying in the rear for three days. Those cans are a grunt's most prized possessions. You'll be sorry, Zeke."
"You're wrong, Doc. My infantry days are over. Sixpack informed me last night that the colonel had honored my request to be the mail clerk for my last three weeks in country. From now on, I'll be sleeping on soft mattresses in Cu Chi. No more humping for this guy."
"Congratulations!" Doc announced.
"I'm happy for you too, Zeke," Frenchie added.
"What luck!" Larry joined the others in snapping up Zeke's discarded treasures.

"You bet your ass it's luck," Zeke declared. "In my eleven months here, I've been sniped at, ambushed, pinned down, and overrun by Charlie. My surviving is just pure luck. Now, all I have to do is lounge around in the security of Cu Chi for three more weeks, and I'm out of here on that Freedom Bird home."

"I'm sorry," Larry mumbled, "I didn't mean it to sound like that."

"Forget it, Larry," Zeke replied. "If you're lucky enough to survive as long as I have, then maybe a break will come your way too."

"What's your plan once you get home?" Doc asked.

"The first thing I'm going to do is sit on a real toilet and flush it a hundred times." Everyone laughed. "Then I'll go to a fancy restaurant and order the biggest steak on the menu."

"Are your folks planning a welcome home party?" Wild Bill asked.

"Maybe. My mom said in her last letter that she was considering one, but would like to combine it with my twentieth birthday party, which is only two weeks later."

"Twenty years old! I thought you were much older than that."

"This war makes us all appear much older than we actually are."

"I'll second that."

John selected a can of fruit cocktail from the dwindling pile in front of Zeke, then moved over by Doc and took a seat on the ground next to him.

"I can't believe Zeke is only nineteen," he said to the black medic.

"I'm just as surprised as you are."

"He might be young, but he sure knows his shit."

"He sure does! Zeke is the only old-timer left in this platoon. Our old L-T, who is now the XO, used to call on him for advice all the time. He's seen most of the VC tactics, and could sometimes spot an ambush before the platoon walked into it."

"Does Zeke have a sixth sense or something?"

"No. He has a special skill that has developed over the months. The same will happen to you down the road, you'll know when it happens. Did you know that Zeke was awarded a Silver Star for Valor a few months back?"

"No, I didn't. What did he do?"

"It happened back in May when our company was in Cambodia. An ambush caught Second Platoon off guard and pinned them down until help arrived. When we joined the fight, Zeke single-handedly took out two of the machine gun bunkers. Then he ran through the hail of gunfire and pulled two wounded men to safety."

"Wow! Did he get hit?"

"No, he didn't, but you know it had to be a miracle."

"Why do you say that?"

"When I saw him later, his rifle had been shattered by bullets, his helmet had three creases in it, both his canteens had holes in them, and the heel of his right boot had been shot off."

"No shit? Somebody must have been watching over him."

"Amen to that."

"We still have some time before leaving, so I'd better take this opportunity to write my folks."

"Good move, Polack. There won't be any time for writing in Cu Chi."

"What do you mean? I thought we were going to have three days of rest and relaxation."

"Call it what you like. Now let me enlighten you, my brother. Cu Chi is the next best thing to being back in the world. Hell, with all the beer parties, barbecues, movies, Service Club, and swimming pools, you won't have time to do anything else."

"Well then, I'd better get started right now."

"Do you need paper or anything?"

"No thanks, Doc, I'm all set."

"Say hello for me."

"Will do." John walked away.

"Where's Sixpack?" Wild Bill asked.

"He and the L-T are over in the Company CP area," Larry replied. "They're probably making arrangements for our pickup on the LZ."

"I don't know," Frenchie emphasized. "They usually don't spend this much time planning a pickup."

"What else can it be? We've been out in the bush twice as long as the other companies in this battalion. Alpha's R&R is overdue!"

"Maybe the brass has canceled the R&R."

"Why would they do that, Zeke?"

"I don't know, but I feel like there's something in the wind."

"I hope you're wrong."

"Here he comes now," Larry pointed to the tall soldier heading their way.

"He doesn't look too happy!"

Sixpack inhaled deeply on a cigarette, threw it hard to the ground, and then drove the heel of his boot into the stick of smoking tobacco, grinding it in the soft dirt.

"Oh shit," Wild Bill uttered, "looks like bad news."

"Okay guys, come on and gather up," Sixpack waved for them to join him. "I know this is going to break your hearts, but we're not going to Cu Chi today."

John dropped his pen before he was even able to write a first word.

"I knew it!" Zeke blurted.

"Why are they changing the plan?" Wild Bill was the first to ask.

"Battalion wants us to hump back to the trail we found a couple of days ago. They're curious about that base camp, and they want Alpha Company to go and check it out."

"Why do we have to hump?" Frenchie asked.

"The brass feels that since we left in choppers, we could surprise the VC by returning on foot."

"That's bullshit!"

"I know, but we have to follow orders. As soon as we are near enough to the camp, the artillery crews on Firebase Kien will fire it up again. All we have to do is go in and count the bodies. The whole mission shouldn't last more than a day or two."

"I'll still be able to go in today, right?" Zeke asked hopefully.

"I'm sorry, Zeke, but the colonel has canceled all returns to the rear until after this mission is over."

His dreams now shattered, Zeke leaned back against the narrow tree, feigning a weak smile, and then laughing hysterically. Each member in the squad glanced over at him, offering a silent look of sympathy.

"Fuck it! It's only two days. Don't you guys worry about me," Zeke hollered, donning his warrior face.

"How far is it to the trail?"

"On the map, it looks like about seven clicks, but the terrain is hilly and the jungle thick. It will be a long, hard hump. We'll be lucky to get there by noon tomorrow."

"Are we getting resupplied before we leave?" Doc asked. "I do need a few supplies for my medical bag."

"Yes, we are. In fact," Sixpack looked at his watch, "the birds will be here in half an hour. Just take enough supplies for two days and be ready to move out by nine."

When the resupply chopper landed, a soldier jumped from the doorway to the ground.

"Junior!" Somebody called from the vicinity of Third Squad.

John turned toward the noisy helicopter and recognized the black PFC as he waved warmly to shadows in the bush. John dropped his gear and moved quickly to intercept him.

"Hey, stranger," John called when he was within earshot. Junior turned his head to see John exiting from a clump of bushes.

"Polack, my man! I see you're still with us."

"My luck has been holding up. What brings you out to the bush?"

"The lead medic on Kien said that my leg is strong enough to hump. So here I am."

"I bet you couldn't wait."

"To be honest, Polack, I missed the bush. Bunker guard was getting to be pretty damn boring. Besides, I have to get rid of these extra pounds," Junior rubbed his belly with both hands.

They both laughed, Junior's dimples flashing deeply.

"You have a long way to go before getting fat, my friend." John pushed a finger into Junior's stomach.

"I hear we're moving out shortly, so I'd better be going. Let's get together when we have a little more time, Polack. Have to talk about getting together in the hometown sometime."

"Okay, bro, take care of yourself."

"You too!"

John slapped the palm of Junior's outstretched hand, and the two men parted company.

Alpha Company was on the move by nine. They had not yet moved one-hundred yards before some of them started voicing their disapproval.

"Why didn't they let us walk part way before getting resupplied?"

"All they think about is body counts."

"It doesn't make sense to me."

"Don't these people in the rear know what it's like to hump in the bush?"

"They're assholes!"

John followed Zeke once again in the column of men. He found the camouflage cover on Zeke's helmet intriguing. On one side, the word "Short," was written in large block letters and colored in with a black marker. The term referred to 'short-timers' who had only weeks or days to go before going home. John was not able to make out the saying written on the opposite side. He quickened his pace and closed the wide gap between himself and Zeke, trying to read the evasive words. He was only one-step away and stumbled, plunging headfirst into a bush. When he looked up, Zeke's eyes glared at him.

"Do you have a problem?"

"No, no problem, Zeke. I just tripped, that's all."

"Be more careful. Charlie can hear that kind of shit." Zeke offered John his hand and pulled him to his feet.

"Are you okay?"

"Yeah, sure. I'll be fine."

"Check the ground quickly and make sure nothing dropped from your ruck, then hurry and catch up."

As Zeke turned to resume humping, John caught a glimpse of the phrase on Zeke's helmet. 'Fighting for peace is like fucking for virginity,' John read quietly. 'That's heavy,' he uttered to himself, repeating the saying a couple more times, as he followed along.

After moving two-thousand meters, the soldiers halted for a break. John moved to the side of the trail and sat next to Doc.

"This is a bitch!"

"It'll get worse."

"I can't keep my pack in a comfortable position. Just when I think everything is okay, a vine snags onto my pack and stops me cold. How many times did you have to unhook me, Doc?"

"At least a dozen", Doc smiled. "But don't let those wait-a-minute vines get you down."

John laughed. "What did you call them?"

"Wait-a-minute vines. Haven't you ever heard of them before? Every grunt who has ever humped in the bush has heard of them. The name's catchy, don't you think?"

"Yeah," John chuckled. "What else do I have to look forward to?"

"Just wait until we hit some bamboo thickets. We'll have to remove our packs and push them in front of us while crawling on our bellies."

"You're shitting me. Wouldn't it just be easier to go around them?"

"Sometimes we do, but most of the time they're so wide, we don't have a choice. I'm not bullshitting, you'll see," Doc promised.

"I hope you're wrong."

Suddenly there was a snapping of fingers and Zeke said, "Let's go!"

The men before him were already on their feet and moving forward. Doc and John helped each other up and joined the procession.

In the next four hours, the company only moved a thousand meters through the thick, musty jungle. The point man had come across a shallow, ten-foot wide stream with slow-moving green and brown water. Captain Fowler decided to have his company follow the stream in an effort to make up some lost time.

While standing in the ankle-deep water during the next break, John felt a stinging sensation on both his neck and waist. He passed it off as perspiration irritating the small cuts caused by the jungle vegetation. Raising his hand up to his neck, he suddenly felt someone grab his wrist.

"Wait a minute, Polack. You have a couple of leeches on your neck," Zeke cautioned.

John panicked and tried to grab at them to pull them off.

"Hold on! Don't do that. Let me squirt some bug juice on them. It'll make them fall off." John winced in pain as the bug juice soaked into his open cuts and sweaty pores.

After the second leech bloated up and fell from his neck, Zeke said, "All set. Check me over will you, Polack?"

"I don't see any on you, Zeke," John stated, taking a quick look up and down Zeke's backside. "How in the hell did they get on me in the first place? Did they crawl up my pants from the water?"

"These are land leeches. You probably picked them up before we even entered the stream. Don't let them scare you. They're more of a nuisance than anything else. If you want to stop any more of them from hitching rides, cover your exposed skin with more bug juice."

At 1100 hours the next morning, First Squad huddled together, chatting nervously about the anticipated mission. Zeke, however, had not joined them. He sat alone in the shadows of a bush, whittling intently on a small tree branch with his Bowie knife. Tan and green shavings collected around his feet as each stroke of the silver blade sent another into the air. The ground surrounding Zeke took on the appearance of a woodshop floor, but nobody in the squad attempted to interrupt him.

"Zeke sure is depressed," Frenchie noted, stealing a glance in his direction.

"I don't blame him. You saw him yesterday morning. He was happy as hell, until Sixpack dropped the bomb on him."

"Why wouldn't they let him go in on the resupply?" Larry asked.

Doc said, "Beats me. If it was my decision, he would have gone in."

"One man isn't going to make a difference on this mission!"

"I don't think that's the reason," Scout pointed out.

"What do you think it is?"

"Captain Fowler knows the mechanical on the trail was Zeke's. Maybe he thinks he's doing Zeke a favor by keeping him out here one more day, so he can see the results of his work."

"Do you think he really cares? Zeke is so short he's become paranoid. All he wants to do is get out of the bush. If the captain thought of this gesture as a favor to Zeke, then he should see how happy Zeke is right now."

"Like the man said yesterday, he's okay and still has his shit together. If we hit anything on that trail, he'll be the first to react."

"I think he will too, Doc."

Sixpack approached the group. "Okay, saddle up! We're moving out in five minutes."

"Is there anything we should know before leaving?" Scout asked, rising to his feet.

"Yeah! The firebase will start firing artillery in a few minutes. So don't dive for cover and start yelling 'incoming'." The group laughed nervously.

"They'll continue to lay it on while we move forward. Then when the rounds stop, a squadron of Cobra helicopters will move in to cover us from the air while we sweep through it."

Zeke still had not joined the group. Sgt. Holmes frowned after looking in his direction.

"Hey Zeke!" The sergeant called. "Are you okay?"

There was no answer. Zeke continued to stare at the ground, drawing circles in the soft dirt with the sharply pointed stick.

Sixpack walked over to him and patted him on the shoulder. "What's bugging you?"

"Don't you know?"

"Don't tell me you're still pissed about not going to the rear yesterday."

"You got it."

"What's the big deal? It's only one more day."

"That's not the point. If any other lifer or officer were in my place, the colonel would have made a special trip in a Loach to pull him out of the field. They give a shit less about me. A Specialist

Fourth Class doesn't rate any special attention. So why should they care?"

"You're making too big an issue out of this. Nobody in that base camp will survive the bombardment that's coming. After we count the bodies, we'll be in Cu Chi in time for dinner."

"Do you honestly believe that?" Zeke questioned. "Sixpack, you've already spent a tour of duty here. Have you ever swept through a base camp after artillery dropped a ton of munitions on it?"

"I know what you're getting at."

"Damn right you know what I'm getting at. Not once have I just been able to go in and count bodies. Those slant-eyed bastards wait for us. Every time we do it, they put us in a world of hurt. What makes you think it'll be any different this time?"

"I don't know how it will turn out. But I'm not going to let that stop me from doing my job. If it means a firefight, then, by God, it will be a firefight. We've all had the proper training and experience to deal with this kind of situation. Just do what your instincts tell you and you'll be fine."

"Bullshit! Training and experience don't mean shit in the Nam. It's all luck. And today I don't feel like I have any left."

"You'll be okay, Zeke. Just keep your cool and don't try anything foolish. I need you. The rest of the guys are counting on you. Sixpack waved toward the squad.

"Yeah, come on, Zeke. You can do it!"

"What's six more hours compared to forty-nine weeks?"

"We need you, Zeke!"

Zeke blushed after hearing the words of encouragement. He smiled nervously, placed the rifle across his shoulder, and moved to join the rest of the men.

"What the hell? I can't let my brothers down. If you need me that much, I'm yours."

Upon reaching the point in the trail where the mechanical ambush had exploded, Lt. Ramsey ordered the First Squad to check the vicinity.

"Look under rocks if you have to. I want this area thoroughly searched. We'll secure both ends of the trail so you won't have to keep looking over your shoulder."

"You got it, L-T." Sixpack turned to the others. "Let's get this done!"

He led the men through the devastated area. One-hundred feet of leveled vegetation was all that remained to the front of the blown claymore mines. The small steel balls damaged several of the larger trees on the opposite side of the trail; bark was missing and white sap was still leaking from the incisions. Five craters along the trail marked the location of each mine, each large enough to bury basketballs. A mixture of brown and red dirt coated the surrounding green vegetation.

"Sarge, I found something," Wild Bill said, looking at the ground on the other side of the trail.

"Looks like wheel impressions from a cart," Sixpack guessed after seeing the ruts in the ground.

"There's two sets," Wild Bill pointed out. "One appears to be coming from the base camp, and the other, which is sunk deeper into the trail, appears to be returning."

"Looks like the dinks came out and picked up the pieces," Zeke declared upon reaching the two men.

"There are puddles of dried blood all over the place. The ambush did some real damage here."

"Hey, guys! Come and take a look at this."

The men rushed over to see what Larry had found. John was the first to arrive, "That's so gross! What do you make of it, Doc?"

"I need a closer look." Doc moved forward, swinging his arms wildly to bat away swarms of flies that had gathered on that portion of the tree. "It's definitely human bone and tissue. There's more over here!" He pointed out several smaller pieces strewn about the area. "The largest piece I can see is about as big as a cigarette lighter."

"Thanks, Doc. Let's all get back onto the trail and try to figure this out."

"How many do you think the ambush caught?" Larry followed Sixpack, pinching his nose with two fingers to escape the stench, his voice sounding an octave or two higher.

"We might have caught a squad or maybe two." Sixpack hesitated, and then turned to see why Larry's voice had changed. "Why in the fuck are you holding your nose?"

"I can't stand the smell. It's like walking through a butcher shop full of spoiled meat."

"It is dead meat. You'll get used to it!"

"The fuck I will."

"I don't like this one bit. There's not one body to be found, yet the evidence is overwhelming that the mechanical blew a bunch of them away."

"That's because there's a lot more VC left and they came out and picked up the pieces, Sixpack. Remember, that mechanical blew during the artillery barrage, so there were survivors, and they're probably waiting for us in the bunkers."

"The artillery in Kien just spent fifteen minutes dropping more rounds on that base camp. They couldn't have survived a second barrage."

"They survived the first time and because of that, they will survive this time too."

"Nobody really knows for sure, Zeke. We'll have to take our chances."

"Don't say I didn't warn you."

"Let's get back to the rest of the platoon," Sixpack suggested, ignoring Zeke's remark.

"What did you find, sergeant?" Lt. Ramsey asked upon their return.

"The whole area is wasted. We found evidence of death, but couldn't find any bodies."

"That's good news!"

"We also found signs of a cart having been on the trail."

"Did you see anyone?"

"No, sir. There are two sets of tracks. One of them is sunk much deeper into the trail, as if a great deal of weight was moved."

"Thank you, sergeant. I will pass that onto the CP. Right now, we had better get a move on. The rest of the company is in position to sweep the base camp."

The platoon had moved up the main trail, veering onto the smaller path that led into the encampment. Nung called to Sixpack, "Sergeant, look!" He pointed to the upper half of a tree on the right side of the trail.

The platform in the tree, where Sixpack and Nung had spotted the enemy lookout earlier, was still in place and unscathed by the many artillery rounds.

"I don't believe it," Sixpack shook his head in disbelief.

When reaching the outer perimeter of the base camp, the rest of the company was already sweeping toward them through the massive area.

The full barrage of artillery had hit here. All in all, First Platoon counted seventeen bunkers; none intact. Unlike the underground complex, they did not find tunnels, caches, or important documents lying around. A strong odor of burnt wood and musty soil hung in the air.

"See how those VC screw with our heads?" Frenchie remarked. "I know we should have had a big body count here, but like always, they just take their dead away and leave us to guess at what happened here."

"I'm with you on that! At least we give them the satisfaction of knowing they hurt us after a fight. All they have to do is count the number of Medevac's coming in to pick up our dead and wounded."

"Let's do some grave hunting!"

"No fucking way, Frenchie," Sixpack replied. "We sit tight until the L-T returns. Maybe we'll get lucky and be able to move out toward the LZ."

"I'll buy that," John remarked.

Lt. Ramsey returned ten minutes later. "There's nothing here so go ahead and break for lunch. Afterwards, we will head north and cut a trail through the jungle to our new LZ. With luck, we'll be in the rear before nightfall."

"All right!" The squad cheered unanimously.

Even Zeke allowed himself to smile as he sat down and prepared to eat his meal of C-Rations.

The company split into platoon-sized elements heading in the same direction, two hundred feet separated each of the four columns.

First Platoon had only moved five hundred feet when coming upon another large, well-used trail. Lt. Ramsey dispatched a squad to investigate while everyone else took a short break.

"Lieutenant, you aren't going to believe this," the squad leader informed him.

"What is it, Hawkins?"

"This is the same trail we've originally been following, it winds around the base camp and moves back in this direction."

The L-T pulled out a map from his pants pocket and studied it. "This part of the trail isn't on the map, either," he informed the young buck sergeant.

"We'd better be careful, sir!"

"Fuck this trail. Let's just get to our LZ." Lt. Ramsey returned the map to his pocket. "Hawkins, have your point men stay on a heading of thirty degrees. The LZ should only be three clicks away."

"Roger that." The black sergeant turned and jogged back toward the front of the thirty-five-man column.

The men in the column were moving along at a leisurely pace when the sudden sound of gunfire and explosions on their right flank forced the men to the ground to seek protective cover.

First Platoon hunkered down and awaited further instructions. The source of the gunfire was unclear, but it sounded like all AK-47 fire, and it was escalating. Seconds later came the distinct sounds of M-16 and M-60 machine guns returning fire - exploding M79 rounds and grenades added to the already hazardous noise levels.

Word passed along the line for each man to keep his head down; Second Platoon stumbled into another bunker complex and set off an ambush. The fight was taking place about two-hundred feet to their right flank. Lt. Ramsey continued to relay information as he received sit reps from the engaging platoon. The captain communicated initial strategy to support Second Platoon.

First Platoon was the column farthest to the left and needed to protect Second Platoon's left flank. Third and Fourth Platoons would do the same on the right side of the battle. When the captain gave the word, each flank was to squeeze toward the center and overpower the ambushers. Sixpack was already crouched and moving down the line of men, stopping at each prone soldier to organize and coordinate individual positions. He intended to create a small horseshoe configuration in order to cover their forward, right and left flanks. Even at that distance, bullets popped overhead and tore apart anything in their paths, many impacting into the ground nearby.

John sprawled on the ground, unable to move. His mind told the body to go, but it would not listen.

Suddenly, numerous dry branches snapped and bushes rustled to their left flank.

Zeke was the first to rise to his feet. "Gooks!" He yelled, firing from the hip in that direction on full automatic.

Screams of both surprise and pain came from the unseen invaders, who quickly retaliated by sending a barrage of hot lead in the direction of Zeke and the First Platoon. Rounds flew overhead in both directions and dirt showered over the men as bullets hit the ground near them. The noise was deafening, making it impossible to communicate verbally.

On instinct, First Platoon reacted quickly. The machine gunners began firing in a wide arc at a knee-high level. Others quickly joined in and fired in the direction of the unseen but advancing enemy. Frenchie fired beehive rounds from his M-79 grenade launcher, Scout tossed grenades, and Sixpack took well-aimed shots at shadows from behind a large tree. Nung and Wild Bill lay prone on the ground, firing their rifles at arm's length above them. Larry still tried to maneuver into position, not yet firing his machine gun.

John made his move to what he thought was a more secure position. Rising to his knees, he dove into a clump of bushes behind an old tree trunk to face the oncoming threat. In his haste, he jammed the barrel of his M-16 into the soft earth and found it tightly lodged under gnarled, protruding roots. As he struggled to free the weapon, bullets began flying in his direction, narrowly missing him and ricocheting from the tree trunk. John was numb with fear. Without access to his gun to defend himself, his sense of vulnerability was overwhelming. He buried his face into the ground, helpless to stop the flow of urine seeping down his leg. He lay motionless until the incoming fire subsided.

Larry's machine gun finally joined the fight. He fired five-second bursts into the jungle to his front, attempting to cover an arc of about forty-five degrees. It was only then that the enemy fire subsided enough for John to free his rifle from the tangle of roots. Dirt and mud were packed tightly into the barrel. He knocked it against the side of the tree a few times, to no avail.

He wondered if the weapon would blow up in his face if he tried to fire it, but there was no alternative. He took a couple of deep breaths, positioned the rifle on the far side of the tree, lowered his head to the ground, and pulled the trigger.

The rifle recoiled, almost falling from his hands. John examined the barrel and found the plug gone. He pointed the rifle in the general direction of the AK-47 shooting and fired three-round bursts from overhead, emptying his first magazine in a matter of seconds.

Red smoke from several exploding canisters around them fogged the area. Snaking lazily through the air, it served to identify the friendly positions for Cobra helicopters, which circled above the firefight.

The ground shook, and debris rained down upon them as the gunships launched rockets into the area where the enemy fire originated.

Incoming fire at the First Platoon suddenly ceased when the first of many rockets exploded in the midst of the enemy.

"Hold your fire! Hold your fire!" The squad leaders yelled repeatedly along the line until the last of the Americans stopped firing his weapon.

First Platoon's fight was temporarily over, their enemies either dead or forced from the area. The rest of the company continued to exchange sporadic gunfire with a concealed enemy; however, the sound of their battle was also winding down.

Sixpack yelled, "Sound off! Anybody hit?"

"I don't know, I can't see anybody else this low to the ground, but I'm okay." Larry responded.

Sixpack conducted a roll call of his squad. All answered but one, there was no reply from Zeke.

"Somebody find Zeke and see if he's okay!"

"Last time I saw him, Sixpack, he was just ahead of me. I'll take a look," Scout offered.

After a few minutes passed, Scout called out from an area twenty feet away, "I found him, but it's not good. He didn't make it."

"Can you pull him back to us?"

"I could with some help. His body is wedged in between some bushes."

"Polack, Frenchie, and Doc, grab a poncho and go give Scout a hand!"

The three men low crawled to where Scout waited.

When John reached the location and saw Zeke's lifeless body, he turned and vomited uncontrollably. The other three men tugged and pulled at the body, trying to free Zeke from the jungle's grasp and lift him onto the poncho.

"Come on, Polack, we don't have time for that!" Frenchie barked.

"He doesn't have a face left," John managed to blurt out.

"I'm sorry about that too, but there's still VC around. So quit looking at him and help us. We've got to get the fuck out of here and get back to the others."

"You're a cold-hearted son of a bitch, Scout!" John said, taking hold of a corner of the poncho.

"No, I'm not," Scout retorted. "When you've seen as many dead bodies as we have, it doesn't affect you anymore."

When Zeke's body was lifted from his deathbed, Scout called to Sixpack, "We have a sick Polack, but we're on our way."

"Move slowly and stay low. We'll cover for you!"

Some of the platoon fired into the jungle behind the men in order to protect the slow moving group during their retreat.

When the four reached the sergeant, he looked down at Zeke's limp body deep within the poncho and bowed his head. "Sorry, Zeke," he said quietly before acknowledging Scout. "The company medics have formed up just outside of the base camp we left earlier today. They are treating the wounded there and setting up a staging area; Medevac's are already on the way. The rest of us will meet up with you in just a bit."

The men started for the LZ. En route, they saw other members of the company carrying soldiers in various fashions. Some of the wounded had their arms draped over a fellow soldier for support and hopped along on one leg. Others walked on their own, unassisted, with gauze bandages tied or taped to different areas of their bodies. Several other four-man teams were struggling toward the aid station with their human cargo lying on ponchos. The parade of casualties continued to pour out of the jungle, moving toward the same location.

The earlier artillery barrages had devastated the original base camp and nearby surrounding area, thus creating an area large enough for the Medevac choppers to land.

The immediate area next to the LZ soon took on the appearance of an open-air aid station. Medics scurried about, using whatever supplies were available to treat the many wounded soldiers. Some of the casualties were still bleeding through their bandages as they rested, smoking cigarettes and talking to friends who offered moral support. Others babbled to themselves or lay in a semi-comatose state. The corpses lay unattended and covered with ponchos in an area out of everyone's way.

The smell of sterile bandages, iodine, dried blood, and dismembered bodies now overrode the earlier stench of burnt wood and vegetation.

John bent over in a clump of bushes and vomited again.

"It gets easier as time goes on," Sixpack assured him after noticing him there. The sergeant slapped John on the back a few times in an attempt to console him.

"Medevac's will start landing in a minute or two. I want you to go and lend a hand in the loading of the wounded."

"I can't."

"What do you mean you can't?"

"I just can't, Sixpack. The sight of the wounded and the smell in the air is making me sick to my stomach."

"This isn't going to be the last time something like this happens. You should be thankful that you're not one of the casualties. Go on now and help them, it's for your own good," Sixpack gave John an encouraging look and pushed him forward.

John resisted and looked up, tears running down his cheeks. "Sixpack, I'm hurting bad. I can't believe Zeke is dead."

"We're all hurting and feel the same way." The sergeant draped his arm over John's shoulders and guided him toward the waiting casualties. "I know you'll never forget him, but you'll get over the hurt soon. Now go and give those people a hand. They need you right now."

John used his shirtsleeves to wipe away the tears, but ended up smearing the saltwater all over his dirt-encrusted face. It would be impossible to disguise the fact that he had been crying. Moving toward the rest of the men, he saw others with the same telltale signs of grief; any embarrassment he felt at that point completely dissolved.

Four helicopters were en route to extract Alpha Company from the field and transport them to Cu Chi for three days of rest and relaxation. Each squad from the First Platoon was in position for pickup; the squad leaders waited to raise their weapons to guide in the birds.

Fourth Platoon remained in position between the bunker complex and LZ, providing security for the extracting platoons, flying out on the last sortie. Artillery guns in Kien were shooting rounds into the complex and surrounding area for the last thirty minutes, intending to inflict as much damage as possible before replacements arrived to sweep through that area.

"On a scale of one to ten, I have to rate this fire fight an eight," Scout volunteered.

"It was indeed a bitch," Wild Bill agreed. "I would have bet we were shooting at each other for over two hours, but I heard somebody say it lasted only thirty minutes."

"How bad did we get hit, Doc?"

"From what I've heard, the company suffered nine killed and Medevac'd twenty wounded. Except for Zeke, First Platoon didn't suffer any other casualties."

"How many did we get?"

"Nobody knows yet. Bravo and Charlie Companies are on their way to relieve us. They're going to sweep through the area and get a body count."

"I hope they have better luck than we did."

"Does anybody know just exactly what went down back there?"

"I don't know for sure, Larry, but I did overhear the officers earlier. It appears that the first base camp we found and destroyed with artillery was only an extension of the main complex, which we found today. The VC were waiting for us, just as Zeke had said they would be. I heard most of the casualties came from the Second Platoon as they triggered the ambush; the rest were from Third and Fourth Platoon. Their efforts overwhelmed the enemy and allowed everybody to pull back. Those survivors in the Second were lucky to have made it out of there."

"Luck? That's what Zeke used to call survival," Larry added matter-of-factly.

Nobody responded.

The artillery barrage stopped when the choppers approached the LZ.

When touching down, members of Bravo Company jumped off, running for the tree line.

"Get some payback for us, Bravo."

"Good luck, guys!"

Some of the Alpha Company grunts just stared at the helicopters and did not even acknowledge their friends from the sister company when they passed. Their eyes held a faraway look – a combination of disbelief, sorrow, exhaustion and relief.

A three-day stand down in Cu Chi did not seem like a big deal anymore. After all, who could party after an experience like this? There might not be a party, but there would be plenty of alcohol, which was the perfect prescription to help one forget.

# CHAPTER TEN

Enthusiastic cooks, clerks, and supply personnel filled the battalion area in Cu Chi, preparing to host those companies returning from the field. Some busied themselves by erecting tents and cots; others separated clean fatigues and miscellaneous equipment onto long eight-foot tables. The cooks, adorned in white aprons and chef hats, were barbecuing hundreds of rib eye steaks on open grills throughout the area. Blue smoke from each rose into the orange-red evening sky, and the scent of barbecue sauce temporarily camouflaged the real stench of Vietnam.

Tents were set up across from the company orderly room. There were no walls, but the large canvas roofs provided sufficient protection from both the rain and sun.

Under each of the five shelters, a center aisle separated twenty-four cots – twelve to a side. Three fifty-five gallon barrels, completely filled with cans of soda, beer and ice sat just inside the entrance. Sweating profusely in the heat, each bead of moisture raced down the side, collecting in a puddle of tepid and muddy water. A fourth empty barrel stood ready to collect the empty cans and garbage.

Several wooden tables were set in a row adjacent to the shower building; the two closest tables held a hundred or more bars of green soap and clean towels. The remaining held piles of clean fatigues and dozens of small Army-issue cans of foot powder.

Choppers began landing in an open field a quarter-mile away. The First Platoon disembarked, following the road toward the battalion area. Their appearance was 'unmilitary' by stateside standards. Their fatigues were looking vile - all covered with mud, sweat, and dried blood. Most trousers were ripped and torn; some severely, exposing the genitals. One could use hair length to distinguish between lifers, Cherries, and those who had been in the field the longest. The commonality was their heavily matted hair and faces coated with layers of mud, salt, and red dirt.

The sight and smell of the infantry soldiers overwhelmed the rear echelon personnel, who tried to distance themselves from these new arrivals.

Frenchie raised his head and sniffed the air like an animal in the wilderness.

"Steaks are on!" He pointed out the blue barbecue smoke rising into the air.

"It looks like they're planning to throw a party for us!"

Scout, Frenchie, and Wild Bill gave a war hoop, and then joined the others in a race for the showers. While running, soldiers dropped their rucksacks in mid-stride and peeled tattered fatigues from their filthy bodies. Naked men - backs and buttocks covered by an assortment of mud, blisters, rashes, and jungle rot - quickly converged on the small building.

"What the hell is going on?" John asked Larry.

"It looks like everyone wants to shower. Shit, you'd think somebody was giving away a million dollars."

"I smell food cooking, so why don't they eat first?"

"Those guys have been in the bush for two months without bathing. Wouldn't you like to clean up before eating something that smells this good?"

"Yeah, right on, Larry. Good point."

"Well, what are we waiting for?"

"We're going to wait for the showers." John pointed to the long line, already forming outside of the building.

In the morning, several pocket transistor radios tuned in to the American channel, sounds of rock and roll vibrated and echoed throughout the area as the Rolling Stones poured it on.

The loud stereophonic music woke Scout first. He sat up on his cot, rubbing both eyes, and then buried his head in the palms of both hands.

Wild Bill and Frenchie, who had been sleeping on the hard ground during the night, were the next to awaken - rising to their feet and stretching.

"That was the best I've slept in the last two months," Wild Bill said triumphantly. "No bugs, guard duty, or going to sleep at seven. Shit, I feel great!"

"Me too!"

"Why do you guys do that?" Doc asked. He sat on the edge of his cot, lacing a boot. "Every time we're in the rear, you both sleep on the ground. What's wrong with these cots?"

"The ground is better," Wild Bill stated. Frenchie nodded in agreement.

"The first time I tried to sleep on one of those, I was awake all night. Those fucking wood frames come alive at night and poke the shit out of you. Every bone and muscle in my body hurt the next morning. No thanks, Doc, you can keep them."

"Would you guys please try to keep it down?" Scout pleaded from the side of his cot.

"What's the matter? Poor baby drink too much last night?"

"I don't think so," Scout replied. "It must be cheap beer."

"What's wrong with cheap beer that's free?"

"Nothing. It's just that I haven't had any for a while and it sort of hit me suddenly."

"Guys," Doc interrupted, "it was cheap beer, but we didn't let that stop us. In fact, I think we outdid ourselves last night!" He kicked an empty beer can across the ground.

The four men surveyed the area. Paper plates with half-eaten steaks sat in a pile on Frenchie's cot, and at least a hundred empty beer cans littered the floor around them.

"It sure was a good time though," Scout managed to utter.

"I'll say," Wild Bill added. "Look at Polack and Larry," he chuckled, pointing to their cots. "Aren't they a pitiful sight? They were the first to pass out and they're still unconscious." They laughed.

"Let's wake them up," Frenchie suggested.

"No, let them sleep it off. I don't think either of them has ever drank that much beer before."

"Look around. Are you blind?" Scout asked. "I don't think any of us has ever put away this much brew."

"Speak for yourself. Last night wasn't any different than a normal Saturday night back in the world," Wild Bill broke in.

"That's because cowboys can't drink and drive during the week," Frenchie mused.

"Wrong!" Wild Bill shot back. "We ride! Besides, if we get stinking drunk, our horses always know the way home. All we have to do is hang on. I bet you can't say that about your cars in the big cities." Wild Bill was always boasting about his ability to use horses as an alternative means of transportation out west - a constant source of amusement among the men.

"I can," Frenchie blurted. "There were times when I was so drunk; I couldn't have made it home without my car knowing the way."

"Wild Bill does have a point. I don't ever recall reading about a four-horse pile up involving a drunken rider," Doc announced.

"You guys are all full of shit!" Wild Bill exclaimed, embarrassed by the laughter.

"Come on, guys, let's get this place cleaned up," Frenchie suggested.

"Why? Are we having company?" Scout continued to rub at his forehead in an attempt to increase the blood circulation.

"We might," Frenchie surmised. "You know those public relations people always come looking for the Cherries whenever we're in the rear after a firefight."

"So what? Our Cherries won't be going anywhere," Wild Bill replied.

"That's true. And even if they could, Polack and Larry wouldn't feel like answering questions," Doc added.

"Fuck the Cherries, and fuck the visitors," Frenchie declared. "This place looks like shit and I can't stand looking at it anymore. Are you going to help me or not?" He began to gather empty beer cans and throw them into the large trashcan.

"Yes, Mother Frenchie!"

Later that Sunday morning, the company assembled for a multi-denominational religious service near a portable stage where a traveling Filipino band had performed the night before.

Chaplain Dunkirk waited patiently behind a lectern in the middle of the stage while soldiers filtered into the benches and bleachers. He paged through a Bible, inserting pieces of paper, marking certain passages he intended to read during the service.

In front of the stage stood nine inverted M-16 rifles, their attached bayonets driven into the ground up to the hilt. A helmet perched atop the stock of each weapon and a pair of jungle boots, facing forward, sat poised to the front of every rifle - each representing a fallen comrade from Alpha Company.

Some soldiers shed tears as they remembered fond memories of those friendships, now lost forever. Others stole solemn glances at the symbols and offered silent testimonials to those killed, whether they knew the fallen personally or not.

When everybody was in place, Chaplain Dunkirk, an older and balding major, cleared his throat and spoke to the congregation.

"Good morning! I have stood before you as a representative of God on many occasions. Together, we not only prayed for His protection and guidance, but we also celebrated with Him on those joyous and festive occasions. Today, we are all here to pray for our deceased friends and fellow soldiers, who have entered into the kingdom of Heaven to join God by His side.

"The death of a close friend is God's way of testing us. It is very difficult to accept that our God is good and all giving when he takes away someone close to us. It is on occasions like this that we must re-affirm our belief and faith in Him.

"We are all part of God's master plan, and each of us has a role during this lifetime. Once that role is complete, God recalls us to his side for all eternity.

"I'm sure we'd all like to live until we're a hundred years old. However, none of us knows what our true role is or how to play it. Therefore, you see, it is impossible to determine when our time will come. It could be today, tomorrow, ten years from now, or even on our ninetieth birthday. Only God knows for sure. We must continue to have faith, not only in our God, but also in ourselves, in one another, and in our country. Without this faith, we are nothing.

"I'll talk more on faith later in the service. Right now, let's bow our heads and pray for our deceased friends." He read the name and rank of each of the nine dead soldiers. Most of the men only knew each other by their first names or nickname, so when they heard the real names of the fallen soldiers spoken aloud for the first time, they seemed strange and unfamiliar.

Fifty minutes later, the chaplain offered a final blessing. "The service has concluded. However, Captain Fowler would like to say a few words before you all leave." He waved a farewell to the men, retrieved his Bible from the lectern, and walked over to the right side of the stage, taking a seat on a nearby chair.

After climbing the six steps to the stage, Alpha Company's commanding officer moved toward the lectern. He placed a few notes onto the surface and then stepped behind it. This resulted in snickers from the congregation.

The officer stood five feet, six inches tall and only the top of his head was visible to those men sitting on the low benches to his front. The microphone on the flexible holder did not bend low enough for him to speak on the public address system. He continued his struggle to manipulate the silver mechanism, which only invited more chuckles from the crowd.

Embarrassed, he finally removed the microphone from its base and stepped out to the front of the lectern.

"I've decided to stand out in front of this speaker's box to address you men, but only as a courtesy to those of you who want to read my lips."

He succeeded with this icebreaker, and the men laughed loudly with relief.

"Now, if I can get serious for a moment, I have a great deal of admiration for you men, and I commend you on your performances during our ambush the other day.

"As you know, we were caught by surprise and suffered dearly as a result of it. These nine men paid the ultimate price." He motioned to the rifles below.

"Later that day, after we were withdrawn, our Sister Companies in the battalion swept through the ambush sight without having to fire a shot.

"There were many caches and hundreds of documents uncovered. It appears that we had stumbled into the Division Headquarters for the VC Seventh Regiment. We're not sure as to the strength of the enemy we encountered during the battle, but the sweep confirmed eighty-seven dead bodies."

A cheer rose from the crowd as the young soldiers congratulated each other.

"Furthermore, there were immense trails of blood leading away from this complex in all directions. Our sister companies will continue their patrols through the area and try to hunt the rest all down.

"Now, for the bad news. This battle has reduced our strength to a level that battalion doesn't feel is effective. So - I know this is going to break your hearts - battalion is recommending that Alpha Company not return to the bush tomorrow."

The crowd was ecstatic. Boony hats flew into the air and cries of joy drowned out the captain's pleading voice. It took several minutes for the crowd to settle down before Captain Fowler could continue.

"Gentlemen! There must be a misunderstanding! I didn't say we weren't going to the field."

The joyous celebration ceased as the men looked to one another, asking if they had heard him correctly.

"That's right! We will be going out into the field tomorrow, but we won't have to hump on patrols for a bit."

Inquisitive looks from the crowd prompted him to explain in further detail.

"Tomorrow, Alpha Company will depart for the Iron Triangle."

A look of anxiety spread across the faces of the old-timers in the group that knew of this evil place.

"As many of you already know, the triangle has a reputation of being the most hostile of all areas within the division's area of operations. Every time our units patrol through this vicinity, heavy opposition meets them. Delta Company and the Corps of Engineers have spent the last week clearing out a large area in the center of it all. We will be joining them tomorrow and help to build a new firebase. The brass has already named it Lynch.

"This firebase is very important, as it will provide added security and firepower to those forces patrolling through the Triangle. We will not have to hump, but after a couple of days of digging and filling sandbags, you will all wish you were back in the bush again.

"Choppers will pick us up at eight in the morning. Enjoy your last day of leisure. That's all I have."

Most of First Platoon cleaned rifles in the tent and prepared equipment for the following day's move.

"That must have been one hell of a mess. Can you imagine piling up eighty-seven bodies?"

"Who knows for sure how many bodies there actually were Larry," Doc answered. "Especially if they were following battalion protocol."

"What are you saying?"

"It's not a secret that the VC carry their dead away with them after a firefight."

"I've been a witness to that myself."

"The policy is something like this. We get credit for a kill if we find a puddle of blood measuring more than four inches in diameter, a weapon found lying in the jungle, and of course, a body always counts."

"Damn, I didn't know that," John confessed. "I always thought a body had to be present."

"As you can see, that's not always the case."

"If that's true, why didn't we get credit for all the blood and body parts from our mechanical ambush?"

"I don't know, Polack. We didn't stick around long enough to measure and count all the dried blood and body parts. Besides, it was a couple of days after the fact anyway."

"Those fucking lifers are the only ones worried about a body count in this goddamn war anyway," Scout volunteered. "Did any of you see the company tote board today?"

"What about it?" Wild Bill asked.

"Major Stone was having the battalion clerk add to the figures while he stood there verifying the numbers."

"So what's the big deal? That's just normal lifer bullshit."

"He was doing this during the church service," Scout replied.

"I still don't see your point."

"The clerk was next to me during the service and we were talking about Zeke, when that lifer motherfucking major came over and yanked him away."

"Are you joking?"

"Wild Bill, I wouldn't joke about something like that. The poor kid didn't even have a chance to ask him if he could wait until after the service."

"What a sorry fucking thing to do."

"I'll say," Doc added. "That shit could have waited."

"That's not all of it," Scout interrupted.

"You mean there's more?" Larry asked.

"Yeah. It was not even five minutes after the clerk had finished that some General showed up. As soon as he stepped out of the jeep, Major Stone guided him to the tote board. The General's face lit up like a flashbulb when he saw the figures. He cracked a big grin and shook the major's hand. Then, as they were walking into the building, the General slapped Major Stone's back a few times as if he was single-handedly responsible for the body count."

"I'd like to know what kind of story he told the General." Wild Bill frowned deeply. "All he did during the ambush was to fly around overhead in that helicopter of his watching the fireworks below. What a jerk! Did your clerk buddy have anything to say after returning?"

"He never did. I did catch a glimpse of him while the captain was talking to us; he was carrying coffee and cake to the major's office." The men could only shake their heads in disbelief.

Just then, a stranger walked into the tent and approached those nearest the entrance.

"Excuse me; I'm looking for PFC's John Kowalski and Larry Nickels."

"It's time to write up the Cherries," Wild Bill teased.

"I'm Kowalski," John raised his hand.

"And I'm Nickels," Larry added from the cot behind John.

"Great! I'd like to take a few minutes of your time to ask some questions."

"Why, and who are you?" Larry asked.

"I'm a reporter and the information will be used for an article in your hometown newspapers."

"Why? What did we do?" John asked.

"You both earned the Combat Infantry Badge during that last firefight. You're heroes and we'd like the people back in your home town to know it."

"I'm not a fucking hero," John quickly protested. "I was scared to death during that ambush and pissed myself. Then, I spent the rest of the day puking my guts out. That doesn't sound like something a hero does."

"Relax, Polack," Doc interrupted. "It's just a formality. We all had similar experiences during our first firefights, but you will get stronger as time goes on. This is a way of letting the people back home know that you are surviving and doing your best over here. It'll also make your family proud to see an article about you busting your cherry."

The group laughed.

"What's this article going to say?"

"Before I answer that, are you aware that the Combat Infantry Badge is the most coveted of all awards eligible to an infantry soldier? Some lifers in the rear areas would do anything to get one."

"He's telling the truth," Wild Bill affirmed.

"Many soldiers in Vietnam will never get one," the reporter continued. "You have to earn it through combat. Moreover, regardless of what you did, or how you felt during the fight, you are still entitled to this award. The article will let the people know who you are, where you are from, what school you attended, and the year you graduated, who your parents are, and where you are located in Vietnam. The rest of the article will relate to the award itself and its origin. It's good publicity, and the article will make your family proud. The format is the same for everybody, so all we have to do is to fill in the blanks."

"What the hell," John conceded, "I'll answer your questions."

"Good! Let's get started."

Wild Bill stopped the PR man before he could leave.
"How about writing a story about our sorry-assed Major Stone and the stunt he pulled today?"

"Why? What happened?"

Wild Bill and Scout related the earlier incident for him, making sure not to leave out any of the details. After several minutes of listening, the reporter closed his notebook and returned it to his shirt pocket.

"I'm sorry, guys, but I can't write a story like that. I can sympathize with you, but we don't have all the facts and don't know what really happened."

"What if I can get them for you?"

"Don't waste your time. Even if I wrote it, the editors would shit-can the article. They would tell me that it was in bad taste, and bad for morale. Besides, that type of behavior has always existed throughout the military, as well as in civilian life. A few assholes can ruin it for everybody else. Just chalk it up to experience and let go of it. Dwell on the good and forget the bad."

"What good can come out of war?" Doc asked the confident reporter.

"Friendship and camaraderie are two that I know for certain."

"I agree that there is a bond that develops, but it's more of a dependency on each other for moral support and strength than anything else. It's the only way any of us will survive this insane war."

"That's the point I'm trying to make. You've all shared your inner feelings with each other at one time or another. I would even bet that you've built such a trust between yourselves that you could confide in one-another and tell tales that you would not dream of telling anyone else. And you really haven't known each other that long."

"The man has a point," Scout broke in. "I grew up with a couple of guys who are still back in the world. I thought we were the closest of friends. But when I think about it now, you guys know more about me than they do."

"I agree," Doc smiled. "You know I'd do anything for you guys. Hell, even Polack and Larry have become part of my life."

"You might not see each other after Vietnam, but I can guarantee you that each of you will remember this bond. So cherish it while you can." The reporter looked at his watch. "I have to go. You guys take care of yourselves."

"You too!"

He turned and walked out of the tent.

Doc stood up and headed to where the other four men sat on two adjacent cots. He extended both arms outward, balled his hands into fists, and positioned one in front of each group.

"Brothers!" he said,

All reached up and hit Doc's fists with their own.

"We are, indeed!"

That afternoon, Bill Sayers, John, and Larry managed to get together for a little R and R. They spent the next couple of hours drinking cold sodas and telling each other about the things they had experienced during the last month with the company. The three young men decided to walk over to the stage where the movie, "Butch Cassidy and the Sundance Kid', was about to start. A western starring Robert Redford and Paul Newman as outlaws, the movie was humorous and entertaining - an effective diversion from the reminders of war around them - and they were reluctant to return to their tents.

John and Larry found that almost everyone in the tent was either sleeping or writing letters. Not even a card game was taking place. For both men it was just too early to sleep, so they dug out their supplies and joined in on the community letter-writing.

Both men were excited about the upcoming article in the local newspaper back home, and wanted to give their families some notice to watch for it. John had kept all his letters simple since arriving in country and had never written about narrow escapes or other dangerous events, tending to write about the weather, or answering questions prompted by TV news shows. One particular question from home was especially upsetting, as his mother asked if it was true that the U.S. was killing innocent women and children. John, taken aback by the inquiry, was afraid to ask any of his fellow soldiers for fear of reprisal by the group. He simply responded that he had never seen the enemy and seriously doubted that any were innocent woman or children.

John bit the bullet and wrote that he had been in his first battle, and because of it, an article would soon appear in the local paper. He wanted to downplay it, writing that the event was a typical occurrence and that every infantry soldier received the award during his tour of duty. However, he already knew the news article would generate a deluge of questions in future letters from home.

When John finished and packed everything away, he lay on his cot and prepared himself for day number fifty-two in Vietnam.

# CHAPTER ELEVEN

At three in the morning, the Division helipad bustled with activity. Battalion Supply needed to have all the equipment and supplies ready for transport prior to the infantry's 0800 departure. Their only lift truck was broken, however, so moving the supplies by hand was the only option. Large nets blanketed the pad and trucks full of supplies sat idly to the side, lighting the area with their headlamps. Pandemonium reigned as rear echelon personnel moved around in mass confusion, carrying crates on their shoulders. Nobody seemed to know where they belonged. Supply sergeants and officers ran around with clipboards, trying desperately to organize the chaos and meet their schedule.

At the deadline, only small portions of the total supplies were ready. The grunts, anxious to leave Cu Chi, became impatient and irritated by this delay.

"What's the deal, Sixpack?" Wild Bill asked.

"It looks like we'll be here awhile, so make yourselves comfortable."

"Why do we have to wait until the supplies are loaded?" Scout whined.

"Because we're flying in Chinooks, and the brass wants to limit the trips."

"Isn't this just like the Army?" Doc commented. "It's always 'hurry up and wait'."

"You got that right," Scout agreed. "Only I wish we could do our waiting in the shade. This hot sun is a bitch."

"Go to sleep and it won't feel so bad."

"That's a great idea, Wild Bill. I can use a couple more hours of sleep."

"Wake us when they're ready to go." Scout and Larry lay on the grass, using their rucksacks as pillows.

"Don't worry about needing a wake-up call. You'll know when the birds arrive," Sixpack smiled and continued to pace on the grass.

The rest of the squad followed suit and tried to get in a few extra winks.

Three hours later, Sixpack strode up to each man, kicking him on the sole of his boot. "Come on, you deadbeats, wake up! Birds are on their way."

"What the fuck?" Scout sat up quickly, unsure of his whereabouts.

"There's nothing like getting a suntan while fully clothed." Wild Bill fanned his damp fatigue shirt in an attempt to cool off his sweaty body.

"I know the feeling. Look at me! I'm soaked to the bone." Scout mimicked Wild Bill in his cooling- off technique.

Others, who had removed their shirts earlier, scratched each other's back to relieve the itching caused by lying bareback on the grass.

After a few minutes, the men in the First Platoon gathered their rucksacks and moved toward one of the large piles of supplies on the tarmac. Progressively louder chopping sounds from beyond alerted them to the approaching helicopters.

The five giant birds - each looking twice the size of a city bus - had two large rotors overhead to carry the ship. They created such a whirlwind during final approach that it temporarily blinded everyone near the landing zone. Of course, the supply personnel were all wearing goggles and seemed immune to the onslaught of debris. Once the birds were down, a large hydraulic ramp on the rear of each helicopter lowered to the ground, enabling each platoon member access to their respective transports. It was still extremely windy and dusty, but the level of visibility was sufficient for the men to move through the dust storm and board the aircraft. They sat on long fold-down planks running the length of the aircraft; their backs leaning into netting that lined the fuselage. Both rows of soldiers faced one another.

In the meantime, the supply personnel were gathering corners of nets and securing them to a towing hook on the bottom of each monster machine. The Chinooks rose straight into the air at a very slow pace until the sling holding the net was taut and the bundle of supplies lifted into the air. The pilots reviewed their control panel gages to verify that the total cargo weight was acceptable and safe for them to fly before tilting the rotors slightly and flying away.

The formation of Chinooks circled over a large, round clearing surrounded by dense jungle. Green heavy-duty construction equipment sat unattended throughout the brown and red dirt-filled clearing. The large helicopters turned into the wind and began their descent. Several piles of debris burned in the northern sector of the clearing and thick black clouds of smoke rose up toward the airborne formation.

"Look at all that smoke! You can see it for miles." John sat near the rear of the aircraft where much of the First Squad could see through the open ramp.

"It's a good beacon for the VC to follow, too," Wild Bill pointed out.

"Just like sending out smoke signals and offering a personal invitation to come and visit us," Scout added.

"What the fuck are we getting ourselves into?" Larry wondered aloud.

Delta Company soldiers manned temporary guard positions encircling the entire clearing. Several massive bulldozers and graders from the Engineering Battalion had created the opening in the heavy jungle. In size, it equaled six combined football fields. The Chinooks first dropped their cargo in the center of it all, and then landed nearby to discharge the human cargo.

Red wooden surveyor stakes stuck up from the ground at fifteen-foot intervals, forming a smaller circle within the huge clearing; this was the actual perimeter of the firebase.

Captain Fowler called the Alpha Company Lieutenants together in a wet and muddy section of the clearing. He did not have any alternative, as most of the clearing was the same. Boots quickly sank into the mush; soldiers struggled to walk through the clearing. Deep sucking sounds accompanied every footstep.

"This isn't going to be a picnic out here. Many of you already know the Triangle has plenty of booby traps, caches, and enemy soldiers. Most supplies and reinforcements come from Cambodia and pass right through this area. Military intelligence calls this area the Ho Chi Minh Trail of the South.

"The VC are already aware of our presence and know what we're trying to accomplish. They have mortared the clearing twice in the last week and have caught some of Delta Company's patrols in ambushes. The Engineers also believe the enemy is slipping into the clearing during the night, because they're finding mines which weren't there the days before.

"If they decide to hit this firebase before it's finished, it could be a bloodbath. Therefore, we need an all-out effort from each of you in preparing this location before nightfall. So, work hard for all our sakes."

Each platoon had the arduous task of building four-man bunkers along a portion of the perimeter. First and Second Squads of First Platoon busied themselves with the actual building, while the other two squads began working on the area to the front of where the bunker line would be. Barbed concertina wire was unrolled and staked in place. The men then placed trip flares, claymore mines, and other early-warning devices in strategic locations.

Wild Bill and John painstakingly worked as a team in building one of the bunkers. Wild Bill dug while John filled sandbags and stacked them to the side. Both their backs were the color of a red, ripened apple, yet they had to continue to sweat and persevere in the backbreaking chore.

"Goddamn clay!" Wild Bill yelled from the depths of a four-foot hole. "Why couldn't they have chosen an area with sand?"

"And make it easier for us? They probably set this up intentionally as a method of cleansing our bodies of all that cheap beer we drank in Cu Chi."

"I'd give anything to be out in the bush right now."

"That was quick. The captain said we wouldn't feel that way for another couple of days."

"Fuck the captain, fuck the Army, and fuck Vietnam." The chant came from deep in the ground, and started over again after a shovel full of dirt was tossed topside.

At 1900, John and Wild Bill completed their fighting position and stepped away to admire their work from a distance.

"Looks great, doesn't it?"

"Not bad. But you have to admit, it was the hardest eight hours we've ever put in."

"I know what you mean. I'm even too exhausted to eat."

"Just hope we're not picked for an ambush patrol tonight."

"Ambush patrol? Why would they send any of us out on ambush teams? We've been working our asses off all day."

"Look around," Wild Bill suggested. "There are too many people in this perimeter and not enough bunkers to protect them."

"I see your point. One mortar round in the right place would wipe out a whole bunch of men, that's for sure."

Both men walked out to the barbed wire, turned around, and then looked over their portion of the perimeter. Scout and Larry were to their left, still working feverishly on their bunker. On the right, both Doc and Frenchie were also admiring their completed work. The two groups waved to one another.

"Not bad for a bunch of rookies!" Frenchie threw a softball-sized rock at their bunker.

"Hey, hey, don't try to knock it down just yet. Let us get at least one night of sleep in it first."

The men laughed.

"They may not be perfect, but at least they'll be a better cover than bushes and trees."

"That's very true, Doc. I can't wait until tomorrow when we can use our new natural air conditioner. It's at least twenty degrees cooler down in the hole right now."

"Wild Bill, next you're going to tell us that room service is available."

The group shared another laugh.

Sixpack returned from the Lieutenant's bunker in the center of the firebase and called out to his squad when close enough, "Come on, guys, we have to talk." Sixpack waved for the men to join him.

"Oh shit," Wild Bill mumbled, "looks like it's time to fuck with the First Squad again." He pulled at the barbwire, letting it snap like a slingshot. "Come on, Polack!"

The two men left the barbed wire and merged with the other two-man teams, converging upon Sixpack's position.

"Don't look so worried," he announced after seeing the distressed looks on their faces. "Delta Company is going out on ambush tonight."

The men exhaled deeply and cheered with delight.

"Personally, I would have preferred the ambush. Tonight, we have to fill in the gaps on the perimeter and fill in those bunkers left unattended when the ambush teams leave. Our squad will take over the bunkers that you've just finished, but only two men will be in each. I know you're all tired, but the firebase will be on fifty percent alert tonight, so one of you will have to be awake at all times."

The men mumbled their disapproval.

"The Mortar Platoon will be firing illumination flares into the sky at fifteen-minute intervals. So keep your heads down, and do not make yourself a target for a sniper. I do not want any unnecessary firing, unless you actually see movement to your front. If hit, watch the wire closely for sappers. If they get through, we can be in a world of hurt. The password for tonight will be 'Champion'. Are there any questions? He paused.

"Okay, let's get ready for the night."

Wild Bill and John sat outside their bunker, leaning against the soft sandbags. John's appetite had improved lately, but he was too tired to heat a meal. Instead, he opened a can of cold beans and franks and nibbled on his spoonful of nourishment. Wild Bill placed a heat tab into an empty C-Ration can and punched several holes into it. After igniting it, he placed a canteen cup full of water on the makeshift stove.

Both were quietly admiring the sun as it set over the jungle.

"You know, this country has its pretty moments. Just look at that orange sun behind the palm trees. If I didn't know better, I'd think we were in paradise." John sighed.

"It is like paradise. If you listen closely, you can even hear the birds and monkeys calling to us from the jungle. I don't recall it ever being this quiet in Cu Chi."

"Maybe it's the calm before the storm!" Wild Bill took a drink from his steaming cup of hot cocoa. "You'll think of this place differently in a couple more hours."

The two men continued to eat and drink in silence for several minutes. Finally, John turned to face his partner for the night.

"Why do the guys call you 'Wild Bill'?"

"You know how it is. Everyone in the Nam either arrived with a nickname or did something to earn it. In my case, the guys started calling me 'Wild Bill' after seeing this picture of me from back home."

He withdrew a wallet from the rubber pouch in his rucksack, extracted a photograph, and handed it to John.

"See what I mean?"

The picture showed a cowboy standing next to a brown and white Appaloosa horse. In the background was a snow-capped mountain range and wild sagebrush; both silhouetted in front of a royal blue, cloudless sky. Shoulder-length brown hair hung from under a black cowboy hat with a silver band. He sported a six-inch long but neatly trimmed dark brown beard that hung over the front of an unbuttoned tan buckskin jacket. A thick, black leather ammo belt encircled his waist; a holster rested on his right hip, its bottom tied to his right thigh with a thin leather strip. A chrome revolver with white pearl handles peeked out of the holster, reflecting the sparkling sunlight in all directions.

"This is you?"

"Yeah, but you wouldn't think so."

"Shit, no. You look like an old west outlaw and twenty years older. Where was this picture taken?"

"In El Paso, Texas. I worked on a ranch there before I was drafted. Man, I can't wait to get back."

"Me neither." John thought about that for a few seconds. "What's your real name?"

"Bill Hickock."

"Get the fuck out of here!"

"That's why they call me 'Wild Bill'."

He placed the picture back into his wallet and returned it to the protective rubber bag inside of his rucksack. Then he leaned back against the bunker and lit a cigarette. Wild Bill drew deeply from the unfiltered stick of tobacco, exhaling the smoke slowly through the wide gap between his two front teeth.

"God, I sure do miss the circuit."

"What circuit?"

"I used to travel on the rodeo circuit all through the western part of the country."

"What are rodeos like?"

"Haven't you ever been to one?"

"Nope. Detroit isn't the kind of place to have a rodeo."

"You don't know what you've been missing. Shit, back home, everyone planned their weekends around the local rodeos."

"We didn't have that luxury."

"I understand. They're not popular where you come from. You know I made half my earnings every year from the circuit."

"What were you selling?"

"I wasn't selling anything; I was a participant."

"You mean roping horses and shit?"

"Yeah. And bronco-busting, cattle-wrestling, and steer-roping."

"Were you good?"

"I have trophies and newspaper articles that say I am."

"Damn! I'm sharing a bunker with a real celebrity."

"Aw, knock off that bullshit, Polack."

"No, seriously, I'm intrigued. Tell me more."

"I'd like to, but it's getting dark. We'd better get ready for our watches."

"How do you want to work it?"

"Let's see," Wild Bill looked at the luminous dial on his watch, "it's almost seven-thirty. How about we each take a two-hour shift on the first watch and then follow with one three-hours long? This way we can both get some sleep."

"Sounds good to me, I'll take the first watch."

"You got it."

First Squad's turn on patrol came the following morning. They were to move toward a trail junction a kilometer to the west of the firebase and set up a day ambush site.

After leaving the wire, they followed a large hard-packed road toward their destination. It was not twenty minutes before an APC patrol forced them from the road. The four Armored Personnel Carriers passed noisily, each carrying a squad of men on top.

"G'day, Mates!" A few of the soldiers called from one of the steel monsters.

All wore strange hats with brims folded up high on one side.

"Who are those guys?"

"They're Aussies and have a base nearby."

"Australian? I didn't know they were here," Larry remarked.

"Shit, yes," Frenchie broke in. "We're not the only people fighting the Communists in this country. I read about it once. The article said that fifteen countries were involved in this war, but I've only seen Koreans, Thais, and Aussies."

"You learn more about this place every day."

"Yeah, and just when you think you know it all, Larry, it's time to go home," Doc added.

"Now that's the way to go out on patrols." John jerked his head in the direction of the departing dust-covered soldiers. "No more humping. Just put your shit inside and ride out your tour."

"Those are iron coffins," Sixpack said matter-of-factly. "Every enemy soldier within a mile can hear you coming. All they have to do is mine the approach and wait for your APC to blow its track. Then he'll finish you off with either a B-40 rocket or RPG. I've seen what they can do to those armored tracks. Everything inside is cut to ribbons. It might look appealing, but you can have them."

As the patrol continued westward, the jungle surrounding them became withered and sparse.

"What happened to this part of the jungle?" John asked. "It looks like somebody sprayed weed killer all over it."

"It is a weed killer," Sixpack replied. "Special planes used to fly all through this country to spray defoliant on the jungle."

"Why did they spray the countryside?"

"To eliminate and uncover all the enemy hiding places. They had names for the operation and for the shit they sprayed, but I can't remember either of them. Hell, during my last tour, I can even remember them spraying while we were patrolling through the jungle below. The shit came down like a monsoon rain and smelled terrible. We used to get skin rashes that itched like hell and breathing problems from inhaling the stuff."

"Was it dangerous?"

"Other than the rashes and stuff, everybody told us the stuff isn't dangerous and not to worry about it."

"This area smells like shit, too!" Scout added.

"Must be the decomposition," Doc reported.

"Dead bodies have smelled better."

The squad arrived at the junction and moved into the decayed underbrush to set up an ambush on line with the trail.

All the porous tree stumps were havens for red ants, spiders, horseflies, and other crawling insects, which feasted on the rotting vegetation. Most of the squad was preoccupied with taking defensive measures against the small insects instead of focusing on the trail. Red ants sting unmercifully; horseflies leave welts after biting their victims, and hundreds of spiders sent chills down the spines of the young men. Every insect spray bottle was empty within the first hour; the precious liquid was used more on the insects than on the men's own bodies. It appeared that the insects were immune to the bug spray. Upon reaching the liquid line on the ground, they only hesitated briefly before moving through it and toward their human prey.

At 1700 hours, the ambush set-up terminated. Everyone stood and wiped hundreds of dead insects from their fatigues before gathering their gear to leave.

On the return to the firebase, the men gently caressed welts, rashes, bruises, and mosquito bites while keeping their eyes on the surrounding jungle for the enemy.

When arriving at the firebase, the men noticed two new semi-luxuries that were not there when leaving that morning: a shower and a toilet. The shower stood in the middle of the compound. Two fifty-five gallon drums hung suspended six and a half feet above a platform that straddled a drainage ditch. Each barrel had a showerhead attached to the underside, helping to distribute the water uniformly. Using the "buddy" system, one would bathe while the other dumped pails full of water into the barrels. Unfortunately, the showerhead did not turn off so there was no way to collect water in the barrel. Whatever went in came right back out, but at a slower rate.

A crowd was already gathered around the shower. Some waited for their turn under the cold, refreshing spray, while others stood only to watch and pass the time of day, like old men in a barbershop. No curtains or walls enclosed the structure - modesty was not an option.

Two new "outhouses" joined the bunkers near the perimeter of the camp. Those too, however, were devoid of walls or curtains to provide privacy. Three fifty-five gallon drums, cut in half, sat under a twenty-inch deep by ten-foot long wooden plank. Three oblong holes were spaced evenly across the face of the plank - one size fit all.

During the initial stages of building up the firebase, these outhouses caused many problems. The main concern was the location, which sat on the edge of the perimeter next to the barbed wire. When using the facilities, you faced the inside of the perimeter leaving your back exposed to the jungle outside of the camp. This made it difficult to concentrate on the duties at hand, as the men continuously turned to keep an eye on the tree line.

Embarrassment was the other concern when trying to take care of business in plain view of everyone in the firebase. Many of the young men developed painful hemorrhoids from not letting nature take its course. They would purposely try to hold their bowel movements until nightfall, when the cover of darkness allowed them to relax in a more private manner.

A few weeks later, First Squad was taking a break during one of their patrols.

"These daily patrols are getting to me," Larry admitted.

"Look at the bright side. At least we're excused from all the bullshit details on the firebase."

"Yeah, like burning shit," Scout chimed in.

"What's that?"

"It's the worst detail in this whole stinking country."

"You only have to watch somebody do it once to know it," Doc added. The men snickered.

"What do you have to do?" Larry asked.

"When we return to the firebase every night, haven't you ever seen those smoking barrels over by the shitters?"

"That's just trash burning, isn't it?"

"Yeah, Larry, it's trash, but its trash from your ass." The others laughed again while Larry and John looked at them curiously.

"That's the shit detail. It starts early in the morning, right after breakfast. Sometimes, there's two people assigned to the detail, but most of the time there's only one. When I had to do it, I was alone." Scout shuddered at the memory.

"It is a motherfucker," Wild Bill emphasized.

"Yes, it is," Doc agreed.

"As I was saying, the first thing on the agenda is to get the barrels out from under the planks. Sometimes they're almost filled to the top." John and Larry looked at Scout in horror.

"Especially if the mess hall served beans the day before," Wild Bill smirked as he watched the two Cherries squirm and turn pale.

"Anyway, they don't give you any gloves or breathing devices. So dragging those cans some forty feet away to an area where it is safe to burn can be a disaster. You can always hold your breath so you don't have to smell the stuff. However, no matter how careful you are in moving them, there's no way of stopping the semi-solid contents from splashing onto you. Once that happens, you just don't give a fuck anymore."

"It's a real bitch too, if you aren't able to come up with a clean set of fatigues," Sixpack chimed in.

"I had to take a shower in mine, but the smell was still there," Wild Bill said, enjoying the show.

Larry and John looked at each other, a repulsed expression on their faces.

Scout continued, "Once you've managed to pull and tug the cans away, you add a combination of diesel fuel and gasoline to them, providing there's enough room. Sometimes, you have to transfer some of it out from one can to another with a bucket to make room. Once that's done, you just throw in a lit match, and move back."

"Is that all you have to do?" Larry asked.

"No, you have to stir it too," John said jokingly.

"Give that man a cigar," Scout announced.

John stopped laughing and flashed an incredulous look.

"That's right, Polack, you have to sit and watch the shit burn all day long. You stir it up every half hour or the fire will go out."

"How do you know when you're done?"

"When there isn't shit left in the can." A chuckle erupted from the men.

"That was a good one, Scout!" Sixpack announced.

"It usually takes until seven in the evening to burn everything up."

"That's one detail I hope that I never get."

"Don't bet on that, Polack. Everyone does it at least once. And when our squad's turn comes up, guess whose names will be on the list."

"Aw, fuck!" The realization hit Larry.

The day ambush team positioned itself near the bend of a well-used trail. The weed killer had not been sprayed on this area yet, so the dense jungle offered good concealment and protection for the men in the First Squad.

Scout and Wild Bill stood on opposite sides of the single line ambush. Both men watched the trail intently while the rest of the squad in between relaxed and daydreamed. Larry wrote a letter to his folks, Sixpack spread a towel out in front of him and used it as a table to play a card game of Solitaire, Frenchie monitored the radio, John and Doc shared a tree trunk to catch a few minutes of sleep.

Suddenly, Scout bolted upright. "Movement, coming this way," he whispered.

The men quietly picked up their weapons and readied themselves for what might be coming.

"No firing until I open up," Sixpack instructed the team.

Five minutes later, a lone Vietnamese came into view walking on the trail. He wore black nylon pants, a blue denim shirt, Ho Chi Minh sandals, and a U.S. boony hat. He pointed his AK-47 up the trail as he proceeded cautiously.

The VC point man was almost in front of Nung's position, when he heard some rustling in the bush and stopped suddenly. He raised an arm, looked behind him, and then moved toward the side of the trail, where the ambush team lay in wait.

The men froze in position as the VC teenager tried to find the source of the noise. Nervous beads of perspiration ran down the faces of each man; fingers tightened their grips on triggers, and all breathing stopped for a moment. He did not venture from the trail to make a visual reconnaissance. After a few sweeps of the jungle, he turned his right ear toward the ambush team and lowered his head, listening. Maybe he could hear what he was unable to see. Finally, having satisfied his curiosity, he returned to the center of the trail and waved for others to follow.

He waited a few minutes before three similarly clad youths came into view from around the bend. They wore conical hats, and carried rucksacks and weapons as well.

When the four men were within the killing zone, Sixpack fired his M-16, the signal for the rest of the squad to open fire. The sound of the ambush was loud enough to reach the firebase, making those soldiers stop working and look anxiously in that direction. The four Vietnamese dropped in their tracks. Larry swept the entire trail with the M-60, Scout and Wild Bill tossed grenades, and Doc, Sixpack, John, and Nung continued to fire on automatic in the direction of the enemy. When there was no return fire, Sixpack yelled, "Hold your fire, hold your fire!"

Scout and Nung jumped from their concealed positions and raced to the bend in the trail. They watched for any enemy reinforcements that might be on their way. Wild Bill and Doc did the same at the opposite end of the trail. Sixpack, Larry, and John rose from the smoky underbrush and moved out toward the corpses on the trail.

The VC were not able to return fire during the ambush; the execution was perfect and took away any chance of their escape. All four enemy soldiers died immediately, their bodies contorted into unthinkable positions. Blood continued to ooze from dozens of holes in their bodies, collecting in small puddles and seeping into the dry, red earth.

Sixpack moved quickly to check the bodies for any signs of life. He found the last enemy soldier in a depression on the far side of the trail.

"We have a live one!" Sixpack announced. "Frenchie, get me a Medevac, and notify the company that we have a POW."

"Roger." Frenchie returned to retrieve his radio.

"Polack, keep an eye on him while I go through their gear."

John hovered over the wounded and unconscious soldier, making certain that his weapon stayed pointed at the man's head.

"If he makes a move to hurt you, waste him," Sixpack emphasized.

"I won't give him the chance."

Frenchie returned to the trail. "Hey Sixpack! The captain said we're to remain here after the Medevac leaves because a team from Intelligence is coming out."

"Why? We can strip the bodies," Sixpack protested.

"I told him that, but he said they would take care of it, so we wouldn't have to carry the stuff back to the firebase."

"Now that's the best idea that man has had since I've been in this company."

"I'm crazy about it too. Gimme five."

It took another month and a half to complete Firebase Lynch. By that time, squad-sized bunkers had replaced the small emplacements and new permanent structures enclosed the showers and outhouses. The officers also managed to build special facilities for "officers only". Two batteries of 105mm Howitzers now called the new firebase home and were set-up next to the two mortar pits.

Reinforcements were arriving periodically to beef up Alpha Company's strength. Billie Joe Johnson, from Alabama, replaced Zeke in the First Squad. The men quickly nicknamed him 'BJ' and assigned him to Larry as an ammo bearer for the machine gun.

The new Cherry sat restlessly near one of the bunkers. His expression was one of awe and his head jerked every which way so as not to miss anything around the firebase.

"What's it like in the field?" He finally asked.

"You'll love it," Larry replied. "All we do is go out on daily ambushes and wait for Charlie to come by."

"Yeah, and we've been lucky too," John added. "We must have killed at least thirty VC since coming here, and haven't lost any of our own people."

The young, backwoods newbie's eyes widened when hearing this report.

"Just be glad that you weren't sent to Delta Company," Scout announced.

"Why?" The tall, wiry kid asked, looking at the outspoken Native American.

"Because they're not as lucky or as good as we are."

The Cherry appeared confused and cast an imploring look to Larry.

"What Scout is saying, BJ, is that Delta Company has only killed a couple VC soldiers while losing a bunch of their own to ambushes and booby traps."

"Wow!" The youngest soldier commented. "You guys must be good."

"We do have our moments," Scout replied.

"How much longer will we be here?"

"Only a couple of more days, we're leaving on Thursday for the Michelin Rubber Plantation."

"To do what?" He asked in a strong southern accent.

"We're going to kill gooks! Jesus, man, you think we're going there to make tires? Don't be such an ignorant motherfucker!"

Doc interrupted, "Don't be so hard on the man, Scout. He just arrived and doesn't know what the Nam is about yet."

"It sure won't take him long," Larry pointed out.

"Who will take over the firebase when we leave?"

"See what I mean? All Cherries ever do is ask questions."

"Don't worry about it, Scout." Doc directed his attention to the newest man in the squad. "Son, the higher brass has determined that this area is too difficult to patrol on foot. Shit, most of the jungle is rotting away around this firebase, so they are replacing us with the Fifth Mechanized Battalion. Their APC's will patrol through this area without a problem. Besides, in the last seven weeks, I haven't felt as comfortable here as I do at Firebase Kien. It'll be a pleasure to go back."

"Why is the jungle rotting?"

"That's a long story for another day!"

"How far away is Firebase Kien?"

Doc shook his head then smiled broadly. "Damn, BJ, I don't know myself. All I can tell you is that it's near the Black Virgin Mountain and in between Tay Ninh and the Parrot's Beak."

"Where's that?"

"I give up!" Doc threw his hands into the air and walked away.

John leaned back against the bunker and smiled, recalling his first few days in the country. Watching and listening to Billie Joe was like a mirrored image of himself just two and a half months earlier.

"Don't worry about the bush, you'll do just fine."

"I have a few more questions; will you answer them for me?"

John thought back to a remark Junior had made on Firebase Kien the night before he left for his first day in the bush: "Someday you'll be able to help out a Cherry and he'll be grateful and thank you for your help and understanding."

John sat upright then called to the new Cherry, "Come over here and sit down. I'll try to answer your questions and help you get organized."

# CHAPTER TWELVE

The Michelin Rubber Plantation was not too far from the Black Virgin Mountain, which the Vietnamese called Nui Ba Dinh. From a distance of several miles, the mountain appeared to be black and laced with white crevices and tears, taking on a marble-like appearance. No other hills or mountains stood between the plantation and Nui Ba Dinh; it towered, tall and alone in the distance, and could be seen for miles.

Stories circulated about that mountain. The Americans had a base at the top of it accessible only by helicopter; a radio relay station boosted communication signals between the military officials in Saigon and the rest of the country. The Army of the Republic of Vietnam (ARVN) had a large compound at the base of the same mountain. They were allies to the Americans, but content staying within their bases instead of patrolling through the jungle. In between these two compounds, the enemy supposedly had an intricate tunnel system, encompassing the entire mountain, top to bottom. It was said that the mountain is so porous that a couple of well-placed thousand-pound bombs could dissolve the mountain into a pile of dirt and stones.

The First Platoon operated on the outskirts of the plantation where several small villages lined the length of the dirt road. The area was sparsely populated and not considered a "Free Fire Zone." A daily curfew existed between dusk and dawn, however. A person caught outside of their village during those hours could be shot and killed.

They shared the road with shuffling villagers who made their way to and from the rubber plantation. Large water buffalo pulled carts filled with pails of dark, sticky liquid collected from the trees within the plantation. Adults moved about in a very quick step balancing long, bent bamboo poles across their shoulders with a full pail attached to each. All but the children wore straw-colored conical hats with traditional black nylon pants and working shirts in various colors.

In the passing villages, children ran about chasing small pigs, chickens and barking dogs. They laughed and had fun, too caught up in what they were doing to notice the line of American soldiers passing by.

"This is just too weird! I would never have imagined that I would be walking on a trail in Vietnam alongside villagers on their way to work." Larry transferred his machine gun to the opposite shoulder so one of the buffalos could not snatch it from him.

"Last time we worked in this plantation, we were on the western side of it and there were very few people around."

"Scout, how do we know which of these people are VC or not?"

"If we had that answer, the war would have been over long ago, my friend."

"I don't understand."

"One way, Polack, is to ask them for their ID. Everyone must carry them to show that they're honest citizens. However, that's the easiest piece of ID to buy on the black market. The VC also carried them – that's why it's so confusing during the day. Everybody's a farmer and villager during the day; some join up with the VC at night."

"I agree with you, Scout, but carrying cards after curfew doesn't mean squat. If we spot anybody moving around after dark, the probability of his or her being VC is very high. So we can shoot them first and not worry about checking ID because he looks suspicious."

"You got that right, Sarge. That's why I prefer the free-fire zones, where we don't have to deal with this bullshit."

"You know these villagers are mostly honest, hardworking people, trying to make a living. Most "imposters" are usually found in those villages outside of major base camps; many even have a job on the base. During my last tour, a Sapper Squad hit our base camp during the night. They created all kinds of havoc, but the next morning, we found one of the base barbers dead in the wire with others from his VC squad."

"Shit, it's like you can't trust anyone," BJ stated after hearing Sixpack tell the story.

"No, you can't, so don't let your guard down, even in areas like this. It only takes guts for one of them to reach down into a bush and come out firing an AK-47 on full automatic. How many of us do you think he can take out?"

"Say no more, Sixpack. We get the message!" The squad members adjusted their rifles, carrying them in a more defensive posture. Some had their weapons hanging from their shoulder by a sling; others held them by the handle, swinging the rifle at arm's length along their sides with each step.

The parade continued with the Americans showing more curiosity in the villagers than the villagers in them.

Sixpack led the column into one of the villages, looking for things that might be suspicious.

"This is the first time I've been in one of these villages. It's a lot different walking through than just glimpsing them from a bus or truck window when I first arrived in country."

Once again they saw old people squatting in front of their straw huts, chewing betel nuts, and occasionally smiling as the Americans passed. Others sneered at them for the interruption and spit on the ground at their feet.

Dogs barked incessantly and chickens scurried about, pecking at the dirt with every other step.

"These are the sorriest excuses for chickens that I've ever seen in my life. Just look at them! They're nothing but skin and bones."

"BJ, they probably eat more than the villagers but are only good for flavoring a pot of water."

"They're mean little fuckers though. This one almost bit my finger off when I reached for it."

Some of the nearby villagers covered their mouths with a hand and chuckled after seeing Larry jump into the air and back away from the small, snapping three-pound bird.

Young boys led the huge water buffalos around, prodding and beating at them with long, thin bamboo sticks. They showed no fear of these massive animals; nonetheless, the Americans gave them a wide berth.

Small children began tagging along and followed the soldiers through the village as if they were Pied Pipers. The little kids ranged in age from about five years old to eight or so, and looked cute wearing pajama bottoms that were too big, continuously tugging and pulling at their waists while struggling to keep up.

"GI souvenir me chop-chop? Cigarettes?" The kids begged for handouts.

BJ handed one of them some of the red licorice he carried. All at once, the kids converged on him.

"Hold on now, I don't have any more to share." BJ held the licorice high into the air; the kids tried climbing up his body to reach the prize.

"You're fucked now. Give them the whole package before they knock your ass over and take it from you anyway." The sight reminded Scout of what life was like on the reservation, as many of the Native Americans lived in poverty and the children there would have done the same thing.

BJ quickly tossed the package off to the side and watched the pack of youths dive toward it in a free for all. This kept them busy for the next five minutes.

Most children under two years old or so were naked and were either sitting on the ground in front of their huts or were carried in the arms of an older sister.

A few boys, who looked to be about twelve, wheeled up on their bikes next to the column of soldiers. They had Styrofoam coolers filled with ice-cold Cokes strapped to back of each bike.

"GI want buy cold Coke? Only one dollar?" They parked their vehicles and set up shop right on the side of the trail.

Some of the soldiers stepped out of line and approached the young hawkers with dollar bills in hand. The bottles were temptingly cold and condensation dripped from them.

"What do you think, Larry? Should we get one? I remember them telling us in training when we got here that we shouldn't because they may be poisoned or have ground glass in them."

"It doesn't seem to be affecting those guys who've already finished their bottles."

"Aw, what the fuck! They look really good and cold. I'd probably pay ten dollars if that was the asking price." Once again, John recalled Junior's words of wisdom back at Kien.

The two of them purchased the last two bottles of Coke.

"This is fucking great!" John tilted his head back and allowed the rest of the cool, refreshing soda to run down his throat.

"Right on!" Larry agreed.

By mid-afternoon, Alpha Company entered the Michelin Rubber Plantation, which was the largest plantation in all of Vietnam. Each rubber tree was evenly spaced twenty feet apart and no matter in which direction you looked, the trees stood in perfect rows for miles. Vegetation between trees was thin and sparse, rising no more than two feet above the ground. Each tree had a pail secured, collecting slowly oozing sap.

After moving easily through the plantation, the column stopped when a farmer approached with his water buffalo-drawn cart of pails. The animal sensed something whenever Americans were around and the old man had trouble controlling the huge beast. It wheezed and stomped its feet, then dug in and tried to pull free from the villager. Finally, the old man raised a stick and swiftly whipped it twice across the animal's snout. This had little effect. The sergeant scanning the villager's ID was apprehensive about the beast possibly breaking away and injuring him or his fellow soldiers. He quickly returned the card and directed the villager to move on. The beast relaxed and settled down to a more docile state once it distanced itself from the soldiers.

"I gotta hand it to that old man - all eighty pounds of him. He handled that water buffalo like I used to break them wild horses back home," Wild Bill said in admiration.

"There's no way I'd try that. Goddamn thing would have stomped me to death."

"Yeah, Polack, it would have been all over for you, especially if you would have whipped his snout like the old man did."

"Wild Bill is probably the only person in this entire column who would have taken on the beast. Everyone else would have been long gone if he had broken free."

"There's no doubt about that, Frenchie, and I'd be at the front of that pack and leading everybody else." Doc continued to steal glances at the departing animal in order to convince himself that the threat of danger had passed.

First Platoon broke off from the main column and veered to the left on an angle of forty-five degrees. They planned to walk through the plantation for another half hour and then try to find a good spot for an NDP.

As they moved along, John looked up and could not believe what he saw in the air. "Hey guys, you better take a look up above."

"Holy shit!" Larry stopped abruptly, scrunching his shoulders as a chill ran down his spine.

"They're all over!" BJ looked upward and walked right into Larry.

Huge spiders, suspended from webs just above their heads, were the largest these men had ever seen. Their bodies, thin and oblong, measured about five inches in length, but when taking the legs into account, these arachnids were probably over a foot long. They each sat in perfectly round webs, suspended between two rubber trees. Most were high in the air, but some almost touched the ground. The size and colors of these spiders fascinated the soldiers; shades of bright yellow, candy apple red and green, reflected the light of a setting sun.

One of the grunts pulled and snapped on a web to get a reaction from the spider. However, the motion did not intimidate the creature, which stayed fixed in the exact center of its home.

"Do they bite?" BJ asked.

"Everything bites," Scout responded.

"Are they poisonous?"

"Not a clue. Care to find out?"

"No way!"

Because of the sparse vegetation, suitable spots for a good night defensive perimeter did not exist anywhere within the plantation. Lt.

Ramsey picked an area with a little more underbrush than he had seen so far and decided to set up for the night. The L-T arranged the perimeter in the shape of a square and assigned each squad a point on the compass so they could defend themselves on all four sides.

Sixpack's Squad set up on the north side of the perimeter. The open area did not provide any protection for the men in the event of a firefight, but at least the low underbrush would afford some concealment from prying eyes, unless somebody stood erect or walked around. It would be another night of moving around on hands and knees.

Most of the interior of the perimeter was bare and the soft brown earth made sleeping easier for the men. They spread ponchos on the ground and covered themselves with the thin - but soft - green liner to create a sleeping position. Pillows consisted of nothing more than towels and balled up shirts. Most soldiers placed their rucksacks and extra supplies on the outer perimeter side of their makeshift beds in hopes of providing some protection if attacked.

The men had to set up mechanical ambushes, trip flares, and manually detonated claymore mines to cover nearby trails before anyone could relax or eat dinner. In the morning, everything had to be dismantled and secured before sunrise so innocent villagers were not hurt after the curfew ended.

"You guys have to be careful to not hurt these rubber trees. We don't want to have to pay the tire company for any damage," Sixpack announced.

"You've got to be joking," Larry said.

"Nope, it's true. This rule even goes back to when the French fought here. The deal is that if any unit is forced into combat within the plantation, the government has to reimburse the rubber company for any damages to its trees."

"That's a stupid fucking rule. We're at war, how can they justify that?"

"Stupid or not, we have to follow it."

"This is unreal and gets more insane every day!"

First Platoon remained within the plantation for the next several days. Squad-sized patrols were dispatched daily to check ID's of nearby workers and to investigate any suspicious-looking trails. Every afternoon at about 1500 hours, the platoon packed it up and moved to a different - but similar - site between the trees. The deployment of defensive measures after curfew, and then securing them before daybreak, had become routine.

During their fourth night there, odd noises occurred around their perimeter; the distinct sound of leaves stirring, twigs breaking, and unfamiliar grunting sounds were alarming. Sixpack scanned the surrounding area with a Starlight scope, seeing only the trees standing silently and nothing else. Most of the soldiers, spooked by this ongoing disruption, remained awake and alert through the night.

There was a break in their routine when the person on watch spotted flashlights out in the field at about ten o'clock at night. The guard woke Lt. Ramsey, and then moved to Sixpack, shaking him out of his slumber. "L-T needs you over by the CP." Sixpack grabbed his weapon and moved over to join the lieutenant.

"What's up, L-T?" Sixpack rubbed the sleep from his eyes and waited for his vision to adjust.

"Night guard spotted flashlights in the fields outside of the plantation. Can't see much, but if you look closely," he placed a hand on the sergeant's shoulder and pointed out toward the flickering lights, "I make out at least six of them."

"I see them, L-T, and don't remember a village in that particular area. But I do recall that field; heavy jungle borders it on the left and at the far end."

"I'll call in a fire mission and we can check it out in the morning." The two men referenced the map and agreed on the coordinates for the first salvo.

Lt. Ramsey called Battalion HQ and waited almost a half hour to obtain clearance for the fire mission. By that time, the lights had long disappeared, but he knew the artillery barrage was still necessary.

Many of the sleeping men were awakened by the commotion around the CP, so when the explosions finally occurred in the clearing about five hundred yards away, few of them were surprised. The L-T called for ten more rounds to impact within that general vicinity.

Two hours later, some of the men heard a motorcycle moving across the open field toward the same area where they saw the flashlights earlier. The sound was deceiving and it was very difficult to pinpoint its exact location as it echoed through the trees. The remainder of the night was quiet and uneventful.

In the morning, Captain Fowler ordered the First Platoon to move out of the plantation and investigate the area that exhibited all the activity during the night.

When the platoon reached the clearing, the men formed up into two columns while crossing the open area.

"It looks like we're walking through an old rice paddy."

"How can you tell?"

Scout pointed to the right and left, and said, "Look over there, do you see the raised ground? Those are old paddy dikes that kept the water in and allowed the villagers to move through the fields."

"Why do you think it's not being used anymore?"

"Look around, BJ, do you see anybody around?"

"I haven't seen anybody since leaving the plantation. In fact, I don't even see any villages nearby."

"This is really old. If there was a village around here, they packed it up and moved out a long time ago."

"This is still a no-fire zone so stay on your toes."

The men soon reached the area where the artillery barrage had hit during the night. Here, the L-T had the platoon form into a single line, so they could sweep through the area and look for signs of the enemy having been there.

The ten small artillery craters were in an area one-half the size of a football field. Fresh, black dirt coated the ground and nearby vegetation. There were no trees in this open area, but the hot steel projectiles shred much of the foliage surrounding each crater. The grunts collected several pieces of jagged steel, no larger than a pack of cigarettes, as souvenirs.

"Man, if there was somebody out here last night, you'd think they couldn't have survived. Just look at all this devastation." John said, sweeping his arm in a half-circle arc.

"It's too weird. I haven't seen any flashlights on the ground or traces of blood anywhere in over an hour that we've been looking."

"If we haven't seen anything yet, then it's unlikely we'll find anything at all, Polack. It's hard to judge distance at night, and I can't guarantee this is exactly where the L-T and I saw those flashlights."

"Yeah, Sixpack, but didn't you say earlier that the lights were long gone before the fire mission? They probably weren't anywhere near this area when the rounds came in."

"That's what I think too, but we had to try anyway."

"We're not too far from the edge of the jungle over there," Larry pointed out to the dense vegetation only two-hundred feet away. "Maybe we should just keep walking until we reach it and poke around over there."

"I don't know. I'm already nervous about being out in the open so close to that tree line; it's the perfect spot for an ambush. Just hang loose and keep looking around here and I'll check with the L-T to see what his plans are." Sixpack walked over to where Lt. Ramsey was standing with his RTO, Bob.

"What are your thoughts about that tree line, L-T?"

"I've been tossing that around myself, Sixpack. We have most of the day left to patrol the area and find a place for the night. Might as well get out of this sun and go take a look."

"When do you want to leave?"

"Instead of all of us going together, I want your squad to recon the area first. Once you've got it secured, the rest of us will come up and join you."

"Sounds like a plan. I'll gather them up and we'll leave in five."

"Good luck!"

The platoon set up an NDP just inside the jungle and next to a well-used trail; Sixpack's Squad had discovered it during their recon of the area. The six-foot wide trail skirted the jungle and continued westerly into the dense thicket, away from the rubber plantation.

The hard packed surface, with its recent activity, intrigued Lt. Ramsey, especially after not seeing anybody in this area during the entire day. The captain agreed that it was suspicious and ordered the L-T to set up an ambush on the trail.

The men placed two mechanicals across the trail - one further west of their position and the other to the east. With trip flares and claymore mines in place, and guard rotation organized, the stage was set for the night.

As BJ had the last watch of the night, he was to wake everyone at 0545; this allowed the men fifteen minutes to dismantle the mechanicals before the curfew ended at 0600.

The Army had issued a prime directive to all field units that mechanical ambushes or trip mechanisms could not remain armed in no-fire zones after the end of curfew; the penalty for failing to comply could result in court martial.

In the morning, BJ did not wake the platoon at the designated time. Instead, a large explosion and dirt raining onto them roused them from their sleep. The time was 0630 hours.

"You dumb shit - you fell asleep!" Sixpack berated the new recruit. BJ, completely disorientated, did not know what to do or what to say. He leaned back against a tree, still holding the handset of the radio in his right hand.

"Our shit's in the wind now!" Sixpack looked out to the trail. "Scout, Frenchie and Nung, get out there and check that eastern ambush." He then looked to BJ. "Pray to God that some poor villager didn't stumble into it."

The colonel was already on the radio reviling the captain because he did not have an answer regarding the explosion from the vicinity of his First Platoon's NDP.

Lt. Ramsey switched to the company radio frequency and called the captain to inform him of their predicament. He was just about to apprise him that the last person on watch had fallen asleep when he was interrupted by sudden bursts of gunfire; rounds ricocheted through the perimeter, sending everyone to the ground for cover.

Suddenly, the three men came crashing back into the perimeter, guns still smoking from firing on the run.

"There's VC on the trail!" Scout hollered. "Don't know how many, but the mechanical didn't get them all. They started shooting at us before we even saw them."

Not another word was necessary before the men bolted into action. The grunts lying closest to the trail began firing out to their front and along the trail to their right. They also triggered two claymore mines, which exploded near the aggressive enemy.

The remaining squads on the other side of the perimeter hunkered down and held their fire, waiting for a clear target to materialize.

After just a few moments, the return fire became sporadic, then finally stopped. Sixpack was already on his feet gathering his squad to go and investigate. The Third Squad moved further east through the dense bush with plans of exiting onto the trail just above the ambush site.

Scout and Nung led the way with Frenchie following close behind. They cautiously stepped out onto the trail and found themselves about seventy-five feet from the blown ambush site.

"Remember, we still have a live mechanical on the trail behind us. Should we disarm it before moving up to check out the other one?"

"No, leave it be, Wild Bill. If we caught the VC in this one while moving west, it may protect us if reinforcements try to come out of the jungle from that direction. We'll get to it later."

The eight men crouched down and ran in single file across the trail, moving further into the elephant grass and away from the jungle. When they were parallel to the ambush site, the grunts spread out and tried to keep five feet between themselves as they proceeded on line toward the trail.

The smell greeted them even before they saw the seven bodies spread along the trail. The first two in the column, having taken the full blast of the single mine ambush, had missing appendages and their torsos were cut to shreds. The other five lay in contorted positions, blood still leaking from bullet holes in their bodies.

Each of the seven corpses were dressed alike and carrying a rucksack, ammo pouch, and AK-47 rifle. Steel pith helmets with a single red star lay strewn about the area. The rucksacks were full and bulging. A mortar tube and base plate lay in the middle of the line of dead enemy soldiers.

"Oh man, these are hardcore NVA soldiers. No wonder they held their ground and shot back at us," Frenchie said while scanning the corpses, his face showing deep concern.

"Looks like they were part of a supply train," Scout volunteered.

"Polack, go back and let the L-T know what we found. Then bring him and the others back here with you." Sixpack prodded at the bodies with his boot, watching for a reaction.

"I'm sure the L-T will be relieved," Scout mentioned.

"No doubt about it. Now all he has to do is to convince the colonel that this was planned so BJ doesn't have to go to the stockade."

Just then, Third Squad stepped out of the jungle and approached the ambush site from the east.

"Looks like we just hit the jackpot," the black squad leader announced when spotting the corpses on the trail.

"Yeah, but those are NVA dudes," a tall, blond former surfer from California stated. "I hope none of their buddies are hangin' out nearby."

"Me too!" Frenchie continued to watch the open field with Wild Bill while the others searched over the bodies.

A rustling from the jungle startled the Third Squad members before they saw John exit with the L-T and the Second Squad. They all gathered along the trail and then crowded around the corpses for a closer look. Some exhibited relief, some moved quickly to the side of the trail and vomited, while others - mostly the old timers - showed concern.

"Sixpack, let's get some people out on security. We don't need anybody walking up on us while we're all together on this trail celebrating," Lt. Ramsey ordered.

Sgt. Holmes conferred with the other squad leaders, then dispatched ten men into various directions. Each of the two-man observation posts (OP's) would set up about two-hundred feet away and monitor the approaches into the area.

After the L-T reported to both the captain and the colonel, the radio traffic on the battalion net became a chatterbox. Calls went out to anyone who needed to know about the ambush. After several minutes, the colonel ordered the L-T to strip the bodies and inventory everything they found. A helicopter and two intelligence experts would arrive at their location within the next two hours.

"These rucks must weigh about a hundred and fifty pounds each. I'm curious as hell to see what's inside of them."

"Unbelievable! How can somebody who weighs so little carry so much weight?"

"No telling how far they had to come, but there's enough stuff here to keep them supplied for several weeks."

They emptied the rucks onto the ground and organized the contents into small groups to the side of the trail. Most were identical and packed with ammunition, food, medical supplies, and varying personal effects. Scout found a map and some official paperwork written in Vietnamese. He handed them to Nung who began to read the special orders.

After scanning through the documents, Nung and Scout approached the L-T with the find. "NVA are on resupply mission and come from area in Cambodia. They travel over twenty-five kilometers and supposed to deliver all supplies not far away from here."

"They would have made it if not for BJ," Frenchie exclaimed.

"Good point. If we would have pulled in the mechanical before six in the morning, they would have walked right past us while we were cooking breakfast."

"Yeah, but these guys would have lit us up if they smelled food cooking. They wouldn't take off like the VC might have."

"That's just too much for me to believe," somebody in the other squad debated. "I'm thinking that they would have been bopping down this trail and chattering up a storm as they humped along. We would have heard them coming and set up a quick ambush."

"I don't think the results would have been the same, and there would have been a good chance that some of us would have gotten hurt." Frenchie replied, not as confident as his brother from the Third Squad.

"We'll never know, will we?"

The seven soldiers had carried the mortar tube, base plate, ten mortar rounds, three-thousand rounds of 7.62mm rounds for the AK-47's, bags of rice, tins of fish and chicken, personal effects, cigarettes, official documents, letters and a map.

The helicopter and intelligence team did not spend more than fifteen minutes on the ground. The two men reviewed the bodies, took several pictures from various angles, and then asked the grunts to load the supplies onto the chopper, taking off without saying another word.

After conferring with Nung about the papers, the L-T looked over his map, and then dispatched a patrol to follow the trail into the jungle for five hundred meters or so. Sixpack assigned the task to John, Scout, Wild Bill, and Nung.

The four men retrieved web gear, grenades, water, and extra ammo, and readied themselves to leave the security of the NDP. Sixpack stepped into their path, "Now don't get cute or try any hero shit out there. Just follow the trail and take notes about what you see. Do not go any further than you have to. I know that I don't have to tell you that there are only four of you, so avoid contact at all costs. Nung, take the point and try to get close to where these NVA were heading. And stay sharp!"

"We'll be cool, and definitely in no hurry," Scout replied as they exited the NDP and stepped onto the trail only a few yards from where the dead NVA soldiers lay. It had been several hours since the mechanical was blown and the corpses were already bloating up with gas and attracting swarms of flies. The stench was unbearable.

The four-man patrol followed the trail alongside the thick vegetation for twenty minutes when it suddenly turned and led into the dense jungle. Once inside, they found it to be cooler under the triple canopy jungle. All were sweating profusely, moving nervously along the trail. Nobody had said a word since leaving the NDP.

About two-hundred steps into the jungle, they came upon a fork in the trail. Nung held up his arm, fist clenched, signaling the others to stay put, and then moved up the right branch toward a small stream. He only walked about thirty feet before bending over on the side of the trail to have a closer look at something on the ground. Nung returned and motioned the group together.

"No can go this way. Beaucoup danger," he whispered.

"What did you see, Nung?"

"Come, I show."

Together, they walked the thirty feet to where Nung had spotted the warning. Something was wrong with the scene and definitely out of place in the middle of a jungle. Seven bricks lay on the ground to the side of the trail. Four of them were stacked neatly in one row, and butted up behind were the remaining three. The space created by the missing brick in the second row formed a "V", whose point faced up that trail.

"See. Is sign for booby traps! Better we no go. We go try other trail for ti-ti (Vietnamese slang for a little bit)."

They quietly returned to the fork and Nung led them up the left trail. The discovery of the booby trap warning heightened their awareness up another notch or two. They slowed their approach in order to watch both the jungle for movement and the trail for trip wires. The slow pace continued for another two-hundred meters when a large cleared area opened up to their front. The ground on the left side of the trail was void of all vegetation and measured about fifty feet square. The trail resumed on the other side of the clearing and continued onward into the jungle. They were halfway across the clearing when they came upon another strange sight. Nung called for them to stop again.

To their right was something resembling a hitching post for horses in the old western movies. Two poles, three feet high and ten feet apart, stuck up from the ground. A third and longer pole ran horizontally – straddling the other two and tied together with vines.

The four men gathered around, glancing at one another with inquisitive looks upon their faces. Shrugging their shoulders and shaking their heads, none had the slightest idea of what it was or what it represented. The ground nearby was hard and smooth and they did not see any horseshoe or hoof prints embedded into the earth.

"Let's head back," Scout whispered. "I'll take the point. Nung, watch our backs."

Scout moved down the trail, followed by the other three men. The small patrol moved slightly faster than they did when coming up the trail, still very quiet in their movements.

All breathed a sigh of relief when they exited the jungle, and returned to the open trail. Now the pace was even faster.

When the patrol returned to the NDP, there was only enough time left to report in with the L-T and grab a quick meal before nightfall.

The L-T had decided to spend another night in the same location, and then dispatch two squads in the morning to investigate what the small patrol had uncovered.

During the night, Larry became very sick. He developed a high fever, and Doc recommended they call for a Medevac to pick him up in the morning. His symptoms were the same as malaria, but something else was ailing him too; Doc could not put his finger on it.

The next morning before Larry left on the dust-off helicopter, Sixpack ordered him and John to switch weapons and ammo. Larry would take the M-16 with him to the hospital and John would now carry the machine gun. John was excited about the having the M-60. He knew that carrying it would be more work, but having such awesome firepower under his control gave him a greater sense of security.

Third and Fourth Squads departed on their patrol shortly after the Medevac helicopter left with Larry. Lieutenant Ramsey's curiosity was piqued and he accompanied them on the patrol up the trail.

John and BJ took this opportunity to tear down the gun to give it a good cleaning and oiling. When the task was finished, they laid out the belts of ammo, cleaned all the dirt from them, and then saturated each with oil. After a half hour, they were pleased enough with the results to pack away the cleaning supplies.

The patrol was gone for only an hour when the sound of a firefight reached the NDP. It came from the same direction as the trails, which meant that the two-squad patrol had made contact. The sound of AK-47 and M-16 fire grew louder and escalated to a fevered pitch, loud single explosions from grenades and M-79 launcher rounds punctuated the rifle fire. Seconds later, the telltale sound of two M-60 machine guns joined in the fray. Those remaining behind knew they had to leave ASAP and reinforce their brothers.

"Grab your shit," Sixpack ordered the two remaining squads, "We move out in thirty seconds."

Sergeant Holmes led the reinforcements up the trail at a fast trot. They were within a hundred feet of turning into the jungle when the other two squads emerged with the L-T. They were also on the run, the L-T motioned for them to turn around and head back in the other direction. It did not take much effort to convince the others to do so. Lt. Ramsey halted everyone after a hundred meters and had them move into the high elephant grass to set up a hasty defensive perimeter. He wanted to be certain the enemy was not following them to the NDP.

"What happened on the trail, L-T?" Sixpack inhaled deeply, trying to catch his breath.

"Charlie was set up at the fork in the trail and waited for us to get close. We weren't quite in the kill zone yet, but they opened up on us anyway."

"How many were there?"

"I'm not sure, but I would guess they had just as many men as we did."

"Why didn't they wait for you to get closer?"

"I think somebody in their group fucked it up, because we heard a misfire several seconds before the shooting started. That gave us all that split second we needed to jump off the trail, find some cover, and return fire. When they broke off the ambush, we kept firing and backing away, then took off at a run when we could."

"Anybody get hurt?"

"It is truly a miracle, but everybody made it out okay."

"So what do you want to do now?"

"First thing we need to do is to get some artillery fire going into that area."

"Good idea. I'll send out a couple of OP's between us and the jungle trail to give us some warning in case they decide to come after us."

The brass denied the request for artillery because of the close proximity to some of the villages in the line of fire. A short round could land in one of them and kill innocent bystanders.

Sixpack returned and could see that the L-T was pissed.

"They won't give us permission to fire artillery."
"Why the fuck not?"
"Villages are in the line of fire."
"We haven't seen one village anywhere near us! This is bullshit!"
"I know."
"What about the gunships?"
"I'll try them next."

Fifteen minutes later, two Cobra gunships arrived and circled over the jungle where the ambush occurred. The pilots switched to the company net in order to speak directly with Lt. Ramsey about the fire mission, informing him that they were unable to see through the triple canopy and wanted the grunts to identify the hostile area with smoke.

This disappointed both Sixpack and the L-T, who informed the pilots that he would have to send his entire platoon back into the jungle to look for viable targets. Both pilots wanted to support the platoon and agreed to remain on station in case they found the enemy.

First Platoon cautiously inched their way back into the jungle, staying low on the side of the trail. After a hand signal, the men quickly stepped off to the left and sought suitable cover. They were not sure if the enemy would fire at them again, but each made sure they were well concealed and protected.

A star cluster flare fired through the triple canopy to show the two Cobra pilots the location of the friendly forces below. It was also the signal for the men to open fire. The four machine gunners, equally spaced through the column, opened fire, and were joined quickly by those with M-16 rifles. The men fired hundreds of rounds at the invisible enemy before the L-T, satisfied with the recon by fire, called for an end to the shooting.

BJ and John smiled proudly to one another as their gun was the only one of four that kept firing without jamming.

Lt. Ramsey sent the pilots a sit rep, informing them that they were now entering the ambush site.

The platoon swept through the area, checking for signs of the enemy. They found blood splattered just beyond the fork and all through the brush in between the two trails. Several blood trails were leading deeper into the jungle and only on the left path, which was not known to be booby-trapped. They continued searching the area for another forty-five minutes, but as always after an ambush, found no bodies left behind.

The L-T called the Cobra pilots to terminate the mission and thanked them for their support. He was also anxious to discuss this area in more detail with the captain and ordered the platoon to return to the NDP.

Upon their arrival, the soldiers moved to their respective areas within the perimeter. It was Third Squad's turn to provide volunteers for the two-man OP's. They organized three teams and moved out within ten minutes.

During this downtime, and especially after a firefight, the weapons were cleaned and oiled. Each squad took turns completing this task while the other three remained on guard and defended the perimeter. It would otherwise be disastrous for the platoon if some NVA happened upon the NDP and caught all of them with their weapons apart.

Some of the men took the opportunity to write home; letters were collected and taken to the rear during every resupply twice a week. A letter home did not require a postage stamp; instead, soldiers printed the word "FREE" in place of a stamp. Rumor had it that if someone wrote a note on the side of a C-Ration box - as long as it had an address and the word "FREE" in place of a stamp - the Postal Service would deliver it. This theory was never tested, however.

Many of the young men laid on the ground with their backs against rucks, reading books or listening to transistor radios with earpieces. All equipment was packed, and weapons were cleaned and ready to move out in a moment's notice.

Lt. Ramsey had a map spread out on the ground and was in the process of making small marks with his grease pencil while listening to the captain on the radio handset. He did not look too happy, succeeding in only transmitting a couple of words before the captain forced him back into a listening mode. When he attempted to talk a second time, the results were the same. Finally, he threw his grease pencil down onto the map and tossed the radio receiver to Bob, who was sitting close by.

"Squad leaders on me!" Sixpack and the other three sergeants dropped what they were doing and immediately moved over to join the L-T.

"The captain wants us to stay in this same position again tonight and dispatch two ambush teams after nightfall to cover the trail near its entry into the jungle."

"L-T, I don't mind the ambushes, but staying here for a third consecutive night isn't too smart."

"I agree, Sixpack, but there was nothing I could do to change his mind."

"Sir, some of the men are already complaining about the smell coming from the trail."

"Sorry, Rock, but there's nothing I can do about that."

"Have your men break off the filters from their cigarettes and give them to Nung. He has some special liquid and can put a drop onto each one. Then your people can put them up their noses. It's worked well for our squad."

"Thanks for the suggestion, Sixpack."

"Which squads are going to pull the ambush tonight?"

"Sixpack, I want your squad to team up with Rock's Second Squad. We will finalize our plans later this afternoon. Plan to leave about 2100 hrs. It will be dark enough by then."

"Hey, Scout, you know I would have volunteered for the ambush if we hadn't been picked ourselves."

"I would have been right behind you, Wild Bill. I'm not too fond of staying in the same place for three nights in a row. This is plain stupid!"

"That will be for the other two squads to worry about."

"Doesn't it strike anybody as odd that nobody came through here to investigate the explosions and shooting? After all, this is supposed to be a populated, no fire zone."

"I thought about that myself, Polack, especially with these villages nearby. You'd think somebody would have shown up by now."

"This reminds me of something a guy told me when I was on road security when I first got in country. The guy told me to be happy when villagers were around; they know when Charlie is in the area and do not want to be caught in the middle when there's going to be a fight. So, this must be a sure sign that the VC are out and about."

"That's why I don't like being in the same place all this time. If the VC are definitely around, then it's certain they know we're here."

The two ambush squads were making final preparations for the night. They rolled up poncho liners and tied them to the back of their ammo belts. There was no need to wear the ponchos, they would make too much noise; it was also highly doubtful that any of them would be lying on the ground anyway. Each man would most likely spend the night wide-awake sitting against a tree, wrapped up in a camouflaged poncho liner, staring into the black night.

It would be too dark for them to set up mechanical ambushes, but they did plan on taking along extra claymores and clackers to cover their small perimeter.

The men shared canteens and filled them to prevent water from sloshing around inside while moving. They also used black electrical tape to secure anything that could rattle or knock into something else. Noise discipline was crucial in the dead of night; the slightest of sounds could carry through the air and alert others to their presence.

The NDP would not set up any mechanicals that night either. They wanted to keep the trails open in the event that either of the ambush teams got into trouble - thus allowing reinforcements the ability to move in quickly in support, or to make a hasty retreat if necessary.

Squad members finished dinner and had last cigarettes before heading out within the hour.

John ate beans and franks from a C-Ration can when he suddenly dropped the can and started to shake as if he had just walked into an ice cold freezer.

"What's up, Polack?"

"I was just thinking back to the four of us on that trail less than thirty-six hours ago. We walked way beyond that fork in the trail."

"Are you wondering why we weren't shot at?"

"Yeah, Scout. You have to wonder if they saw us and just let us go, hoping that a larger group would follow afterwards."

"We'll never know and you can't spend time thinking about those kinds of things. It'll drive you crazy!"

"Did you ever almost get into a car accident and then later when you think about what might have happened, you get all shaky and shit? It's uncontrollable and you can't stop."

"Adrenaline does that to you. It's kind of like getting into a situation where you have to decide whether to stay and fight or run. Your body sends this blast of energy to help you through the panic, and if it's not used, it has to go somewhere. It starts to bleed out and give you those kinds of reactions. That's most likely what's happening to you right now. It happens to everyone and I wouldn't be concerned about it."

"Maybe it was just luck that we got though that one, huh?"

"It's very possible, and no different than those seven enemy bodies laying out on the trail. If we had done our job, they would have been lucky on that day too. Unfortunately, their ticket was pulled and it was time to go."

The two squads quietly departed under the cover of darkness and moved along the trail toward their designated ambush sites just inside the jungle.

John thought to himself that this was surely the spookiest thing he had ever done in his whole life. Pitch black, the light of the partial moon offered little comfort as it rose into the night sky.

At point, Frenchie used a Starlight scope and stopped periodically to check their front. The rest of the grunts in the single file held onto the shoulder strap of the man to his immediate front. It worked well when leading this group of blind men through the inky black terrain.

They slowly grew accustomed to the darkness and could see somewhat in the shadowy environment. Nobody spoke; communications were limited to pushing and pulling of shoulder straps. Even so, they could travel at a satisfactory pace. However, once they turned and entered into the triple canopy, they lost all vision again.

John mentally compared this hump to walking through a Halloween haunted house, where you felt your way along, waiting for something to jump out and surprise you. But getting surprised here could very likely result in death.

Once they reached their destination, the men stepped off the trail and into the thick underbrush. The first order of business was for the men to set out claymore mines covering the trail to their immediate front. Once in place, each member of the ambush team unrolled their spool of electrical wire and backed away to a safe distance. They remained within an arm's length of each other and tried to sit on the ground as quietly as possible. Both squads remained in that position until sunrise.

Every chirp, crack, and croak solicited a reaction from the stealthy soldiers, but as nervous and jumpy as they were, they still managed to maintain noise discipline and did not overreact. They were fully aware that if a firefight was to develop, and it became necessary for the teams to retreat, it could be disastrous.

The next morning, everyone breathed a sigh of relief, thankful that nothing had happened during the night. They waited until seven before starting back to rejoin the balance of the platoon.

As they stepped back onto the trail and began walking toward the exit of the jungle, Nung stopped suddenly and motioned for everyone to get down. There was a hint of wood burning in the air and the sound of laughter and chattering to their left. Nung raised his right hand with two fingers, forming the 'Victory sign'. He pointed to his own eyes, and then extended his arm to point into the bush and raised four fingers. Sixpack was already moving toward the front of the column to where Nung squatted. After watching the explanation, Sixpack rose to his knees and peered through the brush toward the stream. There, he could clearly see four VC, sitting around a small fire on the bank, two AK-47 rifles leaning against a nearby tree.

The Americans were already in a column on the trail; Sixpack used hand signals to organize them into a firing line. Meanwhile, the

RTO quietly informed the rest of the platoon that they had the enemy spotted and would be engaging. On Sixpack's signal, everyone started firing toward the shadows near the stream.

There was a flurry of activity and flashes of movement around the campsite. No one returned fire, and the squads seemed to enjoy being the aggressors for a change. Now it was just a matter of sweeping through the area and counting the bodies.

Suddenly, several enemy soldiers opened fire on the Americans from their left flank. They were well concealed and hidden near the fork of the trail. The last two Americans closest to the enemy, were immediately hit and fell to the ground. No longer sensing a threat to their front, the grunts jumped into the brush and began returning fire. This ambush lasted no more than a minute; the firing stopped just as abruptly as it had begun. Amid the chaos, the RTO did not even have a chance to inform the L-T of the ambush. Nevertheless, there was no mistaking that something was terribly wrong when the sound of AK fire reached the NDP.

The two wounded forward soldiers were crawling along the edge of the trail to safety. When the firing stopped, the squad retreated and carried the two men from the jungle.

Lt. Ramsey was the first to bump into the retreating men out on the main trail. He quickly organized a defensive perimeter and requested a Medevac chopper. Then he began to outline the next plan of action with his squad leaders. The other grunts kept an eye on the jungle.

One of the wounded took a bullet in the left arm, the other in his back. Their wounds were not life threatening, and both men would return to Cu Chi after a short hospital stay.

The plan was to repeat exactly what the platoon did a few days before. Cobra support helicopters would come on station; the grunts would fire several hundred rounds into the jungle and then move in to sweep the area again.

They found blood all around the campfire, and the two weapons still leaning against the tree unscathed. Frenchie and Scout picked them up and slung the rifles over their shoulders. The First Squad continued its sweep and began following the small stream into the jungle. They moved against the flow and began to notice a red tint in the water.

"Blood in the water," Scout pointed out in a whisper, leading the squad upstream. Those following acknowledged him with a quick nod.

The stream was shallow and less than six inches deep; the bottom littered with small stones, leaves and twigs from the surrounding trees. Minnows scurried through the clear liquid and water spiders darted across the top, trying to keep out of the way of the advancing soldiers.

"Looks like someone was dragged through here," Frenchie noted, pointing out the disruption on the streambed. There were three and sometimes four parallel troughs, two inches across, burrowing through the stones and leaves along the fifteen-foot wide stream.

Scout raised his right arm to stop the column. "Sixpack, we've got bodies up ahead."

Sixpack moved forward to join Scout. "We'll check them - the rest of you fan out and see if you can find any more."

"There're two here and another one about twenty feet forward."

"Looks like these bodies were hit multiple times. There's no way they made it this far alone."

"That would account for the skid marks along the bottom of the stream. They were helped or dragged deeper into the jungle."

"I wonder why they dropped them here after carrying them this far?"

"It might have happened when we fired the mad minute before entering the jungle again, they probably needed to get away quickly to save their own asses. Did you also notice that there are no weapons lying near these bodies?"

"It could be the same bunch we opened up on around the campfire; we've got two of their weapons."

"Yeah, but somebody took whatever that third guy was carrying."

"I agree."

"That means there are more of them around here someplace."

After searching the bodies and taking everything of importance with them, the squad followed some new blood trails along the side of the stream. They led away from the stream and finally ended after a hundred feet or so.

"So where did he go?" John asked.

"It looks like he just disappeared."

"That's what's so frustrating about this place. It's like the earth just swallows them up."

"You've probably hit it right on the head," Sixpack said, scanning the nearby area. "Remember that underground tunnel complex and hospital we found earlier? I wouldn't be surprised if there's another one somewhere around here."

The squad concluded the search of the area and formed back up with the rest of the platoon at the fork in the trail. They were running low on ammunition, and the L-T was worried that another prolonged firefight would cause them to run out.

Lt. Ramsey gave the order for the platoon to return to the NDP to bed down once again for the night. He already planned for a resupply of ammo the first thing in the morning. Afterwards, the platoon would return and create a new NDP close to the fork in the trail.

First Platoon had to carry enough rations for the next five days. The captain wanted to minimize their exposure, so they could work effectively in the jungle during that time. The enemy was very aware of the protocol for resupply and knew that if a unit were in the area, helicopters would be landing every three days. The men hoped they would become bolder and come out into the open when they thought no Americans were around.

Every day, they moved deeper into the jungle, following the stream in its westward tract. They set up nightly NDP's near the stream and dispatched ambush teams to watch nearby trails and open areas.

Following a stream provided the men with an ample supply of drinking water, thus cutting down on the weight they carried during the humps. The water looked clear, but upon closer investigation, small, barely visible creatures were swimming in it. Nevertheless, each man filled his canteens and dropped in two iodine tablets, which were used to kill the bacteria in the unsanitary water. It left a bitter taste, but there was no alternative. Some of the luckier warriors had pre-sweetened Kool-Aid sent to them from home, which made for a flavorful thirst quencher. Nobody hoarded their treasure, openly sharing their Kool-Aid canteens with fellow squad members.

During the next five days, the men did not see another human being. The routine of moving daily and sending out ambushes at night without contact was boring the troops. Some soldiers were becoming over-confident and cocky, letting weapons hang to the side during humps and even talking louder than they should.

A resupply was scheduled to take place on the following day, but the colonel asked if the unit could get by for at least one more day, possibly two. He truly believed that his strategy would work and result in some body count.

Sixpack and the other squad leaders checked with their men on food status and found that they could squeak by for another couple of days. When Lt. Ramsey informed the colonel of this, he was very pleased with the feedback.

The next two days proved uneventful for the platoon, as it had been ever since they started following the stream. It was the consensus that the VC were aware of their presence, but were staying underground, or possibly vacated the area all together.

Lt. Ramsey arranged for an early morning resupply in an LZ near their original NDP for this mission. Later that morning, after receiving hot food, clean clothes, ammo, mail, and other supplies, First Platoon would be airlifted to a new Area of Operations (AO), where the colonel believed the potential for kills were promising.

The platoon left early in the morning and humped back to their first night's NDP. Although the men moved at a swift pace with empty rucks and canteens, it still took them three hours to exit the jungle.

It was not long before the men had to pass the seven NVA corpses on the trail for the last time. Not everyone felt the need to look at them; only the Cherries were fascinated and curious enough to do so. Most gagged and some had to step off the trail to vomit. Maggots, flies, and ants were still hard at work trying to devour the decaying bodies; only a small amount of flesh and hair remained on the bleached white bones. The smell was not quite as strong as the week before, nevertheless, it was putrid. The skeletons still lay just as they fell; none of their comrades had returned by to bury them. That was a good sign.

The men showed no remorse - only satisfaction in knowing that these enemy soldiers would never shoot at them again.

When the resupply was over, everyone was actively packing supplies for the new mission. Doc was busier than most as he treated everyone for one ailment or another. He administered creams and ointment to fight ringworm, jungle rot, cuts, and bruises.

The L-T walked around the perimeter congratulating everyone for a job well done. He told them that First Platoon had received credit for twelve enemy soldiers killed, while suffering only two wounded and one illness. Battalion was ecstatic.

First Platoon had been lucky so far, and many of them wondered how long it would last.

# CHAPTER THIRTEEN

Six Huey helicopters, filled with members of the First Platoon, circled in a counter-clockwise direction over a small clearing in the middle of the dense jungle. As the grunts were transfixed on the LZ below, a Loach helicopter flew by as a decoy, skimming over the treetops around the open area and attempting to draw enemy fire from the surrounding tree line. If successful, the early warning helped to identify the location of hidden enemy troops, thus preparing the grunts for a potentially hostile landing under enemy fire.

"You know those guys doing shit like that must have balls as big as watermelons," Frenchie yelled above the noise of the turbine engines.

"You ain't shitting. I'd never fly around like that just waiting for somebody to shoot at me."

"Yeah, but you'll walk along a trail and do the same thing. Those air jockeys think that grunts have big balls. Wild Bill, show us yours!"

Stunned by Frenchie's comment, Wild Bill was unable to respond. John, BJ, and some of the others began to laugh, momentarily relieved from their anxiety. It was short-lived, however, and the laughter stopped abruptly when green tracer rounds began flying through the air. A string of rounds from the tree line trailed the small Loach, the pilot taking evasive action to get away. Several new strings of green reached up from the same portion of the tree line, now targeting the circling Hueys.

"Shit! This mother's hot," Wild Bill cried, quickly turning to face John and BJ. "When the birds land, jump off, and get away from them as quickly as you can. The door gunner will be shooting at the tree line so do not run in front of him. When they lift off, start firing your gun into that same tree line. Okay?"

Both nodded.

The tiny Loach trailed smoke but managed to stay airborne. It dropped a red smoke grenade into the tree line, darted back up into the sky, and then passed on final instructions to the Cobra gunships before limping to base.

Two of the deadly birds dropped out of the sky and made a first pass - one following closely behind the other, both firing mini-guns and rockets into the area with rising red smoke. Debris from the jungle rained onto the LZ as rockets continued to explode on their targets. Meanwhile, the Hueys had maneuvered into position so that their glide path for the insertion would be parallel to that of the supporting Cobras.

The formation was on its final approach, flying only fifty feet above the jungle, when the two Cobras launched a second assault upon the tree line.

As the gunships kept the enemy's head down, the six slicks formed a straight line on final approach into the hot LZ; door gunners on the enemy side of the aircraft fired into the tree line as they neared the ground. Once they touched down, the birds emptied in seconds. Soldiers dropped to the ground, firing their own weapons into the same part of the tree line.

John and BJ felt as if they were running in slow motion. Belts of machine gun ammo, about five hundred rounds each, wrapped them from their chest to their hips. Once clear of the rotors, both dove for the ground. The weight of full rucks, combined with both the machine gun and ammo, nearly knocked the wind out of John. He lay there with heart and lungs pounding wildly. BJ lay next to him with a look of absolute terror on his face.

The pilots knew they were sitting ducks in this hot LZ, and wasted no time leaving. Eager to get back into the air, one took off too soon, forcing the last of the troops to jump six feet to the ground. Luckily, no one was injured.

John extended the two bi-fold legs near the end of the barrel to support the weapon and started to fire his machine gun into the jungle to his front. While firing, BJ, his assistant gunner and ammo bearer, linked the individual belts of ammo together to keep the weapon firing.

The second sortie landed with the next group of Alpha Company grunts. Soldiers jumped off quickly, joining those already on the ground.

Suddenly, a large explosion sounded behind the grunts. A helicopter from the sortie was ablaze; shrill alarms sounded as the bird twirled slowly toward the ground. No sooner did it crash into the jungle at the far edge of the LZ, when there was a second explosion. A blaze of yellow and red flames rose into the sky, culminating in a fog of thick black smoke. Nobody saw the small pieces of fiery steel and aluminum flying across the LZ. Suddenly, there were screams of pain and calls for medics from an area near the crash site - in the same area where Third Squad had taken refuge earlier.

Two RPG rounds had hit the chopper; the crash killed everyone on board instantly. The Cobras responded quickly, launching an assault into the new target area. Artillery rounds also began landing in the jungle on the western side of the LZ.

The ground shook violently as each rocket and artillery round impacted. Three quarters of Alpha Company soldiers were lying on the ground of the open LZ, firing their weapons at the invisible enemy within the jungle. The noise was unbearable and the concussions made the men bounce slightly as if stretched out on a trampoline.

While the battle continued, the last of Alpha Company and the CP landed on the final sortie. Every time the birds came in, the door gunner's machine gun barrels glowed from the extensive firing; it was a wonder they were still functioning.

Once the entire company was on the ground, the grunts spread out and moved into the jungle on the eastern side of the LZ. Security was in place. Word filtered back for the men to sit tight, as fast movers (jets) were on their way to drop bombs.

The Gunships had left the area and returned to Cu Chi for rearming; they would return if needed. It was too late to warn anyone when the jets began their runs. A loud "vroom" noise echoed and an ear-shattering explosion sounded before they became visible. The planes climbed straight up, the sun reflecting from their wings like flashing mirrors. Their bombs were right on target, and the entire western tree line was ablaze. The two Crusaders made two more passes and dropped each load of explosives deeper into the jungle.

The departing sound of the jet engines could still be heard when the captain jumped to his feet, rallying the company to cross the LZ and sweep through the smoking jungle on the other side.

He organized the men into a horseshoe formation, with Second and Third Platoons on the two sides, and Fourth Platoon at the base. First Platoon would stay behind to provide security for the CP, and to take care of loading the dead and wounded onto the Medevac choppers when they arrived.

The three platoons moved quickly toward the tree line hoping to catch the enemy, who may have been shocked and wandering around, disoriented. There had not been a sound from the tree line since the fast movers had dropped their payloads - that served as a confidence booster to those conducting the sweep.

A team from the helicopter squadron was preparing to land for an investigation of the crash site. The bodies of the helicopter crew, pulled earlier from the wreckage, were now lying with those from Alpha Company. Not much remained of the chopper and cargo, and the remains were no longer recognizable.

Lt. Ramsey greeted the squadron members somberly, offering his condolences. After briefing them about the battle, he pointed out the location of the crash site.

The men stopped for a moment at the bodies of their dead team members, offering a quick prayer before heading to the crash site - escorted by Sixpack and four other soldiers.

First Platoon was the leading unit on the ground and therefore, experienced most of the casualties; the other three platoons had only a few. Not counting the four crew members killed on the helicopter, Alpha Company suffered eight dead and fifteen wounded. Less than half of the casualties were from bullet wounds; shrapnel from the crash injured the rest. Some of the more seriously wounded men had pieces of metal protruding from their bodies. The medics dared not remove any for fear of internal bleeding. Instead, they did their best to pack the wound, stop the bleeding, and make the soldiers as comfortable as possible.

John, Wild Bill, and Frenchie walked through the temporary aid station to survey the casualties. They were surprised to come upon Bob, the L-T's RTO.

"Bob, what happened to you?"

He winced in pain, wheezing and breathing heavily, upon hearing his name called. He was shirtless, and had several large pieces of bloody gauze covering the upper portion of his back. "That radio saved my life," Bob said, pointing to the side.

The PRC-25 radio lay on the ground and looked like somebody shot a few rounds of buckshot into it. Bob's rucksack also took a beating.

"Holy shit! Is all that from the crashed chopper?"

Bob nodded his head.

"What the fuck? Were you right next to it?"

"Naw, we were about thirty feet away when it crashed. The L-T and I were close to where the Third Squad had touched down, and it seemed like most everybody around me got hit except for the L-T, who was standing behind me."

"The man owes you his life!" Wild Bill exclaimed.

"Seems that way - he's already stopped by and thanked me ten times," he tried to laugh but could only smile slightly, wincing in pain once again.

"What are they telling you about your back?" John asked.

"Doc thinks my lung is nicked and that's why it's so hard for me to breathe. But other than that, I'll get stitched up and have some R&R at the 93rd Evac (Evacuation Hospital in Long Binh)."

The four of them shook hands. "Good luck to you, Bob - we'll see you when you get back!" The three men continued walking along the line of victims.

John did not know any of the wounded; however, Frenchie and Wild Bill recognized a couple of men and stopped to chat. The visits were brief and they continued toward the line of bodies covered with ponchos.

It was then that the first Medevac chopper touched down to pick up the four seriously wounded soldiers. Just as soon as it lifted off, a second Medevac chopper landed to transport the remaining five out of the field and to the hospital. The rest of the wounded and dead would have to wait for the two helicopters to return.

The wind from the chopper landings had blown the ponchos from the deceased soldiers, leaving their bodies exposed. John and Frenchie ran to gather the coverings and returned with an armful each.

They began draping the corpses when John stopped suddenly upon reaching the middle row of bodies. He dropped the ponchos to the ground, took in a deep breath, and stared in disbelief at the corpse lying at his feet.

"Polack, what's going on? You know this guy?" Wild Bill asked.

A single tear dropped from John's right eye, leaving a trail on his dirt-encrusted face for more to follow.

"Goddammit! John finally mumbled. He dropped to one knee and placed his right hand on the forehead of the dead soldier; brushing it lightly from side to side with three fingers.

"Who is he?" Frenchie asked.

John shook his head and wiped the tears from his face with a shirtsleeve. "This is Junior Brown. He was from Detroit and lived a few miles from my home back in the world." John began picking debris from Junior's black, curly hair, dropping the small twigs, pieces of leaves, and caked mud onto the ground. He looked up to the two, somber men, "This guy took me under his wing on the first day I arrived at Kien. He helped me with my supplies, showed me how to pack my ruck and how to keep it properly balanced for humping in the bush. I spent my first night in the firebase with Junior on bunker guard. He was an excellent teacher - I learned so much during those days with him! Without his help, I would have really suffered when I came out to join the company in the field."

"Sorry, Polack!" Wild Bill and Frenchie left to cover the remaining four bodies, leaving John alone with Junior.

Junior's body was lying at an awkward angle, his head almost severed, the left cheek resting on his shoulder. His fatigue jacket, was completely saturated with blood - still wet to the touch. Had the helicopter not crashed, he would still be alive and sitting here with the rest of First Platoon.

John continued his vigil over the body and smiled as he thought back to those earlier days together. "I will never forget you, Junior," he whispered to the corpse. "I owe you, buddy. I owe you big time. I do promise to look up your family when I get back to the world, and will share my memories of you."

Frenchie and Wild Bill held the extended poncho and moved closer to Junior's corpse. "Hey, man, sorry, but he's got to be covered up," Frenchie offered solemnly.

John reached over and offered Junior a final "dap" on each hand before standing up.

"I'm alright, go ahead," John said in a shaky voice, backing away to give them room.

After the last chopper left with the corpses, the First Squad members headed back to the tree line where the company CP and remaining soldiers were located. Most of them just sat on the ground and relaxed against a tree. They expressed their sorrow and shared their hurt over the death or injury of friends, but silently were relieved that they were not among the injured. It was very quiet; the only sound heard was the squelch from the radios.

The rest of the company returned from their sweep after two hours, finding only spent ammunition. No bodies, blood trails, or bunkers provided evidence of the enemy having been there. Once again, they vanished.

The company would stay in its present location until the team had finished its investigation of the crash site; the grunts took advantage of this break to eat lunch. Many of the soldiers were relieved to be back in a 'free-fire zone'; at least now they could fire at shadows without having to worry about hitting innocent bystanders or requesting clearance to fire.

"This shit ain't right! Those fucking VC pop off some rounds, eliminate half of a platoon, shoot down a chopper, and then di-di (Vietnamese slang for run-away) out of the area before the heavy shit comes in."

"I know, Doc, it's like they're psychic and always keep a step ahead of us. It burns my ass!"

"What happened to that small Loach that got hit?"

"Not a clue, Polack. I was so worried and focused on that hot LZ, that all I was thinking about was how to save my own ass."

"You and everybody else, Scout!"

"I didn't have time to think. I was so scared, my mind went blank, and everything happened in slow motion."

"Did you leave some turds on the chopper?" Wild Bill kidded John.

"I may have, but don't know for sure. Why don't you come over and smell my ass and then tell me if I did?"

A laugh erupted from the small group.

Billy Joe sat off by himself, away from the rest of the squad. They all noticed him at the same time.

"Hey, guys, check out BJ. What's up with him?"

"One of his close friends in the Fourth Platoon was killed today," Doc volunteered.

"He didn't say anything to me about having a friend in the Fourth," John said.

Doc moved closer to the group and reported in a more subdued voice. "Seems BJ and this guy went through Basic Training and AIT together and both ended up here in Alpha Company. They actually both came out to the field on the same resupply chopper."

"I have a buddy like that too; Bill Sayers is in the Third Platoon. Larry and Sixpack both know him."

"I know that's tough; it's like losing a brother."

"Losing Zeke was like losing a brother and I didn't even know him all that long."

"I know what you mean, Polack. A lot of these other guys in the company say that's why they keep to themselves and don't want to know your name or anything about you."

"I've heard the same thing," Scout added.

"These guys will tell you that it's the only way to keep their sanity, and that if you die, then it don't mean nothin' to them."

"Yeah, but you know that's a lot of bullshit, Wild Bill. I'm sure those people don't have any super powers and have emotions just like the rest of us. So when fellow grunts are killed, it has to tear them up inside, whether they show it or not."

"Hey, BJ, come on over and join us," John called to his ammo bearer.

The new recruit looked up and waved him off. "I'm okay right here by myself."

"Well then, we'll have to come and join you."

During the next two days, Alpha Company grunts conducted countless patrols and ambushes. There was no contact, which the grunts were thankful for; however, that did not please the colonel in his desire for body counts.

On the third day, the company commander received orders to move toward a new LZ for an afternoon resupply. Tomorrow, they would move in a different direction and work through an area they had not seen yet. The thought of having to hump heavy rucks once again did not appeal to many in the company, but everyone looked forward to the possibility of getting mail. It had been two and a half weeks without contact from family or friends, and most people there would walk ten miles for the chance to get a letter from home.

That resupply turned out to be one of the best. The battalion cooks put together enough hot food to feed everyone in the company twice. The olive green Thermos containers contained roast beef, potatoes, corn, carrots, and ice-cold applesauce and lemonade.

A defensive perimeter was in place around the LZ and squads rotated through the chow line before returning to their location on the perimeter. The hot food surprise definitely boosted morale for the company. In the past, those types of resupplies only happened on holidays. Everyone appreciated the kind gesture.

Once they had their fill of the fantastic meal, the grunts were given time to draw out new supplies. C-Rations were distributed and packed away, and piles of assorted supplies, including clean uniforms, towels, socks, canteens, foot powder, bootlaces, razor blades, chewing gum, toothpaste, toothbrushes, and all the cigarettes you could carry, were dwindling fast.

Enough special Red Cross packages were available to go around and split between the many squads. These treasures included ink pens, paper, postcards, envelopes, and Christmas cards from children back home.

John's curiosity about the card he received was piqued and he quickly tore open the envelope. It was simple, with a picture of a white candle over a green Christmas wreath on the front cover. Inside, he found a short, hand-written, folded note:

Dear Soldier,
Our Sunday school gave money so we could send packets to you men who are fighting for our country. I hope they can be of use to you and make your Christmas a little merrier. I am ten years old and want to hear from you. Where are you stationed?
Wishing you a Merry Christmas and God's blessing,
Phillip Huntley
R.R. #23
Grand Rapids, Michigan, USA

It was only the middle of October, but the kid's card touched John. He immediately started to write him a return letter:

Dear Phillip,
Thank you for the Christmas card. My name is John and I am only nine years older than you are. I hope when you are my age this war will be over and you will not have to go through what I am today. I live in the Detroit area in Michigan and cannot wait to get home in nine more months. The weather is very hot here – you probably would not like it. Halloween is right around the corner, I hope you have a good costume picked out. I will not see the leaves change color or snow fall while I am here so I hope you can enjoy the upcoming seasons for me. You can keep writing if you want – a letter from home always makes our day. Thanks again for writing, your new friend, John.

He put the letter into one of the new envelopes, addressed it, and lay it on top of his rucksack. Later, somebody would come around to collect the mail, taking it back to the rear with the rest of the unused supplies.

The crowd roared its approval around the perimeter when the company Clerk approached carrying two, over-stuffed, large red nylon bags. The platoon sergeants and squad leaders left their positions and circled around the young clerk, who had already organized the mail by platoons, thus making it easier to distribute.

Sixpack approached the squad with a couple of sealed boxes and dozens of letters for his men.

"Mail call! Listen up for your name. Damn, Polack, this big box and a lot of these letters are for you."

He took the package and nine letters back to his position on the perimeter. He set the package to the side and eagerly tore open the first letter from home. He lay back against his rucksack and started reading the words. When he turned to the next page, a smile slowly developed and then he laughed aloud. John finished and returned the pages to the envelope, tearing open the second one, which was from his girlfriend. While focused on the letter and reading the news from home, John did not notice the other squad members getting restless and whispering among themselves.

Finally, Scout called out, "Hey, Polack, what's in the box?"

"I don't know yet. It's from my mother." John opened the third letter and began reading it.

"When are you going to open it?"

John sighed slowly, then responded, "When I finish reading the rest of these letters."

"Come on, man, some of us didn't get any mail. At least you could open it up and see what's inside."

"Yeah, Polack, aren't you curious to see what she sent?"

John sensed all eyes on him and he became irritated by the interruption. He stopped reading and looked over toward the rest of the squad. "Will you guys just wait until I'm done with these? We have lots of time before we leave. Give me about fifteen more minutes."

It was difficult for John to concentrate on the letters when those around him continued to groan and complain. John was aware that every time a package arrived from home, the normal protocol was for the recipient to get the first pick and then split the bounty with the rest of his squad. This way, everyone got to share in the celebration and receive a bit of the bounty. Nobody would be foolish enough to keep everything to himself too, because it would mean that he would have to carry around the excess weight.

John felt a pang of guilt and looked up from his reading. His fellow squad members looked like anxious kids on Christmas morning, trying to be patient while they waited for the signal to begin opening gifts. The sight was truly pitiful.

He set the letters on the ground and reached for the package. "Okay guys; let's see what my mother sent us."

There was a collective cheer and the men moved in closer to watch the ceremonious opening of the package from home.

"You guys know this is my first goody box from home, so I don't even know what to expect inside."

"We'll love whatever your mom sent."

After the box was unwrapped, and all the crushed paper removed, the treasure lay exposed.

"I'm just going to empty everything on the ground and then we can divvy it up."

First, John lifted a large, round metal tin from the box, opening it to find aluminum foil surrounding dozens of homemade chocolate chip cookies. He took a couple and passed the tin to Scout who was the closest to him.

Ecstatic, they began scarfing them down, like dogs when passed a scrap of meat from the dinner table.

After the box was empty, the group surveyed the selection of gifts on the ground. There were several small cans of Vienna sausages and hot dogs, vacuum-packed cans of peanuts, candy, fruit cocktail, a one-pound jar of instant coffee, magazines, and a couple of copies of the Detroit News Sunday newspaper, complete with comics and inserts.

There was also a five-pound canned ham. Although it could not compare to the lunch they had earlier, it would make for a wonderful squad dinner in a couple of days. The group salvaged all the unused cans of C-Ration pineapple bits from the resupply and then agreed to take turns carrying the ham until the big cook out.

After splitting the bounty and packing the goodies inside their rucksacks, the men gathered all the leftover packaging for disposal, burning the packing paper, boxes, and various wrappings, and then spreading the ashes about. That was standard operating procedure when one had to leave behind anything in the bush with names, addresses, or other written personal information. Wild Bill took the empty metal tin, filled it with stones and dirt, then tossed it into the closest water-filled bomb crater; it sank easily to the bottom of the twenty-foot deep hole. The protocol was necessary to deter Charlie from salvaging anything to use against the Americans later - either as a booby trap or a psychological weapon.

The anticipation of the upcoming ham dinner made the next two days go by rather quickly. The soldiers did not even mind taking turns carrying the extra five pounds of additional weight; the thought of the mouth-watering cookout offset any urge to complain. The perfect opportunity for the culinary feast presented itself on the third night. The squad gathered and laid out their supplies. They then converted several empty C-Ration cans into stoves, punching holes into the sides, thereby providing a flow of oxygen to keep the heat tabs burning. They had ten cans of pineapple bits to use when cooking the ham; Scout opened them and set them to the side. Meanwhile, Wild Bill took the seven stoves and arranged them into a circle large enough to support the can of ham, allowing it to cook evenly in its tin container. Next, he dropped a heat tab into each of the "stoves" and lit them with a match. Everything was now ready for the ham.

John had the privilege of opening the can of ham, accepting it with ceremonial reverence from Wild Bill, who carried it through the last leg of the journey.

He pried the small key from the lid, and then secured it to the metal tab on the seal of the can. Scout, Frenchie, and BJ crowded around him and watched intently as John turned the key like a wind-up music box. The seal broke with a hiss of air; some juice spilled onto his lap and ran down his pant leg.

"Goddamn! What the fuck is that smell?" Wild Bill and the others quickly backed away, leaving John with a perplexed look upon his face. They fanned the air with their arms in an attempt to dissipate the foul odor.

"It smells like a bunch of dead bodies!" Frenchie pinched his nose closed with his thumb and forefinger. "It's the fucking ham! The damn thing's spoiled!"

John dropped the can onto the ground and quickly moved away from it with the rest of the men.

"Shit, man, get away from us. You smell just like the ham." Wild Bill gave John a playful shove away from him.

John looked down to see that the juice from the container had spilled along the entire length of his trousers. He quickly ran to the nearest bomb crater, removed his pants, and jumped into the tepid water. There, he took a handful of mud to use as scrubbing material; he covered the length of one of the pant legs, and rubbed it vigorously against the other. He rinsed the pants thoroughly, took a whiff, and repeated the process once again. John repeated the process several more times until he was satisfied with the results. He climbed out of the hole, put the wet trousers back on, and returned to the group. Scout was in the process of scolding the rest of the squad.

"All of us are a bunch of dumbasses. During the last three days, each of us has carried this can of ham, yet none of us took the time to read the label. Here, look at this," he pointed to some large lettering on the side of the can. "Keep refrigerated."

"Polack, I think you better let your mother know what happened here. There is no refrigeration in the bush. In fact, it had to take at least a couple of weeks for this to get here, and I'm certain it was never chilled again after your mom removed it from the refrigerator."

"I will. I'm sorry, guys. I was really looking forward to our open range cooking tonight, too."

"We all were, Polack, up until ten minutes ago. What a bummer!"

"Yeah, man, thank your mom anyway. Tell her that we were all thrilled and thought that it was nice of her. Too bad this happened."

"We have to bury this shit so it doesn't attract wild animals. Everyone grab a can of pineapple bits and we'll have a toast to Polack's mom."

They raised the cans together in the center of the small circle. Wild Bill made the toast, "To Polack's mom, who is one hell of a fine woman and cookie maker."

"Here - here!"

The next day, the platoon moved into a highly humid area, rich in vegetation, to set up their NDP for the night. They used machetes and Bowie knives to cut out individual sleep areas and rid the ground of roots.

With the perimeter secured, everybody began cooking C-Ration dinners. Desmond Stumps wandered over and joined some of the members of the First Squad. Desi had been in country for several months and hailed from Alabama; he was the point man for the Second Squad.

"Hey y'all, this here sure does look like the same place I saw the biggest varmint of mah life while ova here."

"What's a varmint?" Scout asked.

"It's a big critter!"

"Talk English!"

"Okay. Listen up and let me tell the story 'bout the critter then maybe y'all will understand."

Those nearby coaxed him on. "Yeah, Desi, tell us that story."

"Don't interrup' me then. We found us a place for o'er night jest like this here one. Ah found me a place betweenst some trees and used mah long metal cutting tool to clear out all the stuff growin' there. Whenst I got to the ground, ah had to use mah big bear-skinning knife to cut up all those small roots and things that be stickin' up from the ground. Once that were done, ah rolled out mah poncho and liner and had me a bed soft enough for mah granny to sleep in.

"Bout the time ah finished it were time to make mah supper. Ah put mah sack to the side, fetched a can of pork, beans and weenies. Whoo lordy, mah mouth is fixin' to start waterin' jest at the thought of them vittles. Ya know, they the best vittles o'er here." This drew moans from the others.

"Ah notice a smooth green and brown log to the side of mah sleepin' area, 'bout as big as mah leg." He wrapped his hands around the thigh of his right leg for emphasis. "Ah thought maybe some feller had skinned the bark off this here log and used it fer himself to sit on a while back. So I took mah little stove can and vittles o'er to that log and set down on it whilst mah vittles is heatin' up. Ah wanna tell ya that sumpin' just wan't right wit that log, but ah couldn't put mah finger on it. Ah thought ah felt it movin' and shakin' some, an' thought maybe it were concussions from some bombs fallin' someplace, so ah didn't pay it no never mind.

"Just bout that time, old Arnold come rushin' up, 'OOOWEEEE, Desmond – do ya know what yer sittin' on?' he asked me. His eyeballs looked like they were 'bout to pop out from his head. 'Ya better git up and move o'er here wit me,' he said.

"Well don't ya know that ah was getting de heebie jeebies just a lookin' at his eyeballs and figgering ah better jump up pronto like. Ah moved over by Arnold and looked down at that there log and ah can now see that it was vibratin' some. Arnold pokes mah side and points at mah log and ah foller his finger fer bout ten foot away to a tree. Mercy sakes, it took mah breath away when ah noticed that mah log stretched clear cross that ground from where we was standin' and up into that there tree. It was 'bout then that ah noticed a big snakehead at the end of mah log up in that tree - that rascal's head were bigger 'a mine. It 'peered to be sleepin' whilst it was hangin' onto the ground. Then we saw that it were all swollen up and maybe four times bigger than the rest of it fer bout three feet or so. Now this here swollen part is layin' on the ground bout a foot away from that there tree. Old Arnold guessed that it must have swallered a wild pig since they all around us and is telling that everythin' be alright 'cuz that varmint be filled with vittles and probably would not be movin' for some days. He tells me ah got nuthin' to worry bout and that critter won't bother any of us o'er night. Some of the otherin' were telling that none of 'em were sure but thought it were either a python, a boa constrictor or Anasometin' type of a snake. It were too bad that nobody took pictures of that varmint. Ah would be awfully grateful to know what it were." Everyone listened intently, mesmerized by his story and accent.

"Well, you know old Desmond wanted to shoot that varmint in is head, but the otherin' wouldn't let me. They say that it would give our position away to them Viet Cong fellers and it would be more dangerous than sleepin' wit' that big rascal. That were easy for them to say cause none of 'em are layin' anywhere close to that there tree septin' me." Some of the men squirmed as they imagined themselves in that situation.

"Now ah gotta tell ya that this here night were the worstest of mah whole life. Ah built mahself a small fence twenst that critter and me and jest set there on the ground and kept an eyeball open all the nightlong. It were pitch black and them there shadows played wit' mah head all night. And I know to this day that if that fence made any noise at all during that night, ah would be up and putting some distance betweenst me an that critter.

"But ya know what? In the morning, ah was surprised to find that varmint in the exact same position as it were when it started to git dark the night before. Ah will never ever forget that there night and swear to all y'all that nuthin' in this here bush, even them Viet Cong fellers, has ever scared me more than that there snake. I hopes there ain't any 'round here tonight."

The men laughed and thought it was a funny story, but they could not resist scrutinizing their surroundings and taking a closer look around after Desmond had left to return to his squad.

The monsoon season was beginning in the southern half of Vietnam. It was hot and sunny most of the day, started raining by seven every evening, and continued nonstop until eight the next morning. You could set a watch by this pattern.

"At least the VC won't be out in this kind of weather."

Quick to correct BJ, Nung said, "This VC weather. Rain will cover all noise of moving and wash out all signs on trails. VC stay one place during day and move nighttime. He know American soldiers not like be wet. They all covered with ponchos at night and no hear or see him. GI also complain loud about wetness and VC hear this. This beaucoup danger time for GI's."

What he had said made the others think hard about the possibilities. Could it really be true? Was it possible for them to know where the GI's were bushing and setting up ambushes every night? If so, the monsoon season would be the toughest months of the yearlong tour.

They tried keeping the noise and complaints down to a minimum for as long as possible, but it only lasted a week. The bitching and complaining became progressively louder during the night and increased with the intensity of the hard rain. Rightfully so, there was no protection from the weather in the bush and no way of keeping dry during the night, sleeping soaked to the bone every night soon became a way of life for the troops.

Every morning, the platoon moved to a new NDP, and because their equipment was wet, the added weight made it much more difficult to hump. Even their clothes were heavier. During the moves, the afternoon temperatures and high humidity were unbearable, drying everything in the hot sun. The grunts sweated profusely. Always too hot or too cold, there was never a happy medium during the rainy season.

The constant rain was also rough on the machine gunners. Their lives and those around them depended upon the weapons in a time of need. A jam or misfire during a firefight could be devastating. Therefore, everyone pitched in to help the gunners with their daily ritual of cleaning and oiling the guns, thus, keeping the weapons in dependable working order. Any belts of ammo exposed to the environment had to be cleaned with a toothbrush and oiled thoroughly at least twice a day. Dirt particles, sand, and rust on the linkage would cause the weapon to jam. The platoon was easily going through a gallon of oil each week.

New replacements started arriving - at least one or two on every resupply. During a normal rotation, each squad expected to go out on recon patrols every other day, but because of the eight people lost on the LZ, every squad was now required to go out on daily patrols. At that rate, First Platoon would be back up to full strength within the next two weeks, providing they did not lose anyone before then. Everyone counted the days.

Lt. Ramsey developed pneumonia and was trying to hide it. He was stubborn and insisted on staying with his men, but his constant hacking and coughing jeopardized the platoon. Sixpack had to intercede and asked the captain to give the L-T an order to leave. A Medevac helicopter finally pulled the L-T from the jungle and flew him to the hospital.

With the L-T gone, Sixpack, as the highest-ranking sergeant, assumed command of the First Platoon and quickly promoted Frenchie to replace him as the First Squad team leader. They wondered how long it would remain that way, as Second Lieutenants were at a premium in Vietnam. Usually, their combat tours in the bush averaged eight months, before rotating to a rear job for the last few months. It seemed highly unfair to the enlisted men who sometimes were unable to get out of the bush until a day or two before going home.

During the first night without an officer, a typhoon hit the southern part of Vietnam. The grunts in the field soon found it to be one of the most terrifying experiences they ever encountered. The wind blew so hard through the jungle, that it carried pieces of trees, rocks, and anything else that could become airborne. Some larger trees fell and crashed to the jungle floor, and rain blowing horizontally made it difficult for anyone to see or hear. There was no safe haven or shelter; the men had to ride out the storm.

Sixpack had the men break up into three and four-man teams, ordering them to connect web belts together and secure themselves to the larger trees. The wind pulled the plastic knives from both mechanical ambushes and caused the trip flares to disengage, thus causing unexpected detonations and illuminations around the perimeter. Mother Nature was at her worst, with the panic-stricken men at her mercy.

For once, no one complained about being wet; they were too busy wondering if survival was an option at that point. Each team did everything in their power to stay connected and secured to the trees; the heavy wind buffeted them around like ocean buoys in a hurricane. Some of the soldiers who did not bother changing clothes during the last resupply watched their frayed clothing shred and tear apart. Tabs of material caught in the wind vortex and ripped from their bodies like bandage strips.

Nine hours later, the typhoon wound down and the remaining wind and rain were bearable. It also helped that it was now early morning; the light of day was starting to break through the jungle. Relieved, the teams untied themselves and salvaged what was left of their Night Defensive Position and gear. Doc was already making his rounds and attending to those injured by flying debris during the night. None of the injuries were serious; Doc could treat everyone without having to call in a Medevac.

"Thank you, Jesus!" Frenchie made the sign of the cross and surveyed the area. "I have never experienced anything so terrifying in my entire life."

"You and me both. It was so damn scary, I prayed all night long. Now when I get home there won't be a pot for me to piss in. I told the man upstairs that I'd give everything I own to the church if he got me through this storm in one piece."

"Shit, Wild Bill, there isn't much to give, is there? After all, don't you just own a bunch of flat land and wild sagebrush in Texas?"

"I did up until now, Frenchie. Wild Bill smiled at the ribbing. But you got to admit last night might have been the first night in a long time that many of the guys in this platoon actually prayed."

"I guess you're right. It's been a while for me, but at least it worked and we all made it through that nightmare."

"Amen!"

"I'll take a firefight anytime next to that storm."

John happened to notice that most of Scout's trousers were missing. "Where the fuck is the rest of your pants, Scout? Your fucking balls are hanging out!"

"This is a new fashion statement."

Sixpack strolled over while they were still laughing at the absurdity.

"Hey, Frenchie, get your squad squared away, for Christ's sake."

"Okay Sarge. Come on, troop, let's get things cleaned up. We can talk later."

Several days had passed since the dreadful typhoon. First Platoon was back into the routine of moving every day and pulling ambushes at night.

Alpha Company had been lucky and had no contact with the enemy in quite some time; most of the grunts were thankful. The colonel, on the other hand, wanted to see more results, and increased their visibility by having the companies continuously hump long distances during the day, hoping to find the elusive enemy. Noise discipline was deteriorating, complaints continued about the humps and having to carry sixty to eighty pound rucksacks on tired backs. Some men fell out during the humps, unable to keep up with the pace during the heat and humidity. Some heat stroke victims required a Medevac to transport them to the nearest hospital. Thankfully, waiting for the chopper to arrive gave everyone else a much-needed break.

During the long follow-the-leader marches, many in the column walked along absentmindedly, daydreaming about home, girlfriends, cars, and other diversions. Then in the evening, they would get together and share those thoughts while eating dinner. The troops were so exhausted; many were fast asleep even before darkness set in.

Debates occurred every evening - some over cars, actresses, musical groups, sports teams, and of course, Vietnam. The young men were very passionate about these topics, each person believing his own opinion was the correct one. Sometimes the debates heated up, but all knew when to stop and move on to a different topic. It seemed to be the only way to work off the accumulated adrenaline of the day. Sixpack thought all the inactivity was causing the platoon to lose its sharpness.

November was two weeks old and many of the soldiers from the northern states had not yet accepted the fact that the rest of the year would not offer them a snowy season. The winter months in Vietnam were no different from any other time of the year: hot and muggy.

The captain tried to convince the colonel to withdraw the company and move them to another AO. He told him that Alpha had already patrolled every acre of the area during the last five weeks and had not seen the enemy or fired a single shot. The constant humping wore down his men and some were starting to get sloppy. He warned that even the new Cherries were becoming overconfident, thinking they knew it all.

While the discussion took place, the grunts rested and ate lunch just inside a tree line surrounding a large open clearing. Exhausted, everyone ate their meals quietly, knowing that they would soon be leaving on the next leg of their journey.

The colonel granted the request and Alpha Company would be airlifted into a new area the following morning. In fact, the colonel planned to use the same clearing for their pickup point, which would allow the company to stay where they were until extraction. This was a rare treat and everyone was thankful that there would be no more humping that day.

At night, as usual, the rain started falling just before seven. Luckily, since the men stayed in the same spot for most of the day, many of the grunts had been able to use their ponchos to build tents or some simple shelter against the nightly rain.

John sat under his plastic canopy eating a can of fruit cocktail, when he noticed a small brown snake. It was as thick as an average index finger and about ten inches long, slithering through puddles of mud in between his legs. "Shit!" He shrieked and propelled himself backward against the edge of his shelter.

Those nearby looked over at John in stunned silence, unsure of what the commotion was all about.

Even while jumping back, John kept his eye on the snake and saw it moving away from him.

"Hey, guys, watch out! A snake is heading your way!"

"Aw, shit, what kind?" BJ asked in a panic, picturing the snake in Desmond's story. His wide eyes were frantically scanning the muddy ground between the two positions, watching for ripples.

"I don't know. It was small and brown, and moved pretty fast through the mud."

"Do you see him now?"

"No. You probably scared the shit out of him when you hollered out. He most likely turned and went the other way."

"That ain't funny. I'll find the little bastard."

BJ picked up his rifle and used the stock to club the ground all around his position. The noise sounded like a child splashing through rain puddles on the way home from school. He quickly attracted the attention of the other squad members.

"Beej, what in the fuck are you doing?" Frenchie asked more annoyed than concerned.

"I'm looking for a snake that Polack saw crawling toward me a few minutes ago."

"Is it big?"

"No. He said it was as small around like your finger and maybe twice as long."

"I'm sure it wasn't able to survive all that pounding. You probably knocked it silly and it drowned in the mud. Just let it go; you'll be ok."

"I'm really not sure about that."

BJ and John scanned the area between themselves for several more minutes. Confident that the creature was no longer lurking around, both sat back down and continued to finish their meals.

John finished his fruit, placing the empty can to the side with the rest of the garbage, and then turned to pack the spoon away in his rucksack. He had just lifted the flap on one of the side pouches when he suddenly froze. A terrible stinging sensation buzzed in his left ring finger, and when he glanced down, he saw the rogue snake clamped to his digit.

"Help! I'm bit! Get this motherfucker off me!" John screamed, trying violently to shake the serpent loose. "It won't let go!" The snake held on tight and looked like a small whip cracking in the air.

BJ and Frenchie were already moving toward him, each carrying a knife in their hand; Sixpack and Doc were close behind.

When the snake finally released its grip, it shot through the air, traveling ten feet before landing in a puddle outside of the perimeter.

John bent over and held his finger tightly as if trying to stop a flow of blood. "That fucking snake bit me!"

"Try to find him so we can see if it's poisonous or not," Doc ordered, taking John's hand in his, BJ, Frenchie, and Sixpack moved to the area where the snake might have landed. Using knives, they poked along the ground trying to find the illusive creature.

Meanwhile, Doc examined the two puncture wounds under the beam of his small red-lens flashlight. "It doesn't really look all that bad. How do you feel, Polack?"

"I'm getting real hot and my heart's racing like hell."

"Here, take this," Doc handed him a yellow pill. "It'll help you relax."

John swallowed the pill and immediately vomited it back up along with everything else he had eaten that night. He began shaking uncontrollably. The tremors were so bad that two men had to pin him down on the ground.

"Better call a Medevac, Sixpack. That snake venom is doing a job on him. He's burning up and going into convulsions."

Those nearby consoled John as Sixpack requested an Urgent Medevac, signifying a life and death evacuation. They tore down his canopy and placed him on the poncho, quickly packing his ruck and other belongings. BJ tied one of his ammo bandoliers and his own M-16 to John's ruck; it was now BJ's responsibility to carry the machine gun in John's absence.

The chopper touched down in the LZ within five minutes of receiving the call. Four men loaded John on board while a fifth tossed in his ruck and weapon.

En route to the hospital, the onboard medic gave John a shot and opened an IV line in his arm. Then moving the convulsing soldier onto a stretcher, he tied him down to control the thrashing.

In ten minutes, the Medevac landed at the 93rd Evac Hospital in Long Binh, where doctors awaited his arrival. They pulled him from the chopper and placed him onto a hospital gurney, then quickly wheeled him inside.

First, the doctors stripped him naked and packed him in ice. John closed his eyes, hoping to stop the room from spinning, and then started choking on his own saliva. A nurse reacted quickly, propping his head on some pillows and turning him onto his side.

One of the doctors walked up to the gurney, holding a small book in his hand. "Can you understand what's going on?" He asked in a very concerned but professional voice.

John could only nod his head affirmatively.

"Good! While we are analyzing your blood, I'd like you to look at some pictures of snakes. See if you can recognize the one that bit you."

He turned the page and waited for a few seconds before turning to the next one, each showing a different species. Many looked alike, except for some small distinguishing characteristic.

"Do any of these look familiar?" The doctor continued to turn the pages.

"No," he mumbled weakly. "It was small and brown, but that could be because it was raining and muddy."

"Take your time. Don't pay too much attention to the colors. Concentrate on the shapes and sizes. Note all the different heads."

When he flipped the page, the sight of one of the pictures made John open his eyes wide in recognition and fear. The doctor noted this reaction.

"Is this the snake?"

"Maybe, but I'm not certain. It was so quick."

"We'll check the blood for this type of venom. So, try to relax. We can't treat you until we're sure of the species that bit you. Hang in there, and I'll be back in just a bit."

He returned after what seemed like an eternity. "Luck is on your side, my friend. The picture and blood sample helped us to identify the snake." He produced two syringes filled with a yellowish liquid and stuck one of them into each of John's arms.

"Like I was saying, you're very lucky! The snake that bit you was a Banded Krait, the second most poisonous snake in all of Southeast Asia. Their venom attacks the nervous system, first paralyzing you, and then killing you by suffocation or a heart attack. You'll be all right now. We caught it in time." The doctor gave him a couple of encouraging pats on the leg. "We'll put you in a ward and keep an eye on you for a couple of days. If everything turns out fine, you'll be discharged and can rejoin your unit."

John was unrestrained, dressed in a hospital gown, and then wheeled through a series of corridors into one of the many wards. An orderly placed him onto an upper bunk and covered him with a blanket. A nurse arrived for routine temperature checks and blood pressure readings.

"You're going to be just fine. Enjoy the rest and air conditioning. If you need me, I'll be at my desk in the middle of the ward. Just call out and I'll come over. Get some sleep and I'll see you in the morning."

John looked down at the nurse, very relieved, and mumbled a quiet "thank you".

"You're quite welcome!" she responded cheerfully.

As she walked away, John turned his head and fell asleep.

## CHAPTER FOURTEEN

Spending the night in an air-conditioned hospital ward in Vietnam was not quite what John expected. He envisioned snuggling up in a nice soft bed, lying on clean sheets, covered with warm blankets. He looked forward to having a very peaceful night's sleep, uninterrupted by either guard duty or annoying insects. In the morning, he expected breakfast in bed, taking care of some personal hygiene, and then going back to sleep for as long as he wanted. Only a portion of what he perceived would actually occur.

To begin with, the nurses - although American and gorgeous - were a greater disturbance during the night than the insects had been in the jungle. They woke him every half-hour, prodding and shifting him into a position more suitable for checking his vitals. The nurses seemed sincere in their apologies and whispered softly for him to return to sleep when they finished. It was easy to fall back asleep after the first couple of checks, however, the routine soon got the best of him, and the luxury of sleep would evade him for the rest of the night. When breakfast finally arrived in the morning, he was exhausted and too tired to eat. Nevertheless, he made a feeble attempt at the powdered eggs and dry toast. After a couple of spoonfuls he set the tray aside, opting to wash it all down with watery orange juice.

After collecting the breakfast trays, a nurse ordered him to get out of the bed and make it up. "There will be no sleeping during the day," she ordered. His only option was sitting up in bed. Looking around, he saw many of the other patients already up and making their bunks. With some help, he managed to climb down and start working on his own.

Afterwards, he sat up in bed, pondering his stay while looking over the ward. The vantage point from his bunk offered a view of more than a half of the cross-shaped building. John's section housed patients who were recuperating from illnesses such as malaria, or, as in his case, snakebite. Another section had patients who overdosed on drugs and were in a coma or restrained to their beds while working through the withdrawals.

The "illness section" was comprised of twenty bunks and a TV set in each of the two corners. The American Network in Vietnam played reruns of old favorites from back home, such as Gunsmoke, Laugh-In, Let's Make A Deal and others. In the afternoon, clerks dispensed copies of the Stars and Stripes newspapers to the patients, affording them an opportunity to read instead of watching television. The newspaper was filled with articles about various in-country battles, discovered enemy caches, captured weapons and other articles from around the world.

The nurses' station stood in the center of the cross, thus providing them with an overall view of all four wards. Many patients - those permitted to walk - chose to hang out around the station during the day, watching, talking, or asking questions.

On the second night, a nurse gave John a questionnaire requesting information about his next of kin. The military needed the info to send a telegram, informing the family that he was in the hospital recovering from an injury. A small space at the bottom was available for him to write a personal message if he so desired. He added a short sentence, "I'm okay and doing well. Do not worry! Love, Johnny."

On his fourth day at the hospital, there was some excitement as a General from the First Cav made his rounds through the various wards. He stopped by each patient, sharing small talk and spending a few minutes at every bedside. Before moving on to the next patient, his aide took a Polaroid picture of them talking and gave it to the patients as a remembrance of this historic visit.

John left the hospital on the fifth day after he was admitted. An orderly took him to a room where the gear of every patient was stored while they were recovering. Each item had a tag attached with a large red cross, the owner's name and unit written in black marker. He found his old set of fatigues, helmet, rucksack and rifle, and then pulled them all from the piles. The bottom line on the tag read, "93rd Evac."

John signed out of the hospital and immediately headed for the 90th Replacement Battalion, which was located just across the road. There, he would not have a problem finding a ride back to Cu Chi. Once at the 25th Infantry basecamp, getting back out to the field would be easy; the First Sergeant would make sure of that.

John learned of his luck when reaching the center; a convoy was leaving shortly for Cu Chi with new in-country replacements (Cherries).

The place had not changed a bit since John first arrived in Vietnam three and a half months earlier. He still had some down time, so he headed straight for Alice's restaurant for a mouth-watering cheeseburger.

Two hours later, John climbed onto a truck filled with replacements and became an instant celebrity. His fatigues were filthy, ripped, and smelling; Red Cross cards were still attached to his ruck and weapon. Taking a seat in the middle of the truck bed, he noticed twenty 'kids' - who had not even been in country for two days - surrounding him. They stared at him wide-eyed and intrigued. John was also the only one in the back of the truck carrying a weapon. When the convoy received the signal to move out, John thought about having some fun with the newbies. He pulled out a magazine from the bandolier of ammo and loaded his M-16, sitting silently, watching the terrain from the side of the truck.

"Excuse me, sir." One of the closest Cherries was the first to address him.

"I'm not an officer," John responded nonchalantly.

"I'm sorry. Are you in the infantry?" He asked, but more humbly this time.

"Yeah, I'm a grunt."

"Have you been in the hospital?"

"Did you get wounded?"

"Yeah, I've been in the hospital, and no, I didn't get wounded. I almost died from snakebite. I'm heading back to Cu Chi with you guys so I can get back out to the bush."

"How long have you been in Vietnam?"
"Almost four months."
"Is it really as bad as they say?"
"It all depends. But personally, I'd rather be out there than in some firebase."
"Why is that?"
"When you get there, you'll see what I mean. Those firebases got hit all the time by rockets and mortars and all you can do is hunker down and pray you don't get hit. You also spend much of your waking hours pulling work details of some kind. No thanks, I'd rather stay out in the field where it feels much safer."
"Did you kill anyone yet?" One of them asked boldly.
"I don't really know because I've never personally had an enemy soldier in my sights. When you walk into an ambush, you don't see anybody, but can hear the weapons firing at you. At that point, your only option is to point your rifle in their direction and start shooting back at them. If you manage to find any dead bodies lying in the jungle, you'll never know if it was your bullet that had hit him or not."

There were no more questions after that. Each of them sat, staring silently into space, digesting what they had just heard.

When arriving at the Cu Chi training center, John jumped from the truck, wishing them good luck, and headed to the Wolfhound Battalion area.

The company had been resupplied the day before, forcing John to stay there for the next two days. He was chosen for bunker guard on the first night and then for KP the following night.

On his third day back, a clerk informed John that a resupply chopper was leaving at noon for Alpha Company, and the First Sergeant expected him aboard. With the entire morning available, John was not under any pressure to draw out supplies and pack. He took a well-deserved nap, then packed his ruck, and waited on the pad, ready to go, even before the engines started.

On the way to the bush, John was excited and could not wait to see the rest of his friends. When landing, it was like a family reunion, they all gathered around, wanting to hear about his adventure. When finishing his tale, the squad started bringing John up-to-date on their happenings during the past week.

The day after his Medevac, the squad received two new replacements. BJ grabbed the first one off the chopper and made him his assistant gunner. He was quite happy with the M-60 and asked if it was okay for him to keep it. John was quick to agree, thankful he didn't have to lug the heavy weapon around anymore.

A new Second Lieutenant also arrived and took over the First Platoon.

"What's his name?"

"Lt. Stryker, but we call him Rubber Ducky."

"What kind of nickname is that?"

"Just wait until we move out. He's a real clown, and couldn't lead cows to pasture."

"Sixpack is also back again as our squad leader," Frenchie added.

"How are you feeling, Polack?" Sixpack asked when seeing him with the squad.

"Great, now that I'm back out in the bush."

"Good. How would you feel about being the squad point man for a while?"

"What's wrong with Nung and Scout?"

"Nothing. I just want to give them a break for a while."

John responded without hesitation, "No sweat, Sixpack. I'll give it a try so they can catch a break."

"Good. Here you go," Sixpack handed him a machete and compass. "We'll be moving on a heading of 220 degrees. I want you to follow as close to that course as possible for about two-thousand steps. Just take your time and keep your eyes open. You know the rest of us are depending on you to get us where we're going in one piece."

"I'll get us there. You can count on me."

The entire company was still in a cocky mood; not one person had fired his weapon during the last thirty days. Stored paperback books and transistor radios found their way out of rucksacks; reading and listening to the radio helped them to pass the time. The practice had been taboo for as long as anybody could remember. Yet, none of the officers challenged anyone.

John found that long humps through the thick jungle were the norm every day. The point man had a dual role: first, clearing a path for the rest of the column to follow, and, second, watching for the enemy and booby traps. Wild Bill walked a few steps behind John, keeping an eye overhead, as well as on the surrounding area. John hacked and swore at the stubborn growth and could not help but keep a wary eye out for Banded Krait snakes along the way. He'd finally stumble into an occasional clearing, only to start hacking away some thirty feet later. John kept the column headed in the correct direction, but had lost count of his footsteps long ago.

Sensing his dilemma, Wild Bill came up behind John and whispered, "Don't worry about the footsteps. I've been keeping count. Just focus to your front and in cutting your way through this shit. I've got your back, man!"

The grunts no longer thought of the never-ending jungle as Vietnam. Instead, they imagined themselves trapped in a large, bush-filled box, constantly walking, and never being able to reach the other side.

During one of the following days, Rubber Ducky lived up to his name. After choosing a place to bush for the night, the Cherry L-T wanted to confirm their location. Being quite certain of the coordinates, he asked Firebase Kien to fire a white phosphorous round, expecting it to explode three-hundred meters away and one-hundred feet in the air. Lt. Stryker, stood with compass in hand, ready to take an azimuth on the exploding cloud of white smoke. He was expecting the explosion to the right of their perimeter.

When picking out coordinates for a fire mission, it is essential to know where the firebase is located in relation to your target. If a unit is in the artillery round's trajectory path, a slight miscalculation - or even a shot malfunction - could result in serious injury or death. Unlike High Explosive rounds that detonate on the ground and throw shrapnel in every direction, a white phosphorus-marking round contains powder that ignites in the air. The carrier, a four-inch wide by sixteen-inch long hollow projectile, continues along the line of flight for another two hundred yards. It would not explode upon impact; instead, the projectile would hit the ground at one-hundred miles an hour and continue to bounce and roll until it ran into an immovable object or until the law of physics allowed it to stop on its own. If somebody stood in its path, a direct collision could result in instantaneous death.

The phrase "fire in the hole" sounded around the perimeter, alerting the men. All were aware of the imminent explosion in the air, but they did not know exactly where it would detonate.

They heard a faraway sound of artillery firing to the east; the 105mm artillery round from Kien was on its way. The white phosphorus round exploded harmlessly in the air 150 yards away, the growing white cloud of smoke visible only a split second before they heard the detonation. Unfortunately, the cloud was not on the right side of the perimeter as planned, it exploded to their front.

"Shit, we're not where I thought we were," Rubber Ducky exclaimed. He was pointing his compass in the direction of the smoke, unaware the NDP was in the round's trajectory path.

Suddenly, there was a strange noise, like someone blowing into the top of an empty soda bottle: VROOOM, VROOM, VROOM, the sound became louder as it closed in on First Platoon's perimeter.

Sixpack knew exactly what it was and shouted, "Take cover! Incoming!" He jumped behind a tree, ensuring some protection between himself and the incoming projectile.

Many of the men around the perimeter scrambled for cover; others simply dropped to the ground and covered their heads. The hollow projectile came tumbling through the overhead foliage - hot and smoking. It crashed to the ground and threw up a wave of dirt, before launching back into the air and mowing a path through the thick jungle foliage. The projectile hit a tree and then ricocheted, bounding toward the overnight position of two new Cherries. Both had been sitting on the ground, watching the projectile in awe as it crashed into the center of their NDP. When it suddenly changed course and careened toward them, there was absolutely no time for either to react. The long side of the smoking cylinder was parallel to the ground when it crashed into both of them with a deep thud, knocking them onto their backs. The projectile bounced over the men and tumbled along the ground for twenty or more feet before stopping; the wet jungle foliage hissed loudly under the unwelcome ten-pound object.

Suddenly, screams of pain echoed across the NDP from the two Cherries. Doc and others ran toward the sounds, knowing the men were going to be hurt badly, but hoping for the best. Both had only been in the bush for a couple of weeks, and nobody knew them other than their fellow squad members. Doc and a couple of the other soldiers took field dressings from the Cherries' web harnesses and administered first aid to the shocked men. Doc worked feverishly to stop the flow of blood gushing from the almost severed leg of one of the men. Once the tourniquet was in place, he started checking for other injuries. The other Cherry had a broken right forearm; jagged, white bone, about an inch long, was poking through his skin in between the wrist and elbow. Both men had broken ribs, burns, and lacerations on their upper bodies.

A Medevac chopper with a jungle penetrator arrived within twenty minutes to evacuate the two injured soldiers. Both men were going to live, but it was a costly price to pay for a foolish mistake. The brass called this a "friendly fire" accident.

Rubber Ducky defended himself and blamed the firebase for the error. If he had any remorse, he surely was not showing it.

Similar errors in judgment continued and the platoon members wanted him out before anyone else got hurt. Several men heard through the grapevine that there was a bounty on Lt. Stryker's head. Many hoped he would voluntarily leave the field because if a firefight erupted first, one of the grunts would most likely take a pot shot at him.

John was soon comfortable in his new role as point man and found it to be challenging. He did not have to perform this role every day, as the position alternated between the four squads in the platoon. The best humps were those through light vegetation, where he could focus on his surroundings and not worry about exhausting himself while slashing a path through the jungle.

When First Platoon finally exited the triple canopy jungle, they found the area saturated with trails and showing heavy activity.

During the week, the men set up booby traps and ambushes, but always came up empty.

The company remained in the vicinity for one more week before battalion brought them to Firebase Kien so the men could celebrate Thanksgiving.

It was not Cu Chi, but it was the next best thing, offering the grunts an opportunity to rest up for a couple of days. Sure, Thanksgiving was here, but to the grunts, every holiday was just another routine day in Vietnam.

# CHAPTER FIFTEEN

What a big surprise! When waking on Thanksgiving Day, the grunts found the open area next to the mess tent had changed during the night.

The cooks had erected a large tent with two dozen folding banquet tables set up in six even rows, and enough wooden chairs to seat a hundred people. Individual place settings were on the table in front of each chair – comprised of real plates, silverware, cloth napkins, and a menu on each plate. A banner, strung across the length of the tent, read "HAPPY THANKSGIVING, WOLFHOUNDS – ENJOY!" Several cardboard turkey centerpieces adorned the tables, creating some level of ambiance for celebrating the special occasion.

During the meal, cooks continued to bring platters of turkey, ham, mashed potatoes, peas, green beans, dressing, turkey gravy, cornbread, muffins, and cranberry sauce to the tables. The heaping platters were passed back and forth between the grateful men. Pitchers of coffee, milk, and soda were in ample supply; dessert was fresh apple and pumpkin pie. It was a feast fit for a king, but humbly served to the warriors on this special day.

The stand-down officially ended early Friday morning; Alpha Company was on the move once again. This time, instead of flying out in helicopters to their destination, the grunts humped to a location in the jungle just three clicks west of Kien. Intelligence wanted to confirm rumors of a buildup in that area for a possible attack on the firebase.

Alpha and Bravo Companies would be blocking forces - Alpha lining up east to west and Bravo north to south along their right flank. Charlie Company would sweep through the area, flushing out the enemy and pushing him toward the waiting companies. Mechanical ambushes and trip flares covered potential and expected escape routes.

Four Army snipers also joined Alpha Company on this mission. They chose positions behind their ranks that offered the best view of the approaching routes.

Choppers inserted Echo Company (Recon) into the northern part of the jungle earlier that day in an attempt to locate and maintain surveillance on potential staging areas.

The grunts itched for the firefight that had been a long time coming. They were more excited this time because, for a change, they could sit and wait for the enemy to walk into their ambush, instead of vice versa.

In two days, Charlie Company completed their sweep through the jungle and joined up with Alpha Company. During that time, they had found absolutely no evidence of any buildup or signs of the enemy within the area. Battalion Loach helicopters continuously buzzed overhead at treetop level, but were unsuccessful at drawing fire from the jungle below.

The mission was a bust. The men in the blocking forces remained in place until the next morning, then left for the new AO.

Only Recon remained active within the area, the four-man stealthy teams stayed behind to observe and patrol through the checked areas, ensuring nothing was overlooked. The other companies remained close in case something significant was discovered.

In the morning, Alpha moved to the outskirts of a village within two miles of the firebase. Here, they began the tedious task of searching villagers and checking ID cards again. Once finished, the company continued humping west, repeating the process with each village encountered.

After three days - and now about six miles from the firebase - the company found themselves in an area with dozens of small villages. The search would take several more days to complete. First Platoon traveled the furthest and found an acceptable location for their NDP. It was inside the jungle, providing excellent concealment. They planned on staying there for the next week, dispatching daily patrols to check the many villages.

Only two squads went out on the daily patrols; the other half of the platoon remained within the NDP. OP's were in place outside of the perimeter during the day, an early warning given when observing approaching visitors.

Boredom filled the idle days. Many of the men read and traded paperback books or listened to the American music channel from Saigon on AM radios. Poncho liners served as a playing surface for gin rummy and poker.

On the second day, Nung returned from a patrol with what many considered a luxury in the bush. When reaching his sleeping position, he unpacked a blue nylon hammock and suspended it from two nearby trees. Next, he snatched his poncho from the ground, attached it overhead from the same two trees, and created a canopy, resembling a floating pup tent. It covered the hammock completely, yet provided enough head room underneath to sit upright on the suspended bed. The activity attracted the attention of just about everybody within the NDP. Several soldiers stood nearby, watching Nung work with deep curiosity. He took four small strips of cloth and secured one to each hammock rope by a knot, letting it hang between the hammock material and the tree. When done, he moved his ruck under the hammock, grabbed his poncho liner, and then maneuvered into the hammock, covering himself. After several seconds, Nung raised the side of the poncho roof and projected a wide, pleased smile.

"Nung, where in the fuck did you get that?"

"Villagers sell for ten dollars, MPC."

"No shit! They have any more?"

"Have many to sell. Hammock is same-same used by VC. Now Nung will stay dry during nighttime rain and sleep much better."

"Why do you have those strips of cloth hanging from the ropes of your hammock?"

"Rope get wet when raining, and without pieces hanging, water move to hammock and Nung get wet. Now water stop at knot and fall to ground."

"When can we get some for ourselves?"

"You give MPC and Nung go to village tomorrow."

Several of the men made a mad dash back to their sleep areas, digging out their money from the waterproof containers secured to their rucks. When it was all over, Nung held almost three hundred dollars in MPC notes. Even Rubber Ducky agreed to purchase one.

The next day, Nung returned with a rice sack full of the precious hammocks. After distributing them, everyone got busy, trying to mimic Nung's shelter, sacrificing several green t-shirts to make enough "water stoppers" for the hammocks.

The grunts were in their glory and looked forward to the night. Not sleeping on the hard ground and staying dry were luxuries in the bush, especially during the monsoon season.

Most First Platoon NDP's were located in wooded areas, so it would not be hard for anyone to "tie up" for the night. It would also save time when preparing a sleeping position at the end of the day. With no need to concern themselves with removing all of the obstacles from the ground, it permitted the men an extra hour to read or listen to the radio. The hammocks were compact and portable, and could be stored easily in pants pockets.

The immediate area to their west had an abundance of bomb craters, filled with fresh rainwater now that the monsoon season was well underway. Sixpack designated two of the nearest craters strictly for drinking water, and the next two for bathing. However, each canteen of water still required iodine tablets. At least the grunts no longer had to worry about carrying the excess weight of five canteens or having to ration water for three days until the next resupply.

Once again, Nung came up with another luxury item for the bush: an unscented bar of lye soap. They passed it from person to person, and it barely lasted an entire round. Some grunts who had been in country for a while, passed on the opportunity to bathe. Their rationale was that it was a wasted effort considering their filthy and torn uniforms, and that the cleanliness was sure to attract more insects.

The only item missing was a portable outhouse to bring them closer to civilization.

Over the next several days, members of the First Platoon started trading with the villagers. After each resupply, they collected and saved many of the unwanted C-Rations, the meals incurring nicknames over time. Beans and franks were known as 'beans and baby dicks, lima beans and ham were the ever dreadful 'beans and motherfuckers, and scrambled eggs were simply 'egg chunks,' as the meal was usually solid in the can and had to be chopped apart when heating. Each soldier had to take malaria pills daily. Unfortunate side effects were gas, stomach cramps and diarrhea. Because of this, eating beans did not appeal to the men, so meals that included them were undesirable.

The daily patrols took these unwanted cans of food into the various villages to trade and barter for items they had, ranging from ice-cold drinks and rice to live chickens. Villagers were very excited about the food choices and always seemed willing to work out a deal with the grunts. Whenever a patrol could bring back a chicken or two to the NDP, Nung took on the role of master chef. He used special herbs and spices and cooked over an open fire before shredding the meat and mixing it into cooked rice. There was always enough to feed the entire platoon and the grunts considered these meals a real treat.

Time had moved quickly and the soldiers realized that Christmas was only two weeks away. Greeting cards were not available, so the grunts got creative and made their own. Rubber Ducky ensured that everyone in the platoon would send at least one letter or card home to his family for the holidays.

There had been so much time available during the last few weeks for letter writing that most everyone had run out of things to write home about. Some letters simply read, 'Hello. I am doing OK and everything is fine. Will write more soon. Love, so-and-so.'

The two weeks since leaving Kien had been rather enjoyable. Even Rubber Ducky was content and not bothering anyone. If a new recruit had arrived during this time, he would have been stunned by the amount of free time the soldiers had, and the folks back home would have never believed it.

However, as always, all good things came to an end. First Platoon received word to pack up and get ready to move out later

John Podlaski

that morning. Not wanting to hump the C-Ration cans through the jungle, the platoon traded enough for cold sodas and then buried the rest.

Alpha Company continued moving in a westerly direction and soon found themselves cutting their way through the dense jungle once again. The four platoons still operated separately with missions of their own. First Platoon moved to an area just outside of the free-fire zone and planned to keep a medium-sized village under surveillance. Intel suspected this village to be sympathetic to the VC cause. They were hoping to catch the enemy out in the open and possibly uncover a cache of weapons or food.

Sixpack organized small three-man patrols and sent them to locations providing good vantage points of the village from all directions. The men had to be invisible, and yet keep a close eye on the occupants during the day. Prior to returning to the NDP, mechanical ambushes were set to cover possible avenues of travel to and from the village into the jungle.

The routine continued for three days without the soldiers seeing anything strange or out of place. On the fourth morning, First Platoon was ordered to sweep through the village in force and to search everywhere for tunnels or caches.

When the Americans entered the village just after daylight, they were surprised to find the villagers expecting them. The first village hut had a large cardboard sign attached to the wall that read, 'Alpha Wolfhounds – Go Home'.

"Looks like they have the welcome mat out," Sixpack smirked.

"How in the fuck do they know about us?"

"Yeah, this ain't right. It just ain't right!" Scout mumbled.

"They seem to know all about us and we don't know a damn thing about them!"

"They've got intelligence groups, too. And if what our brass suspects is true, we could be in a world of hurt."

Rubber Ducky was beside himself and it was evident that the sign shook him up. He started pacing back and forth in front of the group, unsure of what to do next.

Sixpack instructed everyone to split up into three-man teams again and to check out every hut, container, and especially under each bed, for evidence of the enemy being there. The L-T quickly joined up with Sixpack and stayed close to him.

The villagers were not happy to see the grunts searching through their possessions. Some offered ugly sneers in retaliation to their invasion of privacy; others wore a sinister and amused glare on their faces as if mocking the soldiers for their efforts.

Not one villager resisted or spoke, even when prompted by Nung to answer his questions. They appeared defiant but did not do anything to threaten the soldiers.

The grunts were very cautious and yet very thorough. Many of them had bayonets attached to the end of their M-16's, and, using the weapon as a probe, they poked into large containers of rice, bales of hay, into the ground under beds, and into the straw walls and roofs of the huts.

It took almost six hours to complete the sweep, and once again, the grunts came up empty handed.

"Shit, they knew we were coming so they must have hidden everything."

"Where, Polack? We looked everywhere."

"I don't know. Maybe they came in during the night and carried everything away into the jungle."

"That does make sense, but we won't be able to prove it."

"Wait a minute, Polack, you may have hit on something," Sixpack stated and called over the L-T. "Polack thinks the VC moved everything out of the village during the night. It all makes sense now when you think about it. They knew we were here and most likely the position of our mechanicals, so they only had to go around them. I think we should leave our NDP for a new one and then set up nightly ambush teams around the village for the next few days."

"I like that plan." The L-T responded. "However, we've got to get resupplied before we can pull off something like that."

"Agreed. Run this past the captain and see if he'll sanction it. We can set up for the resupply right here and then move out, heading back the way we came in, and circle back later."

The captain liked the idea, too, but felt it was too large of an undertaking for a single platoon, so he dispatched Second Platoon to link up with them. Both were to meet after the resupply, about a mile away, in the jungle and out of sight of the village. There, the two groups formulated plans for the nightly ambushes and moved closer to the village.

Both the first and second nights were quiet. A full moon shone, which helped with their night movements and deployment, but they feared the VC were aware of their plan and were choosing to stay away.

Just after one in the morning on the third night, one of the villagers on a bicycle triggered a mechanical ambush on one of the trails leading away from the village. He was carrying a pouch with papers that warned the nearby VC to stay away until the Americans left the area. The papers also stated that they knew the Wolfhounds had the village under surveillance and had ambush teams within the vicinity. The villagers would let them know when it was safe for them to enter.

"How in the fuck do they do this? Why don't we just go in and tear that place apart?" Frenchie asked, visibly upset. "Those cock suckers are all VC sympathizers!"

"It won't do us any good. We now know there aren't any military supplies there, and there surely aren't any VC around either. This message proved it," Sixpack held up the letter as proof.

"I just wish I could get my hands on them. They're all playing us for fools."

"Right on, Frenchie! They're all Commies in my book." Wild Bill pumped his fist into the air to support his brother.

"Look, guys, we're still in a no fire zone, but we were justified in killing this guy because he violated the curfew. We can't just go into that village and rough everyone up. It would be wrong and we'd all suffer the consequences eventually. You can't cover shit like that up."

"Fuck it, Sixpack! At least it would get us out of this stinking war. Besides, what can the brass say if we just burn down a couple of the hooches? At least it'll show the villagers that we're pissed."

"The brass may not say anything, but it'll turn the good villagers against us, -if there are any there - and make us play right into the Communists' hands. You people know the enemy preaches to the villagers that we are really the aggressors in this country, anxious to burn and pillage their land. Just keep cool. We'll eventually catch them."

"I hate to admit it, but that makes sense."

"I know it does, Frenchie. You learn from your mistakes. Ever heard the saying 'once burned, twice shy'?"

"What kind of mistakes are you talking about, Sixpack?"

"On my last tour, the company I was with made a mistake. It was almost the same situation, except that there was a sniper there. We jumped to conclusions and burned down most of the friendly village. The next time we came back into that area, we lost a bunch of good men. The VC had convinced some of the villagers to join them for revenge. Afterwards, they went out of their way to booby trap and ambush us every chance they got."

"What makes you think the same thing will happen again?"

"I don't know, but I've got to spend another eight months in this country and I'm positive we'll be working in this area again sooner or later. I'd rather not take that chance."

"Aw, Sarge, I thought you were all gung-ho and shit!"

"No, I'm not, but you all ought to take a look at yourselves. Things that you used to overlook are starting to bug you. Most of you are short and have less than two months to go before going home. I know you've all been through a lot of shit in the last ten months and the lack of action lately is getting to some of you. You guys need to stop being so restless and keep a cool head. Remember what happened to Zeke when he lost his head?"

"Yeah, literally," Scout muttered, snickering.

"You're an asshole!" Sixpack's face harbored a scowl and he bit at his lower lip. "You just better keep your shit in order. The first of you motherfuckers that gets out of line, I'll personally kick your ass."

"Oh yeah? Come on, motherfucker!" Scout challenged and moved closer to the sergeant.

"I don't believe it. Sixpack's turning into a real lifer."

"Frenchie!" Sixpack looked at him with glaring eyes. "I'm no more a lifer than you are. I'm just interested in living and keeping you all alive and in one piece. I may not have anybody back home waiting for me, but I do know that you all have wives and girlfriends waiting. What you do when you get out of the bush, I could give a fuck less. But right now, you do as I say!"

Doc stepped in and stood next to Sixpack, facing the angry pair. "He's right. Go and cool off somewhere. If you want to pursue this any further, then come see me and I'll hear you out. Come on now, we're all brothers here and need to keep our shit tight. There is absolutely no reason whatsoever, to be talking shit to each other like you are. The enemy's out there!" Doc pointed toward the village.

"Okay, Doc. You've always been straight with us. I'm good with it."

"Thanks, Scout. Now see if you can talk some sense into your buddy, Frenchie."

"No need to. I'm okay for the moment."

BJ and John stood dumbfounded and could not understand why the men were so agitated all of a sudden. They sat there the entire time listening, but were too afraid to interfere. They were shocked, as it was the first time that such fallout had occurred within this tight knit squad, and it worried them. The next few hours were spent in a sullen air.

An announcement that afternoon brought the troops some much-needed relief. Alpha Company would return to Cu Chi and had an excellent chance of seeing the Bob Hope Christmas Show the following week. Battalion wanted the Wolfhound Company to patrol through a couple of suspect areas first and then hump to Kien, which would only take a little more than three days. A hurried resupply would take place later that afternoon so the company could get moving and cover the planned three-mile hump before nightfall.

Frenchie and Scout approached Sixpack and Doc during the resupply and made an awkward attempt to apologize for their behavior. Both admitted that getting short was beginning to affect them. It was not the lack of contact during the last month that was upsetting, but instead, it was an uneasy feeling, a sense of foreboding that something bad was going to happen soon. Then again, maybe it was just short-timer's paranoia.

The men made amends and everything was back to normal by the time the company left the LZ. The total distance to Kien was almost ten miles. It would be tough-going in some areas, but nobody complained, as they looked forward to seeing the famous comedian and the usual bevy of beautiful American women who accompanied him on these USO tours. Most every soldier in the column had seen Bob Hope's Vietnam Christmas Show on TV during the last couple of years, but actually seeing the show in person would be an exhilarating experience. Each man already fantasized about the show, thinking of ways to be visible on television. Surely, friends and family would be watching from home, and seeing them on TV would be a wonderful Christmas gift.

The route to the firebase would take the company through the same area where the suspected large enemy buildup had been two weeks earlier.

As there had been no earlier signs of the enemy, the troops' confidence level remained high. They expected a trouble-free hump.

On that first night, each platoon dispatched a five-man team to ambush different nearby trails. Since First Squad stayed behind, they gained an extra hour to read or listen to Christmas carols on transistor radios. The songs felt surreal and out of place in these surroundings, like hearing them in July. It was difficult to get in the holiday spirit, and it was hard to believe that Christmas Day was only five days away.

At 0300, the CP lost contact with Third Platoon's ambush team. They tried several times to reach them, suspecting radio trouble since there had been no report of weapons firing or exploding mechanicals. They would have to wait for the answer when the team returned to the NDP in the morning.

Four hours later, all ambush teams had returned except for the team from Third Platoon. The concern for them grew as word quickly spread throughout the company.

"Dumb shits probably overslept like our own BJ did a little while back."

"I don't think so, Frenchie. I'll bet you ten bucks they got lost."

"You're on, Wild Bill. I heard that Lt. Carlisle went out on that ambush. He's the best navigator in the company so the coordinates he sent in last night had to be accurate within ten meters."

"Aw, shit, I didn't know that. Bet's off!"

"No way, bro, you want to pay now or later?"

"Let's see how it shakes out."

First Squad joined three other squads from the company to search for the missing team. During the briefing, they referred to a map showing both their current location and the circled tentative location of the ambush team; six hundred meters separated the two red X's. Each search team would target the identical coordinates, approaching from different directions. They would travel light and should reach the destination within forty minutes.

Sixpack's Squad had the most direct route and stopped every two-hundred meters to fire a green handheld flare into the air; the other three teams followed suit. Standard practice was for a lost squad without communications to respond with a star cluster flare of their own after seeing a green flare. After eight flares, there was still no response from the missing five men.

It took almost an hour for the First Squad to reach the general area of the ambush site. The other teams were still en route and were about fifteen minutes out.

John was on point and beginning to feel uneasy. There was a hint of death in the air and it became more pronounced as they advanced. His mind raced, trying to make sense of it all.

He felt a slight tug across his right shin and immediately froze in place. His breathing stopped as he realized what had just happened. A microsecond later, the disengaged trip wire allowed the circuit to complete and sent an electrical charge to the mechanical ambush. When he heard a popping sound, he braced himself for what may have very well been his last second alive. However, nothing happened. John turned his head, surprised to find himself standing alone on the trail; the squad had already sought protective cover. Hearing no explosion, they filtered back onto the trail and approached their point man.

"Polack, don't move!" Sixpack cautioned. "I don't know what you hit, but just stay right where you are."

Too shaken to answer, John remained frozen in place. Sixpack and Wild Bill approached him very slowly, making certain to step in the same footprints that John had originally left on the trail.

"Did you step on something or trip something?" Wild Bill asked. Both he and Sixpack used knives to probe into the ground beneath John's feet.

"I think I tripped something because I felt it brush against my leg."

Confident that John was not standing on a pressure release mine or booby trap, the two men stood back up and returned the knives to their scabbards.

"Okay, there's nothing under your feet. You can move now," Wild Bill slapped John across the back. John inhaled deeply and took a few unsteady steps to the side of the trail.

"Look around for a trip wire. It had to be attached to something." Sixpack inched his way up the trail, looking everything over with a keen eye.

The rest of the men scoured the two sides of the trail, looking for the thin strand of wire.

Frenchie was ten feet away and standing just off to the right side of the trail. "I found it!" Upon hearing this, the rest of the squad joined him.

"Jesus!" Sixpack was surprised to see what Frenchie had discovered. "You guys keep your eyes open. Something's really wrong here."

The two men were looking at a stake in the ground with pieces of metal attached to it with rubber bands. A set of wires led back into the jungle; one was only two feet long, blackened at the end, and lying there on the ground just in front of a claymore mine. Four other mines were daisy chained together in the mechanical ambush. The blasting cap had somehow fallen out of the lead claymore and exploded harmlessly when John hit the trip wire. Had it been in place, the entire squad might have perished.

"Polack, you are one lucky motherfucker. I hope you have nine lives."

"Thanks, Scout, but I don't plan on making shit like this a habit. I'll have to start keeping count of these close encounters."

The men quickly disconnected the mines, gathering the supplies to carry back with them to the NDP.

"This is some spooky shit, Sixpack. VC didn't put this booby trap together; it belonged to the missing team." Frenchie's voice quivered and he looked on edge.

Sixpack paced nervously and replied, "I agree that it belonged to the missing team, but two things are bothering me: why didn't they take it down, and why wasn't the blasting cap secured in the claymore? Keep your eyes open, people. Their night ambush position was around here somewhere."

Just then, Fourth Platoon's search team stepped out of the jungle and onto the trail and joined up with the First Squad. Sixpack took a few minutes to brief them before the eight men joined the others in searching through the jungle on both sides of the trail.

Suddenly, 150 feet away from the location of the mechanical, John came upon a sight that literally sent shockwaves through his body. He found the missing ambush team lying in the bush just four feet off the trail. They were not lost and did not have radio trouble. Each of them was parallel to the trail and spaced about five feet apart.

"I found the missing squad!" John shouted. "They're all over here!"

The search parties exited the jungle and jogged up the trail toward John. Sixpack was the first to arrive.

The first man they came upon was lying on his poncho. A deep slice across his throat from ear to ear nearly severed his head. The once green camouflage liner, still covering the man, had turned a shade of dark burgundy, almost black. The second, third, and fourth men were all found the same way. When they approached the last man, John dropped his rifle to the ground as he recognized the corpse of Bill Sayers. He was not lying on the ground and covered with a bloody poncho liner. Instead, he sat on the ground, propped against a tree. His eyes were wide with surprise, and his mouth hung open as if he were trying to call for help. The handle of his own Bowie knife was sticking out of his chest, surrounded by a crust of dried blood.

"God, no! Not Bill! Please don't let it be!"

Sixpack placed his hands on John's shoulders. "Easy, Polack. We're too late to help them. There's nothing we can do for Bill and the others."

"Oh, my God!"

Sixpack summoned Frenchie and Wild Bill. "Take Polack off to the side and keep him quiet."

John's mind went blank and he seemed to fall into a semi-comatose state. He sat quietly with the two men while Sgt. Holmes reported their findings back to the company CP.

During the discovery, the remaining two squads had emerged from the jungle and converged on the ambush site. The squad from the Third Platoon had a hard time accepting that their L-T and four other close friends were dead. They shed tears, offered prayers, and gave condolences all around.

The four Squads formed a defensive perimeter around the ambush sight so choppers could evacuate the dead soldiers. Not much remained aside from the bodies, as the enemy had taken their weapons, ammo, rucksacks, and radio.

Sixpack walked over to the three soldiers sitting together to the side of the trail. "How's the Polack doing?"

"He hasn't said a word since we've been sitting here with him."

Sixpack got on a knee and put a hand on John's shoulder. "Polack, talk to me! You okay?"

He blinked several times in an attempt to hold back tears and then looked into Sixpack's eyes. "I'll be all right."

"Are you sure?"

"Yeah, yeah, I'm alright. I'm sure it would have been different if I'd heard about his death, but actually being the first to see him did a job on me."

"I know you guys were very close. I'm sorry though, but you have to let it go. Bill's not going to be the last friend of yours that's going to die in this war. There will be others, so you have to learn how to block out the emotions and live with the hurt, otherwise you'll drive yourself crazy."

Frenchie and Will Bill nodded in agreement.

"Hang tough, Polack. Be happy you're still alive."

"Anybody figure out what happened to them?"

"The consensus is that a Squad of sappers took them out. This wasn't a coincidence. I bet they were followed and then watched while getting into position and setting the mechanical ambush. Some of us believe they took the blasting cap out and either forgot about it or were in a rush to get away. They took everything else and we can't figure why they didn't take the claymores."

"So they didn't even have a chance to fight back, did they?"

"Doesn't look like it. Looks like Bill was on guard duty and had the radio, so he had to be the first to go. They probably came up from behind to get him out of the way and then killed the others while they were asleep."

"Can somebody really be that quiet?"

"Sappers are the best and are very patient. They crawl through the barbwire, disconnect claymore's and trip flares, and enter firebases during the middle of the night. Once inside, they remain invisible and usually try to blow up command bunkers. Most of them are good enough to escape afterwards without being seen."

At that moment, the lead element of the Third Platoon exited the jungle not far from the ambush sight. They wanted to investigate the area and take care of the bodies themselves.

Seeing this, Sixpack stood and turned to go meet with them. Before leaving, he stopped and spoke to John, "I promise you this: we will get even for what has happened here. Mark my words." He then moved quickly to join up with the staff sergeant who was leading the column of Third Platoon soldiers.

The First Squad approached and gathered around the three men sitting on the ground. Doc was the last to arrive.

"Polack, you've been through a terrible shock. If you want, I can send you to the rear and arrange for the Battalion Aid station to give you something to help you through this ordeal. Just say the word."

"That's alright, Doc. I want to stay out here with the rest of my friends and make those guys pay for what they did to Bill."

"Now hold on. If you start thinking like that, you'll be the next one killed around here."

"You don't have to worry about me. I'm not trying to be John Wayne."

"No problem, then?"

"No problem, scout's honor." He raised his right hand showing three fingers of the traditional Boy Scout salute.

Since it was so close to Christmas, John wondered if the Army would wait until after the holidays to notify Bill's family. If not, it would certainly be the worst Christmas of their lives, and he hoped they would pull through it okay. He could not even imagine the pain they would soon be experiencing.

He thought about his own family and wondered how they might react to the news if he died. It would probably kill both of his parents, who had already lost most of their families during World War II.

It finally hit him that he too, would be dead if the mechanical he tripped earlier in the day was armed. John looked up to the sky and made the sign of the cross, thanking God for the extra chance.

Battalion canceled Alpha's trip into Cu Chi to see Bob Hope. Instead, the men were to remain in the bush and find those responsible for the killings. If anyone felt disappointed, they were not showing it - it was something they would have volunteered to do anyway.

A countrywide cease-fire was in effect on Christmas Day, and both sides stopped fighting to celebrate the holiday. Alpha Company settled into the jungle next to a large clearing and would remain in place for the next two days.

Two choppers landed during the company resupply. The second was loaded with hot food canisters and ice-cold sodas. Battalion cooks arrived to feed the troops with a meal similar to the one they enjoyed on Thanksgiving Day, but this time the dining room was the jungle floor and there were no fancy decorations.

It was a lazy day and most of the men listened to the Bob Hope Christmas Show on their radios. Some sat together in small groups to share in the laughter as Bob joked about the government and politics. Sometimes it was difficult to hear the female guests speak or sing as the cheering and catcalls from the audience drowned them out. Miss America was a big hit; they pictured her standing there on the stage in her bathing suit and sash. The soldiers thoroughly enjoyed the radio show, although listening to the American humor was also a bittersweet experience for the young men. Waves of homesickness washed over them as they recalled past Christmases spent with their families or girlfriends. Nevertheless, the entertainment was a distraction from the reasons why they were there – if only for one day.

When the cease-fire ended, the grunts got serious again, and packed away all paperback books, radios, and cards deep into their rucksacks. They were ready to avenge the deaths of their brothers.

# CHAPTER SIXTEEN

The cease-fire came and went without incident. The Stars and Stripes newspapers reported, however, that the Communists had numerous violations throughout the country.
In Alpha Company's AO, the grunts had a feeling that the enemy was well aware that a witch-hunt was underway and remained out of sight. The sensation continued for the entire week after Christmas.
On New Year's Day, 1971, the company received word that Delta Company was engaged in heavy fighting and needed help. Alpha was the closest unit, and helicopters were already en route to pick up the reinforcements.
Delta Company had been working in a banana plantation for most of the past week, and that morning a patrol member tripped a vicious booby trap while going up a hill. The buried 105mm artillery round exploded and sent shrapnel in many directions; three soldiers died and four were critically wounded.
Unaware of a well-camouflaged base camp at the top of the hill, Delta Company remained in position and waited patiently for the Medevac helicopters.
When two finally landed on a plateau, fellow soldiers rushed the dead and wounded onto the waiting birds. However, before the Hueys had a chance to lift off, the enemy surprised everyone by opening up on them from the top of the hill. The enemy concentrated their heavy automatic fire and RPG's on the two helicopters. The first chopper carrying the wounded soldiers managed to avoid major damage and escaped the ambush. The second bird also managed to lift off, but returned to the ground, trailing thick black smoke after sustaining several hits to the engine.

Luckily, the pilot was able to land and power down behind a small hillock three-hundred yards away.

The ambush and heavy gunfire scattered many of the company soldiers who retreated downhill. As a result, many were without their gear and extra ammunition. In their haste to reach safety, they left all equipment behind.

When regrouping at the base of the hill, the Delta Commander requested an artillery fire mission targeting the summit. This afforded him an opportunity to assess the threat and formulate an attack plan.

During the barrage, dozens of soldiers tried inching their way up the hill to retrieve the left-behind gear. They managed to reach the general area, but then came under intense fire once again, forcing them back downhill for a second time. Fortunately, they secured a third of the gear.

The artillery rounds did not seem to be affecting the attackers - their rate of fire was still as aggressive as at the onset. The captain terminated the barrage and then requested a squadron of Huey Gunships and Cobras to help relieve the pressure. Knowing the VC were well dug-in, rockets and mini-guns could focus on those reinforced areas; a lull in the firing would provide the grunts with another opportunity for an assault. This time they were successful and gained a foothold halfway up the hill - returning fire, but not able to advance any further. The summit was just three hundred feet away, but the gunships had exhausted their armaments and left the battle to re-arm. Another push to the top would have to wait until they returned.

While the exchange of gunfire continued, several volunteers took it upon themselves to go and look for their wounded brothers and other survivors along the hillside. They successfully located a dozen critically injured soldiers and dragged them to the bottom of the hill, where the medics began treating the men. The fact that only five American soldiers had died in this battle thus far was surprising and encouraging.

Medevac choppers made repeated attempts to land and pull out more of the wounded, but the firing of heavy weapons kept them away. Thankfully, the injured were holding up. If not, it would have been deadly to try to carry them through the kill zone to an area where the choppers could land.

The gunships returned after thirty minutes and pounded the hilltop again. Confident the protective shield would suffice, Medevac choppers tried once again to land near the wounded.

The enemy's heavy weapon fire subsided when the Cobra rockets finally succeeded in destroying some of the reinforced bunkers; the unarmed medical choppers began landing and collecting the wounded. When lifting off, they banked tightly around the hill to whirl clear of the firing.

When the assault choppers pulled out to refuel a second time, the entrenched enemy let loose with mortars, walking the rounds downhill over the hunkered-down men and into the first aid area. Fortunately, the choppers had extracted all the wounded and the Delta medics had vacated that area by then.

Five hundred meters on the opposite side of the hill, Alpha Company troops were landing in a small valley clearing, shielded from the besieged hilltop by another larger hill. They were relying on the element of surprise, hoping the enemy did not see the choppers or hear them land. Their plan was to climb the muddy hill and come up behind the enemy while Delta Company and the attacking gunships were distracting them.

Alpha found a good-sized trail leading to the summit, but decided against following it, especially since Delta had already hit a booby trap on the other side.

Because of the muck and slippery conditions, they were forced to move slowly up the hillside. Finally, they managed to crawl and pick their way halfway up without confronting the enemy or his booby traps. Suddenly, gunfire behind the two lead squads sent everyone diving for cover. Half of the First Platoon had already passed when two VC emerged from spider holes on their left flank, opening fire on the advancing file of men. Sixpack immediately cut one of them down and an exploding grenade silenced the other. Rubber Ducky and three other soldiers sustained wounds in this exchange but their injuries were not critical. Rubber Ducky was shot in his right thigh - a through and through wound that luckily missed bone and major arteries. However, the second Lieutenant went into shock before Doc had a chance to reach him.

After a quick evaluation, Doc asked for an escort then sent him and the other three wounded men to the bottom of the hill. Alpha Company continued their ascent, knowing the element of surprise was now gone.

Meanwhile, Delta Company had fought their way up the hill, finally reaching the summit. Only sporadic fire continued as Delta started a cautious sweep across the hilltop.

Alpha Company was still having a difficult time climbing the hill. On the way up, many grunts were losing their footing and sliding down the muddy hillside, taking anybody they fell into along. The men were still finding spider holes and could not advance without checking them first. Thankfully, all were vacant; nevertheless, for those uncovering the hole, it was a nerve-wracking experience. It took them more than an hour to climb the six hundred feet to the top and link up with Delta Company.

Not much remained of the jungle canopy; many of the tree stumps were still smoldering from the intense heat of the bombardment. Without camouflage, the hilltop sat naked and fully exposed from above and below.

It was surprising to everyone that of the thirty-seven enemy bodies counted, seventeen were females. Evidently, the women were active participants in the battle, as all were armed and died with weapons at their sides. Many of the soldiers had a difficult time accepting the fact that a large group of females had joined in the battle against the Americans. The enemy totaled slightly more than a platoon in size, yet held off two aggressive American Infantry Companies under a hail of artillery and gunship attacks for a period of almost six hours.

The Wolfhounds received credit for all thirty-seven kills. The enemy on the other hand, had reduced the American's headcount by twenty-six, ten permanently.

The hilltop soon transformed into a high volume traffic center. The battalion Commander and some of his staff were in the first chopper to touch down. Subsequent arrivals included intelligence teams, dogs and their handlers, photographers, and representatives of the press. The grunts wondered if it might be necessary to bring air traffic controllers out on the next inbound chopper.

The Intelligence folks and dog teams searched through the remaining rubble, hungry for any uncovered information. To alleviate the crowding on the hilltop, the brass ordered platoon-sized recon patrols to leave the summit and patrol through the surrounding jungle.

First Platoon descended from the hilltop, now a popular attraction, and crossed through a small valley before climbing to the top of an adjoining hill. It was not as high as the former hill, but covered with heavier vegetation and underbrush. When they cleared a path across the summit to the edge, the battle site was clearly visible seven hundred meters away. The scarred hilltop buzzed with activity, with choppers still landing and lifting off.

It was evident that this new hilltop had not had any visitors for quite some time; the men did not find any trails or cleared out areas. Every step required the swing of a machete to clear a path through the overgrown brush. Striking out, the captain directed the men to follow a ridgeline on the far side of the hill down to the valley floor. This part of the valley consisted of tall elephant grass and small clumps of vegetation - nothing to impede their forward progress in returning to - what was now known as - Hill 200.

Back on flat ground, the men had moved only two hundred meters from the base of the hill, when they unknowingly wandered into an area hit some time ago by powdered CS gas. It was impossible to know how wide of an area had been contaminated; the powder remained unnoticed and had lain dormant on the ground since then. Foot traffic activated the powder, creating newly airborne gas. Startled, the men wondered why their vision was blurry, their eyes were tearing, and it was becoming difficult for them to breathe. The parade moved on, disrupting the particles of powder on the ground and dispersing more gas into the air, worsening everyone's conditions. Minutes after their initial symptoms appeared, the captain realized it was CS gas.

"We're being gassed! Everyone high tail it out of here as fast as you can!"

The thirty-two men tried vacating the area as quickly as possible. In their haste, they twisted ankles and knees, and some soldiers tripped over one another to get away. Those coming up from behind latched onto the men who were limping or could not see and helped move them along.

The mad dash ended after fifty yards or so when the effects of the gas began to subside. The men began assisting each other, flushing the noxious powder from their eyes. All continued to cough, some violently, until they could discharge the chemical from their throats and lungs. The grunts also learned that if they were not careful while brushing the powder from their hair and clothes, the CS gas would become airborne once again.

When the crises was over, the men began joking and laughing about the experience.

"Did you guys catch the face Polack was making back there? It was so twisted up, I didn't even recognize him."

"Hell, Frenchie, I didn't see you laughing back there!"

"That's the fastest I moved in a while. Kind of reminded me of what we went through in boot camp."

"You're full of shit, BJ. We expected it back then. Now tell me any of you knew this was going to happen."

"That's the first time I've experienced CS gas," John added.

"How is that possible? Nobody gets excused from the gas chamber in Basic."

"Yeah, you're full of shit, Polack."

"No, it's true. See this long scar on my neck?" He pointed to the four-inch scar across the left side of his neck. "A few days before we were supposed to go to the chamber, four guys broke out of the stockade at Fort Knox and came through our company training area to hassle and rob us. Some of us started to fight them, but didn't know they were hiding box cutter straight razors in their hands. Two of them cornered me between our barrack wall and the hand railing on the slab just outside of the door. One of them swung at my head and I jumped back, thinking that I cleared his reach. Both felons backed away quickly and then attacked another nearby recruit. I ran inside, grabbed my folding shovel from my web belt, and was on my way back outside when my bunkmate stopped me, pushing me down on the nearest bunk. I remember him telling me that I was bleeding profusely from a cut across my throat. This was news to me as I wasn't feeling any pain and don't remember being cut. But, when I looked down at my t-shirt and shorts, I saw they were soaked with blood.

"My buddy ran to get some gauze from the nearest web belt and quickly covered the wound and wrapped it tightly. Meanwhile, some of the other grunts in the barracks came over to see what all the commotion was about and saw all the blood. One of the squad leaders ran to the Orderly Room and told the sergeant on duty. He quickly arranged for an ambulance to take me to the hospital.

"They told me I was lucky, because the razor had just nicked my jugular vein; a millimeter more and I would have bled to death. I needed thirty stitches, both inside and out, to close the wound properly. Afterwards, a couple of MP's took me over to their headquarters where they interrogated me about the assault. That lasted most of the night, and I got back to the barracks about four in the morning. The DI and captain of the training company let me sleep for the rest of the day, excusing me from training for the next week. But I did spend some of the time doing KP.

"So, is that a good enough story for you to believe that I missed the gas chamber in Basic?"

"Damn, Polack. What happened to the motherfuckers that cut you?"

"I heard a couple of days later they were caught and would be prosecuted. I didn't have to testify or do anything else because they had my story, witnesses, and pictures of my wound as evidence."

"Did they put you in another training company?"

"No, we were almost at the end of the program anyway and I was allowed to take the PT tests - which I passed - and then graduated with everyone else."

"Okay, good enough story, Polack. I stand corrected. You are the first of those I know in the Army who's never experienced the gas chamber in Basic Training. But you guys have to admit that what just happened to us is still funnier than shit."

They all agreed and started laughing once again, pointing to one another and making faces.

It was almost five in the afternoon when the First Platoon neared the base of Hill 200. The captain instructed them to pick an area nearby for their NDP and settle in for the night. He also cautioned them that other patrols were still out for another hour; mechanicals were not to be setup until the last possible moment.

The grunts located a spot where the banana trees provided shade from the low-setting sun. The ground had soft, shallow vegetation, which provided some cushion for their makeshift beds for the night. John and many others chose to lie down and rest for a short period, postponing dinner until later.

Nung climbed one of the banana trees and brought down a bunch of small bananas, passing out the pickle-sized treats to those nearby. Wild Bill walked toward John with a few of the yellow fruits to share.

"Holy shit, Polack, don't move!" He dropped the bananas to the ground.

"Why? What's wrong?" He asked, startled and concerned, but careful not to move.

"Man, you have got the biggest tarantula I've ever seen crawling up your leg."

John lifted his head and saw a softball-sized, furry black creature moving up his leg.

"Get this thing off of me," he pleaded though clenched teeth.

"Just lay still and maybe he'll crawl off you. If you move real sudden-like and scare him, he might bite you."

John was praying that he would not need a Medevac pick-up because another jungle creature bit him. He lay absolutely still.

"Hey, guys! Come over and look at this!" Wild Bill called to the rest of the squad.

"Jesus Christ. That's one big, motherfucking spider!" Frenchie said upon his arrival. He was holding a large Bowie knife in his right hand.

"Where did that come from?"

"BJ, you don't know shit do you? We are in a banana plantation. Tarantulas are banana spiders. They thrive in this shit."

John could feel the presence of the huge arachnid on his leg as it made its way up his body. It continued on its course until reaching his waist.

"Guys, I'm scared shitless here. Please do something to get this thing off me!"

"We can't. If we try to pick it off with a branch or machete, it will really piss him off. They're very delicate and can feel sensations easily. Let it go, eventually, it'll walk right off."

John felt his heart beating so hard and fast that he thought his chest was going to explode. He broke out in a cold sweat as the spider continued its upward trek. When reaching his chest, it paused once again. John was terrified, hoping that his heaving chest would not scare the creature into biting him.

It traveled upwards on his neck; John braced himself, clamping his lips together. When one of its legs reached up and brushed the bare skin of his chin, it sent a chill down his spine, causing him to shiver.

"Don't move. He'll be off in a minute," Frenchie cautioned. He and Scout knelt down, each pinning John's shoulders to the ground, restricting his movement.

He could feel each of its eight legs on his face now and closed his eyes tightly until it crossed over. It paused for a third time on his forehead. John dared not open his eyes in fear of what he might see. He felt the tarantula moving again, slowly maneuvering through the strands of his hair. It tickled, and he felt an uncontrollable urge to reach up and scratch his head. However, Frenchie and Scout saw him starting to move and quickly secured his arms as well.

Seconds later, when the spider finally crawled off of him, the men yanked John to his feet quickly. Hearing a sharp crack behind him, John turned to see that Wild Bill had smashed the spider with John's steel helmet.

"Relax, Polack, it's over," Wild Bill took some banana leaves and wiped off the helmet before handing it to the quivering soldier.

"What a fucking relief! I'll bet I aged twenty years during those last ten minutes."

"You handled it well, Polack. I just hope there aren't any more of them wandering around here tonight."

"Fuck you, Scout. You just had to be a smartass and say something like that." John looked the ground over and moved some long leaves from around the nearest banana tree. "I don't ever want to be this close to another spider again for as long as I live." They all laughed.

"Come on, let's celebrate. I've got some extra fruit cocktail we can share," Frenchie suggested.

"What's the occasion?"

"Polack's continued stretch of good luck!"

The following day, John led the way as the First Platoon moved toward their new NDP location, traveling at a good pace because of the thin vegetation in the area. The men humped for over an hour without a break and began complaining loudly. In order to keep the peace, Sixpack stopped the column when reaching the far edge of the valley. John moved as far away from the banana trees as possible; he did not want to relive another confrontation with a tarantula.

After the break, they continued at a relaxed pace until John came upon a trail heading in the same direction. There, First and Third Squads switched positions in the column. The new point man and three other squads passed John; he fell in behind the last man and First Squad was now bringing up the rear.

Two hours had passed and they found themselves still moving along the side of the same trail. Nung, who was the last man in the long column, passed up word for them to stop. Sixpack immediately broke away from his place in the column. Moving back to join up with Nung, the column of men took a break and broke out cigarettes, sharing with those who did not have any. A minute later, a single, light blue cloud of smoke formed, hovering above the smoking men on the trail.

"Sergeant! I think maybe VC follow," he informed Sixpack.

"How many, Nung?"

"Not for sure, maybe only one man."

"Wild Bill, Frenchie, I need you both." They stood up and walked over to where the sergeant squatted with Nung.

"Nung thinks we're being followed by one or more VC. So when the platoon gets up to move out, I want the two of you and

Nung to hide out here on the side of the trail and if our watcher comes by, grab his ass!"

"Right on, Sarge. We'll get the little fucker."

"I want him alive, so don't get trigger-happy and waste him."

Sixpack then called the captain on the radio to inform him of their current situation.

While rising to their feet after the break, everyone created more noise than usual, covering up the sounds of the three men sneaking into their hiding places. When the column moved forward, Sixpack and the men, bringing up the rear had to fight the urge to look backwards, thus, spooking the trail watcher.

After ten minutes, Sixpack heard Frenchie calling from a distance, "We got the little fucker!" The column halted once again.

The four men were moving up the trail towards the rest of the platoon at a fast pace. Nung had secured the young enemy soldier; one hand held the bound man's arms tightly behind his back, and the other grasped a crop of the man's hair, pulling on it so he faced upward when walking. Wild Bill carried Nung's M-16 and the AK-47 as he led the way. Frenchie followed slightly to the side of the trio, keeping his rifle trained on the new prisoner's head. When they reached Sixpack, Nung threw the prisoner to the ground at his feet.

"Mr. Victor Charles at your service, just as promised," Wild Bill tossed the AK-47 to Sixpack.

The man's nose was bleeding, and his upper lip and right eye were also red and beginning to swell, yet he exhibited a look of defiance that under different circumstances might have been intimidating.

"Nung, ask him what unit he's from," Sixpack ordered. Nung started jabbering at the man in rapid- fire Vietnamese but did not seem to be getting anywhere.

"He is very stubborn. No want talk."

Without warning, Nung punched the prisoner in the side of his head. He staggered and fell to his back; Nung then jumped onto the man, straddling his chest. He yelled viciously at the VC and got in three more punches before Sixpack and John pulled him from the prisoner.

His lip and a gash over his eye were both bleeding now along with his nose. He looked up to Sixpack, said a few words in Vietnamese, and started to cry. Nung pulled out his towel, wiped at the blood on the man's face, then pulled him to his feet.

"He say he ready to talk."

"Good. Ask him again what unit he's from."

"He say 274 VC Regiment."

"Where is he going?"

"He say he moving back to area where many men wait to fight. He want make sure that he watch us because we go same way."

Handing Nung his map, Sixpack said, "Have him point out on the map where this staging area is."

Nung unfolded the map, pointing out their current position to the prisoner. They mumbled back and forth, as Nung touched different spots on the map.

"Is here," Nung, pointed out the location.

"Ask him how many men are there."

"He say he not know. He just say beaucoup men."

"Okay. Frisk him and make sure he's clean." Sixpack turned to his RTO and said, "Get the captain on the horn."

Nung offered the prisoner some water from his canteen as they continued jabbering. Captain Fowler wanted to meet up with First Platoon, and asked Sixpack to move up the trail about five-hundred feet so they could meet halfway. After assuring him that he would not be hurt anymore, the prisoner spilled his guts to Nung.

The captain, his CP and Third Platoon met up at the rendezvous point with Sixpack's men. Many of the men from the Third Platoon were Cherries and crowded around for a look at the live prisoner. Sixpack's men had to step in to keep them all at a safe distance.

"What happened to his face? It looks like he took a beating." Captain Fowler asked when seeing the prisoner for the first time.

"The men had to run him down and when they tackled him, his face fell against a big rock."

"These rocks have five fingers attached?"

"No, sir, it was just a simple round, big, gray rock."

The captain noticed Nung's bloody knuckles. "Did you fall against the same rock, Nung?"

"Yes, Dai Uy (Vietnamese for captain), both VC and Nung hit beaucoup rock same same time."

"Very well, you better go and have that looked at."

"Yes, Dai Uy!" Nung bowed and left the officer, walking along the column of men to find Doc.

Upon hearing what the young VC soldier had divulged to the men, the captain excitedly relayed the information to the Battalion Commander, who immediately dispatched a team from Cu Chi to retrieve the prisoner.

Meanwhile, the artillery liaison in the CP passed on the coordinates of the suspected camp and prepared Firebase Kien for an artillery fire mission.

Captain Fowler asked Sixpack to take the First Platoon and head for that area to sniff around and see what they could find. The Third Platoon would follow on their heels as soon as the prisoner was on his way to the rear.

It was almost four clicks to the suspected enemy camp and the trail they had been following would get them to within two-hundred meters of their target. Captain Fowler suggested they follow it and estimated that they could reach their objective in just over an hour.

As the First Platoon prepared to leave, they heard the sound of artillery rounds landing in the distance as the bombardment began.

Delta Company was patrolling in an area just north of the suspected enemy staging area, and had volunteered to assist as needed. They agreed to block the northern escape route and maneuvered their people quickly to setup on line. Delta Company was in place within twenty minutes; the blocking line of men was just five-hundred meters away from where the artillery shells were exploding.

First Platoon had made good time toward their objective; artillery rounds continued whistling overhead and erupting in ground-shaking explosions. The noise was louder and more bone-jarring the closer they got. When reaching the spot where the platoon had to step off the trail for the final leg of the journey, Sixpack informed the captain, who called an end to the fire mission. The short wait allowed the men an opportunity to catch their breath before entering the jungle.

Suddenly, they heard gunfire to the north - predominately M-16's with an occasional pop of an AK-47, mimicking a mad minute, and then stopping.

Sixpack was not going to move his men until he knew exactly what happened during that last confrontation. They sat tight, keeping their eyes open for any movement heading their way.

Captain Fowler called to inform Sixpack that the artillery had flushed a group of VC from the area and straight into the gun sights of Delta Company. They were running full tilt and were taken by surprise by the ambush; many died immediately. Some of the VC returned a few rounds before falling themselves, yet others fled to the west. Delta just started their sweep of the area and counted twelve bodies so far.

First Platoon was in a precarious position, as the prisoner's information had proven to be somewhat correct. It was no longer simply a mission to check out a rumor. Now, with the probability of finding enemy soldiers in the complex, the men had to rethink their approach and do so at a high level of alert. Third Platoon was still some thirty minutes away; First could not wait that long to begin the sweep.

Sixpack split the platoon into two columns, twenty feet apart, and sent four flankers to the sides. The men sweated profusely as they inched forward, expecting the enemy to open fire on them at any second. They were uncertain if any of those staying behind even survived the shelling; the grunts were pessimistic and prepared for a worst-case scenario.

John was on point, leading the left column. Scout, Frenchie, Nung, Wild Bill, BJ and his assistant gunner, Doc, Sixpack, and the radio operator were following close behind. Half of the Second Squad fell in behind them, those remaining moved out as flankers to the left of the column. A mirror-image formation, comprised of the remaining two squads, kept pace with John's column, twenty feet to their right.

The men waited patiently for the gunships to arrive before entering the complex. Artillery stood by to support when called upon. Delta Company also remained in a position to reinforce the sweeping platoon if needed. John was the first to step out of the jungle and into the staging area. The captured VC soldier had not lied; the complex was definitely there. He passed the first of many destroyed bunkers and used hand signals to those behind him, pointing to bunkers that needed checking. Some were still intact; the logs, dirt, and leaf-covered roofs rose up and were only two feet above the ground. Some of the passing grunts tossed in grenades, which exploded seconds after shouting out a warning: "Fire in the hole!" After each explosion, three soldiers shot rounds into the bunkers and then crept down the earthen steps and through the narrow entrances, expecting bodies inside.

They counted eleven bunkers in total, and because of the camp's overall size, it was highly unlikely that this was a staging area for 'beaucoup men'. Well-camouflaged from above, it encompassed an area no more than one acre.

Traces of blood were evident throughout the area; some blood trails led away from the camp and to the west. As usual, they were not able to find one dead body in or near the staging area. They did find food supplies, but no weapons, papers, or anything else of value.

The platoon, using bricks of C-4 plastic explosive, destroyed the three remaining intact bunkers. Their sweep continued for another one-hundred meters beyond the bunker complex. Blood traces had ended, there were no signs of shallow graves, and nothing stood out in the green jungle vegetation.

Satisfied with the thoroughness of the sweep, Sixpack informed the captain of their accomplished mission - they were moving now to link up with Third Platoon on the main trail. The officer, in turn, informed Delta Company that First Platoon had completed its mission, thanking them for their help and wishing them well.

Captain Fowler received orders from battalion to move his company into the area west of the complex, to look for signs of the fleeing enemy soldiers.

They spent three days patrolling through the area - the search grid extended four kilometers beyond the complex. It was an exhausting and futile attempt to seek out an invisible and silent enemy.

Late in the afternoon of the fourth day, First Platoon changed direction and began humping toward the former bunker complex. The captain wanted the area booby trapped in the event of VC returning and rebuilding the camp. The plan was for the First Platoon to spend the night nearby, setting ambush teams on the approaches, then dispatching a squad first thing in the morning to set up a few mechanical ambushes within the complex. The task was not expected to take more than an hour; afterwards, the platoon would leave the area, and join up with the rest of the company later in the day.

In the morning, Third Squad left the NDP right after breakfast, heading toward the former enemy complex with enough supplies to build four booby traps; the rest of the platoon stayed put until their return. Many of the men accepted this potential hour-long pause as an opportunity to write letters, the first such chance in a week. It was very quiet and an appropriate setting to do so.

John was addressing an envelope to his girlfriend when the sound of gunfire, coming from the direction of the base camp, shattered the serenity. Without hesitation, the remaining members of the platoon snatched up web gear, ammunition, and weapons, then moved quickly in support of the eight soldiers fighting in the base camp.

Moments earlier, the Third Squad had entered the complex, moving almost to the center, before the point man noticed some of the bunkers already in a state of repair. He raised his arm, everyone taking a knee, before making them aware of his discovery. While scanning the area, another member noticed a small campfire not far away, a pot of boiling water and smoking food hanging above the flame.

"Guys, we're not alone here and need to get the fuck out quickly," the squad leader whispered to the others, pointing out the campfire.

Slowly, they began backing up across the complex, hoping the enemy did not spot them during their retreat. Their luck ran out when an enemy soldier exited a bunker near the campfire; surprise was exhibited by everyone. There was a slight hesitation on both sides, but the VC soldier was first to holler out a warning and then fired a burst from his AK-47 at them. Within seconds, other VC joined him, firing from different areas within the complex. All at once, as if receiving an identical mental suggestion, the eight Americans dove into the nearest bunker and returned fire on their attackers.

The reinforcements arrived within minutes, finding Third Squad pinned down between them and the enemy. Firing from this vantage point would be too much of a risk to the squad inside the bunker. The back-up support remained unnoticed, the enemy focusing on the single bunker with the Americans inside. Sixpack dispatched two squads through the surrounding underbrush in an attempt to flank the enemy soldiers and stop the siege. The men were almost in place when the VC caught sight of their movement and opened up on them as well.

Charlie was firing from four bunkers on the northern side of the complex. The trapped American soldiers, now aware of reinforcements arriving, began screaming hysterically from inside the bunker to let them know their location.

Gunships had responded to Sixpack's call for support, but he learned they could not help because of the squad's close proximity to the enemy. It seemed the only option available was to rescue the pinned down squad and then move to a safe distance, allowing the gunships to use their mini guns and rockets.

In between volleys, Sixpack communicated with the besieged men and coordinated a plan for getting them out. Two of the men in the bunker had wounds, but they were not serious and the soldiers could walk with some assistance.

The three machine gun teams spread out and found defendable positions, despite the intense incoming fire. On Sixpack's signal, they opened fire, concentrating on the closest enemy bunkers. The platoon also fired their two remaining LAW's, blowing large holes into two of the shelters, but failed to silence the guns inside. Now, the grunts fired through the large holes and into the small firing slots, hoping for a lucky shot or ricochet to silence them.

The Americans had been firing steadily for over two minutes, yet there was no movement from the Third Squad. They had ignored the signal to exit the bunker and join up with them.

"Don't those fuckers know they're supposed to be coming out during this cover fire? What the fuck's their problem?" Wild Bill called loudly to John, who had already fired four magazines himself during the last few minutes.

"Goddammit, guys, we can't keep this up forever!" He called out. "Un-ass that bunker, come on!"

Still there was no movement from the trapped men. The level of firing continued in hopes they would try to rush to safety. Suddenly, Wild Bill rose from behind his tree and ran, zigzagging toward the bunker, diving headfirst through the opening.

Firing intensified as some of the men switched to full automatic and increased the rate of fire toward their aggressors. Seconds later, one by one, seven men emerged from the bunker, running wildly out of the complex and into the concealment of the jungle. Wild Bill then stepped out of the bunker with a man across his shoulders like a fire fighter; he was firing at the enemy with one hand, while racing across the thirty feet of open ground. The men watching this rescue were in awe of his bravery and focused on keeping the enemy's head down until Wild Bill reached safety. Once clear, Sixpack tossed a red smoke grenade as close to the four bunkers as possible, then withdrew with the rest of his men to the main trail.

The gunships had an all clear and began their runs on the bunker complex using the red smoke as a beacon. As the rockets and mini-guns fired, the platoon members retreated to their NDP, where Sixpack requested a Medevac for the two wounded soldiers, and a resupply of ammo.

Captain Fowler already had the rest of the company moving to reinforce and support the First Platoon; his estimated time of arrival was in a little more than an hour.

When the gunships exhausted their ammo and fuel, artillery took over in the interim, pounding at the complex until the gunships returned with a fresh load of ordinance to expend.

The assault on the base camp continued for an hour, the gunships and artillery alternating their fire. Nung was the first to spot the rest of Alpha Company and CP jogging on the trail toward their NDP. Once together, the men took a knee, catching their breath while the officers formulated a plan. Twenty minutes later, they were in position and preparing to sweep through the camp once again.

Prior to entering the complex, one platoon fired their weapons into the general direction of the bunkers for thirty seconds. There was no return fire and the men moved cautiously toward their objective. The First Platoon, especially those in the Third Squad, was hoping the VC had vacated the complex as before; one narrow escape already was enough for the day.

Once inside the camp perimeter, the men found it extremely cramped, forcing the troops to bunch up. The Platoon Leaders immediately dispatched half of their men into the surrounding jungle, securing the perimeter, while the rest of the men searched through the complex.

The damage was much more intense than the first time. Once again, they found no resistance, but the results were much different. This time, they counted sixteen bodies - most found in the destroyed bunkers and four discovered outside of the perimeter, killed during their attempt to flee. The four killed outside of the perimeter wore NVA uniforms, and the remaining corpses sported typical VC black pajamas and Ho Chi Minh sandals; an AK-47 rifle lay within an arm's reach of each body.

The only American casualties were the two men from Third Squad. The battle was a surprise to both sides, but for a change, the men of Alpha Company were victorious and satisfied–at least for the moment.

# CHAPTER SEVENTEEN

By mid-February, major changes within First Squad had taken place. Most prominently, Frenchie, Wild Bill, and Scout finished their tours and went home in one piece.

Their last night in the bush together turned out to be a pleasant experience. Wild Bill managed to get his hands on some LRRP meals - lightweight, dehydrated meals primarily used by the long-range recon patrols. The dry and powdery food mixture came in vacuum-packed aluminum foil pouches. After tearing off the perforated top, simply adding hot water and stirring the mixture created a unique and tasty meal. He had enough packs for the whole First Squad, thus providing them with an entirely new eating experience in the bush. Every meal included beef with rice, noodles, or cubed potatoes, in a rich, creamy sauce. John and the others especially enjoyed the spaghetti and meatball dinner. The ration packs also included a chocolate bar with a slight cookie-like texture. It, too, was a special treat and very much appreciated. The men saved cans of pound cake and fruit cocktail for the celebration dinner. It turned out to be one hell of a party considering the circumstances.

After dinner, the men proposed toasts of hot chocolate to celebrate their friendship and to a successful future. They exchanged addresses, promising to keep in touch and possibly visit one another back in the world at some future date.

In the morning, as the three of them readied themselves for their final chopper ride out of the jungle, the men all hugged and some shed tears. Although promising to keep in touch, unfortunately, this would be the last time any of them heard or saw one another again.

Doc was supposed to leave two weeks earlier than the trio did, but he extended his tour for six more months so he could get an early discharge from the Army. After what he had experienced in Vietnam so far, he did not want to serve his remaining year of military obligation at some stateside post. Although this choice placed him in a more dangerous position, Doc no longer had the temperament or patience to spit shine boots and take orders from officers fresh out of ROTC. Most had never been to Vietnam and he did not want to have to listen to them preach about how to fight a war. His goal was to continue in medicine, and he wanted to achieve that goal at his own pace as a civilian.

Wild Bill received the Bronze Star with a "V" device for Valor for his action during the ambush at the enemy base camp. His snap decision to rescue the Third Squad from that bunker had potentially saved many lives. He later said that he did it so they could all get the hell out of there. He insisted that he did not intend for his actions to be heroic; he was merely "impatient".

Sixpack, Doc, and John were the "old timers" now, with BJ not far behind. Cherries would be looking to them for guidance and direction. In the last week alone, the platoon had received four replacements, one being a lieutenant. Sergeant Holmes spent most of his spare time with the new L-T and the other three men went to the First Squad.

Lieutenant Alphonso Rodriguez was not a Cherry, having spent five months in county with another Army unit. He transferred to the Wolfhounds from the First Cavalry; the division was pulling out of Vietnam per Nixon's early withdrawal program to end the war. The L-T preferred to be called Rod unless in the company of other officers. He was bitter about not going home with the men in his unit, but everyone with less than seven months in country - regardless of rank - remained in Vietnam and transferred to other units.

Jim Mitchum hailed from Dallas, Texas. A big, robust fellow with sandy blond hair, he was a perfect fit for the machine gun team, and the squad promptly nicknamed him Tex.

Cherries – A Vietnam War Novel

Danny Jigelewski hailed from Atlantic City, New Jersey; the others quickly dubbed him 'Ski'. He was a former gang member and tried to look tough in front of everyone. Ski told them – in his heavy New Jersey accent - that prior to coming to the Army, it was common for him and his gang to be involved in street fights at least once a week. Back then, he said, it was always about protecting your turf - similar to what the Americans were doing in Vietnam. He was ready to start all over again with this group, his "new gang." John and Doc looked at one other and rolled their eyes. "Let's see how he does under fire," John whispered.

"Yeah, I bet he just can't wait."

Malcolm Dupree was a black man from Jackson, Mississippi; his wrists and neck were already adorned with several shoelace braids and crosses. The first person he approached was Doc. Although he was also black, Doc did not share in any of the extreme so-called "black power" attitudes or rituals. Others with the same skin color would have certainly labeled him an "Uncle Tom." When Malcolm approached him for some dap, he was surprised when Doc simply offered his hand for a traditional handshake. Taken aback and unsure of his next move, he reached out and clasped Doc's hand anyway, shaking it warmly. Back in the rear, Top had already outfitted him with an M-79 and ammo vest.

The First Squad was complete again, but now mostly comprised of Cherries. It was not the best of all worlds, but at least the extra bodies would help share in the daily tasks.

On their first four patrols, there was no contact with the enemy. The new Cherries were trying hard to learn the ropes, their confidence growing with each patrol.

After the next resupply, the L-T and Sixpack approached John with a piece of paper. He suspected something was up and sat upright in his hammock.

"Congratulations, Polack! You are now a Specialist Fourth Class (Spec 4), officially promoted this past Monday. Here are your orders confirming it." Rod handed the official document to John and then offered his hand to shake.

"Jeez, you're gonna be rich now. What are you going to do with all that power and money?" Sixpack cajoled.

John, surprised by this, quickly scanned the document. His highlighted name stood out from the others on the filled page. All the names listed were Wolfhounds; he would have to take a closer look at the other fifty names later.

He looked at the men, "Thanks, guys! This really is a surprise. I sure can use the extra money every month, and don't worry, I won't let the power go to my head and start abusing the Cherries."

They laughed, happy for the recognition shown to their fellow Wolfhound.

For two weeks, First Platoon patrolled through the Boi Loi Woods. The area once had a reputation of being as treacherous and notorious as the Iron Triangle, but nothing had happened of late to justify its reputation. The men returned to their ritual of never-ending patrols over the same terrain, repeatedly.

Ski was John's new slack man whenever walking point. John had this job for over four months and felt comfortable in the position; he was also good at his job. During that time, he had personally uncovered several booby traps, thus saving many from getting hurt. His new slack man had taken to the role in earnest and assured John that he would always have his back.

The two men were leading the First Squad down a well-used trail when John suddenly raised his fist in the air to stop the file. He squatted, examining fresh Ho Chi Minh sandal prints crossing the trail. Nung and Sixpack came forward to join John in the evaluation of the footprints in the mud.

Nung was the first to voice his opinion, "Only one VC cross trail no more than maybe one hour before."

"I agree. What do you think, Polack, want to track him?"

"Yeah. It looks like the path he made through the jungle will be easy enough to follow."

John led the way, looking for broken twigs and leaves that may have fallen to the ground when the VC had passed earlier. A few steps close behind, Ski watched for signs of movement to John's front and to their sides. The extra set of eyes was a big help as John primarily focused on the ground. Occasionally, he came upon another fresh set of footprints on the soft ground. However, the further they traveled, the wider the spacing of the footprints became, hinting that the VC was starting to run.

John signaled for another stop and then waited for Sixpack.

"He's running now, and probably knows we're on his tail."

"You can never tell, Polack. He may also be setting us up."

"I see a clearing up ahead. Stay here and I'll go up and have a look around."

"Okay, but don't get too far ahead of us. I want you back in no more than five minutes."

"See you in a short." John rose and moved cautiously up the trail toward the clearing. When he reached the edge of it, he noted that a dropped bomb was responsible for creating the small open area. The twenty-foot wide crater, filled to the top with water, sat directly in the center of the clearing; waist-high swaying grass encircled it and extended out for several feet to the jungle's edge. Scanning the area, a sudden and quick movement on the other side of the pond caught his eye, surprising him. The rustling was roughly at the eleven o'clock position from where he stood. John's heart skipped a beat and he froze in place, his eyes locked onto that specific area. Just then, a young VC soldier stood up with a canteen held to his lips. He took a long drink of water, not realizing somebody was watching him.

John hesitated for a second, and then switched his rifle to full automatic, firing, even before bringing the stock up to his shoulder. The kid heard the loud click made by the weapon's selector switch and dropped quickly into the high grass and out of sight, before John was even able to fire. John fired several short bursts into the area where he last saw the man. Changing magazines, he increased the arc, extending his bursts to cover as much of the area on the other side of the crater as possible. The rest of the squad quickly formed at his side, weapons ready, facing the clearing.

"What's up?"

"I had a VC in my sights on the other side of that bomb crater, but he dropped into the grass before I could get a clean shot off. Now I don't have a clue where he may be and don't know if I hit him or not."

The squad split in two, circling around the bomb crater from both sides, cautiously approaching the spot where their point man saw the VC soldier. John was the first to find the VC's canteen lying on the ground and noted that a bullet traveled through the plastic vessel. Water was still seeping from the opening and quickly soaking into the earth.

"You may have hit him. Maybe he fell into the water."

"I didn't hear a splash, Malcolm."

Ski called out from ten feet beyond, "I found some blood on the trail here, leading deeper into the jungle."

Fresh blood droplets were visible on leaves at the entrance of the four-foot wide pathway.

"Let's see if we can find him!" Sixpack motioned up the trail with his rifle to the men standing around.

John resumed his position at point, continuing to follow the fresh blood spots along the trail. After a hundred feet or so, the splotches thinned out and then finally ended forty feet later. The men searched the immediate area for the enemy soldier, who might have either left the trail or fallen dead beside it.

Satisfied he was nowhere around, the squad backtracked along the trail, looking for signs that may have been missed earlier, possibly showing where their elusive quarry may have left the trail.

John discovered a couple of bloody leaves on the ground next to a small pathway leading away from the trail. He hadn't noticed it earlier as he was focused on the thin trail of blood on the ground. This was the evidence they were looking for; John called Sixpack forward.

"Check this out. It looks like he backtracked and ducked up this trail."

"Okay, let's take it slow."

John started up the small pathway but did not see any more blood after the first dozen steps. He continued forward, his eyes intently searching the ground for any telltale sign, Ski following only one step behind. Suddenly, John felt the pull of fishing line across his chest and heard a pinging sound.

"Booby trap!" John yelled. Turning quickly, he gave a surprised Ski a hard shove backwards. Losing his balance after a couple of steps, Ski fell to the ground. John instinctively covered his head with his arms and dove into the foliage, away from the "ping" sound, almost landing on top of Ski. The rest of the squad members immediately sought cover after hearing John's warning. An explosion filled the air.

John felt a burning sensation in his right arm even before hearing the explosion or hitting the ground. Turning onto his back, he noted that he was bleeding in several spots, the pain searing like somebody was holding lit cigarettes against his skin.

"Doc, I'm hit!" he called out from his prone position.

Seven other men rose from the ground and tried to assess what might have just happened. Sixpack, BJ, and Tex looked through the area and then provided security while Doc checked on his new patient. The medic made a quick diagnosis and started working on the wounds.

"It ain't bad, Polack. Shit, you'll be back with us before you know it."

Ski stood next to Doc, looking down at John, his face showing concern. The gang member then took a knee next to Doc and held out his hand to John. "Hey, man, I owe you one. When you pushed me out of the way, you saved my life."

Doc looked over to Ski. "The Polack did that?"

"Yeah, he shoved me backwards and yelled 'booby trap' before it went off. I was caught off guard and fell right on my ass."

"Are you hit?"

"I don't think so. Do you see anything?" Ski stood and turned in a complete circle.

"Nope, don't see a thing."

Ski bent over and grabbed John's good hand, shaking it reverently. "I'm serious, man. Thank you so much."

"I don't even remember doing that. It must have been instinct. I'm glad you're not hurt."

Sixpack exited the area where the booby trap had exploded. "Man, that's twice you lucked out. Your elusive friend planted a grenade with a trip wire in a tree."

"What do you mean "lucked out"? Shit, I'm hit."

"That ain't shit. Fucking scratches is all. A few stitches and your ass will be right back out here with the rest of us."

"It might not look that bad to you, but it sure hurts like hell."

"It looks like he got even with you for shooting him."

"Damn, how far away from the path did he set it - twenty feet?"

"Shit, no. It should have killed you. He laid it in a tree about chest high right next to the trail. I guess he was expecting you to be watching the ground and set the wire up high where you weren't looking. When you pulled on the trip wire and the pin came out, the grenade was supposed to fall out toward you; instead, it dropped behind the tree, which absorbed most of the blast. That's why I said you lucked out again."

"Jeez, thanks."

"What do you think, Doc? Will he live?"

"Oh, hell, yes. There's a lot of blood but it's not bad at all. He caught three pieces of shrapnel in his right arm. The surgeons will dig out the steel and patch him up as good as new. Go ahead and request a dust off, but make it a routine."

Within minutes, Doc had the injured man's arm bandaged and they all returned to the main trail to wait for the Medevac. The soldiers sat to the side smoking cigarettes. Sixpack received word that a chopper was on its way and should arrive shortly to pick up the wounded warrior.

"Well, Polack, you got your first Purple Heart. How does it feel?"

"Fuck the Purple Heart. That was one award I was hoping not to get while here. I'm glad though, that it wasn't worse."

"You'll heal up fine and after you get the stitches out, we'll probably all meet up in Cu Chi and drink some beers together."

"What do you mean, Sixpack?"

"We're about due to pull an R&R soon - maybe even this week!"

"Really?"

"Yeah, if we get there before you, we'll save you a few beers."

"Thanks a lot."

John was on his second Medevac trip to the 93rd Evac in Long Binh. This time the ride was much more pleasant, under the circumstances. He could relax, knowing his condition was not one of life or death.

The burning sensation in his arm stopped after the embedded hot steel cooled off. All that remained was an aching reminder of the injury that throbbed with every heartbeat. He was confident that it would pass once he received a shot of painkiller at the hospital.

When landing at the Evac hospital, the same scenario played out as the last time he arrived. A crew waited, but instead of a gurney, they had a wheelchair ready this time.

After removing the shrapnel, the surgeon closed the wounds with several stitches each. John was resting comfortably in the ward within an hour of his arrival.

In the morning, the same surgeon cleared John and released him from the hospital. Now familiar with the area, he walked across the road to the 90th Replacement Center, wondering if a repeat performance would take place with the Cherries on the ride to Cu Chi. This time he played his experience down, however, saving the newbies from a nightmare that night. He didn't feel the need to mention his Purple Heart to them. He laid back, relaxing, and quickly fell asleep, leaving the Cherries filled with curiosity.

Upon his return to the division base camp, the battalion aid station changed John's bandages every morning, keeping his wounds clean, adding antibiotics to prevent infection.

Alpha Company flew in to Cu Chi on John's fourth day at the base camp. The men were talking excitedly about their upcoming in-country R&R at a place called Vung Tau, a town located on the shores of the South China Sea, not too far from Saigon. There, the grunts could forget their fears for two whole days. John was released and able to join the company on the short vacation. The medics instructed him to keep the wounds dry, giving him a small satchel of ointment and bandages to take along on the R&R.

After arriving in Vung Tau, the men quickly claimed their bunks in the R&R barracks, donned bathing suits, and then rushed out to go swimming in the South China Sea. Every person wore identical trunks and carried a fresh green towel. It was surreal to see over 150 soldiers in yellow bathing suits, rushing all at once toward the sea, frolicking through the sand like groups of kids. They kicked sand at one-another, tackled best friends, and then dunked one another in between the massive rolling waves. John sat in the warm sun, watching all of the fun, and suddenly wished his girlfriend were there to see it all. An intense wave of homesickness filled him once again, as he thought back to all of the summer afternoons they shared at the beach on Belle Isle in Detroit. He thought, too, how much his ol' buddy Bill Sayers would have loved swimming in the South China Sea.

John was one of the last to venture out onto the sand and did not plan to join in the roughhousing with the others. Instead, he sat on the sand just a few feet from the crashing surf. After a short period, he entered the sea and tried with great difficulty to walk along the shoreline in shallow water no deeper than his knees. He found the water refreshing, squatting down to a height where the waves washed over him, remaining protective of his arm and raising it high enough to keep it dry. The salty taste of the sea spray surprised John. As a Michigander, many fresh water lakes surrounded him, but he had never been in an ocean before. The taste reminded him of those times when he had a sore throat and his mother forced him to gargle with warm salt water.

John wandered along the shoreline and unexpectedly experienced a sensation that he never had before. Even though he was in shallow water, he felt a force pulling his feet away from the beach as the waves returned to the sea. He dug his heels into the sand, hoping to stop his skid into deeper water. It proved to be a futile attempt. His feet continued forming shallow trenches along the soft, sandy bottom, the current pulling him away from shore, becoming stronger with each step. John had always been a strong swimmer, participating on swim teams during his youth, but he was not sure if just letting go was the right thing to do at this moment. He started to panic and called out for help.

Two nearby soldiers were just passing when they heard him call out.

"Hey, man, what's up?" One of them shouted over the sound of the pounding surf.

"There's an undertow or something here in the water and it's pulling me away from the beach! I can't make it stop or get away!"

"Relax, man, you're caught in a riptide. You have to walk out of it."

"I've been trying to do that!"

"Don't try to walk to the beach, man. Stay in the water and walk along the shoreline until you don't feel the pull anymore."

John turned and moved nervously in the direction he'd come earlier. The two soldiers on the beach were only about fifteen feet away, remaining on the sand and watching his progress. It took all of his physical strength, but after completing twenty of the hardest steps he ever took through water, he found the pull suddenly gone and his panic subsided. He turned and quickly exited the sea without any effort.

"Thanks guys, I thought I was a goner!"

Both soldiers were familiar with riptides. "You did luck out, because some riptides will pull a person out to sea a mile from shore. We'll notify the folks monitoring the beach so they post warning signs for everybody else. Are you okay?"

"Yeah, I'm fine now. Thanks again!" John walked over to his towel and dropped onto it. Exhausted, his legs were cramping from his muscular tug of war with the sea.

Massaging his legs and working out the cramps, he continued watching the others out in the water. The waves were higher than he had ever seen in his life and many of the men bodysurfed to the shoreline. Thrilled, they jumped back into the water and swam out to catch the next big wave.

Groups of young soldiers, with friends riding upon their shoulders, were battling each other in a show of strength and balance in the waist deep water. Those knocked over, moved to the side, and continued watching the action until the last pair of men remained standing. It was good to see the guys lose themselves in the friendly competition. Roughhousing like any teenagers on a summer weekend, the war seemed a million miles away.

During the next two days, the men occupied themselves with floorshows, drinking, and whoring around; cash paid for the latter. Prior to leaving Cu Chi, the Alpha Company grunts had to sit through classes about preventative measures to take before having sex with the town hookers - many had venereal diseases, which ran rampant throughout the area. Officers also told them stories about a certain strain of VD called the Black Clap. There was no protection from it; even condoms were not effective, and there was no cure. It was said that if GI's caught this strain, the government relocated them to some god-forsaken island out in the ocean, where nobody would ever hear from them again. That was enough to convince many in the group to abstain from such activities in fear of catching the dreaded disease.

The air-conditioned barracks alone were worth the trip to Vung Tau. If a person didn't want to go outside, he could opt to stay in the barracks, enjoying the coolness during the day. At night, however, the ocean breeze cooled the town, making it very comfortable for the nightly movies on the beach, the outdoor floor shows, or just sitting and relaxing at a sidewalk bar or restaurant.

It was a wonderful time, but just like any vacation, it was over much too fast. The men departed Vung Tau by truck in the early afternoon, arriving in Cu Chi just in time for dinner. The following morning, it was business as usual, preparing for new missions.

Rod approached John that evening. "You know, Polack, maybe you should consider giving up the point for a while. I need a good RTO to handle the radio. How would you like to try carrying it for a while?"

He stood there and considered the offer for a brief moment before consenting. Carrying the radio would be more work at night, but in return, he would not have to pull night guard or go out on patrols unless the L-T was going. It was a no-brainer.

"Okay, I'll give it a try."

"Good. First, you need a clearance from the medics. Let them check you out and if they say you can return to the bush, then stop by and see Top. He'll brief you on your new job and give you all the charts, pencils, and supplies you'll need. You'll be my personal RTO, which means that in the field you go where I go. Does that bother you?"

"Hell, no! It'll be something different for me, and I'm sure it'll be a little more exciting. At least I'll have an idea of what's happening out in the bush instead of guessing about it all the time."

"That's true. Thanks for taking it on. I'll see you in the morning."

Battalion medics did not see any problems with John's arm. The stitches had dissolved and the wounds were healing nicely. They gave him a clean bill of health and a note lifting the restriction to give to Top.

After meeting with the First Sergeant and receiving the new supplies, he found it necessary to rearrange his rucksack and pack things differently. The radio came with a dedicated, quick release aluminum frame, which now required that he secure his rucksack over the back of the radio. If he had to move quickly or go out on light patrols, the rucksack could be detached in a snap. The added weight of the radio and two spare batteries increased his load by twenty-six pounds, but that wasn't much different from the M60 machine gun.

Excited with the new toy, John sat on his cot reading over the material while everyone else was busy socking down that last beer. He was afraid of becoming a burden in the bush and wanted to be certain of doing everything correctly. He experimented with the code indicator, making up coordinates, coding them, and then double-checking for errors before repeating the process again.

He turned on the radio and switched to the different frequencies in the area; he listed all of them on a notepad. He tuned in on the gunship frequency, Medevac frequency, and then to the various company frequencies, listening for a few minutes on each channel. The chatter was routine, nothing of interest going on.

Content that he would do well, he set everything to the side and waited for morning to arrive.

## CHAPTER EIGHTEEN

Humping with the radio was much more difficult than John had expected; the extra twenty-six pounds felt more like a hundred. The backpack hung heavily from his shoulders; the thinner straps dug deeper into muscle with every step, cutting off the flow of blood, and numbing both arms. Only an occasional tingle reminded him that his arms were even still there. The extra padding of the towel around his neck did nothing to help cushion the weight.

Originally, John didn't think that carrying the radio would be a big deal because the M-60 machine gun weighed more. However, when carrying the gun, he was able to switch over to his other shoulder whenever one started hurting. The radio, on the other hand, sat right in the middle of his back, with the combined weight evenly distributed over both shoulders. He occasionally bounced the backpack upwards, grabbing onto the straps - pulling them forward, shifting it to a slightly different position, allowing a brief reprieve to his aching arms and shoulders.

When out in the bush, the RTO needed to monitor his company frequency at all times, whether on the move or bushed for the night. At the start of the hump, John held the handset against his ear constantly, but this method did not last long. The constant rubbing, his numbing arms, and the hissing static of the radio made it an almost impossible task. This method was also dangerous as it prevented him from hearing sounds and noises around him, thereby, making him extremely nervous. During a break, one of the other RTO's suggested that John remove his grenades from the rings on the shoulder harness and, instead, attach the handset there. After turning up the squelch and eliminating the white noise and static,

John was able to hear both the conversations on the radio and the sounds of the jungle around him, much to his relief.

Every RTO carried two different styles of antennae when out in the field. A small, flexible, thin whip antenna, three feet long, would bend and give when moving through the heavy bush - this was much preferred and used most of the time. Sometimes, when signals were strong due to the close proximity of the units, the radio operators folded the whip antenna over and tucked the end into a loop on the utility straps. Every RTO preferred this method when on the move, especially in high grass or short underbrush; everyone was otherwise concealed, but the radio antenna stuck upward like a submarine's periscope. The opportunity elated enemy snipers when seeing a bouncing antenna moving across a field; once in the crosshairs, he only needed to drop about three feet and fire off a few rounds. Many RTO's lost their lives this way, falling dead before even hearing the shots. Unfortunately, Alpha Company's units seldom operated close to one another, usually spreading across the entire AO, thus, making it necessary for the operators to extend their antenna fully to hear one another. During times like that, many RTO's were extremely jumpy.

The other antenna, an extendable version, enabled long distance communication, and was used at night or when staying in a location for an extended period. It consisted of ten, two-foot sections of thin walled, three-eighths steel tubing; stretchable twine inside of the hollow tubes held the pieces together, providing a level of tension similar to that of a stretched rubber band. One end of each tube was oil-canned, telescoping over the other end of the following tube, like male and female connectors. An RTO held the base in his hand and let the tubes fall to the ground. With a little shaking and coaxing, the twenty-foot antenna assembled itself, the operator threading it through the overhead foliage before securing it to the radio.

The most hectic part of an RTO's day was when the units stopped and began setting up their NDP for the night. After designating a central guard position, radio operators followed a set protocol, completing all the steps, before preparing their own sleeping areas or dinner. They disconnected rucksacks – leaving them in their potential sleep area, then relocated the radio to the watch area and swapped out the antennae. By that time, the L-T had their coordinates available, which needed to be encrypted and forwarded to the Company CP. His final task of the day was to record the locations of the other platoons and ambush squads, and plot their locations on a map with a grease pencil. Afterwards, they could set up a sleep area and cook dinner. If the NDP was in a wooded section, then having a hammock usually cut their set-up time in half. When the RTO finished with his radio duties, most of the other soldiers had already constructed their sleeping positions and finished eating dinner. Someone always volunteered to step in and monitor the radio while the operators readied themselves for the night.

The Platoon CP, consisting only of John and the L-T, were not part of a specific squad. Instead, they rotated every three days and attached themselves to a different squad after the resupply. Although his time in the evening was limited, John tried to join in on the nightly BS sessions. On those occasions when the CP attached to the First Squad, however, he made it a point to catch up on lost time with his closest friends.

The first two weeks of March had passed slowly, and the company moved around very little. The higher brass designated Alpha Company as the battalion reactionary force, keeping them on standby and within fifteen minutes of the nearest landing zone. If one of their sister companies ran into trouble, choppers airlifted the men to the hot spot, where they provided whatever support was necessary.

During those two weeks, Rod and John spent the time getting to know one another better. John really enjoyed the opportunity to get to know guys who lived across the country from his Michigan home.

"What did you do before joining the service, Rod?"

"Actually, my civilian days ended a week after graduating from high school in Hollywood, California."

"Wow, Hollywood? Did you get to see all the movie stars and stuff?"

"You'd see some of them walking down the street occasionally, in certain restaurants, or driving by in their expensive cars and limos. I only met one star face-to-face. I took my prom date to the Brown

Derby Restaurant. John Wayne was sitting at the next table and I had an opportunity to introduce myself and shake his hand. He even called me 'pilgrim'."

"Wow, that's really cool! Is he as big as they say?"

"Hell, yes. He was like a giant next to me."

"He's my favorite actor. Did you see his Green Beret movie a couple of years ago?

"Yeah, I saw the movie, but I think it was more of a political statement than a war movie."

"How so?"

"Well, back then, people didn't know that much about Vietnam; it seemed like the government endorsed the movie to justify the U.S. sending soldiers here to stop communism. Shit like that happens with the Special Forces groups all the time, but the movie didn't even give a hint on what us grunts are doing here.

"I never looked at it that way, but it does make sense. Let's get back to the movie stars."

"It wasn't that big of a deal, Polack. They're ordinary people, just like us."

"That's because you saw them all the time. I just think it would be so far out to actually meet one."

"Most of them are kind of uppity though, and don't want to be bothered. You can just imagine what it'd be like to have fans constantly interrupting them for autographs and asking to pose for pictures. They have no privacy and gather a crowd wherever they go. I'm sure they just want to be normal like the rest of us."

"Yeah, but sometimes the stars forget that fans are the ones who made them famous. Without them, the stars would just fade away."

"That's true to an extent, but hell, fans even chase after the ones who had short careers."

"What did you do after high school?"

"I went straight to West Point."

"West Point? Wow, that must have been tough."

"It was, especially during the first couple of years. Imagine Basic Training, but twice as difficult and lasting all four years there. My last two years there were the best, though."

"Were the initiations as bad as they say they are?"

"Shit, Polack. We were slaves to the upper classmen, and forced to pull their details. They fucked with us every chance they could. One person ordered us to do something, and then another would order us to do something different. When the first person came back, he chewed our ass out for not doing what he requested; the penalty was demerits and extra details. We were always in a state of confusion and punished for one thing or another.

"Besides having classes all day, my first year was filled with daily physical training, constant military drills, harassment, intimidation, extra drills and details, and homework; needless to say, we got very little sleep in between all that."

"God, it must have been a real bitch."

"That's not the half of it. I also played football, so I had to put up with the bullshit from the senior players too."

"Didn't you get preferential treatment there because of your sports involvement?"

"Are you kidding? If a cadet couldn't maintain a B average in his studies, then he couldn't participate in the sports programs. West Point wanted to produce the best in everything. If you didn't measure up to their high standards, you got booted out."

"I don't think I could have taken all that shit."

"I don't know how I managed either. But, looking back, it was well worth it. I've had it pretty easy since receiving my commission, and things will only get better when I get back to the states after Nam. With my combat duty and West Point background, I should make full bird by the time I retire."

"So you're gonna stay in the Army?"

"I'd be a fool not to."

"How long do you think you'll be staying out here in the bush?"

"I really don't know. Normally, lieutenants spend six to eight months in a front line unit then get withdrawn to some rear job. Next week, I'll have my six months in. You know, there's a strong rumor circulating about the 25th Division pulling out of the Nam in a month and returning to Hawaii. So I don't know what'll really happen."

"No shit? That's the first time I heard that rumor. Why would they go to Hawaii?"

"That's where their stateside home base is."

"Does that mean we'll all go to Hawaii?"

"I really don't know. First, we need to find out what the criteria is going to be. In the Cav, everyone with seven months in country could leave with the Division. The rest, like me, were reassigned to other units."

"Cool! That means I'll be able to leave with them!"

"Now, just hold on a minute, Polack. I don't even know if it's going to happen, let alone how it'll play out. I just mentioned it because you may have heard the rumor. Just don't go getting your hopes up."

"How can I not? Only having to stay here for one more month would be like a dream come true."

"I wouldn't think about it that way if I were you - just plan on spending a full year here. The military doesn't usually repeat itself and is very creative in making some of their decisions. If the criterion is different than that of the First Cav and you end up not going to Hawaii as you expected, you might go off the deep end, get sloppy, and maybe even get yourself killed."

"It's okay to hope though, right?"

"Yeah, Polack, hoping is okay, as long as you aren't disappointed with the results."

Nevertheless, John rolled the thoughts around in his head and was optimistic about the possibility of making the cut.

"Rod, now that you've worked with us for a couple of weeks, how do you compare us with the Cav?"

"There's no comparison, because it's an entirely different story here. You grunts spend an awful lot of time walking over the same terrain chasing the enemy away. The only time you make contact and get a body count is when you stumble into one of their base camps. The First Cav is air mobile, and we would CA (combat assault) into an area, and hunt down gooks that were spotted from the air.

We always had running firefights and hasty ambushes, catching the enemy by surprise with dozens of helicopters at our disposal all the time. Sometimes, we would land, be extracted, and moved somewhere else after four hours. Down here with the Twenty-Fifth, there's just too much walking around and chasing ghosts."

The next few days turned out to be just as Rod had described. Alpha Company humped on endlessly, looking for the invisible enemy. The VC stayed well hidden, avoiding the Americans at all costs. The grunts still suffered casualties requiring Medevacs, but this was limited to heatstroke and heat exhaustion only.

The rumors about the division leaving Nam grew stronger every day, and ranged from ordering a full pullout to a total reassignment.

Beautiful Hawaii was suddenly a general topic of conversations. People had their own visions of the paradise. Some romanticized it - imagining themselves lying peacefully on a beach and listening to the rolling surf of the ocean, others planned sightseeing trips to dramatic waterfalls and volcanoes, or to view tropical birds in flower-laden, fragrant jungles. Humping the boonies was no longer a concern, nor was eating out of cans and sleeping on the ground. Pulling stateside duty in a tropical utopia was a dream in itself. As civilians, many of the men wished to visit Hawaii, but few could afford the high cost of air fare and travel expenses. For most of the men, this was a once in a lifetime opportunity. Excitement ran rampant.

John was beginning to feel guilty about not going out on the small recon patrols. Besides, staying behind and monitoring the radio was boring, and the excitement just was not there anymore.

He pleaded with Rod, asking for permission to go out on daily patrols with First Squad whenever they were traveling together. At first, the L-T was reluctant, but seeing John's continued disappointment, Rod finally approved his request and even monitored the radio in his absence.

The First Squad members were always happy when John joined them on their short patrols; it seemed like old times again. The guys also appreciated his experience in the event that they ran into the enemy while out on patrol. It was a great change of pace but short-lived.

After a week, the official word came down from Division - and most of the rumors had come true. Alpha Company would return to

Cu Chi in eleven days and begin out-processing. The men were ecstatic, as the war was finally ending for them.

# CHAPTER NINETEEN

The battalion lifers still wanted one last battle before leaving the country, so running up a body count became their top priority. Some of the pacifists would say that their strategic game of toy soldiers was quickly ending, so it was an opportunity to make the headlines and go home in style.

As it turned out, each company's final mission was to revisit whichever area had resulted in their highest body counts during the last four months. It was ironic that they did not consider the fact that these companies also lost many men in the same battles.

Alpha Company would revisit the area where they lost Zeke. The majority of the lower-ranking soldiers did not even know they were back in that same area of operations, because all of the terrain they patrolled looked the same. It was also important to note that since that earlier battle, sixty percent of the Alpha Company's grunts were new troops, fresh from the states. None of them knew Zeke or were aware of the earlier fights; half had not been in a firefight yet. The old timers were concerned about the risk factor, especially since Captain Fowler decided that the company would operate in platoon-sized units during that last week and a half.

For the first three days, Rod and John attached themselves to the First Squad. On their first break together, John moved over and sat next to Sixpack; Rod busied himself with a compass and his map.

"I've seen some familiar sights already, Sixpack, and it's bringing back some bad memories I have of this place."

"Yeah, same goes for me. It does worry me, though, that we had to come back to this place anyway, and this time, with so many Cherries. Only you, Doc, and I really know what this AO did to a bunch of good guys."

"I know what you mean. I'm scared shitless. It's unbelievable that with only ten days left in this fucking hellhole, the brass was so concerned about running up the body counts. Have you seen the activity on the trail? There are VC out there! If I was in command, I'd pull everyone out of the field and let them hole-up somewhere where it's safe."

"I've seen the signs too, but I'm just hoping the VC stay out of our way so we don't have to lose anybody else."

"Do you remember, Sarge, this is the same area where Larry and I had our Cherry busted and survived our first firefight? I sure don't want it to be the place where I have my last one. I'd be the happiest motherfucker in the world if I never saw another enemy soldier or had to fire my weapon again."

"You and I both, buddy," his voice trailed off and he stared into the sky, deep in thought.

"Hey Sixpack!"

"What?" He seemed agitated with John's disturbance.

"Do you think the VC knows we're leaving the country?"

"You can bet your sweet ass they do. If they were smart, they'd stay out of our way for the next week and a few days. The ARVN will most likely take over this area after we leave. The VC should get ready for a big shootout with them."

"Ha, that's a joke. You know as well as I do they very seldom go out into the field and they just stay put in their base camps."

"Yeah, I know that too. There's only one thing bothering me about this area - no other friendly forces have been here since we last left; the enemy had plenty of time to rebuild their little camps or even add new ones. I just hope Rod doesn't walk us right into one of them."

"Why don't you go fill the L-T in about this place? Maybe he'll let us skate and just hunker down someplace for a while."

"I doubt it, but I'll talk to him anyway."

"I'm kind of tight with him. You want me to go with you?"

"Naw, it'll be more official if I go alone."

As soon as Sixpack walked away, Doc slid over. "How're you holding up, Polack?"

"Shit, Doc. Look at me; I'm shaking like a leaf." He held his arm out to show a slight tremor in his hand.

"I don't blame you. I didn't extend my tour to come back to this shitty place. There's something evil in the air here. I got a weird feeling that some of us ain't gonna leave this place alive."

"Aw, come on, Doc. Don't start that kind of shit."

"I'm serious. Just look at all those Cherries over there," he pointed to the young soldiers sitting alongside the trail. "They don't have a clue about this place, and I know for a fact that most of them haven't even been in a firefight yet." Doc paused and looked down at the ground. "At least the last time we were here, we had all seasoned vets with us."

"Yeah, and the VC still kicked our asses."

"Exactly. What do you think this bunch is going to do under fire?"

"I sure the fuck hope they don't freeze up or turn tail and run."

"Me neither. I wish the L-T would use his head and keep us sitting tight for a while."

"I mentioned the same thing to Sixpack. He went over to talk to Rod about it. I think that may be a possibility."

"I hope so. Hey, gotta go, I'll catch up with ya' later."

"Okay. Stay cool, Doc."

Sixpack returned a short time later with a grin on his face. "He bought into it. We're moving off the trail right here."

John smiled broadly. "All right, Sixpack - way to go!"

"Take a bow yourself. I wasn't even thinking about speaking up; you planted the seed and I just ran with it."

It was only three in the afternoon, but Rod sent word down the column to pull off the large trail and set up an NDP. Some of the old timers smiled at the change in plans.

Once settled in, four LP teams of two moved out in different directions, two-hundred feet outside the perimeter, watching and listening to the surrounding jungle.

At 1800 hours, John sent their current coordinates to the CP, informing them it was their NDP for the night. The nearest platoon was three clicks away so there was no risk of bumping into them.

There were no other pathways intersecting the larger trail they were following; mechanical ambushes covered the approaches from both directions. Both sides of the trail were dense jungle, requiring the point man to cut a path to their NDP. The men also planned to set up several manually operated claymore mines and trip flares between the NDP and the main trail itself. Overall, the location was quite a find; the soldiers were very satisfied with the outcome.

The following day, First Platoon stayed put, rotating the LP's every two hours. Rod had already informed the captain that patrols were out and the only evidence found so far were signs of usage on the main trail. He was also pleased that they had left mechanical ambushes on the trail. Captain Fowler wished Rod happy hunting and signed off.

The soldiers knew they had a good thing going and maintained strict noise discipline, conducting necessary conversations only in a whisper. They spent idle time cleaning weapons, reading, sleeping, writing letters, or listening to transistor radios with earphones. The quietness was unsettling, however. The enemy knew Americans were in the vicinity, the landing choppers having announced their arrival the day before. Some of the old timers actually believed the enemy knew their whereabouts, but were choosing not to engage them yet.

Most of the troops wrote letters home expressing their excitement about the division pulling out of Vietnam and returning to the states through Hawaii. The soldiers repeated the same information to everyone in their address books; hands were cramping and the men had to take breaks before starting on the next one. Everyone asked those back home to say a few prayers on their behalf.

That evening, John sent the same coordinates to the CP, then learned that the other platoons were continuing their movements throughout the area and staying in new locations for the night. They had all been lucky so far, not one encountering the enemy during the past two days. Perhaps it was true that the VC were really trying to avoid the Americans.

On the morning of the fourth day, First Platoon packed everything up and left their home of the previous three nights, heading back to their original LZ for resupply. Seeing no movement on the trail during this time, Sixpack and the L-T felt it was safe, allowing the men to travel on it during their return to the LZ. Fourth Squad had the point and the single file of men moved slowly, maintaining a distance of ten feet between one another. It was an easy hump, as every rucksack and canteen was almost empty.

First Squad brought up the rear of the column, with Rod and John positioning themselves between the First and Second Squads. When the troops were within a hundred feet of the clearing, they suddenly heard two earsplitting explosions, seconds apart. The ground shook and soldiers instinctively dropped, seeking protective cover. They heard no rifle fire, but did hear cries for help and movement on the trail ahead. Through the settling dust and smoke cloud, they were able to make out soldiers lying on the ground, writhing in pain, some trying to stand or crawl to the side of the trail. The concussions were so loud, they temporarily deafened those closest to the explosions; others further back were dazed by a piercing ringing in their ears.

"Medic! Help! We got people hurt up here!" someone called.

"Come on, Polack," the L-T raced to the front of the column.

Stunned, John got to his feet and rushed to join Rod, with Sixpack and Doc close behind him.

When reaching the front of the column, Doc jumped into action, assessing each man, spending only seconds before moving on to the next one. Doc called to Sixpack and others with instructions on how to stabilize the wounded soldiers. If they had no pulse, he did nothing and moved forward. They applied tourniquets to legs and arms, and bandages wherever needed.

"Polack, get us some Medevacs. We've got six urgent, and four routine," Rod called out.

John quickly informed the CP of the booby trap and requested Medevacs to their location.

"Sixpack, send out some men and get this fucking LZ secured. Tell them to watch out for more booby traps."

Sixpack picked ten men and sent them scurrying across the LZ to secure the tree line on the other side. Then, he ordered two men back the way they came to secure the rear. Some of the new

Cherries stood around looking confused, not sure what to do next, seemingly in shock.

"You guys!" Rod pointed to the group. "Get your heads out of your asses and give Doc and the others a hand with the wounded. Get some ponchos for litters, then help move the injured up to the LZ."

A few jumped quickly toward the wounded, relieved to be of some assistance. Others began searching under the rucksacks of the downed soldiers, gathering up the available ponchos. John remained on his feet, a step behind Rod wherever he went.

It took fifteen minutes to transport the casualties to the LZ. Friends of those wounded knelt beside them, offering words of consolation, while Doc continuously checked over his patients.

The radio handset came alive and a quivering voice called out, "Sierra-one, this is Angel-five-zero, on your net, come in." The helicopter pilot's voice sounded like he was slapping at his throat while talking.

"This is Sierra-one, over," John replied into the handset.

"Roger. We are your angels of mercy. Our ETA is three minutes."

"Roger, Angel-five-zero, standing by."

John announced, "Birds will be here in three minutes. Get ready!"

"Sierra-one, Angel-five-zero. What is the extent of your wounded?"

"Sierra-one, we have six on litters for urgent Medevac; two have sucking chest wounds and four are amputations. Four others are routine and are currently stable with upper and lower body wounds. We also have two KIA, over."

"Roger, we'll take your two sucking chest wounds and one of the amputees on this first pick-up. Angel-five-five will touch down behind me and take the other three urgent. We will return for the others within fifteen minutes. Go ahead and pop smoke."

"Pop smoke, James!" John instructed one of the two guides on the LZ. James pulled the pin from his canister and tossed it several feet behind him.

"Angel-five-zero, smoke is out."

"Roger, we identify yellow smoke."

"That's affirmative."

"Roger that. We have you in visual. Is the LZ cold?"

"That's affirmative."

"Sierra-one, we'll be coming in from the west. Have those wounded ready so we can get them out as quickly as possible."

"Wilco, out."

While John stood at the edge of the tree line watching the two birds on their approach, his radio came to life once again. "Sierra-one, Lightning-six-niner, over."

"This is Sierra-one."

"Roger, Sierra-one, what's the status of your LZ for our angels of mercy?"

He looked up, surprised to see two Cobras circling overhead. "This is Sierra-one. It's cold, over."

"Roger. We will remain on station until all your wounded have been evacuated. If you need anything, just let us know."

"Wilco. Sierra-one, out."

Ten minutes later, Angel-five-zero called to inform John that he was three minutes out and planning to evacuate the remaining wounded.

Seconds after leaving the LZ, the Medevac called to John, "Sierra-one, this is Angel-five-zero. I will be leaving your net in a minute. Your wounded are in the best of hands at the 93rd Evac Hospital. A team from Graves Registration will be coming out within the hour to pick up your KIA."

"Roger".

"Angel-five-zero, appreciate what you did."

"No problem. Glad we could help. Hope all of your people make it. Good luck! Angel-five-zero is clear this net."

"Sierra-one, Lightning-six-niner."

"Go ahead, Lightning-six-niner."

"Roger. We will be leaving the area and heading back to our coop. Is there anything you need before we leave?" John looked to Rod, who shook his head negatively.

"That's a negative. Thanks for hanging around."

"Roger. Take it easy down there. Lightning-six-niner, out."

The earlier sense of foreboding felt by many of the old timers was well-founded. It was now clear the enemy did not want to fight the Americans head on, but left a calling card for them instead.

The VC purposely booby-trapped the trail, knowing the Americans might return to the LZ for either a resupply or a pick-up. Claymore mines were part of their booby trap; two of them went off immediately and the third detonated a few seconds later. The entire Fourth Squad, except for the uninjured point man and his backup, had been in the blast zone.

Sixpack approached Rod and John. "Are either of you wondering why the first two guys in the column weren't hurt?"

"Is it possible they may have stepped over a trip wire and the third guy in the line tripped it?" John asked.

"It's highly unlikely for something like that to happen."

"Something just isn't right with this booby trap, Sixpack. We know they used claymores. Let's organize a search and poke around through the brush on both sides of the trail."

Sixpack took four men and moved into the brush on one side of the trail while the L-T, John, and four others entered the jungle on the other side.

Ski was the first to spot a pair of brown wires running along the ground, not far from the exploded mines, heading deeper into the jungle.

"Sixpack, L-T, I found something," Ski called out, waving for the men to join him.

Sixpack closed in on his position as the L-T and John crossed the trail, moving toward them.

Without saying another word, the four men followed the wires for fifty feet, suddenly stopping when reaching a small cleared out area in the jungle. On the ground lay three empty C-Ration cans, some scraps of paper, and two clackers (devices to detonate the mines) attached to the end of the two pair of wires.

"The mines were manually detonated by whoever was sitting here and waiting patiently for us to come by. He let the first two guys pass and then blew the mines separately, hoping to catch the L-T and RTO in the killing zone."

"Motherfuckers!" Rod angrily kicked at the C-Ration tins. Sixpack interceded and quickly took a hold of the officer. "Easy, Rod, haven't you learned not to kick at things in the bush? They might be booby-trapped!"

Rod hesitated, and then realizing his error, looked apologetically at the tall sergeant, "Aw shit, Sixpack. Sorry about that. Thanks!"

"Little cock-suckers blew the mines and then just slipped away during all the confusion."

Rod suddenly looked up as if having an eureka moment. "Sixpack, we need to stop the resupply and move someplace else. No telling how many of them are watching us right now."

"That's a hell of an idea, Rod. I'll gather the troops while you and Polack find another place and call in the new coordinates."

They knew of a suitable LZ about two clicks to their north, away from the trail and anybody who might be watching them. All agreed that moving somewhere else was the best idea, especially after discovering the clackers. Had they not found them, the resupply would have taken place as scheduled, and God knows what might have happened next when the chopper landed and everyone bunched up out in the open. Mortars would have been a solid choice, thus avoiding physical contact with the Americans, possibly hitting a helicopter and dozens of troops with well-placed rounds.

When humping to the new resupply LZ, First Platoon chose to cut a path through the jungle instead of following one of the wide trails. It was still dangerous choosing this approach, because of the possibility of stumbling into a fortified bunker complex before reaching the LZ. This hump wreaked havoc on everyone's nerves, and those walking up front felt extremely jumpy and were overly cautious. It took almost all afternoon to reach the LZ for their resupply.

Because of First Platoon's ambush, Captain Fowler issued a new directive to the company, changing the SOP (Standard Operating Procedure). He had heard from many others about their premonitions and feelings about the VC watching them. He suggested his men play a game of hide-and-seek, hoping to outsmart the enemy. The plan was for each platoon to set up their NDP and go about their normal practices for that time of the day. They must be convincing in their actions, making it appear that they were staying there for the night. Then, at about 2200 hours, the platoons would quietly pack up, and under the cover of darkness, move to a new location. The daily patrols looked for suitable locations no closer than three-hundred meters from the current NDP. When settled into their new locations, FSB Kien's artillery unit would fire H&I (Harassment and Intimidation) rounds all around them to keep the enemy off balance. The next morning, every platoon would lay out mechanical ambushes to cover all the avenues of approach to their day lager area. They remained in place for the day, and then moved again under the cover of darkness to yet another new location. The H&I firing would start up again later that night.

The game of hide-and-seek worked well for three days, but then it was time for them to be resupplied. Everyone worried that when the helicopter touched down, a red beacon would go off in the LZ, alerting the surrounding VC to their location.

Once again, the captain showed his creativity and scheduled a fly-by resupply for the company. He arranged to use several helicopters for this new scheme. All would fly at tree top level throughout the AO, some feigning landings in open fields, returning quickly and resuming flights at treetop level. The resupply would take place without any of the birds actually touching down. The crew would kick out food, water, and ammunition at treetop level from the moving birds, aiming for each platoon's NDP. They hoped the charade was successful and would keep the VC guessing as to everyone's whereabouts.

The Wolfhounds only had four remaining days in the bush before returning to Cu Chi and going home. During that time, small patrols went out during the early morning hours to set up mechanical ambushes on surrounding trails and paths. At last count, First Platoon had managed to leave ten of the powerful booby traps 'live' and abandoned; their locations passed through normal channels to the ARVN.

Alpha Company had been fortunate during the last several days. They did not have to fire a shot and nobody else got hurt. Nevertheless, it was an unusually stressful period.

Cherries – A Vietnam War Novel

Their last night in the bush was the worst, and everyone suffered equally. It was like a nightmare: sitting up in the pitch-black darkness, wide-awake, sweating profusely, hearing strange noises, their minds reeling, and being too afraid to move or close their eyes to sleep. Everyone's grip on their sanity began slipping before the night was even half over. Many of the men chose to lean against trees and watch the surrounding area all night. The platoon operated on one-hundred percent alert, yet nobody had ordered it.

They heard the explosions of three different mechanicals during the night. These made the men feel even more restless, knowing the VC were on the prowl. The enemies' intelligence channels were just as good as the Americans', so there was little doubt that the Communists were unaware of the Wolfhounds leaving in the morning. Some speculated that the enemy was moving into ambush positions around the many LZ's and would wait until the choppers landed to withdraw the troops. Then, they would attempt to kill as many grunts as possible while they were out in the open.

None of the grunts wanted to be the final casualty in the field; that night they had grenades within arm's reach and weapons sitting ready on their laps.

When the light of morning finally arrived, each man lay in the same position as he had the night before. The anxiety suffered by all during that fearful night was now evident on their faces. It was still too early, however, to celebrate and breathe a sigh of relief.

The soldiers packed and were ready to move out when given the word. Still spooked, not one of them attempted to light heat tabs and warm food or water, lest the enemy smell it and come looking for the source. Instead, they sat quietly, glancing at one another, speaking with only their eyes. There was an occasional wink just to show moral support.

At 0800, First Platoon received the nod to move out toward their LZ; birds would be arriving in thirty minutes. They only had to travel two-hundred meters, but it seemed to take forever for them to cover that short distance. Overly cautious - like Cherries on their first patrol - they arrived with only five minutes to spare.

Everyone was paranoid during the withdrawal, praying that an ambush would not erupt at any second. As a precaution, the door gunners fired hundreds of rounds into the tree line on both sides of the LZ during their final approach and when lifting off, not stopping until the birds were safely away. If the VC were waiting in the bush, the tactic surely kept their heads down.

There was no return fire, which was cause for a celebration. A loud cheer erupted from every chopper once they were heading for Cu Chi. For many, this was their last flight on a helicopter - and Mother Nature gave them a present. The passing terrain had taken on an aura of shimmering, brilliant colors; they sparkled and winked in the clear early morning sunlight, offering a beautiful, non-threatening vision of what a Pacific island paradise might look like.

The final airlift of Alpha Company was uneventful and every soldier made it back to Cu Chi safely. When exiting the chopper and clearing the rotor wash, the warriors stopped and turned for a final look at their chariots. Heaving a deep sigh of relief, the infantry soldiers came to attention and saluted the pilots. The grunts held the airmen in high esteem, as the pilots had always been there for them in their time of need.

It was finally over! There would be no more humping, ambushes, eating C-Rations, and having to carry the weight of another person on your back. Goodbye Vietnam! Good riddance, and good luck!

They soon discovered, however, that the war was not over for everyone.

# CHAPTER TWENTY

In Cu Chi, the grunts learned firsthand about those rumors circulating during the last few weeks in the bush - some were true, but others were way out in left field. Yes, it was correct that the 25th Division was pulling out of Vietnam and returning to Hawaii, but not everyone was receiving an invitation to come along.

The official cutoff time was nine months, and only those soldiers with nine - or more months - in country were leaving with the division. Some of the men in this grouping were receiving early discharges from the service, returning home as civilians. Another portion received orders to various stateside bases, reporting after a thirty-day leave; the luckiest ones would be relocating to Hawaii with the division flags. The unlucky ones who had less than nine months in country, were transferring to other units within Vietnam - the same destiny as Rod when the First Cav went home. Clerks were distributing the new orders on the following day.

John, Sixpack, BJ, and many of the others in the First Platoon did not have the minimum time in country; they were transferring elsewhere in Vietnam to continue fighting the Communists. All were required to return weapons, rucksacks, and all other military supplies received since their arrival in the 25th Division. The supply sergeant and his staff reviewed, verified serial numbers, and accounted for all equipment originally signed out to everyone. The troops would have to wait until arriving at their new duty station for weapons and other supplies needed for the bush.

Those men scheduled to leave Vietnam celebrated everywhere within the base. The PX sold out their entire inventory of beer and liquor, and all the clubs (Enlisted Men's Club, Non-Commissioned

Officers Club, and the Officer's Club) already had long lines of people waiting to enter. Those remaining in country were not in a partying mood and spent their time within the battalion area. Most of the First Platoon sat around on cots in assigned tents.

"This blows! They wouldn't even let us keep a poncho liner to cover up with tonight."

"It is a bitch, but what are you gonna do, Polack?"

"It's just like it was when we first arrived in country, Sarge. Only this time, we're not Cherries anymore. We've already danced with the devil and I, for one, don't really feel comfortable without my rifle."

"Don't lose any sleep over it, buddy. I think they're doing this more to protect us from ourselves. This is the perfect time for someone to go off the deep end after drinking all night, especially someone not going home who might feel there was nothing to lose. Would it surprise you if a person planned to get even with someone or shot an officer for not letting him leave this hellhole?"

"You've got a good point, Sixpack. I'm not too happy about staying here, but I heard some guys missed the cut off date by only days and the officers won't let them go home."

"No shit? That is a hard one to swallow. They would probably be the ones to do what Sixpack just mentioned."

"Just keep your chin up, we'll all find out tomorrow where destiny will take us."

"It'd be nice if they kept us all together. I've been getting used to you guys."

"Don't count on that happening, Ski. I think the brass will scatter us all to the wind. We'll just have to wait and see." John replied.

Sixpack closed up his sea bag, comfortable that all his treasures were still inside. "You guys do know that we have a formation first thing tomorrow morning? The colonel wants to talk to us before leaving."

"Yeah, we heard all about it, Sixpack."

"Good. There's also going to be some special parade and presentation. After all that, we'll get our marching orders. This will all happen very quickly, so be prepared!"

After a short parade to retire the battalion colors and pass on the baton to the ARVN, the Battalion Commander, Colonel Bill Morgan, walked to the podium and a quiet hush fell upon the crowd.

"Gentlemen, I'd like to thank you all personally for a job well done. You should all be very proud of your accomplishments. Let me take a few moments to share some facts with you. First, I would like to say that since March 1, 1968, the Wolfhounds had killed 4,165 of the enemy and captured 585. Your extreme efforts made it possible to uncover several tons of munitions, firearms, and food staples in many caches throughout the jungle. You have dealt the enemy a terrible blow and severely restricted his attempts to force a Communist regime upon the people of South Vietnam. Our campaigns last May and June in Cambodia were highly successful. We destroyed many of their staging and supply areas, eliminated their sanctuaries, lessened their power with the people, and destroyed their morale. If not for these successes, our foe would have had ample supplies, would be more motivated, and would be highly effective in missions against us. Unfortunately, we too, have suffered high losses during the same period, but far fewer than those suffered by our enemy. At this time, I would like to ask for a moment of silence in remembrance of our fallen comrades, who have paid the ultimate price and had given their lives so that others may be free."

Heads bowed, and some men made a sign of the cross before saying a small silent prayer in their memory. After a brief moment of silence, he continued, "The Wolfhound organization is a proud and fierce fighting machine. I was exceptionally proud to have served with you in the First Battalion. Even though some of you are leaving for other units, remember in your heart that you will always be a Wolfhound. As a remembrance of this service, I have a small token for each of you. I have in my hand a scroll dedicated to all Wolfhounds. It briefly outlines the history of the First Battalion since their arrival in Vietnam. Please keep this remembrance and look back at it ten years from now. I guarantee you will get cold chills and feel proud all over again. For those of you going back to the states with the division or to other stateside bases, brace yourself, because stateside duty is nothing like this. You all remember that spit shine stuff, don't you?"

Snickers and war whoops arose from the crowd.

"And to those of you who are, unfortunately, staying behind, you'll receive your orders for reassignment immediately following this ceremony. Wolfhounds, I wish you all the luck in the world, and God's protection for a safe return home to your families. God bless you all. Gentlemen, I salute you." He raised his arm and held a salute to the men standing in groups before him. The men quickly came to attention and returned the colonel's salute. When he dropped his arm, Colonel Morgan turned and left the podium.

The crowd cheered wildly for a couple of minutes, and then it was over. Upon leaving the area, clerks handed out the souvenir scrolls to each soldier walking by. Some unrolled the scroll, stopping to read it, however, most everyone else hurried back to their company areas, anxious to find out where they were going next.

For those leaving with the division, their orders read to report to their new duty station, Hawaii, after a thirty-day leave. They would begin out-processing tomorrow and leave the country before the end of the week. Those reassigned would start out-processing immediately and leave for their new units in the morning.

John opened his orders and after a moment of reading, dropped the document onto his cot. "I'm fucked now!"

"How so, Polack?"

He retrieved the document, reading it aloud, "It says here that I'm to report to my next duty station in Phu Bai, Republic of South Vietnam, where I will be assigned to the 101st Airborne Division."

"Where the fuck is Phu Bai?"

"My orders say the same thing."

"Me too!"

"Hey, I'm going there, too."

"Looks like a bunch of us are all going together," Ski confirmed after several other members in the First Platoon reported.

"What's so bad about the 101st?"

"Ski, ever since I've been in Nam, everything I've either heard or read in the military newspapers about the 101st was that they were always getting their asses kicked somewhere up north. It's also very mountainous there and close to the border of North Vietnam (DMZ)."

"It can't be any worse than what we've been through," BJ added.

"No, guys, I think this is going to be a whole new world up there and the way of fighting is also going to be different."

"You may be a hundred percent correct about what you're saying, Polack, but until I get there and see for myself, I'm not going to get worked up over this. I still got eight months left and it'll just be like joining another new gang."

"I wish I could look at things the way you do, Ski. It would make it all that much easier for me. But looking at the bright side - with this many of us going to the same place – there's an excellent chance of some of us staying together in the new units."

"Hey Malcolm, where are you and BJ reassigned to?"

"Some place called Chu Lai in the Central Highlands with the Americal Division."

"Me too," hollered Tex. "Where is Chu Lai?"

"It's in the Central Highlands."

"Where's that?"

"How the fuck do I know? Where's Phu Bai?"

"It's up north."

"Up north where?"

"Somebody find a map of this fucking country so we can see where the fuck we're going!"

Sixpack walked into the tent and threw a rolled up map of Vietnam onto his cot. "Here's a map, knock yourselves out, guys."

There was a mad scramble, everyone gathering around for the geography lesson.

"Who's going up north to the 101st with me?" Sixpack asked. A dozen hands shot into the air.

"All right! We're leaving for Bien Hoa Airport tomorrow morning at 0800 hours. And for those of you not knowing the date - tomorrow is Tuesday, March twenty-fourth."

"Sixpack, any idea what happened to the L-T?"

"Not a clue, Polack. I haven't seen him since arriving in Cu Chi."

"Neither have I. Isn't that strange?"

"Not really. Remember, we're back in the rear and he's probably lying around with the other officers and getting shit-faced with them at the Officer's Club."

"Yeah, you're probably right."

That night, First Platoon had a going-away party to celebrate their time together – one last hurrah. Doc was the luckiest in the group, as the government granted him an early discharge from the military. If all went as planned, Doc would be a civilian by the end of the week. He was ecstatic and the men were all very happy for him.

Before things really got going and the beer started flowing, the grunts exchanged addresses and agreed to follow the same plan: when known, they would mail the new in-country addresses to the parents of their friends and they, in turn, would forward the information to the grunts in the next family letter to the war zone.

In the morning, most of the men still felt the effects of the late night party. Some still tried not to stagger when they walked, and it was obvious that they found the harsh sunlight unbearable. Others were fighting nausea; all were not looking forward to a bumpy truck ride and then flying in a cargo plane.

Almost one-hundred soldiers from the battalion were going to the 101st Airborne; many friends accompanied them to the waiting area. Some of them were leaving for home or other units themselves later in the day. The transportation, a caravan of four Deuce and a Half trucks, turned the corner, stopping next to the group. The men said their last goodbyes and hugged one more time before climbing aboard the trucks. Thirty seconds later the vehicles whisked the soldiers away, leaving Cu Chi for the very last time.

John opened his duffel bag and pulled out the souvenir scroll from the colonel, unrolling it, and then admiring the document. At the very top was the Wolfhound crest - a raised gold wolfhound head profiled on a black background. The Latin words, 'Nec Aspera Terrent' (roughly translated meant, 'And They Fear No Hardship') stood out in gold letters below the head. A thin gold line framed the black and gold crest.

It read as follows:

## KOLCHAK – KING OF ALL WOLFHOUNDS
## GREETINGS

To all true Pups, wherever ye may be:

Know ye that from the hazardous environs on Cu Chi, across the Saigon River, from the perimeters of Fire Support Bases Lynch, Kien, Beverly, and Carol, come a staunch and true bearer of the crest, who has washed the jungles of the Ho Bo, the Boi Loi, the Michelin Rubber, the Iron Triangle and Cambodia with the sweat of righteous terror, dared the treacherous crossing of QL 1, bathed in the semi-solid waters of a monsoon-filled bomb crater and had, through arduous practice, developed the gunship flinch to the satisfaction of his superiors.

Be it further known that since this gallant challenger of Hanoi's agrarian reformers and the Viet Cong local roustabouts has looked unblinkingly into the tunnel mouths of the enemy, known the ecstasy of being a sniper's target and the object of suppressive fires, has been duly initiated into the association of the air-lifted, ambushed, and smoke grenade asphyxiated and accepted into intimacy by the virtuous sisters.

Be it therefore proclaimed that
**John Kowalski**
Has been found worthy to be admitted to the
**OMNIPOTENT ORDER OF KOLCHAK AS A REGAL BARKER**

Be it therefore ordered that all Wolfhound Warriors get all the honor and respect to which he is entitled.

Signed, (with a paw print)
Kolchak V
King of all Wolfhounds

John, pleasantly surprised by the contents of the scroll, smiled broadly. He didn't quite understand some of the terms, but he got the general picture.

"Did any of you guys get to read what's in this scroll?" He asked those sitting around him.

"Yeah, I did," replied a couple of soldiers sitting across from him. "It's pretty cool, isn't it?"

"Hell, yes! It's almost like a summary of everything I've done since being here."

Sixpack finished reading John's scroll and handed it back to him. "I couldn't have summed it up any better myself. It's a nice keepsake."

"This is a treasure!" John reverently returned it to his duffel for safekeeping, and could not wait to show it to his family and friends when he returned home.

## CHAPTER TWENTY-ONE

The replacement center in Phu Bai was almost becoming overcrowded. Experienced soldiers were arriving from various locations in-country; new replacements were still arriving from the states - hundreds of Cherries came in on as many as three flights a day.
"None of this makes sense to me. Why are so many new guys still coming into the country when entire divisions are going home?"
"It's not for us to understand, Polack. We're only supposed to follow orders and do what the brass and politicians want us to do."
"This is stupid! All those guys in the 25th had lots of experience and were battle-hardened. If the politicians want to shorten the war, they should have sent them here with us instead of sending in more Cherries."
"Cool it, Polack. Just let it go. It's something you don't need to worry about."
"He's right though, Sixpack. The President is telling people back home that entire divisions are withdrawing from Vietnam. I remember seeing the parades and ceremonies on TV back in Cu Chi. The media was showing all these guys leaving on jet planes, but they weren't showing all the replacements that came in on those same planes."
"All that pacification shit they're talking about is bullshit, too."
"There isn't anything that you can do about it. So just focus on staying alive and doing what you're told until it's time for you to go home, too."

The entire American concentration of troops was now operating in the northern most part of the country. Since the First Cav and the

25th Division had pulled out of the war, the responsibility for securing much of the southern half of the country rested in the hands of the ARVN. Only small units of Americans were actively involved in those areas surrounding Saigon. However, the northern half was swarming with Marines, the 101st Airborne, and the Americal Divisions.

The in-country transfers were only in Phu Bai for a couple of hours before receiving new orders. Sixpack, John, and a half dozen former Wolfhounds were staying together in the 1st Battalion, 501st Infantry Brigade; the group was traveling north to Camp Vandergrift in the morning.

Sixpack and John returned to the barracks where they had left their duffel bags earlier. John reached in and pulled out a paperback book, then lay back against his duffel to read.

"Goddammit! Fucking sons of bitches!" Sixpack hollered, frantically searching through his duffel bag.

"What's wrong?" John asked, startled by his uncharacteristic outburst.

"Some sorry, no good bastard stole my six-pack of brew!"

"Are you sure it's gone?"

"Yes, I'm sure. Somebody rifled through my shit and took it."

"So what's the big deal? Just go to the PX and buy some more."

"Polack, it's not the same. I brought it over with me from the states. It's been my good luck charm since I've been here."

"Come on, Sarge, you're not superstitious are you?"

"No, I'm not superstitious, but look who's asking? Why in the fuck do you have that fifty-caliber bullet hanging from your neck on that chain?"

"For good luck, too, I guess. But, this is different. I wear it all the time, and I made it back in Kien before going out into the bush on my first mission. I haven't taken it off my neck since. You never took your beer with you in the bush."

"It was a good luck charm for me, too, asshole, but I didn't have to carry it with me. How would you feel if somebody stole your necklace or if you lost it out in the bush?"

John pondered this last question for only a second. "I'd be really bummed out. I'm sorry, Sixpack, I didn't realize..."

Sixpack interrupted, "Fuck it. Don't mean nothin'. Just forget about the whole thing."

"Is there anything I can do?"

"I told you to just forget it! I want to be alone right now. Do you mind?"

"No, of course not. I'll go out and take a walk. I'll catch up with you later." John took his paperback with him and left the barracks.

The next morning, forty soldiers left for Camp Vandergrift on a Chinook helicopter. John sat near the rear of the bird, watching the surrounding countryside through the opened boarding ramp. The sight was pathetic. The valleys lay scorched and the ground was pitted with bomb craters from hundreds of B-52 bombs. Huge mountains, covered with jungle growth, stretched to the north as far as one could see; they, too, showed the scars of war. To the east, the South China Sea glistened, the blue-green color extending to the horizon. Their destination, Camp Vandergrift, was located several miles south of the DMZ; the flight would take almost thirty minutes.

John tensed as he suddenly had the thought that his upcoming experiences could be far worse than anything he had ever encountered while fighting in the south.

He leaned toward Sixpack and yelled above the loud noise of the vibrating aircraft, "Why do you think they need so many replacements up here?"

"Probably because they get their asses kicked all the time."

"That's not what I was hoping to hear."

"Oh, well!"

"Geeze, thanks."

John couldn't understand why Sixpack was taking out his frustrations on him. It wasn't his fault that somebody stole his beer, and he hoped Sixpack's attitude changed soon.

Vandergrift was a large base camp similar to Cu Chi, but the similarities ended there. Vehicles bounced along muddy, chuckholed dirt roads throughout the camp. Long strips of metal planking, half buried in the mud, served as sidewalks. No beautiful buildings were lining the base; instead, everything was underground and surrounded by sandbags. There was no green grass and no 'Keep Off' signs posted - just craters filled with mud everywhere, reminders of the mortar barrages and 122mm rockets that routinely landed within the compound. Parts of once-filled sandbags and burnt timber littered the muddy ground near destroyed bunkers. Work crews were feverishly attending to them, filling sandbags and laying new timber, trying to make it functional by nightfall. There was no PX, service club, swimming pool, or radio phones to call home in this base camp.

Every person walking around wore a bulletproof vest and carried a bandolier of ammo and a weapon with him. Looking around, John knew right away that in this basecamp nobody locked their weapons in the armory overnight. He was anxious to get his, and wondered how much longer he would have to wait.

The environment could not have been more depressing. It was completely different from how they lived and what they were accustomed to during the past months in Cu Chi, and even in the fire support bases. The night and day difference between the two locations was jaw-dropping for the new arrivals.

A clerk rushed the group over to the battalion area, drawing out flak jackets, weapons, and ammo from the supply bunker. The XO appeared to be overwhelmed with his current task, as if assigning replacements to a new company was something he didn't have time to do right then. Knowing that bunkers were always in need of repair, therefore, he assigned the entire group to that detail until he found the time to continue distributing equipment. Because Sixpack was the highest-ranking NCO (Non-Commissioned Officer) in the group, the XO placed him in charge of the work detail and then pointed out which bunkers required their attention.

The day continued without any changes or updates, and the mundane task of filling sandbags seemed never-ending.

Later that first night, the enemy fired several rockets into the perimeter within the span of an hour; they landed randomly and in no particular pattern. Everyone inside the bunkers awaited the next explosion, praying it did not land on top of them. Mortar flares were fired repeatedly into the air, ignited above the compound and then floated downward; they were suspended by small parachutes, which illuminated the terrain beyond the perimeter.

Those manning the perimeter concentrated to their front, watching for enemy movement in the flickering light. Ground attacks were rare against larger bases, but as a precaution, the camp commander doubled the perimeter security for the rest of the night.

At 0230 hours, Medevac helicopters landed within the perimeter, evacuating the dead and wounded. Two bunkers had received direct hits, imploding them; those inside never had a chance. Flying shrapnel also wounded several other soldiers, caught out in the open – two men caught shrapnel while standing in the entrance of their bunkers.

Fires burned throughout the camp as timber and vehicles smoldered after direct hits. Small groups of soldiers were fighting the fires with pails of water and shovels full of dirt and mud.

Repairing bunker damage was a top priority, addressed immediately by those inside and by neighbors nearby. Other damage not affecting security or safety could wait until morning.

At 0500 hours, the NVA started firing mortars into the perimeter, walking them around indiscriminately. Once again, there was a mad dash for the bunkers as everyone dropped what they were doing. Sadly, the men had no other recourse but to just sit there and wait for the barrage to end.

The mortar and artillery pits suddenly came alive; flares lit up the sky again and the big guns shot 105mm explosive rounds at the mortar flashes in the distance. These gunners were the only ones fortunate enough to be able to return fire - everyone else inside the perimeter had to wait until acquiring a visible target of their own.

The barrage lasted over thirty minutes and stopped shortly before daybreak. It was a long, nerve-fraying night for everyone within the camp.

The next day, the entire camp busied itself repairing the damage from the night before. Some were lucky enough to catch up on missed sleep; others, who were not so lucky, felt totally spent and walked around as if they were on 'automatic pilot'.

After breakfast the following morning, John ran into the XO.

"Excuse me, sir, but have you got a minute?"

"What can I do for you, Specialist?"

"My nerves have had it, sir. The 25th Division was nothing like this. I have almost nine months in country. Is there any way of getting a rear job in this division?"

"What's your MOS (Military Occupation Specialty), soldier?"

"11B40, sir."

"That's infantry, troop. Take it from me, you'll be better off in the field."

"If this is some kind of sign of what it's like out there, then I really don't think so, sir."

"I do. Some companies in the boonies have not seen action in months. That's the safest place to be right now. If it were possible for me to be there, I'd leave on the next chopper."

"You're serious?"

"Take my word for it. I have no reason to lie to you. Matter of fact, I envy you because you're going to the field."

"I believe you, sir. Do you have any idea when we will ship to our outfits? My mother doesn't have my new address yet."

"I think most of you transferred guys will be leaving in a couple of days."

"Okay, thanks, sir."

"Anytime, soldier."

John still had his reservations about whether to believe the XO or not and decided to seek out the reenlistment bunker. After asking half-dozen guys - who thought him to be crazy - he eventually found it.

He stepped down into the bunker to find a First Sergeant going over some paperwork at a desk.

"Have a seat. I'll be with you in a minute," he said without looking up.

John sat on a wooden folding chair and waited for his eyes to adjust to the dimness inside. A large crash in the corner caused him to jump up and fumble with his rifle.

"Easy, son. I didn't mean to startle you," the First Sergeant said. "I wasn't thinking when I threw my helmet at the rat."

"Pardon me?"

"The rat. You know what a rat is, don't you?"

"Yeah," he answered, still unsure as to what to do next.

"Well, these fucking rats have a tunnel complex under this place. You don't know where they will turn up next. When you're lucky enough to spot one, you just throw the first thing you can lay your hands on. It's not bad during the day, but it's a real terror at night. They climb in bed with you, looking for food."

John shuddered inwardly.

"That's odd. I've been here two days and haven't seen one yet."

"You're lucky. You must be in one of the newer bunkers."

"Yeah, I am."

"Well, you'll see them soon enough. Just prepare yourself. Now, what can I do for you?"

"I'd like some information about reenlisting."

"Okay. What information can I give you?"

"Can I pick any job in the Army when I reenlist?"

"It all depends on if you're qualified or not."

"I feel that I'm qualified for a clerk typist position. In high school, I had two years of typing and finished the course at fifty-six words a minute."

"That sure makes you qualified enough, but why in the hell would you want to reenlist as a clerk typist?"

"Top, I was stationed with the 25th Division down south and got transferred here just this week. I've been in Nam for eight and a half months, but didn't have enough time in country to go home with the division. Since being in country, we've always heard that the 101st was losing many men during the battles taking place up here. To be honest, I'm scared and don't want to be killed after all I've been through already. I'll do anything to get out of the field."

"I can't say that your reason isn't justified, but I don't think reenlistment is the answer. Have you really thought things through?"

"What do you mean, sir?"

"First, let me ask you something. Did you originally enlist in the Army, or were you drafted?"

"I was drafted, sir."

"Are you looking forward to getting out of the service when your two years are up?"

"I was."

"You do know that if you reenlist, you'll have to give up another four years of your life to Uncle Sam."

"I know, but I guess it'll be worth it, just so I don't have to go out in the bush again."

"Now that's the wrong answer, troop. I wouldn't recommend reenlistment to anyone unless he planned to make a career out of the Army."

"You mean you won't let me?"

"I didn't say that. I just said that I would not recommend it. In your case, I think if you reenlist, you'll come to regret it. I know there's been a lot of fighting up here and many good men have lost their lives, but it's no different here than it was down south. I think I can help solve your problem. Let me ask you another question. When you first came to Vietnam, were you as frightened as you are now?"

"I don't know. Yeah, I guess so. But it was only because of not knowing what to expect."

"Don't you think you're in that same position now?"

"I'm not sure," John answered after some hesitation.

"Okay. Now just think for a minute. If you would have reenlisted when you first came into the country, would you have regretted it today?"

"I probably would have. It wasn't very bad down there. Our base camps were the most secure in the country. Entire companies returned regularly for R&R; genuine relaxation without having to worry about anything. We never had our bases rocketed and mortared like up here."

"Then why do you want to reenlist to get a job in a base camp up here?"

"I don't know."

"Look, son. Let me give you some statistics. Almost seventy-five percent of all the casualties up here occur in the rear areas because of the rockets and mortars. Some ground pounders in the bush have not fired a weapon in three months. Would you believe it if I told you that some of the rear echelon troops want to re-up just to get into the infantry and to get away from these base camps? They are just as afraid of dying as you are and will do anything to find a more secure job in this war. So you see - you're better off to stay right where you are."

"You aren't trying to bullshit me are you, Top?"

"I've got no reason to bullshit you. There's nothing in it for me by trying to keep you in the infantry. Now that we've had a chance to talk, I'd like you to think about our discussion before you consider reenlisting. Take all the time you need because it will be a very important decision that could affect your future. Go out into the field, spend some time there, and see just what it's really like. Then if you still want to reenlist, I'll be more than happy to accommodate you."

"Okay, Top that seems fair. You've changed my mind for now. Thanks for your time."

"That's quite all right. Good luck and take care, soldier."

"I'll do my best."

John turned to leave the bunker when Top called out, "Next time you come in here, be sure it's what you really want. I won't try to change your mind then."

"Fair enough, Top, thanks for the break."

"Airborne!" He called out enthusiastically.

"All the way," John said smartly, replying with the correct formal response. He smiled, and finally walked out of the bunker.

Outside, he noticed that many of the soldiers moving about wore jump wing patches on their camouflage fatigue jackets, identifying them as jump-qualified, a gung-ho bunch that loved parachuting from airplanes. He wondered if they actually jumped from planes here in Vietnam. After his talk with the First Sergeant, he looked forward to seeing what the conditions were like out in the field, and hoped he could still use his hammock during the night.

The recent arrivals finally received orders to their new companies, and, as if by fate, John and Sixpack stayed together; both assigned to Alpha Company, First Platoon.

After lunch, John, Sixpack, and a dozen other soldiers – two being former Wolfhounds – boarded a Deuce and a Half, and prepared to leave Camp Vandergrift on a rough ride to the battalion Fire Support Base Carroll. There, they would pull bunker guard until called to leave for the bush.

FSB Carroll was roughly five miles northeast of their current location but the ride out of Vandergrift to the main highway alone was enough to scramble brains. The truck hit every possible pothole on the dirt road; some of the passengers thought the driver was doing this intentionally. They were moving less than five miles per hour, yet the occupants bounced around the troop-transport from one side to the other, bruising their bodies on the side rails and floors. Before leaving, they had strapped their steel helmets securely onto their heads, which actually saved the men from bashing their heads. Any bystander watching these soldiers pass might have thought it was somewhat comical, but truth be told, if anyone had actually fallen from the vehicle, he would have been seriously hurt, even at that slow speed. Knowing what they did by then, if given a choice, they would have all opted to walk to the main road instead.

Once the big truck reached the paved two-lane highway, the ride was slightly bumpy but bearable; however, it was only a few minutes before they stopped altogether. Up ahead, a mine-sweeping team was checking the road for mines buried during the night. With all of the delays, it took two and a half hours to reach the firebase.

Fire Support Base Carroll was a small, well-fortified position on the top of a knoll overlooking the paved highway. There were seventeen bunkers on the perimeter and twice as many small fighting positions in between each of them.

The firebase housed a battery of 105mm artillery guns, two 81mm mortar pits, and a small helipad to accommodate a Loach helicopter. One-hundred defenders already protected this firebase, and adding to the total might overcrowd the positions. The truck driver pointed out the commo bunker and directed the new arrivals to check in there. This bunker also doubled as the battalion orderly room. A First Sergeant was expecting them, already standing outside patiently waiting for them to arrive. A large and muscular man with a square jaw and an intimidating look, some men joked that he looked very much like 'Sgt. Rock' in the DC Comics Universe.

"Gentlemen, welcome to Alpha Company!" He greeted the small group. "I am First Sergeant Trombley. As you men are all in-country transfers, I do not really have to tell you what it is like in this country. I do have a small speech to make, however, so bear with me," a partial smile crept across his face. "You are now part of the 101st Airborne Division, the most highly decorated and the fiercest fighting unit in this country. I can see that none of you is Airborne-qualified and you may not know how we operate in the bush, so forget everything you did in your former units. Our methods might seem strange at first, but you will catch onto them in due time. When in the bush, I expect you to perform your duties without hesitation and to conduct yourselves in a manner befitting this unit. We will not tolerate cowards or malingers here. You are now in an airborne unit and expected to play by our rules. Are there any questions?"

"Just one," John said meekly, raising his hand.

"What is it, soldier? Speak up," he scowled.

"When are we going out to the bush?"

"In two days," the First Sergeant responded without hesitation. He cleared his throat and continued. "I know many of you are anxious to get the rest of your supplies, and we'll do that just as soon as I finish with this orientation. Whenever you are in the firebase, you will be on ready alert at all times."

"What do you mean by ready alert?" someone else asked.

John hoped that a Cherry asked that question, otherwise, the First Sergeant would think they were all a bunch of assholes.

Sergeant Trombley expected such a question, but glared at the man for a second anyway before answering. "Ready alert means just that. After you receive the rest of your supplies, go and check out the bunkers and foxholes around the perimeter. Some of them are six-man positions, others four-man. Find a vacancy and move in. Pack all your shit and be ready to move out on a moment's notice. There is always a chance of a sister unit getting into trouble and needing help. The faster we get there, the better their chances of survival. Guard duty will be your only responsibility during these next two days. In the bunkers, at least two men must be awake and on guard at all times, and that means around the clock. Did that answer your question?"

"Yes, sir, it did," the unidentified soldier answered.

Top did not like his response and blew it off. "Are there any more questions?" He looked them over and gave the impression that he would pounce on the next person to open his mouth. There were no further questions.

"In that case, follow me to the supply bunker."

With new supplies in hand, Sixpack and John walked around the perimeter until they found a bunker that appeared to be empty. They walked in and found three people huddled in a corner - smoking weed. Their entrance did not surprise the men, and they did not attempt to hide what they were doing.

"Wow, man, check this out," one of the three managed to say. He pointed toward the opening and strained to see through the blue haze, as if thinking John and Sixpack had just materialized from thin air.

"Yeah, far out. Peace, brother," a second man said, making a feeble attempt to raise his arm and flash a peace sign.

"What in the fuck are you guys doing?" Sixpack took a step closer to the three men.

"Toking on some weed, man. You want a hit? There's plenty to go around."

"Fuck no, I don't want a hit." Sixpack looked at John, "These fuckers are so far gone they don't even know where they're at."

"Man, who cares?"

"I care. I'm not staying in a bunker full of potheads."

"We're not potheads. We're just peace-loving people."

"Fuck you all!" Sixpack backed up to the bunker entrance. "Come on, Polack!"

"Polack? What the fuck is a Polack?" The three men laughed hard; one lost his balance and fell onto the other two. All three buckled to the ground together, still laughing.

John stood and watched in disbelief. "These guys are supposed to be on guard duty protecting the camp. They're so stoned that if a ground attack happened right now, they'd probably just laugh at the attacking soldiers."

"Ground attack? Where do you think we are, man - in Vietnam someplace?" More laughter erupted from the trio.

John turned and walked to the doorway. "I'm coming, Sixpack!"

"Shit, you guys, they got beer. Don't go, man!" one of the three stoners implored from the heap on the ground.

Sixpack stopped suddenly and then turned to flip off the hopeless youths. "We've got to find a bunker that's far away from these shitheads. Come on, Polack!"

They both exited and continued their search for new living quarters. They had walked clear around to the other side of the perimeter before finding another bunker that looked as if it might have some extra room inside.

They poked their heads through the entrance to see who might be inside before making a move to enter. Four soldiers were inside; two played a game of checkers on a small crate, one was writing letters, and the fourth was cleaning his weapon and looking out at the highway to their front.

"Is there any room in here for two more?" Sixpack asked.

"Why, hell yes, Sarge, come on in. The more, the merrier."

They entered what would become their new home for the next two days and stowed their gear in a corner.

"I'm Larry Holmes; they call me Sixpack. My friend here is John Kowalski, better known as 'the Polack'." They shook hands all around and the new bunker mates introduced themselves.

The two checker players were Dan and Bill, Peter was writing letters and Albert was on guard duty. All four were short-timers, leaving for Phu Bai in three days to process out of the country and go home.

They sat together shooting the shit for the next few hours. John and Sixpack exchanged stories with the foursome, hoping to learn as much as possible about the conditions out in the field and the type of operations they conducted. All the shit the two new arrivals had been through with the 25th surprised the foursome. It was nothing like that up here, the four men assured them, and it had been very quiet in the bush ever since leaving the A Shau Valley some four months ago. In fact, their weapons were spotless, but the foursome admitted they were not even sure if the rifles would fire; it had been that long. They informed the two newcomers that the hardest thing they would have to endure was the never ending humping up and down the mountains.

During the sharing of information, John's ears perked up when his new hosts talked about a soldier nicknamed 'Professor'. He carried a radio in the Company CP and was going home in a week. His departure would create a vacancy, one that John very much coveted. He would check into it first thing in the morning.

After breakfast, John walked over to the communications bunker and found the First Sergeant there.

"Excuse me, Top, got a minute?"

"What's on your mind, troop?"

"I heard there's a radio-carrier in the Company CP nicknamed Professor, who will be going home in a few days. What's the chance of my taking his place when he comes out of the field?"

"You know how to operate a radio?"

"I do, and think I'm pretty good at it. I carried one in the 25th for two months."

Top thought about it for a few seconds. "I'll tell you what, how about I give you a small test?"

"Sure, that's fine; what do you have in mind?"

"Report back here at 1800 hours. I'll let you work the radios tonight. If you can convince me that you're as good as you say, then I'll talk to the captain about it."

"It's a deal. I'll see you later."

He was excited and anxious to tell Sixpack the good news. His friend was happy for him, but seemed disappointed that they would not be together in the field.

John stood outside of the communications bunker and smoked a couple of cigarettes during the next ten minutes. He wanted to walk into the bunker precisely at 1800 to show Top he was both dependable and punctual.

Top told him that the various units would be calling in their NDP locations shortly; he would have to decipher the coordinates and plot them on the hanging wall map. The First Sergeant said that he expected him to handle anything that might come up during the night, emergency or not.

During the night, John had to contact the various units in the field for situation reports every hour. This was going to be a breeze, as he had already done it hundreds of times.

The First Sergeant relieved him at 0600. John's eyes were bloodshot and burning from the twelve-hour shift. His relief noted all the unit locations plotted neatly on the wall map, and he was delighted when John handed him a log that he had maintained during the night. It listed every call made, the time of the call, the call sign, and reason for the call. John identified anything out of the ordinary with an asterisk.

Top also noticed that John policed the immediate area on that side of the bunker. All the gear was organized and the floor swept clean of mud and cigarette butts.

Top was impressed with his organizational skills and performance. "You did good, son. You do know that nobody here wants to carry a radio because of the excess weight in the mountains. Are you sure you still want to do this?"

"I am."

"Okay. I won't promise you anything, but I'll talk to the captain the first chance I get."

"I'd appreciate that, Top."

"That's quite all right. Go and get some sleep. You look like the walking dead. I'll come and find you when I've talked to the captain."

"Thank you, Top." John left and walked to his bunker, which was not too far away. In retrospect, it was quite a battle to stay awake during the night with nothing else to do but listen to the radio. The opportunity to clean and organize helped pass the time, and it would be the only chance to show his mettle.

John returned to his bunker and tried to get some sleep. He was overly tired and anxious to hear back from Top about the opportunity. He had a restless morning, tossing and turning; his mind was in overdrive, and he was unable to think about anything else except carrying the radio again. He was also worried, and

343

wondered what he would do if the captain refused to grant his request.

Before nightfall, the Alpha Company replacements received word from the company clerk that the company would be arriving in Phu Bai the following morning for three days of R&R. They were to catch a ride on the morning convoy and join up with the company there. This would be an ideal opportunity for everyone to get to know one another before heading back into the bush on their next mission.

All the new recruits were excited. Phu Bai would be a welcome relief where they wouldn't have to worry about staying up all night and filling sandbags during the day. They would all be able to relax and get a chance to fit in as the 'new guys' before leaving for the bush.

The convoy arrived four hours before Alpha Company was due to land; Top greeted them at the R&R center. The new arrivals immediately went to work helping to erect tents, readying charcoal in the many barbecues, and filling trashcans with cans of soda and beer. The cooks added ice thirty minutes before their arrival. The men would also help to barbecue steaks and pass out ice-cold drinks to the arriving warriors. They worked non-stop to have everything ready for the arrivals.

John got his first look at the captain when they stood face-to-face when John was helping in the chow line. The officer reached in with a paper plate and waited for John to transfer a barbecued steak from the grill. For some reason, John thought his appearance resembled that of a professor. He was much older than expected, his clothes oversized, large rimmed glasses with bifocals hung from a lanyard around his neck, and his green boony hat looked more like something someone might wear on a fishing trip. His tightly-clamped teeth held a Sherlock Holmes-style pipe in place, with puffs of cherry-enhanced smoke dissipating into the air. Standing at six-foot, six-inches tall, he towered over the rest of the troops. With a kind and understanding look upon his face, he appeared more like everyone's father instead of an Army Airborne Captain.

"Thank you, troop," he responded after receiving his steak from John.

"No problem, sir!" The captain moved ahead to the next serving station. More excited than ever at the prospect of carrying a radio again, John looked forward to hearing back from the First Sergeant.

After dinner, the new replacements began intermingling with the rest of the company. Nobody told stories about seeing the enemy or recent firefights. Instead, they griped and bitched about the extremely steep slopes of the mountains they had to hump during this last mission. Some related their personal experiences of seeing a fellow soldier sliding or toppling down the mountainside, taking everybody in his path along for a ride. The story evoked laughter from those nearby. Others complained about the length of time it took to go up and down the high mountains – sometimes up to three days each way. This resulted in the men spending numerous nights on the steep slopes; nobody could sleep because they fought gravity all night long.

John stood alone, looking for somebody he might know from his earlier days in training. With what he had heard so far, it seemed that everything the First Sergeant said about reenlisting was true. Suddenly, he felt a hand grip his shoulder.

"This is the young man I was telling you about." John turned to see Top and the captain standing behind him.

"Top tells me you're campaigning to be my new RTO. Is this true?"

"Yes sir." John had to look up six inches to see into the man's eyes.

"You know this is not an easy job."

"I know that, sir, but I can guarantee you'll be pleased."

"You've got your mind made up then?"

"Yes, sir, if you'll have me."

The First Sergeant and the captain looked at one another and smiled. "Alright, you got the job. What's your name, son?"

He smiled proudly, "Specialist Fourth Class John Kowalski, sir."

"Have you got a nickname?"

"Everybody's been calling me 'Polack' since Basic Training."

"That's kind of degrading, isn't it?"

"I don't mind it, sir. It sure sounds better than 'Ski'."

"Okay, 'Polack' it is. Glad to have you aboard." He extended his arm and the two men shook hands. "I'm Captain Robertson. I might have some nicknames floating around the company, but you can just call me 'Cap'."

"Thank you for the opportunity, Cap."

"I'm sure you'll do very well. Top will get you squared away later with a new radio and gear. Then you can meet the rest of the members in the CP. Right now, try to enjoy yourself. I don't know when we'll ever make it back here again. See you soon!"

"Okay, Cap."

He was so excited about the decision, he felt like doing a cartwheel. He scanned the area looking for Sixpack to tell him the good news. Unable to find him in the large open field, he walked back to the tent area and found the sergeant deeply involved in a conversation with members of his new squad. He stopped momentarily, stepping away from the group when seeing John approach.

"Sixpack, the captain accepted me into the CP!"

"That's really great, Polack. I'm happy for you!"

"You going to the CP?" One of squad members asked.

"Yep," he replied proudly.

"Man, they're just a bunch of lazy motherfuckers. Why would you want to get in with them?"

"I carried a radio for the platoon L-T when humping the bush with Sixpack. It was great knowing what was going on around me. Now stepping up into the CP is like being promoted."

"Yeah, we understand. It's a way for you to sit on your ass and not have to go out on patrols with the rest of us."

"Stow it, Joe," Sixpack cautioned. "Polack has seen his share of shit and probably more than any of you sitting here. He has walked point for months, carried the M-60 machine gun and a radio before our division left for home. There's nobody up here that I would rather have at my side. He knows his shit and he'll take good care of us while in the CP. So lay off!"

"Thanks, Sixpack," John said, relieved and grateful that his friend was so supportive. He snuck a glance at the nearby soldiers;

the lecture seemed to appease them and they watched him with some interest.

"That's okay kid, keep in touch!"

"Sorry, man," Joe put out his hand. "Welcome to the Screaming Eagles!"

"Yeah, good luck!"

"Keep an eye on them guys and don't let them get over on you. They're a sneaky bunch!"

"Thanks guys! Good luck to you, too!" John said and then walked away and out of the tent.

It was no different here than it was down south as each segment of the company, from squad size and up, kept to themselves. To locate the CP, John peered into each tent as he passed, hoping to spot a group of radios and their handlers. Instead, he bumped into Top, who led him to a bunker near the orderly room.

Once inside, it was clear the group had special privileges in Phu Bai. Each man had a cot - complete with a pillow and mattress - positioned along two of the sandbagged walls. A thirty-gallon can half filled with ice-cold pop and beer stood sweating just inside the doorway. An oscillating fan in the far corner circulated the musty air through the bunker, making it feel somewhat comfortable inside. A worktable and bench were against the right wall; four radios sat atop, and a spotlight overhead provided enough illumination to light the entire living area. Compared to the rest of the company accommodations, this was a five-star establishment. Four soldiers sat around, each busy with his own agenda. Top got their attention as soon as the two men walked through the doorway.

"Gentlemen, let me introduce you to the Professor's replacement. This is John - uh, what's your last name?"

"Kowalski."

"Aw, shit. Just call him 'Polack'," Top said with a smile.

"This here is the Professor." A tall, gangly guy with thick glasses and jet-black hair lay on his cot, deeply involved in a book. He dropped it quickly and reached up to shake hands.

"Sorry I won't be able to go out with you and show you the ropes," Professor said sarcastically. "But I will share everything I know with you during the next couple of days here."

"What more can I ask for? Thanks, Professor. Good to meet you."

"Next, we have Cotton Top." The First Sergeant pointed to a soldier who looked like he couldn't be more than fifteen years old. He sat on one of the cots writing letters. His short, nubby haircut and light blond hair must have accounted for his nickname.

"Glad to meet you," he replied in a boyish voice, waving in acknowledgement.

John nodded his head and returned the wave.

"This old bastard is Fuzzy." At the other extreme, that soldier looked to be at least fifty years old. "He's attached to the company CP, but is an artillery forward observer by trade. Fuzzy is our liaison in the field, coordinating the artillery fire missions and directing fast movers when they're supporting us. He doesn't carry a radio but helps out with the monitoring whenever he can."

Fuzzy offered an informal salute and went back to reading his book.

"And last, but not least, we have Stud."

A well-built and muscular soldier got up and heartily shook John's hand.

"One word of caution before I leave," Top looked at John with a smirk, "Don't ask Stud why he's called that unless you have a couple of hours to listen."

"Well, since you brought it up…"

Top cut him off abruptly. "Never mind, I've heard this story before. I'll leave you guys to get acquainted and see you later." Top strutted out of the bunker leaving the five men to themselves.

The beer flowed nonstop, and with never-ending discussions, the party turned into an all-night event.

Before the night ended, John knew more about his radio partners than he had thought possible, especially Stud. Each of them had at one time carried a radio in one of the rifle platoons and volunteered for the CP when the openings came up. They were all short-timers, none having more than four months left in their tours.

The next day, a rumor surfaced in the R&R center, upsetting everyone in the company. They heard that they were going back into the A Shau Valley to run patrols. It had been four months since last humping through the valley, and Alpha Company had lost almost a third of their men during a month-long period. The valley was a notoriously vicious area; Bastogne overlooked it from the east and several other firebases - Birmingham, Currahee, and Blaze - bordered on the west. A sister battalion fought a major battle the previous year on a hill that was later nicknamed 'Hamburger Hill'. Many men lost their lives during that siege; it too, was located in the Valley.

Later in the day, the rumor proved to be true. As the depressing news spread, the partying ended as if somebody suddenly flicked off a light switch. Instead, many of the soldiers began preparing for the upcoming mission, even though they had one more day remaining of their R&R.

When Alpha Company drew out supplies for the mission, each man requested additional field dressings for potential wounds, and plenty of extra ammunition. One by one, they visited the firing range and test-fired their weapons to ensure they were in proper working order.

The men readied themselves mentally and physically for the big fight that they knew was coming. John knew all too well how they felt; he felt the same way before heading into the Iron Triangle and the area where Zeke died. He did not have firsthand knowledge regarding the valley, but had a deep respect for the opinions of those who had been there.

## CHAPTER TWENTY-TWO

A quiet hush fell over the grunts as they boarded the choppers for their ride into the A Shau Valley. Only a handful of soldiers were veterans of the last campaign; those troops were focused and ready to face the devil. The other soldiers were naïve as to its dangers, but felt extremely nervous because of all the stories they had heard in the last day and a half.

It had been two weeks since John and Sixpack last carried a rucksack. Neither of them expected the total weight to be any different from the load they carried down south. They anticipated an adjustment period of only a day or two before getting a feel for humping in the mountains. Both found their assessment to be way off-base, mentally cussing out the brass and everyone else they passed, while walking toward the helipad.

SOP (standard operating procedure) for the Airborne infantry specified that each trooper would carry four days of rations instead of three, and six canteens of water instead of two, due to a lack of water in the mountains. Thousands of bomb craters existed in the bush, but without rain, only a thin layer of muddy slime existed on the bottom. The monsoon season was still a few weeks away for the northern part of Vietnam. When it arrived, it would take at least two weeks of heavy rain to fill the craters, and another week afterwards for the sludge to filter to the bottom. Only then, would there be enough water available, and fewer canteens would be needed.

A fifteen-pound flak jacket and steel helmet was part of the new wardrobe, adding to the total weight. The metallic-lined vest only covered a portion of the shoulders and did not provide a suitable cushion for the ruck straps, making it more difficult to carry. The grunts tried using what little cushion was available to support the straps, but when the ruck shifted, the straps fell off and dug into the edges of their shoulders. In the bush, the Wolfhounds always wore boony hats in place of the unpopular, heavy steel helmets, which caused headaches and stiff necks. In the Airborne, they wore helmets strapped snuggly under their chins at all times. In addition, John had to carry the radio and spare batteries; all combined to about an extra ninety pounds of weight. It was difficult enough to stay balanced on flat ground, let alone humping up the slope of a mountain. This would be a completely new experience for the former Wolfhounds.

Each of the four platoons were to land on different hilltops overlooking the valley. The plan was for the men to start working their way downhill, linking up on the valley floor on the following day. The Company CP attached itself to the Third Platoon for the first four days of the mission.

John had not been airborne for more than five minutes, but was already shivering and soaked with sweat. The cool, rushing air battered his sweaty body, causing his muscles to cramp and spasm. He tried hard to clear his mind and to think of something more pleasant to help control his fear and nervousness. He rubbed at his legs vigorously in an attempt to stop the spasms.

The first sortie of the Third Platoon had successfully inserted half their troops onto the LZ without incident. They secured the hilltop, and waited for the rest of the platoon and Company CP to land in the next flight. John listened to the radio, keeping the captain informed of the landings and their reported status. So far, all had been routine with no sign of the enemy.

Looking out of the chopper doorway, John saw the approaching landing zone on the top of a mountain. From this distance, it looked like the top of a friar or monk's head, bald in the middle, with thick, bushy growth surrounding it. The clearing was only large enough to accommodate one chopper at a time, but each of the pilots had performed this type of insertion more times than they could remember. The four choppers flew in a vertical line, spaced evenly apart, and stacked at different altitudes. The execution and timing for each landing was perfect; each bird was on the ground for no more than ten seconds to allow the passengers to jump out and move away. Briefly touching down like hummingbirds to blossoms, the copters just cleared the LZ when the next one landed. With enough choppers in a flight, the choreographed landing process placed sixty soldiers on the ground in a little over a minute. It was a remarkable and efficient process.

Upon landing, the five members of the CP moved to a designated corner of the LZ. John started calling the other platoons, establishing contact with them, Cotton Top relayed information over the battalion net to the officers at Camp Vandergrift, and Stud and Fuzzy coordinated their pre-set targets with the firebase.

The plan was to send out five-man recon teams from each platoon to check the immediate area and locate a safe route down the mountainside. Once that route was established, each platoon began its long descent from the hilltop, continuing until it was necessary to stop for the night.

It was difficult to determine just how many times the army had used this LZ up until that day. Beyond the clear landing zone, paths led into the surrounding vegetation from every direction. Alongside these paths, past soldiers had created dozens of sleeping positions inside the thick clumps of foliage. The ground was clear of obstacles, the overhead jungle offering some protection from the elements. A four-foot wide foxhole, dug three feet into the earth, was located at the rear of each "cave."

These areas were filthy, looking like a public park after an all-night rock concert. Empty C-Ration cans, cardboard boxes, plastic utensils, and even a few crumpled letters from home littered the landscape. Much of the refuse lay inside the foxholes, but the surrounding bushes, too, took on the appearance of trash-covered Christmas trees with wind-blown debris trapped within the branches and foliage. It was an unsightly mess, but nobody dared to touch anything for fear of it being booby-trapped.

The sound of gunfire to the west of Third Platoon's location suddenly shattered the sense of order. Green tracers ricocheted from the mountainside, rising high into the air. The intensity increased as red tracer-rounds joined the green ones in a macabre dance across the skies. A new, deep, base staccato sound also erupted from the same location, keeping pace with everyone's pounding heart. The soldiers shifted about nervously, faces registering worry.

"Eagle-one, this is Eagle-six, over," John heard from his handset.

"This is Eagle-one, go ahead," he responded.

"Roger. Any idea what is going on? That shooting is awfully close to us."

"That's a negative, Eagle-Six. Ram-four is checking on it now. I'll let you know the minute I hear something."

"Wilco, Eagle-six, out."

Cotton Top was Ram-Four; his ear was glued to the battalion radio handset since the firefight began. He took notes on a pad and collected whatever information he could from the discussions going back and forth between the unit in contact and Battalion HQ. Intermittently, Cotton Top broke away, providing an update to the others before quickly returning the receiver to his ear.

"Charlie Company ran into a fortified position with a heavy 51-caliber machine gun. The NVA have them pinned down and they are requesting air support. Don't know how many casualties yet but they're calling for Medevacs too."

"Polack, get on the horn and notify all the platoons to bring their recon patrols back to base and sit tight," Cap ordered, then moved closer to Cotton Top, listening in on the net with him.

As John relayed the information across the company net, those nearby stopped their chatter and quieted down so as not to miss any details.

The noise of Charlie Company's firefight continued in the distance, when suddenly there was an explosion on the next hill, where the First Platoon had landed earlier.

"Polack, call the First Platoon and find out what that was," Cap said, alarmed and looking anxiously between the two radio operators.

"Eagle-niner, this is Eagle-one, over."

"Uh, this is Eagle-niner, go ahead," a nervous voice responded.

"Roger, Eagle-niner, what was that explosion near your position, over?"

"Don't know yet, Eagle-one. I think our recon patrol hit something on the way back in. We're checking it out now. Let you know when we know something, over."

"Roger. Eagle-one, standing by."

There was a lot of fidgeting around on the hilltop. The soldiers had already felt edgy about the nearby firefight, and when the explosions began getting closer, they were naturally impatient to learn any news. When the recon squad returned to Third Platoon's hilltop, the men updated the squad members with what they knew up to that point. Their faces betrayed them; all were deeply affected.

"Eagle-one, this is Eagle-niner, over."

"Finally!" John grabbed the headset and depressed the squelch button, "Go ahead, Eagle-niner."

"Roger, Eagle-one. Recon patrol hit a booby trap just before they got the word to stop and turn back. We need a Medevac for the wounded, over."

"Wilco, Eagle-niner. How do you classify the wounded?"

"We've got two KIA, one urgent, and one priority."

"Roger. Stand by."

John updated the CP and requested the Medevac. Cotton Top immediately informed battalion of the situation while Stud and Fuzzy dialed up the Medevac frequency to make a call for help, quickly relaying the coordinates and priorities over the net.

"Inform the First Platoon that birds will be there in about five minutes," Stud called out.

"Eagle-niner, ETA of Medevac is zero-five. Do you copy?"

"Roger. ETA zero-five. Eagle-niner, standing by."

Several explosions and intermittent burring sounds, lasting several seconds each, suddenly drowned out Charlie Company's gunfire.

Cobra gunships joined Charlie Company's fight, firing rockets and mini-guns into the enemy's fortified positions. They were visible in the distance, circling slowly above the pinned down Americans, and then suddenly diving into the fracas like mad hornets. Green tracers rose from the ground, trying to follow the diving aircraft during its attack. White puffs of smoke, appearing every couple of seconds, were evidence of the Cobra firing pairs of rockets at the enemy. A solid red line raced to the ground from the mini-gun housed in the nose of the helicopter, remaining intact for several seconds before stopping suddenly at the end of its dive. The Cobra climbed back into the sky and joined other circling gunships, awaiting their turn for another run at the NVA. From this distance, it looked like the gunships were diving directly into the enemy fire, but none appeared to be hit. Either the NVA were firing with their heads down or the pilots were doing one hell of a job in avoiding the hot lead.

The effective gunships allowed Charlie Company to evacuate their dead and wounded to an area where a Medevac could land and pull the injured from the fight.

As John monitored the radio and watched the distant battle, First Platoon's Medevac came onto the company net, requesting smoke to identify the platoon's location. Several seconds later, a thread of green smoke snaked out of the jungle to the side of the hilltop, rising into the air not more than five-hundred meters away. The evacuation was soon over, with the wounded en route to the hospital within minutes.

"Eagle-one, this is Eagle-niner, over."

"Go ahead, Eagle-niner."

"Dust-off complete. Eagle-niner actual is requesting permission to move to a different location."

"Eagle-one, wait one."

John passed on the request to Cap, who quickly pulled out his map and began studying it. "Tell them I'll get back to them within a few minutes. Meanwhile, ask them for the nicknames of their casualties and how bad they were hurt."

"Eagle-niner, Eagle-one actual wants the nicknames of your casualties and the extent of their injuries."

"Roger Eagle-one, wait one." John had his pad and pencil ready to record the information. "Eagle-one, this is Eagle-niner, are you ready to copy?

"Affirmative, Eagle-niner, go ahead."

"The two KIA are Baker and Mr. Flowers. Beanpole had upper body wounds with a sucking chest wound, and Sixpack suffered a traumatic amputation of both legs, just below his knees."

John's heart skipped a beat. He hoped there was another Sixpack in the First Platoon.

"Eagle-niner, is this 'Sixpack' the same hard striper who just arrived?"

"That's affirmative."

John was stunned and momentarily rendered speechless at the news of his friend. The handset fell to the ground, and he buried his face into his hands. He began to sob and mumbled under his breath, "Fucking assholes, why did they have to take his beer?"

He dropped to his knees and started punching at his rucksack, slowly alternating his fists as tears ran down his cheeks.

"Goddamn it! Goddamn it!" He repeated, with each hit on the rucksack. He continued for several more seconds before he stopped, too emotionally drained to continue.

Those nearby were caught by surprise at John's rage, and watched in disbelief. He appeared to be undergoing a total mental breakdown. He sat on his heels, hands with palms resting on top of each thigh, rocking slowly back and forth. "Fucking assholes," he mumbled once more. His eyes were glazed and distant.

Before anyone else could react, Cap was behind him, holding him tightly in a bear hug.

"Easy, Polack, easy now! Come on, son, talk to me. What just happened?"

John suddenly stopped, turned his head, and looked directly into the eyes of those soldiers staring back at him. When he noticed the captain had him in a bear hug, he slowly returned to reality, aware of his responsibility to the young soldiers who watched him. "I'll be okay, Cap, he said quietly. Sorry for the meltdown."

"Are you sure?"

"Yeah, I'm sure."

Cap released him, and stepped back. John used his shirtsleeve to wipe the moisture from his face.

"Polack, you just scared the shit out of us. What the hell happened?"

"Sixpack lost his legs." John took a deep breath. The others, still stupefied, continued to watch and listen closely.

"Who's Sixpack?"

"He's my close buddy." He took a few deeper breaths, trying to regain his composure.

"Polack, tell me what happened to First Platoon," Cap requested, compassion filling his eyes.

"They had a five-man recon patrol down a ways from the hilltop and were about ready to return when they hit a booby trap." He stopped, taking a couple deeper breaths before continuing, "Baker and Mr. Flowers are KIA, Beanpole caught some shrapnel in his upper body and his lung is punctured, and my friend, Sixpack, lost both his legs below the knees." John's voice broke.

The expression on Cap's face showed that he, too, was deeply affected, but was struggling to maintain his composure.

Cap cursed under his breath, lowering his head and shaking it from side to side. "What a waste. Did you know Mr. Flowers' wife just gave birth to a baby girl last week? It was their first. Now she'll never know her daddy. Thank God that your buddy will most likely survive."

"He didn't have much of a life outside of the Army and was planning to make this a career. Now without legs…"

"I'm sorry, Polack. That's the price of this fucking war."

"What will happen to my friend now, Cap?"

"They'll most likely send him to Japan to get patched up, and then back to the states for rehabilitation in one of the VA hospitals near his hometown. He'll pull through this okay, you'll see."

"God, I hope so."

"Now tell me what that talk about beer was all about."

"When I first arrived in country, Sixpack told me that he brought a six-pack of beer over with him from the states as a good luck charm. In fact, that's how he got his nickname. His duffle bag was stored with everybody else's in the rear supply at Cu Chi and nobody bothered it. His plan was to drink the beer on his return to the world - celebrating on the freedom bird for surviving his second tour. On the first night we got up here to the 101st, somebody rifled his gear and stole the beer from his personal belongings. It broke his heart!"

"I guess I understand now. That was really low! Will you be okay or do you want Fuzzy to take over the radio for a while?"

"No, I'll be okay. I just need a couple of minutes to get my head back together."

"Yeah, go ahead. Call me if you need me," he said, and then left to rejoin Cotton Top at his radio.

The rest of the perimeter soon returned to normal. After hearing John's whole story, the men were sympathetic and now fully understood why he went berserk as he did. For some looking on, scenes like this had already played out countless times. They were well aware that nothing could ease the pain of their brother soldier; one could only offer condolences for their loss and move on. There was a catch phrase in Vietnam that was gaining popularity, and many soldiers had already added it to their vocabulary: "Fuck it - don't mean nothin'". It was the cure-all phrase for numbing emotions when hearing bad news or seeing a fellow soldier get hurt. Many of the men had it written in marker across their helmet covers. It was an excellent façade for hiding how they actually felt in front of others.

John wondered how many more of his friends would get hurt in the war and how much more of this hell he could take. He could already see the evil in A Shau Valley. If the valley lived up to its reputation, then the bloodshed was only beginning, and surviving the mission would take a whole lot of luck.

An hour later, the captain ordered platoons to begin their descent into the valley. They continued hacking and cutting a path down the side of the mountain until it was too dark to continue. It was only late afternoon, but the heavy jungle foliage and tremendous height of the trees made it appear closer to dusk. Cap ordered all movement to cease and the platoons to set up NDP's in their current positions.

From his experience as a radio operator, John knew that this part of the day would be his busiest. He dropped in his tracks and immediately began receiving the coded locations from the other three platoons. While decoding them and plotting the locations on a map, he was puzzled by the sight of the men digging foxholes into the side of the hill.

"Hey, Cap?"

"What do you need, Polack?"

"Why is everyone digging foxholes?"

"This is SOP and we do it every night. Matter of fact, you better get busy and start digging yours. The map-plotting can wait until after you're done."

John waited a moment until this new bit of information sunk in. He was dumbfounded and never had to carry the fold-up shovel in the south. His large Bowie knife was always sufficient to clear away brush and dig small latrine holes. He had never questioned why it was necessary to carry it up in the mountains. Up until then, he could only recall using a shovel in Vietnam twice. The first time was when he helped to build Firebase Lynch, and the second was a few weeks ago when repairing the bunkers in FSB Vandergrift.

The slope was quite steep; most of the men in the Third Platoon had already tied their rucks to nearby trees to keep them from rolling downhill during the night and hitting trip flares. At least the earth was soft in the spot where John started to dig. Without clay, digging his first foxhole in the brush was quick and easy. When he finished, he hung the radio on a low tree branch nearby and monitored from the depth of his foxhole.

Awake, the soldiers sat on the steep sloping ground and propped their feet against the trees below them. It was, however, a different story at night. The foxholes were only two to three feet wide; some of the men sat inside and slept with their backs against one of the walls. Those preferring to lie flat and stretch out on the ground found it difficult to remain in that position. John and others caught themselves during the night and awakened just in time to stop their slide downhill. After having repeated the exercise in futility a few more times, John changed his strategy and moved his sleeping position behind the large tree where he had tied his ruck earlier. He was somewhat successful in not waking anymore during the night, and still found himself wrapped sideways around the same tree in the morning. Strangely enough, he was amused to find that he was not the only one to wake up in the morning in that position.

Later that morning, the Third Platoon continued their descent to the valley floor. On two different occasions, they found their paths ending abruptly in a sheer drop off greater than fifty feet. This caused a further delay, forcing the men to retrace their steps and seek out a less dangerous route. Many of them incurred numerous scrapes and bruises on the difficult trek after losing their balance and sliding into a boulder or tree. It took the platoon until the late afternoon to complete their downward hump.

Two platoons from Alpha Company had already reached the valley floor much earlier and sent out recon patrols to survey the immediate area. John was quite surprised with their findings when hearing their report over the radio.

Fourth Platoon was furthest away and due west of the rest of the company. They had stumbled onto a large, well-used trail; deep ruts along its length implied that heavily laden carts used the trail to move heavy equipment and supplies. They were well-concealed from the air by fishing nets strung from trees overhead and covered with a layer of leaves and brush. This camouflage enabled the enemy supply trains to move openly any time during the light of day.

Second Platoon found a stream with four man-made pedestrian crossings; each was comprised of tightly packed stones, rising up from the streambed to within a foot of the surface. The stream was three feet deep, the current was lazy and slow, and the milky, brown-colored water covered any sign of the ten-foot wide underwater stone bridges. Engineered perfectly, the current offered no hint of these crossings and continued to flow unobstructed without generating a ripple. The four crossings were evenly spaced along three-hundred feet of the stream, and each had trails leading into the jungle from both sides. All exhibited signs of heavy use, as evidenced by deep tire marks and footprints embedded in the mud.

Neither of the remaining two platoons had an opportunity to send out recon patrols, as their steep descents from the mountains took them most of the day. Cap arranged for the platoons to all link up in the morning and further investigate the two areas of interest.

Darkness closed in quickly on the Third Platoon, thwarting their efforts to find a decent location for an NDP. For the second night in a row, they began setting up a small perimeter; digging foxholes, putting out trip flares and claymore mines, eating, and determining guard rotation before total darkness fell upon them. The ground rose slightly, but the terrain was nothing as treacherous as the night before; it would be much easier to sleep tonight.

At 0300 hours, explosions echoing loudly through the valley awakened the Third Platoon. Spaced ten seconds apart, they had difficulty pinpointing the origin.

John jumped quickly from under his poncho liner and sprinted to where Fuzzy was monitoring the radios during his watch. They heard a faint whisper on the company frequency - too garbled to understand. They adjusted the volume and squelch of the radio, but the transmission remained broken and distorted. John keyed the handset several times, hoping to break contact so he could identify and help the caller. He picked up the radio by its strap and moved it around to different locations in hopes of picking up the weak signal. The entire CP had their large telescopic antennae installed on radios, which would have helped with signal strength if the antennae did not tangle easily in the overhead foliage. Finally, after a slight pause, John heard the word 'Eagle', loud and clear. It was the only word spoken, but the squelch and static had returned, which meant the net was clear and no one was transmitting any longer. John took this opportunity to call out and try to establish contact with the caller.

"This is Eagle-one. Unit in trouble, please respond and identify, over." He paused for ten seconds, and then repeated the call.

After four attempts, the RTO in the First Platoon called, "Eagle-one, this is Eagle-niner. I thought I was able to make out Eagle-seven on that last transmission but it was too weak to be sure."

"Roger, Eagle-niner, thanks."

As the distant explosions continued, John attempted to reach Eagle-seven.

"Cotton Top, call HQ and let them know we've got a unit in trouble and it's not responding," Cap whispered. John continued his attempts to establish contact with the Second Platoon.

Suddenly, a cry for help interrupted the static on the radio. "Eagle-one, Eagle-one, we're being mortared."

"Who is being mortared? Please identify yourself!"

"My name is Ralph and I'm in the Second Platoon."

"Ralph, your call sign is Eagle-seven, what is your situation?"

"I don't know. I was asleep when the mortars started to hit. I kept my head down and continued calling out but nobody was answering me. All I can hear around the perimeter are screams for help. I finally got up enough nerve to crawl over to the L-T's foxhole, and found him and the RTO in bad shape. I'm on his radio now but I don't know what to do next. The mortars are still dropping on us. Can you help me?"

"Hold on, Eagle-seven."

The entire CP gathered around John, anxious to hear his report. When he finished telling them about the Second Platoon, Fuzzy asked for the handset so he could talk to Eagle-seven.

"Eagle-seven, this is Tac-one. Are you still there?"

"Yeah, I'm still here!"

"Okay, Eagle-seven, can you hear the tubes firing?"

"Yes sir."

"This is Tac-one. Which direction are they coming from?"

"Tac-one, I don't have a compass."

"Roger, Eagle-seven. I know where you are, but I just need to know if the firing you hear is coming from the mountain you came down or from a different direction. Listen closely."

"Tac-one, my back is to the mountain and they're shooting from my front."

"Roger, Eagle-seven. I am going to call in some artillery near your position. The first one is going to be a flare. After it pops, use it as a marker to guide me to the tubes. You are going to have to tell me whether to go right, left, or whatever, and how far. Have you got that?"

"Okay, Tac-one."

"Eagle-seven, I know you're scared, but you're going to have to raise your head up out of that foxhole for just a second for me to be able to help you. Are you okay with that?"

"I have no choice."

"Okay, Eagle-seven, hang in there; it'll only be a couple of minutes."

Fuzzy turned on his red lens flashlight and looked over the map. He gave the information to Stud, who quickly passed it along on the artillery frequency.

Only one minute expired when Stud whispered, "Shot out!"

"Eagle-seven, this is Tac-one. The flare is on the way. Watch for it and try to estimate where the tube is compared to where it pops."

"Tac-one, the flare is out to my front, but not far enough. I would say to add about two-hundred feet and then maybe go left about the same amount."

"Eagle-seven, the next one is going to be a high explosive round. You will hear where it hits. So, the plan is the same as before. Give me an adjustment afterwards."

"Shot out," Stud informed Fuzzy.

"Eagle-seven, heads up, it's on the way."

"Tac-one, they're close. Maybe add fifty feet and come back to the right a little."

After the next explosion, Eagle-seven called back in alarm, "Tac-one, when that round landed, there was a second explosion. Did you shoot twice?"

"Negative, Eagle-seven. It sounds like a secondary explosion. Perhaps you heard ammo explode. Keep your head down and I'm going to shoot a bunch of rounds in that same area. They'll move around a little, but don't get excited. They won't land near you."

"Thanks, Tac-one. The mortar has already stopped."

"That's okay, Eagle-seven. We're just going to make sure it stays out of commission. Hold tight. Rounds are on the way."

The twelve-round barrage began and sounded like a ferocious thunderstorm had just begun. The exceptionally loud claps of thunder sounded only microseconds before bright splashes of light interrupted the total darkness.

A new voice called over the company radio. "Eagle-one, this is Eagle-seven-six, over."

"This is Eagle-one, go ahead."

"Roger. We've got casualties here and need Medevacs ASAP."

"Eagle-seven-six, how many wounded do you have?"

"I don't know. We are still checking foxholes. So far, it looks like six KIA and about the same amount wounded. All of them urgent."

"Roger. Will contact dust-offs and get back to you with an ETA. Let me know when you have a final tally."

"Wilco, out."

The survivors in the Second Platoon knew it would be too risky for the Medevac helicopters to pull each wounded man up by cable through the thick valley foliage. It would take extra time that none of them could afford.

The surviving sergeant in charge got the men to begin dismantling their claymore mines and using the C-4 plastic explosive to blow away some of the trees. The birds needed a clear area of at least ninety feet to maneuver and land safely. It only took the group twenty minutes to create a suitable landing zone; the remaining tree stumps did not pose a hazard to a ship, which could drop vertically into the LZ.

It took close to an hour to evacuate the wounded and corpses. The final tally was seven killed, eleven wounded, and three missing - totaling almost half the platoon.

After looking at all the variables, the consensus was that the recon patrol had been spotted earlier in the day by the stream and then followed back to their NDP. The shooting had been too accurate to be the result of guesswork. Of the twenty-some rounds that hit, just two landed outside of their small perimeter.

Only twenty-three men survived the barrage, but not all escaped injury. Almost every one of them had minor wounds that required cleaning and bandaging, but none of them were serious enough to require evacuation from the field. As a result, they were stuck with picking up the pieces and carrying on after the assault.

Cap became concerned about their drastically weakened condition, but it was too risky for the Third Platoon to hump over a mile to link up with them. Too many things could go wrong in attempting such a rescue. Instead, he asked them to carry whatever they could and return to the mountain the same way they came earlier to get to their NDP. He wanted them to put as much distance as was feasible between themselves and the area where the mortars fired – and as quickly as possible. At first light, each platoon would move in that direction and link up with them at the base of their mountain.

Third Platoon was the last to arrive at the company gathering. Cap did not even stop to drop his equipment; instead, he sought out Ralph, the young man who directed the artillery fire the night before, saving the lives of twenty-three men. He found a very frightened eighteen year-old who had only been in Vietnam for three weeks. Ralph was still shaking when Cap reached him. Only then, did the older man remove his equipment and take a knee in front of Ralph. When he noticed the captain, Ralph was embarrassed and quickly jumped to his feet.

"At ease, troop, you don't have to stand up!"

"Sorry, sir, I didn't see you there."

"Ralph, you don't have to apologize for anything. I am so grateful for what you did last night and had to find you so I could thank you face-to-face. What you did was an unselfish act of bravery. Your courage saved the rest of the platoon, and certainly saved those already wounded; some would not have survived if the choppers didn't arrive when they did. That was also some good shooting as it seems you knocked out that mortar team after only a couple of fire adjustments."

Ralph was still shaky and seemed to be uncomfortable as the center of attention.

"When we return to the firebase, I'm going to submit your name for a Silver Star for Valor. Had you stayed in your foxhole and cowered in fear, we would most likely not be here having this chat. I want to thank you once again, and if you don't mind, it would give me great pleasure to shake your hand."

Cap extended his hand and the two men shook heartily. The officer then turned, retrieving his gear, and with John in tow, returned to the CP. Surprised by Cap's announcement, others began congratulating Ralph, previously unaware of his act of bravery. Humbled, Ralph brushed off the praise insisting that he had just done his job and nothing more.

Captain Robertson was more determined than ever to check out the stream and crossings. He was angered by the NVA watching his men and then targeting them for mortar attacks during the night. The captain organized the company into four separate columns and had them follow a route perpendicular to the stream. Their movement would allow the company to clear a three-hundred foot wide area through the jungle to the stream. En route, they expected to cross through the area where the mortars had fired from the night before. If all went according to plan, the columns would all reach the stream at the same time.

When passing through the area where the artillery barrage had hit, the damage was widespread and devastating. It looked like a hurricane passed through this area; shredded parts of the former jungle were piled high in spots, making it difficult for the men to traverse the area. The men came upon a single crater larger than the rest, looking as if a much more powerful explosion had created it. The ground and surrounding area was blackened and bare of vegetation for thirty feet around. Upon closer investigation, they also found pieces of human flesh clinging to foliage and littering the ground at the far end of the western diameter. They surmised this to be where the secondary explosion occurred, annihilating the mortar crew. There was no sign of the tube itself or its base plate - both perhaps blown across the valley by the explosion. It was impossible to determine the number of enemy soldiers destroyed by the blast; nevertheless, the sight did bring a smile to the faces of the Second Platoon survivors.

When reaching the stream, those members of the Second Platoon who had crossed the day before found that nothing had changed since their last visit. The ground was still undisturbed and showed no evidence of recent foot traffic.

They began searching through the immediate area when a distant rumbling noise further upstream got their attention. Cap sent the First Platoon on a recon patrol to find the source. They dropped their packs and split into two groups, walking upstream with two squads on each side of the slowly moving, muddy water.

As they moved forward, the rumbling noise grew louder and more pronounced. After walking close to a quarter of a mile, they glimpsed a beautiful waterfall through the trees just a short distance away. The water cascaded over large boulders and fell thirty or so feet to the stream. The men were relieved to find the source of the unfamiliar sound. Even from this distance, they felt the cool mist of the waterfall surround them. The vaporized water offered a brief, pleasant respite from the jungle heat as it settled onto their bare arms and faces. The men stood entranced and were reluctant to move.

Their ecstasy ended abruptly when the point man spotted what he thought to be soap bubbles floating on the water. They informed Cap of this observation; he responded that it might be foam created from the falling water. However, he directed them to proceed cautiously and see what else they could find.

The patrol did not have to move too far before coming upon a nearly-hidden pool at the base of the mountain. About twenty-five feet in diameter, it sat in a large natural crater, with gentle rapids leading away in three directions and feeding the streams.

Both columns stopped abruptly and dropped to a knee when hearing laughter and loud voices from under the roaring waterfall, the point men moving forward cautiously for a closer look. To their surprise, ten enemy soldiers were near or in the pool. Two uniformed guards stood near the rim of the crater, but paid no attention to the surrounding area. Instead, they cajoled with the other eight naked soldiers bathing in the water.

Both point men returned to their groups and whispered their findings to the waiting men. The Lieutenant immediately called the CP.

"Eagle-one, this is Eagle-niner actual, over."

"This is Eagle-one, go ahead."

"Be advised that we have ten November Victor Alpha (NVA) in the open and will engage in one-mike (minute), over."

John informed Cap, and he quickly took the handset from him.

"This is Eagle-One actual, talk to me."

"Roger, one actual, we located enemy soldiers in a pond at the base of a waterfall. They're bathing and have posted armed guards on both sides."

"Have you been seen?"

"Negative. They are making too much noise and the guards are not paying attention. They will be totally surprised."

"Roger, niner actual. Be careful and good hunting. Eagle-one actual, standing by."

Thirty seconds later, a ferocious deluge of gunfire burst forth toward the crater; it started suddenly and did not change in tempo, every weapon firing on automatic.

Both armed guards on the rim of the crater were the first to go; small puffs of smoke arose from different areas across their upper torsos as dozens of bullets found their mark. The two remained standing for a few seconds during this onslaught, appearing to mimic a marionette's spastic movements. When the firing shifted to the pool, the two lifeless bodies of the armed guards collapsed to the ground and slid downhill into the water.

The ambush totally surprised the bathing soldiers, panicking the group. Some swam with purpose toward the edges of the pond; others dove deep underwater hoping to find refuge. Small geysers appeared throughout the pool as hundreds of red-hot steel projectiles hit the water; many of the rounds found the frantic swimmers, preventing them from reaching the edge. Some of the bodies bobbed in the angry and rough water when bullets found them again. Two remaining enemy soldiers ducked under water, trying to find a last minute haven in the murky depths. They lived a minute longer than the others, and died quickly when breaking through the surface, gasping to replenish their supply of oxygen.

After thirty seconds, the L-T called for a halt in the firing and then dispatched one squad to watch the trail leading away from the pool. He did not want another group of NVA to walk up and surprise them. Meanwhile, two soldiers kept their eye on the floating corpses, watching for movement, while the rest of the squad gathered weapons and searched through the enemy supplies.

The smell of gunpowder hung heavily in the air, a bluish-white cloud of smoke billowed slowly before eventually dissipating a few minutes later. All the bodies were drifting on the surface, some face up and some face down. The brown, soapy water had turned to crimson - dark where blood had collected and much lighter near the base of the waterfall where fresh water was beginning to rinse away the signs of death.

Only five minutes had expired since the opening volley. The L-T took the radio handset from the RTO.

"Eagle-one actual, this is Eagle-niner actual, over."

"Go ahead, niner actual."

"Roger, engagement successful. No casualties and no survivors."

"Great job! What is your ETA back to my position?"

"Unknown at this time. We are searching through their packs and tossing everything we do not keep into the pond. It is quite deep and should hide the equipment for months. Will let you know when we're done."

"Eagle-one actual, roger, out."

In their search around the waterfall, First Platoon did not find anything of substance within the stowed gear. They located only two rucksacks, packed with soap, towels and clothing, and ten AK-47 rifles with bandoliers of ammo. This concerned the grunts, strongly suggesting a base camp or staging area was nearby. They quickly tossed everything into the water, placed a call to the CP, and then moved out to rejoin the company.

The enemy's mistake in using soap had given them away. Had the point men not spotted bubbles flowing in the stream, the platoon might not have caught them so unprepared.

When moving back downstream, the current carried continuous ribbons of crimson-colored water, keeping pace with the platoon as they quickly tried to put some distance between themselves and the waterfall.

When Cap received the earlier call from the First Platoon informing him of enemy soldiers in the open, he had gathered the rest of the company and moved them away from the stream crossings and closer to the waterfall. When the firing started, the men halted, waiting patiently in a reactionary mode until the platoon returned safely.

Now, that everyone was together again, the men took a break while the L-T briefed Cap about their find. There were no documents or souvenirs to share, and the fact that they only found soap, towels and clothes within the rucksacks could mean that First Platoon had stumbled upon a regularly-used enemy bathing pool. The NVA's high level of confidence and lack of security indicated that their 'home' was very near.

Cotton Top was keeping battalion informed ever since the initial call from the First Platoon, sharing their theory of a nearby base camp or staging area. This piece of information piqued their interest and the planners began working on a mission right away.

When Alpha Company returned to the area where the underwater stone bridges were located, they were quick to note wet ground and muddy footprints leading into the jungle on the other side of the stream. A group of people had evidently been in a hurry to get across while the Americans were upstream.

The platoon leaders quickly dispatched a squad to recon just inside the jungle on both sides of the stream, while the officers took a closer look at the area around the crossings.

John looked over to Cap and said, "This is really weird, it seems like enemy soldiers are all around us."

"I agree. But I'm guessing that this particular group is trying to evade us and keep out of our way for an especially sinister reason. Who knows? They might be hustling up some kind of an ambush as we speak."

"Why don't we leave some mechanicals set up here and move away to a different location?"

"What do you mean by mechanicals?"

"You know, booby traps with claymores."

"I've heard of them, but we've never used them since I've been here. I doubt if anyone even knows how to make one."

"I do."

"You do? How does it work?" Cap asked, intrigued.

"You set up a string of mines to cover a certain area and connect them to each other with detonation cord and blasting caps. Then you set a trip-wire somewhere in the middle and hook the entire thing to a six-volt battery. When the wire is tripped, the mines explode."

"And you can make these?"

"Yep. I only need the right supplies."

"Okay. Talk to Fuzzy and have him get you what you need. He'll make sure it comes out on our resupply tomorrow."

This excited Cap. It was something new for him and might even give his company a slight edge in the valley.

John solicited the help of others while waiting for the resupply and started to make some of the components for the mechanical ambush. Cotton Top and Fuzzy both helped. They cut off the tops from several c-ration cans, and then bent them in half, wriggling each one back and forth until they broke in two. Using large Bowie knives, they punched out small holes into each of the lid halves and plastic knives. Others whittled away at finger-thick pieces of tree branches, sharpening the eighteen-inch long stakes like huge pencils. When done, they had enough supplies to build ten small mechanical ambushes.

After the resupply, some of the guys in the Third Platoon were anxious to be involved, and asked if they could help in preparing the rest of the equipment. John split up the work and supervised these volunteers after some instruction. The most dangerous job was cutting the detonation cord into twelve-foot long sections and crimping blasting caps onto each end. It was important to keep them away from electrical devices, fires, and to handle them gently. The bright and sunny weather would make this process go smoothly. If a storm was approaching, static electricity alone could detonate a blasting cap. By itself, these were nothing more than firecrackers, but when attached to a detonation cord, there would be a major explosion. For that night, they would only need to prepare six of the sections for the three ambushes.

Some of the men worked with the thin, clear line, wrapping twenty-five feet around the top of each stake like a fishing reel, and then securing the end to a plastic knife. A rubber band held the utensil to the stake.

The project went quickly, and, after John tested and double-checked his work, he informed Cap that all pieces were ready. Cap was anxious to move out and get the ambushes set up, and since the Third Platoon personnel helped with most of the work, he thought it only fair that they help to set them up. The men divided all the fabricated supplies, nine claymore mines, and three six-volt batteries between themselves and prepared to move out. Fuzzy would monitor the company frequency and keep in contact with the RTO of the Third Platoon: Eagle-five.

At the stream, the men only took a few minutes to determine which of the paths offered the best opportunity for a successful ambush.

John and four volunteers moved up one of the paths into the jungle; Cap followed closely behind with a notepad and pencil in hand. When finding a suitable spot, John instructed his students on where to place the mines, spacing them ten feet apart and back about two feet from the trail. Each claymore mine has two ports, which made it easy to daisy chain the mines for simultaneous detonation.

The plan was going well. The group of young soldiers were eager to learn, and Cap was favorably impressed by John's technical knowledge.

"That's it for this one. She's all set to go," John said with a wide grin. The other volunteers smiled, also pleased.

"Is that all there is to it?"

"That's it."

"Damn, there's nothing to it! Do you mind if I hook up the next one?"

"Be my guest, Cap."

When setting up the ambush on the next trail, Cap read from his notes and directed the same volunteers in the systematic process. This time, the set-up went much faster as less explanation was necessary. Cap walked through the shin high trip wire and both John and Cap were pleased with the outcome. Cap unrolled the long length of cord, all five men took cover, and he successfully made the final connection to the battery.

The group placed the third mechanical to cover a trail on the other side of the stream. John only supervised the volunteers and allowed them to set up this last ambush by themselves. Later, he thought, they would be able to help in the training of others in the company so that each platoon could do it successfully.

Third Platoon gathered on the main trail and then started their mile long hike back to the NDP. Upon their return, there was excitement in the air as they waited for the sound of exploding claymore mines, which they expected at any moment.

They were disappointed when nothing happened during the first night. Some of the men had doubts about the ambush, questioning the reliability of the components and of the possibility that the NVA had dismantled the booby traps. The comments swayed Cap, and he decided to send out the Third Platoon again after breakfast. They would check on the three ambushes and scout the immediate vicinity for activity.

Suddenly, the sound of a distant explosion took everyone by surprise. There was a moment of panic before the men realized that it was one of the mechanical ambushes detonating. Those around the perimeter smiled and began congratulating each other with high fives. Cap stood up and walked over to where John had been eating breakfast. He was halfway there when a second loud explosion sounded from the same vicinity.

"Goddamn, Polack, we're tearing them up!" Cap was jubilant.

"You don't know how good that makes me feel. I was beginning to have my doubts, but now…"

A third explosion stopped John in mid-sentence.

Everyone was stunned for a few seconds, amazed that all three ambushes had blown within a five-minute period.

"Holy shit! I can't believe it! Has something like this ever happened before, Polack?"

"Never, Cap. This is a first for me."

Imploring faces looked toward the CP; the men were anxious to check out the results of their work.

"Is it possible that the first ambush could have set off the others?"

"It would be highly unlikely, Cap - unless something was blown into the air and fell exactly onto the trip wire of the other two. You also have to consider that animals like wild boars or monkeys could trip ambushes; I've seen that happen a few times before."

Cap contacted the platoon leaders and informed them that the Third Platoon would be going to check on the ambushes. The others would remain in place and on standby, ready to support them if they ran into trouble. They all relished the thought of catching NVA in booby traps for a change, and waited patiently to hear the results.

When the platoon was within fifty meters of the first blown ambush, the men stopped and Cap ordered a 'mad minute', directed toward the ambush sites on both sides of the stream. Almost forty weapons, M-16's and M-60 machine guns fired a barrage of flying lead relentlessly through the areas to their front. When the firing stopped, the men split into three separate groups and advanced slowly toward the three ambush sites.

The results were the same at all three. The exploding claymore mines had destroyed the area surrounding the ambush locations and bodies littered the ground at each of the sites. In total, they counted seventeen dead NVA soldiers in full battle gear. Except for their pith helmets, they were dressed similarly to the Americans: wearing fatigues, web gear, and boots, and they carried rucksacks stuffed to capacity. The enemy soldiers were sprawled on the ground in various positions and had internal organs exposed and missing limbs. The green and brown foliage on the other side of the trail was speckled in red - human tissue and blood were still dripping to the ground. Fragments of white bone hit nearby trees, leaving the bark looking as if buckshot had been fired into it.

The first order of business was to strip the equipment and search the bodies before leaving the area.

Billy Ray, one of the squad leaders, was the first to attempt to remove one of the rucksacks and struggled, getting nowhere. "Steven, come here and help me remove this rucksack. It weighs almost twice as much as mine," he said, frustrated.

The point man from New Jersey walked over to help the sergeant. "Damn, this shit is heavy. What do you suppose is in here, Sarge?" Both men struggled to remove the pack.

"We'll find out if we can ever get this thing off."

Finally, the squad leader used a Bowie knife to cut through the straps to remove the ruck from the corpse; they lifted it to the side and set it down next to the body. Billy Ray untied the straps, opened the covered flap, and began withdrawing items, handing them to Steve, who separated them into piles next to him.

Meanwhile, several other soldiers moved toward the other corpses and teamed up to remove those rucksacks, repeating the actions of Billy Ray and Steve.

"Look at all this shit these little guys carried. We got fish, rice, canned goods, cigarettes, ammunition, a change of uniform, cleaning gear, a wallet, and all their personal belongings."

"It must be the standard pack for all of them, Steve. This one has the identical stuff inside."

The L-T was correct; the contents of all the rucksacks were identical.

The odor was overwhelming; the stench of raw flesh and coppery - smelling blood engulfed the air. The sights and smells did not affect the old timers like John and some of the others, who, sadly, had to become accustomed to the bloodshed. The Cherries, on the other hand, had all vomited at one time or another, since encountering the carnage.

"Cap, you and the L-T need to see this," Sarge said, leading them back across the stream to the trail on the other side. "Check this shit out!"

The ruins of four bicycles, heavily laden with supplies, lay where they fell. The handlebars were extremely long, extending back to where a seat should have been. That must have made it easier for the porter to stabilize and maneuver the two-wheeled supply vehicle. Every inch of the frame had something tied to it; sacks filled with rice and fish, two mortar tubes and bases, mortar rounds, and extra weapons spilled over the trail.

"Now that's something you don't see in the jungle every day," the L-T said.

"This is the first time for me, Cap. I've never seen anything like this down south."

"This is a major supply route through the country, Polack; nothing I see here surprises me. Now if we knew of their final destination, that would be icing on the cake."

"You want me to take a patrol up the trail a ways to see what we can find?" The Spanish sergeant nicknamed 'Beast' asked.

"No!" Cap responded. "These supplies are for more soldiers than we have ourselves right now. Let's be patient and continue leaving mechanicals on these trails to see what develops."

This turned out to be one of the larger finds in the battalion during the last few months. It took the men almost the entire day to separate and evacuate all the equipment by chopper. Three new mechanical ambushes were set up further up the trails before the men packed up and headed back to the NDP.

Alpha Company spent the next two weeks patrolling through that part of the valley, hoping to find signs of the perceived NVA base camp. They were unsuccessful in locating it, but had much better results with the deployed mechanical ambushes, adding to the body counts and confiscated supplies.

The soldiers only fired weapons before checking blown ambushes and did not sustain any casualties during that time. It was a new record for Alpha Company in the A Shau Valley.

The other companies in the Valley were not as fortunate, as they continued to be mortared, encountered booby traps, and walked into ambushes. At times, Medevac helicopters evacuated the wounded from that company's area of operations as many as three times in a single day.

Alpha Company heard gunfire and explosions all around them every day, but none close enough to pose a threat or even worry about.

During the third week in the valley, the frequency of blown mechanicals dropped to zero; this necessitated patrols to return to the ambush sites, dismantle the mines and then set them up again in a new location. This exercise was repeated daily.

The Battalion Intelligence Group suspected the enemy might have either redirected their supply routes or stopped them altogether in fear of the dreaded American booby traps. When the week ended without having added to the body counts, the battalion brass ordered Alpha Company back into the mountains to resume patrols there.

The company started to lose men in the mountains every day, but not because of hostilities. Instead, Mother Nature had waged a battle against the grunts. Calls for Medevacs were requested daily as soldiers suffered from heat exhaustion, heatstroke, deep lacerations, and sprains that occurred when some lost their footing and fell down the uncertain slopes. Spinal injuries were also on the rise, as many soldiers wrenched their backs when the heavy rucksacks shifted unexpectedly during a slip or fall. John and the others lost weight rapidly, mostly due to dehydration. Their thigh and calf muscles burned and screamed from the exertion, only to cramp and tighten up when taking a break. Dealing with muscle spasms and charley horses became part of their nightly ritual.

After two weeks of climbing up and down the mountainside without any signs of the enemy, battalion withdrew Alpha Company from the Valley. It had been a very successful mission, with fifty-two kills credited to the company. The men were ecstatic to leave the Valley.

Alpha Company's new mission was to become a diversionary force in an area to the west of the main highway between Quang Tri and Camp Carroll. Fire Support Base Barbara was several miles west of the American base; Charlie Company moved into the FSB to reinforce those soldiers already there. Intelligence had received word of a large force massing in the area and planning to attack the firebase.

Cap and his warriors were to patrol through the area south of the FSB, looking for signs of the buildup. Intelligence had already cautioned the company that the force may be battalion-sized or larger, and if engaged, the Americans were to withdraw to a more defensible location and wait for reinforcements to arrive.

"What is a diversionary force?" Cotton Top asked.

"You don't know?" John asked.

"No, really, I've never heard the term before."

"It's a ploy to divert the enemy's attention elsewhere. In our case, we're going to be the decoys used to flush out the enemy and expose them before they have a chance to hit the firebase."

"That's fucked up, Polack!"

"On top of that, we won't be able to leave any mechanicals set up and armed during our patrols."

"Why not? Those ambushes work great and they cover our backs."

"I know they do, but the higher ups are worried that if we run into this large force out there somewhere and have to make a hasty retreat, we might run into our own claymores on our way back."

Cotton Top nodded soberly, uncomfortable with the plan.

During the first day, they found signs of new enemy activity throughout the area, and discovered two recently used staging areas. The NVA soldiers themselves, however, remained hidden.

Over the next three days, Alpha continued sending out numerous patrols in every direction, but they always returned without finding any new evidence of the large suspected force. The men began voicing their opinions, letting everyone within earshot know they were tired of these endless patrols, looking for an enemy that did not exist. Most of the men already believed there was no truth to the intelligence information about the buildup and possible attack on the firebase. They soon found out how wrong they were.

The NVA soldiers had been watching the decoy company for days, refusing to take the bait. Instead, they remained very stealthy, evading the many patrols and skulking around their positions undetected.

Just after midnight on the fourth night, a full-scale assault launched against Charlie Company and the protectors of Firebase Barbara. Mortars and rockets slammed into the firebase for an hour before the ground assault began.

During this barrage, sappers were moving through the barbed wire toward the perimeter, using Bangalore torpedoes to blow holes through the mass of barbed wire. The men in the bunkers kept their heads down and did not seem to be aware of the enemy activity in the wire around the firebase. These sappers created clear pathways for the attacking forces, granting direct access over the berm and into the compound.

The sound of whistles and trumpets blowing from the surrounding jungle announced the start of the ground attack. Hoards of enemy soldiers advanced on the firebase from three different directions. In a wild-eyed frenzy and screaming insanely, they ascended the hill toward the firebase, weapons firing on full automatic. Charlie Company defenders did all they could to slow down the onslaught of feverish attackers. Some claymore mines still worked and quickly blew as the scourge continued pushing forward through the pathways in the wire. The base Mortar Platoon kept the area lit with flares and fired high explosive rounds into the advancing enemy on the hillside.

The 105mm artillery guns leveled their barrels and waited for enemy soldiers to breach the perimeter. Their chambers, loaded with beehive rounds were now giant shotguns - ready to shoot thousands of steel darts at point blank range into the advancing forces.

M-60 machine gunners around the perimeter soon started to have misfires as barrels overheated from continuous firing; the troops were almost out of oil to keep the barrels cool, with no spares seemingly anywhere nearby.

As the ammunition dwindled, a short pause in the firing enabled some of the NVA to infiltrate into the compound. A number of Charlie Company men inside the perimeter were surprised and had to resort to hand-to-hand combat to save their own lives. Others were not so lucky, as passing enemy soldiers threw satchel charges into their bunkers en route to the Command Bunker in the center of the compound.

Cobra helicopters soon arrived and fired at the enemy running rampant outside the perimeter. Jet fighters also came on station, dropping bombs and napalm into the jungle areas surrounding the camp.

After two hours of intense fighting, the raging battle tapered off and enemy soldiers retreated into the surrounding jungle. Both sides suffered many casualties in this ferocious battle, but the guardians of Fire Support Base Barbara refused to give up.

While the fight was taking place, Alpha Company left their NDP and moved into a blocking position, about a mile away from the firebase. There, they placed a dozen strobe lights onto the ground, pointing upward into the black sky along the front line of soldiers. Fuzzy and Stud had already alerted the aircraft circling overhead of the friendly forces blocking the enemy's route of retreat. They also informed the birds that the line of strobe lights extended along the length of their ambush. Overhead aircraft commanders marked the location of the skirmish line, promising the men on the ground that they would engage enemy soldiers well to their front.

One of the Air Commanders informed Cap that a large group of retreating soldiers was coming their way. Prior to taking the defensive stand, the company had set up ten mechanical ambushes fifty meters to their front and fifty meters on each flank, hoping this first line of defense would stop most of them before the actual shooting started.

Alpha's soldiers had completed their foxholes in record time, sliding into them, and packing dirt firmly to the front of the hole to ensure a clear line of fire.

While waiting for the aggressors to arrive, the firebase fired artillery and 81mm mortars in the direction of the fleeing NVA, flanking them to funnel the retreating group toward Alpha's killing zone.

It was not a long wait until the first of the beaten and weary NVA forces arrived. Nobody in the blocking force could see them, but could hear them crashing through the jungle as if chased by ghosts.

A group of seven NVA tripped one of the mechanicals and fell dead. Those running behind them continued to push forward, thinking the mortars from the firebase had found them. When a second ambush detonated, they finally realized that they had entered a minefield. They came to a stop, assessed their options, and then changed the route, choosing to follow a path leading across Alpha's front. The grunts had been sitting nervously and waiting for the order to open fire.

Cotton Top gave battalion a clear picture on the radio of what was taking place to their front. He also received word that Alpha was to hold their fire until the rest of the reactionary force was in position. Bravo and Delta Companies airlifted into an LZ a mile away and were currently flanking Alpha's line on both sides; they were only minutes away from being in position.

Artillery was on standby and ready to fire at the enemy soldiers, and Cobra gunships returned with a fresh and full complement of armaments. When everybody was in place, the gunships would begin their attack, scattering the NVA toward the infantry blocking positions.

The Alpha Company men were watching the enemy closely from their foxholes. Some had been counting the shadows as they crossed through their field of fire. One of the Third Platoon members whispered that he had counted eighty-six so far. He may have missed some or even counted others twice; it was not important because everyone could plainly see dozens of soldiers out there. John knelt in his foxhole, the handset glued to his ear. He peered over the lip at the shadows to his front, hoping that nobody would be trigger-happy and start shooting before everything was in place.

The column of enemy soldiers suddenly stopped and each person quickly squatted low to the ground at the sound of approaching helicopters. The enemy soldiers were confident that the black of night would hide them; they squatted and waited until the birds passed harmlessly overhead.

On a signal from battalion, the strobe lights turned on. The Cobra gunships immediately began their strafing runs on the stalled column of NVA, flying from right to left well in front of the blocking forces lines. Mini-guns buzzed and rockets fired in pairs, signaling the start of the ambush. At the same time, Alpha Company opened fire. They could not physically see the soldiers through the smoke and darkness, but fired their weapons from the rim of their foxholes and toward their front. The Americans kept their heads down, not taking any chances that would make them a lucky target for the other side.

The NVA, surprised by this swift action, was unable to return fire. Just then, artillery rounds began raining down on top of them. After several salvos, the rounds began moving away from Alpha Company's line, exploding further away, in an attempt to block any retreat in that direction, thereby, effectively trapping them.

There was mass confusion within the enemy ranks. Many refrained from firing and sought shelter instead. They took off at a fast run through the raining steel, only to drop dead onto the ground after just a few meters.

The massacre was over in fifteen minutes when it was clear that no more shadows were moving through the area. The Cobras continued their surveillance from overhead, looking for a reason to start firing again. There were no survivors, and Barbara got some payback.

Alpha Company remained in the immediate vicinity with the other two companies for another two days, chasing down those stragglers retreating toward Laos. Then, as a reward, the brass pulled Alpha Company from the jungle by chopper, flying them to a new base for some well-deserved R&R.

There was much speculation and discussion between the Alpha Company grunts as to where they were going. Most agreed that none of the firebases up in this part of the country would qualify as a suitable location for R&R, especially with all the recent activity around some of them. If given a choice, many of the men would have preferred to remain in the field, where in their opinion, it was much safer in retrospect. However, when considering a place that qualified as an R&R reward, Phu Bai, Da Nang, and China Beach topped the list of probable locations.

The group had worked very hard in the bush during the last five weeks, and welcomed an opportunity to sleep soundly through the night, take showers, and eat normal chow for a couple of days – their definition of a very merited R&R.

Nevertheless, on the day of the scheduled pick up, the men learned they were joining the rest of the battalion at Camp Books near Da Nang. No one in the company had ever heard of Camp Books or patrolled through that area around Da Nang.

Upon their arrival, the grunts learned that Camp Books was a Marine base camp. The jarheads were going home and vacating many camps in the area. The 1st Battalion would secure this base during their withdrawal and stay there until the ARVN's took it over.

The grunts soon discovered that the area surrounding Books had been friendly and quite secure for some time now. After hearing this, they really looked forward to the much-deserved rest.

Mail finally caught up to the moving soldiers at Camp Books. Letters from home were a big deal and when received, everything else could wait. The men were filthy, smelled, wore tattered clothing, and had scruffy beards that needed to be shaved. They were hungry, thirsty, and some required medical attention.

However, sweet words from loved ones had arrived. The top priority now was to find a private place in the shade to read them.

John looked through his mail and then remembered that he had not taken the time to send his new address to the parents of his former Wolfhound friends. He assumed the same had happened to everyone else but BJ - John's mother informed him in one of the letters of his new address in the 173rd Infantry, Americal Division. He left those addresses at Phu Bai with his personal gear, but promised himself to make every effort to contact them in the near future.

## CHAPTER TWENTY-THREE

Camp Books was a refreshing change. The area assigned to Alpha Company had all the luxuries of home. The barracks had beds with sheets and pillows, and electricity to power dozens of fans and radios left behind by the Marines. In the day room, troops had access to a refrigerated soda pop machine, a TV, and a pool table. The latrines were equipped with all the modern conveniences, including hot and cold running water. A mess hall operated by the battalion cooks served three hot meals a day. What more could a grunt ask for?

After two days of R&R, the colonel assigned Alpha Company to bunker guard. They were responsible for securing two and a half miles of the extensive perimeter. There were just enough bodies available to fulfill this obligation, with the men working two twelve-hour shifts.

The CP's responsibility did not change much. They continued to monitor the radios and bunker phones, and battalion headquarters expected situation reports regularly. The four men in the CP also took on the role of goodwill ambassadors, and every four hours one of them drove a jeep along Alpha Company's sector of the perimeter, delivering hot coffee, cold pop, and sandwiches to those people in the bunkers. Extremely appreciative of this kind gesture, the grunts welcomed the opportunity to learn more about those "lazy" people in the CP.

Every person in the company worked a mandatory twelve-hour shift each day, resulting in an equal amount of time off to catch up on sleep, read, shoot pool, or just lounge around the barracks.

It was, indeed, a serious change of pace for the grunts; many never had an opportunity like this since they arrived in country. Compared to what they had endured so far, this was paradise.

The inactivity, however, soon bored the battalion lifers, and they began making drastic changes - mirroring stateside duty before the week was even over. Company formations now took place every day in the morning and evening, to accommodate both bunker guard shifts. Every person was required to shave daily and get a haircut once a week. Boots had to be polished, beds had to be made daily with square corners, barracks cleaned, and an officer performed walk through inspections every other day. Battalion officers banned the wearing of non-military issued clothing and jewelry when in the camp; this did not go over well with the militant 'brothers' who continued to wear small items in defiance to the rule.

Since these inspections began, polishing muddy, worn-out boots, cleaning barracks, and policing the grounds consumed most off-duty time, not leaving much time for sleeping or other personal activities. The men began taking advantage of their time on guard duty to sleep and catch up on reading or letter-writing. There were always two men in each bunker, so taking turns on watch was not a problem,

As if this constant state of flux and order-changing was not confusing enough, the rules changed again after the second week - this time, however, it was to the young soldiers' advantage. When the Marines ran the camp, they employed young hooch boys and girls from the nearby village to take care of all the cleaning, paying as little as five dollars a week. Battalion granted the men permission to rehire these young, enthusiastic workers; four to each barrack, they worked long hours to please their new camp employers. They polished jungle boots, washed clothing and linen, and kept the barracks and grounds immaculate. The money spent was well worth it and the men regained some of the leisure time they had lost a week earlier.

Life on the base soon bored the soldiers; nothing new happened outside of bunker guard, and the novelty quickly wore off.

At the end of the first month, John was on radio watch in the CP when Cap approached with good news. "Polack, I'd like you to know that I've recommended you for promotion to sergeant."

"No shit?"

"Yeah, no shit!"

"Thank you, Cap, that's great news! When will I get my stripes?"

"You'll have to earn them. If all goes well, you should be scheduled to stand in front of the review board within a week."

"Review board? What's that all about?"

"Didn't you know that promotion to E-5 and above had to be approved by a review board?"

"No, I didn't. What do they do?"

"They'll ask you questions about military procedures and weapons, judge you on your appearance, and the military manner in which you conduct yourself during the interview."

"You mean I have to go in front of them and answer questions?"

"You sure do."

"Who's on this board?"

"Normally, there are five officers from the battalion who sit on a board like this, usually meeting about once a month."

"Is that all there is to it? After the interview I get my stripes?"

"I'm afraid it's not that easy. It's really a test. You'll need to know your shit and be able to impress the hell out of them."

"Why is that?"

"Polack, just because you go in front of the board doesn't mean an automatic promotion."

"It doesn't?"

"Hell no! There might be one-hundred soldiers going in front of that board, but division may only have twenty allocations available within the battalion. After the board interviews you, they'll rate you - like in the Olympics - and place you in line according to your score. If there are only twenty openings available, then the top twenty will get the stripes."

"How in the hell do I study for something like that?"

"Go see Top. He's got some manuals in his bookcase that might help you."

"Thank you, Cap. I'll go and visit him after my watch is over."

"Okay, let me know if you need anything." Cap walked to the doorway, stopping before opening the screen door. "Hey, Polack?"

John looked at Cap standing in the doorway; the captain gave John the thumbs up sign. "Good luck," he said and then exited the building.

Later when John arrived at Top's hooch, he knocked on the door, entering when the First Sergeant acknowledged him. Top sat at his desk, holding a couple of books in his outstretched left hand.

"Hey, Top, Cap asked me to come and see you about some books."

"They're right here," he nodded toward the two Army manuals in his hand and pushed them toward John.

"How did you know I was going to ask for them?"

"It's part of my job to know everything that's going on around here."

"Shit, you got ESP or something?"

"No, I don't," he replied, chuckling. "Cap was in here a little while ago and asked me if I had any books to help with your exam. When I showed him these, he said he was going over to talk to you."

"Will these books tell me what I need to know for the board interview?"

"They should. Ninety percent of the questions and answers come from these books."

"Way to go, Top!" John cheered enthusiastically.

"You know you're the only candidate for E-5 representing Alpha Company, so you take these books and you study 'em really hard. If you need help, then come and see me. I want you on top of that promotion list. It'll be a plus for Alpha Company."

"Why will it be a plus for the company?"

"Polack, it's just like being a parent. The things your kids do always reflect back on you. If your kids are wild and raunchy, then other adults will blame the parents for not giving a shit and raising their kids poorly. In our case, if you pass, it'll show battalion that those of us in Alpha Company are doing our job and training you properly."

"Makes sense - what kind of chance do you think I have?"

"Your chance of making it will be the same as everybody else facing the board. You have an edge though, as there are not too many of these manuals floating around. Just study hard. I think you'll make a fine NCO."

"Okay, Top. Thanks for your help."

"No problem, son. It will be a snap. Now get the fuck out of my hooch. I'm sure you have better things to do than standing here all goo-goo eyed."

John was startled and did not expect him to react this way. "I'm going, I'm going," he replied and back-stepped toward the door.

"Haven't you forgotten something, troop?"

"No, I don't think so..." he stammered. "I thanked you, and I do have the books," John motioned to the books in his hand.

"That's not what I meant, shit-for-brains. What do you say when you leave the presence of an officer or NCO in this fine division?"

John thought for a second, then answered with a grin when it suddenly came to him: "Airborne, Top!"

"All the way! Now wipe that shit-eating grin off your face and get the fuck out of here."

John rushed through the doorway, and once outside, turned to look inside. Top was shaking his head and laughing. He got a big kick out of needling people, and John never knew if he was serious or just toying with him.

The Army manuals were the driest reading material John had ever read. The manuals contained technical information, rules, regulations, strategy, and logical theory. At times, it took him almost an hour just to get through one page, because he kept nodding off while reading. John soon learned that it was much easier to scan through the manuals, spending a few moments reading the unfamiliar pages. By the end of the week, he had paged through each book three times and was comfortable with the knowledge he had gained.

When his turn came to face the board, John presented himself sharply, and successfully answered every question with little or no hesitation. The manuals had been a great help for the technical and regulatory answers, but the rest of the answers only required common sense and good judgment. The officers asked the last question forty minutes later. After his final response, the board members congratulated him and wished him well. Dismissed, John saluted and then executed a precision about face before walking out of the room.

He was very pleased with the interview and felt confident that he would place near the top of the list. Now, he just needed to remain patient and wait for the posted results.

John knocked on Top's door to return the manuals, but there was no answer. Peering through the screen door, he saw the hooch was vacant. Against his better judgment, he opened the door and quickly placed the manuals in the center of the desk. Then, taking a blank sheet of paper from the stack next to the typewriter, he scrawled a quick note: 'It was a snap! Thanks for all your help, Top - AIRBORNE!' He placed it face-up on top of the books, and made a beeline for the door.

The battalion was on Books for six weeks when another rumor surfaced about them leaving the base camp and returning to the field. It was quite unsettling to hear that a majority of the grunts were hoping the rumor was true; they had their fill of spit and polish, welcoming the chance to duck bullets and kill Communists again.

During his stay on the hill, John had made numerous observations regarding the men in the battalion. The 'stoners' and 'peaceniks' were comfortable with life in the camp and preferred to stay, if given the opportunity. On the other end of the spectrum, the boozers - beer and whiskey drinkers - were more aggressive and sometimes appeared masochistic. Lifers and Cherries fell somewhere in between. The short timers, on the other hand, were a paranoid group; with only weeks left before going home, they never wanted to set foot into the bush again. John fell into the last category with only six weeks remaining in Vietnam; the current assignment suited him just fine.

All during that next week, small groups of ARVN soldiers were arriving daily by trucks and began replacing Americans in bunkers around the perimeter. Once again, the rumor started to play itself out as the first of the battalion's companies left Camp Books and returned to the bush. Alpha Company had not yet received the official word, but the handwriting was on the wall; only the day and destination were missing.

Alpha Company learned over the weekend that their life of luxury was ending on Monday. The grunts were to surrender everything accumulated during their stay on Books, giving all the supplies to the ARVN when they took over; nobody could use or wanted to carry any of the stuff in the bush anyway.

Many of the men resented the decision to leave behind those treasures that helped make their stay more comfortable and civilized. Of course, they followed orders and turned everything over to the supply clerk, but, according to a unanimous and surreptitious plan, the electric fans, radios, etc., had all been methodically disassembled. They had combined all the electrical cords from the fans into one large box, while fan blades, motors, and protective covers filled several other boxes.

It was not the intent of the men to destroy everything out of spite before leaving the camp, but they acted out of principal. The ARVN had a sleazy reputation, and the Americans were well aware that anything left behind would end up on the Black Market within days.

On Sunday, the last day in the camp, some of the Alpha Company men raided the day room after dinner. They removed the rear cover from the television set and used a wooden broom handle to pry off the plug from the picture tube. Even though the power cord was unplugged, a bright arcing spark jumped out when the plug disengaged. Luckily, one of the young men was knowledgeable enough to know that tubes stored electricity, and thus, took precautions. One of the men severed the plug from the bundle of wires, discarding it, and then reattached the rear cover.

Next, the men staged a mini-Olympics event and collected all the pool cues and balls, taking them to the perimeter. They invented games using the equipment. One guy from the First Platoon received a gold medal for throwing his javelin (pool stick) the furthest.

Alpha Company was the last company of grunts to leave Camp Books. While waiting on the helicopter pad for their transportation to the bush, several discussions took place relating to their former treasures. If the officers were aware of the men's mischief the night before, they offered no hint or said anything about it.

Not one person in Alpha had any idea of what the other units might have done with their items during their last night in the camp. Those Alpha men, taking the boxes to supply on the last day, recalled seeing very little of the luxuries stored in supply. Therefore, they had to assume that the rest of the battalion had left everything behind in the barracks for the next group to enjoy. If this were true, the ARVN must be celebrating and waiting to take possession of the rest of the bounty after Alpha Company left the base.

Laughter was contagious across the chopper pad as speculation spread about the baffled looks on the ARVN's faces when they opened the many cartons of Alpha Company's surrendered treasures. All agreed it would have been priceless to witness that and most were sorry they would miss it.

## CHAPTER TWENTY-FOUR

Alpha Company was air lifted to another notorious destination called Happy Valley. Not too far from Da Nang, the area was less hostile at that time than it was earlier in the war. After landing, they joined up with the rest of the battalion - already providing security for the Marines - who had a firebase on a nearby hilltop overlooking the valley. The Marines were required to dismantle everything before they could vacate the hill and go home.

The Airborne Battalion planned to stay close by for up to a week until the Marines had destroyed every bunker and piece of unnecessary equipment. Nothing was to remain for either the enemy or the ARVN. If either of them wanted to move onto the hilltop, they would have to rebuild from scratch.

Non-stop activity hummed in the firebase and the Marines worked hard and long hours to complete the task. The daily sounds of explosions and overhead Marine helicopters continued to be a distraction to those on the valley floor running patrols around the base of their hill.

From their vantage point, the grunts could not see the actual activity in the firebase. The bunkers, visible earlier in the week, were now gone; The Marines used the dirt from sandbags to fill in the holes and then burned the empty bags in a large bonfire. Dozens of helicopters filled the sky daily, pulling out salvaged lumber, artillery guns, and anything else of value from the hilltop. The rolls of barbed wire, mines, and trip flares on the perimeter remained in place until the very end. On that last day, scores of Marines spilled over the side of the hill, working in small groups to remove the last of the perimeter defenses. It was the first time those in the valley actually saw the soldiers above. It was like watching an anthill from below; every dark figure moving continuously, dozens traveling back and forth over the crest of the hilltop at any given time. Some accidents occurred when the trip flares ignited, but as there were no injuries, nobody cared.

It was close to mid-afternoon when the last helicopter filled with Marines took off from the hilltop location. The real estate was now up for grabs.

The week passed without incident and many of the airborne grunts wondered why the enemy had not taken advantage of the situation. Artillery, mortars, and rockets could have been devastating to the Marines, especially if the enemy had waited until that last day after the Marines destroyed everything on the hilltop. They were exceptionally lucky.

After the first week back in the bush, battalion continued moving the companies further south each day. Not looking for anything in particular, it was their way of sending a message to the enemy that Americans were still actively patrolling through the area. After finding absolutely no signs of the enemy during the next several days, Alpha Company was withdrawn from the field and flown to the airbase in Da Nang.

Their stay was extremely short. A dozen Deuce and a Half trucks and several APC's awaited them at the edge of the airfield, the convoy leaving as soon as Alpha Company climbed onboard. The convoy traveled north on the main highway, stopping after thirty miles to drop off the Alpha Company grunts at yet another firebase; the rest of the convoy then continued to their final destination, Firebase Tomahawk. Unbeknownst to the grunts, this firebase was located on top of a mountain and they would have to walk up the steep, mile-long trail to reach it.

When arriving, the grunts stood next to a towering mountain on the side of the highway; a vertical, ten-foot wide dirt track snaked along and ringed the mountainside all the way up to the top and Firebase Tomahawk. It angered the grunts when the truck drivers informed them that the trucks would not transport them up to the top, and instead, they would have to make the treacherous journey on foot.

Walking up the trail was so much different than climbing the mountains in the bush. Out there, the going was slow and handholds were plentiful to help pull a person up. Time was not normally an issue, and some hills had taken days to climb. On this ascending dusty trail, however, the pace was much faster and more difficult. The brass expected the company to reach the summit within an hour and Cap was pushing the men upwards, but after only fifteen minutes, many of them could not continue. Most had trouble catching their breath in the thin mountain air, some suffered from cramps in their sides, thighs and calves, and every once in awhile - just like dominoes - they all fell out to the inside of the trail. Even the captain was unable to continue and needed to take a break with his men.

A bulldozer had cut this trail into the side of the mountain, and just beyond the outer edge, the earth fell away in a sheer drop off. The soldiers instinctively stayed to the inside of the lane and now fully understood why they were not able to ride the trucks to the top. Nobody risked walking in the loose gravel to the outside of the path, for fear of slipping and falling over the side.

The view was incredible from the trail, becoming more scenic the higher they climbed. The countryside below was mostly rice paddies and small villages, and, because there were no nearby hills or dense jungles, one could see for several miles.

It took almost an hour and a half for the last man to cross the finish line on the summit. It was the most difficult climb ever for many of the troops; some compared the experience to Basic Training in Fort Knox, Kentucky when they continuously marched up the two murderous hills called 'Agony' and 'Misery'. Once reaching the top, they found the surrounding scenery breathtaking. From a mile up, there were no signs of war below and the 360-degree view extended for miles in every direction. To the north, a large mountain range loomed in the distance; the highway they traveled earlier snaked through the pass. On the east, the South China Sea glistened like a mirror, reflecting the sparkling sun in every direction. Small sampans and fishing boats motored around near shore, and not a single military ship was on the horizon. The western and southern most views extended for several miles until the mountains and surrounding jungle took over the landscape. This was truly a magnificent gift from Mother Nature; the hilltop took on the appearance of a tourist stop as dozens of cameras captured the vistas from every direction.

Standing only a few miles away from the ocean, one could view the seascape as it continued far to the north. Mountains rose behind smaller verdant hills, dwarfed them and jutted out into the blue-green ocean. Far below, the miles of rice paddies formed a multicolored checkerboard, stretching across the plains until touching the ocean's edge.

The firebase, on the other hand, was in total juxtaposition to the natural beauty of the Vietnamese countryside. Everything was in a state of disrepair and falling apart. Huge piles of garbage lay exposed throughout the area, left to rot in the hot sun. There was nowhere to escape from the awful stench permeating through the firebase.

During this first night, the new inhabitants would find themselves in a very different battle - one that would cause additional nightmares in the days and years to come. Uninterrupted sleep during the night, and waking rested and refreshed, would not be an option while in Firebase Tomahawk. Every person on the hill became a reluctant participant in this battle, from the highest-ranking officer to the lowest grade of enlisted man. The rotting garbage dump was providing plenty of nourishment for the camp's other tenants during the past several weeks of vacancy. Hundreds of hungry rats scurried about the hilltop after darkness set in, following the scent of this appetizing feast.

Ongoing screams filled the night as rats fell from overhead rafters and onto unsuspecting sleeping soldiers. The grunts were in a stupor, thinking that one of the other men in the bunker must have thrown something onto them while asleep. When the realization hit that a rat as large as an alley cat shared the cot with them, no two reactions were alike. Those soldiers from the city were more apt to scream out in sheer panic and cower in fear. The country boys, however, were not intimidated by the invasion, and immediately fought back with whatever weapon they could lay their hands on. Shots rang out as surprised soldiers instinctively aimed at the extremely furtive creatures before realizing their actions were putting others in danger. Still others used machetes, steel helmets, folding shovels, and even boots to disable or kill the invaders.

In the morning, dozens of carcasses lay on the ground outside of bunkers or hung from clotheslines by their tails. The rats spared no one during the night and everybody had a story to share during breakfast.

"Let me tell you 'bout my experience last night," one soldier recounted. "Some screams from the other bunkers woke me up and I sat there for a minute to get a clear head. I thought I was seeing things when I looked over at Cecil. At first, I thought a cat had wandered into the bunker and found a place to rest on Cecil's chest. It looked like the cat had a deformation or some kind of disease because his tail did not have any fur on it. About that time, it turned and looked at me straight in the eye. That's when I noticed it was a big goddamn rat. I froze in place and couldn't do anything but watch. The rat turned back to face Cecil, its nose and whiskers twitching like crazy. It crept up to Cecil's mouth and started sniffing around his lips. Then suddenly, the rat's tongue came out and started licking at the corner of Cecil's mouth, intent on getting to the dried food or something else from earlier in the day." Clarence stopped for a minute while those around him shuddered at the thought and made comments.

"Ooooweee, rat tongue lickin' on the motherfucker. Goddamn!"

"You know I couldn't just sit there and watch. My ass would have been long gone," said another at the table.

"I've been licked by many things in my life, but never a rat. That's got to be a weird sensation!"

"I sure never want to find out."

"Me neither. Go ahead Clarence, what happened next?"

"The nibbling at his lips must have woken Cecil because he opened his eyes and blinked several times to see clearly. When he looked down and saw the rat's head only inches away, his eyes bugged open in fear and he screamed as if his ass was on fire. It was so shrill and sudden that it scared both the rat and me. Cecil was fast though, and I have to give him credit, he snapped his poncho liner and catapulted that rat onto the floor in the center of the bunker.

And, just that fast, he jumped out of his cot with a Bowie knife and proceeded to stab that creature until it was dead. Needless to say, neither of us could sleep anymore for the rest of the night."

"Damn! That is one bad mother fucker, maybe we all need to move in with Cecil," one of the men commented. They laughed nervously at the comment.

"Hey dig this," another soldier at the table began. "Me and Kevin had to go and piss during the night and headed to the latrine with our flashlight beams leading the way. We both thought we were seeing things because everywhere we looked there were glowing red dots. We were stumped and stopped to figure it out. Then, these red dots started moving around randomly in pairs. Something bumped into my leg and startled me. When I shined the light around our feet, several rats ran away. That's when it dawned on us that the rats had us surrounded. That scene was so bad, man. We booked like hell back to our bunker and barricaded the doorway to keep the bastards out."

Unfortunately, four men, bitten during the night, awaited evacuation to the nearest hospital. This news heightened the fear in many but also made them aware of how vigilant they now had to be during the night.

In the daylight, only a few rats moved around in the garbage dump. The thousands of others rested and stayed hidden in obscure areas or underground in burrows, waiting for darkness to arrive.

In an attempt to turn things around, Cap came up with an idea. He was sure it would interest the soldiers enough to get involved and help clean the hill of the vile creatures. After breakfast, he called the men together and rolled out his idea.

"We are going to start a contest tomorrow to see who can kill the largest rat on the hill." The men looked at one another in disbelief. "We'll start tonight and the competition will continue until the day we leave this hill. The only rule is that you use common sense and good judgment. I do not want to see anyone get hurt during this contest, but you are free to use whatever you have at your disposal to win. The deadline every morning will be 0800 hours; make sure you tag your submissions then lay them out on the ground outside of the

Commo Bunker. If you find that there is already one there bigger than yours..."

One of the black soldiers in formation called out, "Ain't nobody here got one bigger than mine, this is a complete package," he cupped his hand around his crotch and shook it a few times. "Yep, you can just give me the prize right now."

This solicited laughter and comments from those around him.

"Like I was saying," Cap continued when the chatter stopped, "if there is already a rat tagged and it's bigger than your rat, then don't bother entering it. Go and dump it in the trash or throw it off the side of the hill. The CP will judge all entries during breakfast and will measure from the tip of its tail to the tip of its nose. I heard that some rodents running through our camp last night were as big as cats, and know that it would make more sense to use weight as a qualifier, however, we don't have a scale so we will judge the length instead."

"What does the winner get?" Someone called from the crowd.

"I was getting to that, and I think you'll really like this. The daily winner will be exempt from all details during the day and will receive twelve, ice-cold beers to do whatever he would like with them. If you want to sell them or give them away, that is up to you. Now this is where I think it will be interesting. The names of all the daily winners will go into a hat, and I will pick one grand prizewinner on our last day here. Odds of winning will depend on how many days we are going to be here. Nobody knows that, and if we leave at the end of the week, the odds of winning would be better than leaving at the end of the month - unless one of you continues to win many of the daily contests. The grand prize winner will get a three-day R&R to China Beach and I'll even throw in fifty bucks in MPC to spend as you like."

Loud cheering erupted in the ranks. They were already planning and sharing strategies.

"When does the winner get to go to China Beach?"

"He can leave on the next day if he wants. It'll be his call."

The commotion continued within the formation. The men could not believe this exciting prospect and many were anxious to get started.

"There's one last thing I forgot to mention, and this is really important. All entries submitted for the contest must be in one piece from tail to nose. Do not alter the bodies and try to make them longer, and do not enter anything pieced together like a puzzle. Are we clear?"

"Airborne!" The group shouted.

"All the way, men! Good hunting!"

Early the next morning, several carcasses were already on display before daylight arrived. They were long, but eventually replaced by larger entries during the last hour of the daily contest. Six entries were found to be so close that each had to be measured several times and the lengths confirmed by others. Only one-eighth of an inch separated the winner from second place and measured exactly twenty-nine inches in length.

The winner quickly dispensed the twelve beers between his squad members and admitted that they were supporting him during this hunt and deserved a cold one. However, he also made it clear that he was going to China Beach alone. When looking over the carcasses on the ground, the thought of creatures that size stalking them at night was mind-blowing and sent shivers down spines.

The men of Alpha Company killed and burned almost one thousand rats during that first week on Tomahawk. The contest was an excellent motivator for reducing the rat population, however, there were still more than enough of the rodents roaming the hill to keep men awake and frightened during the night.

It was here, with three weeks left in country, that John learned he had passed the exam and was now a sergeant. The posted list of 122 names showed John Kowalski's name as second on the list; only the top twenty-four candidates received promotions to fill the allotted slots within the battalion. It was time to celebrate, and he quickly returned to the Commo Bunker to inform his fellow CP members.

Cap and Top had been watching John's reaction while he read the newly posted document. They could tell he was excited and energized by the news, and as he read, his movements were somewhat awkward. It looked like he wanted to rush away and let others know of the promotion, but felt compelled to stay there until he finished reading every word. He even touched the list a couple of times and rubbed a finger across his name, wanting to confirm that it was really him. When done, his feet could not move fast enough to carry him back to the bunker.

The two observers allowed John several moments to celebrate the news of his promotion before heading over to the Commo Bunker on the other side of the compound.

"I'm proud of that boy. He did well, considering."

"Yes, he did, Top. I knew he had it in him to do well; otherwise, I wouldn't have nominated him for the advance. It's just going to break his heart when I give him the news."

"It probably will, but he'll soon get over it, Cap. There really is no alternative and we have to make decisions for the betterment of this company. Seems the boy has a level head, and at this point, he's our only option."

The two men stopped briefly outside of the entrance to the commo bunker. "You ready for this, Top?"

"Let's do it."

Cap and Top stepped through the bunker entrance and saw John inside, slapping high fives with everyone. A cigarette dangled from his lips and a wide grin was making it difficult to keep it in place. Fuzzy had drawn a set of yellow sergeant stripes on a piece of paper, and then using a razor blade, trimmed around the border of both designs before attaching them with straight pins to each arm. Cotton Top and Stud came to attention and repeatedly saluted the new sergeant in mock military fashion. They were laughing and having fun. Suddenly, Cotton Top noticed the two men standing just inside of the entrance. He stopped quickly, "Um, guys," he whispered, and gestured with a nod toward the entrance of the bunker.

"Good morning, Cap, First Sergeant," Cotton Top was first to acknowledge.

"Good morning, men! I see we are too late for the promotion ceremony. Care to start over?"

"No sir, sorry, sir."

"We're just giving you a hard time. Congratulations, John!" Both men held out their right hands. "Glad to see you made it. I cannot think of anybody more deserving. Well done!"

"Thanks, Cap," John shook his hand warmly. "I couldn't have done it without your recommendation and Top's help." John then reached over to Top and shook his hand.

"Am I supposed to salute you now?" The First Sergeant asked. This cut the ice and the laughter returned.

"I don't think that's necessary, Top, but thanks anyway."

"We'll let you get back to your celebration in just a few minutes, but we need to discuss something personal with you first. Would you mind taking a break and stepping outside with us?"

"Did I do something wrong?"

"Oh no, not at all." The three men walked through the doorway and moved off to the side for some privacy.

"I'm sorry to put a damper on your celebration, but I've got some news that might disturb you."

"What is it, Cap?" John's heart skipped a beat and his pulse quickened. He shuffled his feet nervously, waiting for Cap to speak again. His thoughts raced to his family back home.

"First off, let me tell you that I see you as a very level-headed and quick-thinking person. You've been a great help to me since joining the CP and have made my job much easier. You're an excellent radio operator and it'll be hard to replace you. However, I also feel that you're a good leader and I desperately need your help right now."

Hearing the word 'replace' bothered John, and he sensed bad news was on the way. "How can I help you, Cap?"

Without wasting a second, Cap responded, "I'm going to reassign you to the First Platoon as their temporary leader."

John was stunned, knowing that he heard the captain correctly. "Why do something like that? You know I've only got two and a half weeks left before going home."

"I know that, but I'm afraid I have no choice in the matter. First Platoon has been without an NCO since your friend, Sixpack, got hurt."

"They've gotten by since then, so why now?"

"I've a lot of faith in you, John. You have more experience in the bush than anyone else in the First Platoon. Their Lieutenant has only been in country for a few weeks and has not been out in the field yet. He is fresh out of ROTC and seems quite cocky and sure of himself. I don't want him to be the cause of somebody getting hurt."

"What difference does that make on this hill?"

"If we were staying here, I wouldn't even bother you with this issue, but we're going back out into the bush the day after tomorrow."

"I understand, but the bush has been awfully quiet around these firebases, and not one enemy soldier has been spotted anywhere in the last several weeks."

"John, we're going back into the A Shau Valley."

John reacted to the news as if being slapped across the face.

"I'm too short for this shit!"

"None of us are happy about it, but orders are orders. I really don't want to have a Cherry Lieutenant leading the First Platoon, especially in the Valley. We'll be working separately in platoon-sized elements and staying in separate NDP's. I do not want to lose anybody on this mission because of carelessness and inexperience. This is where I feel you can be a great help to me."

"Just what are you expecting of me?"

"You'll be the Lieutenant's right hand man. I'll tell him that he is still in command of the platoon, but on this mission, he's going to have to clear everything through you first, and I'll make it clear to him that you have the final say-so."

"What good can I do in only two weeks?"

"I don't know how many weeks we'll be in that area, but it would be suicide to let the First Platoon operate in the Valley without a capable and trustworthy leader. The L-T will need guidance and direction. I don't know a better way than on-the-job training."

"Cap, there's got to be another NCO in the company who knows the valley better than I do and can even stay with the First Platoon for the long term. Why not consider him?"

"We have, and without going into the details, you'll just have to accept my word that there is nobody else to choose for the short-term."

"And I'm your best choice?"

"John, we've read your record from the 25th and can see that you were involved in just about every facet of operating in the bush. Christ, you even earned the Bronze Star because of what you know and what you did. I think the new L-T can learn a great deal from you during those two weeks. Follow your instincts and help save a few more lives before you go home."

"How is the new L-T with this scenario?"

"He doesn't know yet, but won't have a choice in the matter. In fact, only a select few on this hill even know we're leaving in a couple of days."

"Cap, both you and Top have been very good to me since I've come to the company. I'd like to help you out, but I really don't think I'm qualified to do what you are asking."

"You are more qualified than you know. I have the utmost respect for your judgment and know that you'll be successful."

"I don't have a choice, do I?"

"No son, you don't."

"Okay, Cap, I only hope my luck continues to hold out."

"You'll do fine without luck!"

"When do I go?"

"Why don't you go back to your celebration inside, I'll even send over some cold beer. Take a couple of hours to party and then gather all your gear and come to see me. I'll take you over and introduce you to the L-T and the rest of your new team."

John was not at all comfortable with the decision but acknowledged the officer with an affirmative shake of his head.

"Thank you, John!" Both men walked away, leaving the heavy-hearted young man to his own apprehensions.

He leaned against the sandbags of the bunker as his thoughts tumbled forward, crashing into his consciousness like a runaway freight train. 'I'm not qualified to lead a platoon. Other people must see a different side of me that I don't see. I'm a loner and have only had to worry about saving my own ass. Now I have to worry about the safety and well-being of an entire platoon. Earlier in my tour, I was a know-it-all and was unafraid to take chances, often taking more risks than I should have, especially when walking point. Now

Cherries – A Vietnam War Novel

that I'm short, I feel like a Cherry all over again - experienced or not. These are going to be the longest two weeks of my life. I hope I don't get overly cautious or paranoid in the bush. That would be dangerous too, and I might overlook something obvious and cause someone to get hurt. If that happened, I'll have to live with that on my conscience for the rest of my life.'

Of late, the bush was quiet when the Americans were out on patrols. Very few units had engaged the enemy, and even then, the firefights were brief. It looked like the enemy was targeting only the ARVN's and beating them up daily. Some of the American soldiers had garnered the opinion that the NVA had purposely tried to stay out of their way, hoping the lack of contact would send the 101st home sooner.

When leaving the hill with the First Platoon, John was fully loaded with enough supplies for four days. He carried a compass around his neck and had two maps stuffed into his trouser pocket. He was pleased that his load felt much lighter and more comfortable overall, without carrying the extra weight of the twenty-six pound radio and spare batteries.

When the birds unloaded First Platoon at their destination, John took readings from his compass to confirm his location. He also looked around to familiarize himself with some of the outstanding landmarks, indicating them on the map for future reference. Once away from the LZ, he would take a reading from any two such landmarks to pinpoint his location on the map. However, the method would not work in triple canopy jungles, so he had to depend on marking rounds from a nearby artillery source.

First Platoon's challenge was to cross the valley and climb to the top of Hill 373. The mountain looked just like any other and was only five-hundred meters away on the map; however, it took most of the day to reach, as a smaller hill stood between the men and their final destination.

On a topical map of the area, the hills were referenced by their elevation in meters, unless, of course, a firebase stood on top. Other hills - such as Hamburger Hill - received its name after fighting a significant battle to roust the enemy from on top. That particular fight lasted several days; soldiers often referred to the battle as a 'meat grinder', thus the origin of the moniker. Pork Chop Hill was another example of a hill made infamous during the Korean War.

When First Platoon reached the base of Hill 373, John and the L-T had their first disagreement. Lieutenant Bozolynsky insisted on sending the entire platoon up the hill at the same time in case the NVA were waiting for them. John, on the other hand, did not want to risk the entire platoon, and explained that he thought it much safer for them to commit only one squad. The most experienced point man, Chris, was in the Third Squad and had a reputation of being an excellent tracker with good instincts. It made perfect sense to send that squad up, and, if they saw any signs of danger en route, they could retreat without getting the entire platoon trapped. The L-T's face was beet red, either from rising blood pressure or embarrassment, and he was unable to provide a clear reason to support his stand. He conceded to John who quickly dispatched the recon team.

The hill had seen much activity over time and many pathways led up and down from the thousand-foot high summit. It was not part of a mountain chain, but it did overshadow many other isolated hills in this part of the valley. The slope and rising ridgelines were not as steep as other hills in the area, thus, allowing the recon patrol to move swiftly to the top.

Forty minutes later, a lone runner descended and rejoined the balance of the platoon. They found nothing out of place on the way up, the summit was now secured, and the squad waited for the remaining soldiers.

When the platoon was together on top, Chris appeared anxious while waiting for John and Lt. 'Bozo' to join him.

"Sir, I found some enemy signs on the back side of the hill. Can you and the sergeant follow me so you can have a look for yourselves?"

The two men followed Chris to the opposite side of the hilltop.

"I found these after sending the runner down to get you." He pointed to the dusty ground; several boot imprints headed downhill.

"What's your opinion?" John asked.

"I think somebody was up here, saw us when we first came up, and then bugged out when they saw we weren't leaving."

"They do look fresh. What do you think, L-T?"

"They're boot prints; somebody from your squad must have come to this side of the hill and walked around before you came over here."

"L-T, those aren't GI boot prints." John stepped into the dust just to the side of the other footprints. "See, the design is different, and the feet are much smaller."

'Bozo' took a knee and looked over the prints. "Okay, I see the difference now, but what makes you think these are recent? They look like they've been here a while."

"How about mine, L-T? Do these look old to you, too?"

Before 'Bozo' could respond, Chris interrupted. "Sarge, come and take a look at this. It might shed some light and help determine the age of these prints." All three walked another ten feet down the pathway where Chris knelt down and grabbed part of a bush, pulling the branches upward. "What do you think about this?"

Several twigs were broken and the fractures were still fresh to the touch. Chris dropped the branch and pointed out several more on shrubbery leading downhill.

"This is not a good sign."

"What do you mean, sergeant?"

"L-T, the breaks are still moist, which means this happened within the last hour or so. I'm not sure just how many people were here, but it's certain they left this hilltop in a hurry after spotting us."

"So that means they're gone, and most likely won't return, because we're here now. This is good news and should make our job easier."

Chris and John looked at one another and saw the disappointment in each other's eyes. Both were quite aware of trouble brewing, and Chris' opinion would only fall upon the L-T's deaf ears. Therefore, it was up to John to convince Bozo of the great risk to the platoon. Darkness was coming fast and they did not have a plan yet. "Lieutenant, we need to talk. Chris, you can rejoin your squad and I'll get with everybody else in a few."

Chris left the two men to talk.

"L-T, take a walk with me." They walked over to the path on the side of the hill near the disrupted shrubbery. "Sir, the enemy knows we're up here."

"So what's the big deal, sergeant?"

"L-T, you have to trust in what I'm trying to tell you. The First Platoon is going to be in deep shit if we stay on top of this hill tonight."

"You know our orders, sergeant. We're supposed to stay on this hill for the next three days and send out patrols."

"We can still do that, but we need to outsmart Charlie so we don't get hurt tonight."

"What's so unusual about tonight?"

"First, let's review the facts. We find boot prints and evidence of a hasty retreat. So, there may have only been a couple of scouts on lookout, watching the valley from up here. That's most likely the reason they didn't fire at our people, and instead, beat a path off the hill. Second, they're most likely part of a larger group, and what they'll do next depends on what our next move will be."

"What makes you think something will happen?"

"I don't know. It's just a hunch. They most certainly saw us land earlier today and now they know we're up here. If we continue downhill after them, they may booby trap our advance or spring an ambush on us. And if we choose to stay up here, they'll most likely set us up for a mortar barrage tonight."

"We'll just have to dig our foxholes a little deeper and stay put right here."

"L-T, why put the men at risk? Not only does the enemy know we're here, they most likely know exactly how many of us there are. Their strength is unknown, and we don't know where they are. We need a plan for the night."

"What do you suggest we do, Big Shot?"

This caught John off guard; he didn't understand the L-T's hostility or ignorance in this matter, and he wondered why the L-T resented him so much. He was just doing what was he was asked to do.

"I'm pretty sure they're watching us now, so we should give them every indication that we're staying on the hilltop tonight.

We'll dig our foxholes, put out trip flares and claymores like we normally do when preparing an NDP. Then after it gets dark, we take our gear and silently move back down to the base of the hill the way we came up earlier. There, we can set up a small perimeter for the night and also keep an eye on the trails around the hill."

"And just what do you hope to accomplish by doing this?"

"When they mortar us tonight, we'll be in a much better position to direct artillery onto them without having to duck mortar rounds from deep inside of a foxhole. We'll hear the tube firing and can silence it. Coordinates can be pre-planned with the CP and referenced during the fire mission."

"And what if they don't mortar us tonight? What then?"

"Well, shit, sir, we just move back up in the morning, foxholes will already be dug. Then, we can dispatch our patrols and stay there tomorrow night. We've got nothing to lose."

"I think it's all a waste of time. I say we stay up here tonight."

"Lieutenant, they did us huge favors by letting us know they were up here. Had that not happened, the situation would be much different and I would not be pressing the issue. I thought we could work together, but I will go over your head if I have to. This is a serious situation and you need to use a little common sense."

Both men rose and stood toe to toe. "You're not calling anyone. I'm in charge of this platoon, and until you outrank me, you'll do as I say." The Lieutenant's voice grew louder, attracting the attention of many of the soldiers nearby. Chris had already briefed his squad and many of the others in the platoon, so they had an idea of what the argument entailed.

John maintained his cool and kept his voice at a normal level. "Look, sir, I do fully understand that you're in charge, but right now you're just a hard-headed asshole that happens to be an officer. I've seen shit like this repeatedly during my eleven months here and have learned much more about our enemy than you did in ROTC. People survive by instincts and hunches here in the Nam. I've only got a couple of weeks left in this hellhole, and plan to take every necessary precaution to make certain I stay alive along with everybody else on this hilltop. I will not tolerate some college-educated ROTC graduate thinking he knows better."

"Watch your mouth, sergeant. I could have you busted to private for talking to me that way."

"You know, I don't really give a fuck, sir. You do what you have to do. Just show me some consideration by letting me do my job."

"Let you do your job? Shit, soldier, you're trying to do mine."

"Call it what you like, sir. All I'm trying to do is to keep every member of this platoon alive until it's time for me to go home, and I'll do that with or without your help."

He did not respond. Instead, he kept looking at the ground and scowled, shuffling his feet back and forth in the dirt.

"Sir, I'm trying to keep you alive, too."

The L-T angrily kicked a stone across the top of the hill and got into John's face with fire in his eyes.

"You know, sergeant, I don't like you or your attitude. I think you're just a smartass nineteen-year-old punk. You think you're hot shit because you've been here so long. Well, I'm not buying it. You kissed the captain's ass while you were in the CP, and now that you've made sergeant, he's letting you feel your rank a little before you go home."

"Are you finished yet, sir?" John interrupted.

"No, I'm not."

"Too fucking bad! I don't have time to argue with you anymore. It's getting late and these people need to know the plan."

John turned to leave and the L-T took hold of his arm. "The plan is that we are staying on top tonight!"

The young sergeant exploded. "You're really a stubborn bastard, aren't you! Why are you not able to get it through your thick skull that I'm trying to help you? I didn't want to be here, but the captain felt I might be able to teach you something about the jungle. But, you don't want to learn! All you give a fuck about is your rank. You want to play your little game of war and make decisions based on what you learned in a book back in college. Well, mister, this is not a fucking game. People are dying out here. Have you ever seen a fellow soldier blown to pieces? What're you gonna do when somebody dies in this platoon because you made a dumbass mistake? Are you gonna say you're sorry and not make the same dumbass mistake again? When it's too late? And do you think your troops will follow you into battle knowing that you'll get them killed? I won't let you lead these men to their death!"

John walked away, heading toward the RTO to call the captain. As he passed the Cherries, many of them sat with their eyes wide and mouths agape in awe, never before hearing a confrontation like that between an officer and an enlisted man. It was also clear that the soldiers who'd been in country for a while agreed with John; they gave him a silent 'thumbs up' signal when making eye contact.

John had the radio receiver and was ready to make the call when the L-T stopped him.

"Hold on, sergeant. We'll do it your way tonight. But if nothing happens, you'll regret it."

"Regret it? What are you gonna do, send me to Vietnam? Do not threaten me, sir. You don't know what I'm capable of doing." John hesitated for just a moment, drew a breath, and then smiled broadly, looking the Lieutenant straight in the eye. "Thanks for supporting my plan, sir. I'm sure you'll find it much safer this way."

Bozo bit his tongue. "We'll see."

"I'll get everything organized right away. I suggest you inform the captain on what we've found and what we intend to do tonight."

"Yes, sergeant," the L-T responded sarcastically.

John just let Bozo's attitude slide and gathered the squad leaders to inform them of their plans for that night. He wanted everyone to be obvious in their actions, giving the enemy the perception that they were staying on the hill that night. The grunts would dig foxholes, prepare sleeping positions, and generally make themselves seen from below. Then, when darkness descended, he wanted some of the men to flick lighters and smoke cigarettes in the open without making it too obvious. Their intent was to make the enemy feel that the Americans were not feeling threatened and were comfortable for the night.

After he shared the plan, John studied his map and chose eight reference locations surrounding the hill, assigning each a number. He helped the RTO cypher the coordinates and then got on the horn with Fuzzy to arrange the preset targets. This allowed for a much faster response from the firebase artillery when calling for the fire mission.

After an hour passed, John sat down next to the L-T at his sleep position to review the plan and preset artillery map coordinates. Surprisingly, the L-T appeared to be a little more receptive and supportive than earlier.

A little after nine, the young sergeant was comfortable that it was dark enough to execute the second half of the plan, calling for the men to move down to the base of the hill. They stayed low to the ground when moving across the hilltop so as not to create a silhouette against the twilighted sky, thus exposing them to whoever might be watching.

The men moved cautiously through the dim light of night, surprisingly quiet as they moved along the path downhill. Thirty minutes later, they reached the valley floor and silently dispersed into the surrounding foliage on the side of the hill.

The L-T and John stayed awake long after the main group bedded down for the night. When midnight arrived without incident, he whispered to John in the darkness,

"So much for your hunch, sergeant - is it okay if I go to sleep now or will I miss something?" John could hear the sinister tone in the L-T's voice.

"Do what you want, sir."

"Eating crow leaves a bitter taste, doesn't it?"

"Sir, just get off my ass."

"I'm not on it yet."

John was sure there was a smirk on the L-T's face when he turned away to lie down. He was ticked off and wanted to avoid any further confrontation with Bozo, so he picked up his equipment and moved next to the RTO about fifteen feet away.

He had heard stories during his tour about men rebelling against their leaders and taking action into their own hands. They called it 'fragging' in Vietnam, which was severe retribution for arrogance, stupidity, and the lack of common sense - resulting in serious injury or death to the men following orders. Obviously, survival was paramount in war, and repeated action by somebody purposely putting you in harm's way without remorse received swift and immediate punishment. The action was a permanent solution.

In the bush, firefights and mortar attacks were the preferred backdrops for many of these deliberate assassinations. In the rear areas, some of these disgruntled soldiers tossed grenades into officer shitters and into their quarters when the opportunity presented itself. John did not personally know of any such events occurring in the units he had been in, but his recent dealings with Bozo made him realize why someone would even consider committing such a despicable act.

During Basic Training and Advanced Infantry Training, an individual who regularly got the platoon in trouble and made them suffer for something he did were given a 'blanket party' as a warning that his fellow platoon members were unhappy with him and wanted him to straighten up. The message, delivered during the wee hours of the night when everyone was asleep, was a message never forgotten. Several individuals participated in the doling out of this punishment. They placed a bar of soap into a towel, and then holding it by the four corners, created a 'swinging persuader'. The procedure was choreographed by one person directing the others. Two people carried a blanket to cover the target and hold him down while the others beat him about the body with the swinging bars of soap. It usually lasted for less than a minute and then everybody quickly retreated to their bunks, feigning sleep. When the target pulled the blanket off, no one was standing there. Sometimes these warnings worked immediately and the message was understood. However, there were times when a second blanket party was necessary before it finally sank in. Drill Sergeants noticed bruises on a recruit but never questioned or intervened in this process.

A little after three in the morning, the two guys on radio-watch shook John awake. "Sarge, Sarge, wake up!"

John sat up quickly, trying to focus in the total darkness. "What is it?"

"We just heard tubes firing to our front."

The hilltop above suddenly exploded as mortar rounds began landing; one exploded every ten seconds. The grunts were wide-awake after the first round detonated, continuing to watch the light show above.

John unfolded his map, covered himself with his poncho liner, and then turned on his red lens flashlight to review his preset locations. He took a compass reading and saw that it was very close to preset six.

"How far away do you guys place those tubes?" He asked from underneath the blanket.

"I'd guess about three hundred meters," responded one of the two men.

John uncovered and saw the L-T already moving toward them on his hands and knees.

"Better call in for the big guns to silence those tubes. Tell Fuzzy to reference preset six, then add one-hundred and move left one-hundred from that location. You can adjust the fire after the first rounds hit."

Initially, John could see a look of disbelief on the L-T's face in the flash of each explosion. He could not believe that the lieutenant actually smiled when reaching for the radio handset. The L-T called in the mission to Stud, who was already in contact with the artillery unit on the nearby firebase. Three artillery rounds landed in the expected location, but the mortar tubes continued to fire. The L-T added another fifty and left fifty. Seconds later the next barrage came in and the mortars stopped. The sequence was repeated twice more before the fire mission was terminated.

"I just wanted to make sure we got them," the L-T said meekly after the end of the fire mission.

"Good shooting, sir!" Several men offered up whispered congratulations.

He was all smiles now and scooted up close to John so that no one else could hear their conversation. "Sergeant, I'm sorry. You were right."

"No need to apologize. Just help me to do my job."

"You got it."

John felt good about what had just happened. Twelve mortar rounds exploded on the hilltop; not one person was hurt, and it looked like the Lieutenant had finally seen the light. It was turning out to be a great day.

The two men got along just fine from then on. No more bickering or threats to each other, and the L-T showed more trust and respect for John's suggestions. They finally worked together as a team.

It was like that for the next two weeks. First Platoon moved from mountain to mountain, changing tactics and direction from every hilltop.

Unfortunately, unbeknownst to them, they set a clear and predictable pattern to their movements.

Resupply had occurred three times since arriving in the valley, thus exposing their position each time. Those NVA scouts hiding out in the hills and jungles monitored First Platoon's location and daily route of travel; it would not take much thought to predict where the next resupply would take place.

The platoon had been very lucky so far, and had managed to kill eight NVA soldiers with mechanical ambushes during those last two weeks. They had yet to encounter a booby trap or fire their weapons, and fortunately, suffered no casualties.

John was nervous during his last resupply in the field, with the war officially being over for him in just two days. He hoped the lucky streak continued, but made no assumptions.

After the resupply was complete, First Platoon crossed the hilltop and followed a ridge leading to the valley floor. They were only thirty minutes into their hump when the lead squad triggered a booby trap. Providentially, the tripwire pulled the grenade into a tree before exploding, thus shielding the men from the explosion and most of the shrapnel. Two men suffered minor wounds; the medics attended to them while the file of men continued their descent. The point man was now exceptionally vigilant, and several minutes later came upon a second trip wire. Upon investigation, they found another grenade attached to the second trip wire. They cut the wire and continued forward, but shifted their line of travel to a higher portion of the ridge. They moved less than one-hundred steps when Chris discovered a third trip wire, once again attached to a grenade.

The L-T and John felt this to be much too much of a coincidence and were apprehensive about continuing along the same route. They decided against venturing any further and returned to the hilltop.

Only two options remained at that time: first, spend the night in the current location where the resupply had taken place; or second, move downhill the way they came up earlier, then set up their NDP in the valley.

They found the hilltop unsuitable for their needs. The ground was extremely hard and rocky, making it an unlikely candidate for an NDP. After a short break, they moved off the hilltop for a second time.

Their movement stopped after descending 150 feet, and finding yet another booby-trap. This time, however, it was on the same trail they had created when climbing to the top earlier. It finally dawned on the men that the enemy had them trapped on the god-forsaken hilltop. After discussing their situation with Cap over the radio, he suggested that the First Platoon remain on the hill until morning when choppers could evacuate them from their prison and drop them onto a new hilltop. John would remain on board and fly to the rear to begin out-processing and leave for home.

There was little doubt in anyone's mind that plenty of trouble was coming their way after dark. John and the L-T repeated the exercise from their first night together and chose preset targets for artillery, then called them in to Fuzzy. Meanwhile, everybody else tried desperately to dig a hole in the rock-hard ground. Their only rewards were small oval holes no more than a foot deep, and blisters that broke and bled. Unlike the other hilltops, this one had higher brush and thicker foliage around the crest of the hill, which made it impossible for anyone to see the activity on the hilltop from below. One or two of the men had given up and had already scouted out the conditions fifty feet down the side of the hill.

"Sir, Mikey and I scooted down the hill a bit and found the ground much softer and easier to dig in. We should consider moving off the hilltop and ring the hill down where it's softer."

"How far down?"

"Fifty feet, sir."

"You know, L-T, they make a good point", John agreed.

"We can sneak down, dig foxholes, and then set up some claymores and trip flares all around the perimeter. We've got enough bodies to set up a ring of foxholes about every twenty feet or so."

"What about the booby traps that were left for us?"

"The men will have to probe the ground as they're moving downward and inform anybody if something is found."

"Isn't that dangerous?"

"Being on this very hilltop without any protection will be more dangerous."

"Sarge," Mikey interrupted, "it'll be perfect down below because there are some outcroppings of rocks there. We can set up under them and have some kind of overhead protection when the mortars start dropping on the hill."

"Are you willing to take the risk with all the booby traps we've found so far?"

"L-T, we've already gone there and back and haven't seen anything big that could really hurt us – they've only used grenades."

"Let me get the squad leaders together and see if we have their support. Mikey, I already know your decision. I'll be back in a short."

John gathered the men around and explained the options. There was no need for discussion; everyone thought the plan was an excellent idea, even if it meant being alone all night with their closest neighbor twenty feet away.

Maintaining a low profile, each man crawled down the hillside to his assigned location. It was true; the earth was much softer and easier to dig in there. Not everyone was fortunate enough to find rock outcroppings close by, but nevertheless, they dug their foxholes deep enough to protect them during what would surely be a sleepless night. They collected and used dead tree limbs, large rocks, and anything else they could find to fortify their positions. Trip flares and claymores were set out only ten feet to their front - dangerously close - but that was as far as anyone cared to venture out in the thick vegetation. In addition, they could trigger the mines from deep within their foxholes.

When nightfall arrived, the men were confident that they had been stealthy enough in setting up their NDP. The thick shrubbery and high vegetation provided excellent concealment for all of their activity and movement. Of course, since they would not be able to communicate with each other above a whisper, they would be on one-hundred percent alert and tasked with protecting their portion of the wide perimeter. The L-T would initiate a signal and send it around the perimeter once an hour to ensure everybody was awake and okay. They did not expect a ground attack, as the heavy vegetation made that highly unlikely. Instead, they were more concerned about the expected mortars and rockets that would be raining down upon them very soon.

John felt exceptionally tense at having to spend his last night in the bush in this kind of a situation. He was frightened - much more so than on his very first night in the bush. The sergeant prayed, asking God to watch over him on this - his final night - in the field. This was not how his life was supposed to end.

He thought of Zeke, Bill Sayers, Junior, and Sixpack, remembering how their lives had affected his. He also thought about those fellow Wolfhounds who had transferred to other units, wondering how they were making out. They were all his friends and brothers and he hoped to see them again sometime during his lifetime.

Once again, his thoughts traveled back to his family and girlfriend, who were anxiously waiting for him to come home. He was aware that - if he were lucky enough to survive this night - the folks back home would never have any understanding of all that he'd been through.

At midnight, the sound of mortar tubes firing from the jungle below interrupted his reflections. Everyone on the side of the hilltop knew the mortars would hit within seconds. They prepared for the worst, and then cringed in fear when the rounds began exploding on the hilltop above. Some of the men pulled their bulky rucksacks into their foxholes, employing them as shields. There were no screams of pain from the men around the perimeter; instead, some of the newer Cherries could be heard emotionally calling out for their mothers. The barrage lasted ten minutes, focusing on the center of the hilltop. Their luck continued to hold out, not one person was hurt thus far.

The L-T was directing artillery, using the preset positions that he and John had plotted earlier. They were not sure if the artillery rounds found the mortar team or not; however, the rounds landed close enough to scare the enemy away for now.

An hour later, a second barrage began. Most assumed it was in response to not seeing Medevac choppers arrive to evacuate the wounded. The mortar team tried once again to find the Americans, now firing from a different location in the valley. This time, the shooters moved the rounds across the hilltop and over the sides near their foxholes. First Platoon responded with an artillery barrage of its own, silencing the tube after only two salvos. The Americans had been spared a second time – nobody was hurt.

At 0230, a third attempt to inflict damage upon the Americans failed once again. This time, the mortars focused more to the side of the hill, moving them down toward the valley. Some secondary explosions were heard - most likely their own booby-traps exploding harmlessly below them.

The L-T had reacted each time the tube fired and continued to fine-tune his return fire, moving the rounds around in an attempt to find the mortars. Overall, the enemy had fired over thirty rounds during their three barrages, and the Americans had fired twice that many artillery shells back at them. Both sides were unsuccessful in finding one-another, so their luck continued to hold.

Daybreak was only a few hours away and John counted the hours left in the field. Quiet once again, it was anybody's guess what would happen next. All hoped the mortar crew had given up for the night and would not pursue their attempts to find the dug-in platoon. They needed to remain vigilant, as sufficient time remained for enemy sappers to creep up and find them.

A whisper sounded from John's neighbor to the left, "Sarge, you okay?"

"I'm good!"

"L-T wants a sit-rep from the perimeter. He also says to stay on your toes and watch downhill for movement. Pass it on."

"Got it!" John communicated with his other neighbor and found him to be in good shape, too. The men relayed the message from hole to hole, until it came back to the L-T again.

A sudden and loud noise in the valley instantly drew the attention of those soldiers that were in position on the northern side of the hill. It sounded like a rush of air, similar to the sound a bottle rocket makes after lighting the fuse, but decibels louder. After a few seconds, another such loud 'swooshing' sound reached the men from the same area. "Rockets! I saw two pairs firing away from us," whispered John's neighbor. "The L-T also saw them launch and will engage with artillery."

John looked out from his foxhole, quite concerned about the rockets, as they were a first for him. He had neither witnessed a launch nor seen the effects afterwards.

Two back-to-back explosions, mere seconds apart, sounded on a hilltop about a mile away from the First Platoon's location. The detonations were much louder than artillery, even from that distance. A light flickered on the horizon, the bright glow on that hilltop growing as the seconds ticked away. Suddenly, the first of several artillery rounds landed in the valley, six-hundred or so meters away, near the suspected rocket launchers. There were no secondary explosions and the fire mission terminated after three salvos into that area.

A loud whisper startled John, "Sergeant, the L-T wants you to meet him on top of the hill."

John's curiosity was aroused and he wondered why the L-T would even want to meet on the hilltop with all the rockets and mortars firing throughout the valley. He put on his ammo harness, took his flashlight, map, and weapon, and started to ascend the fifty feet to the summit along the pathway they had created earlier. The L-T was waiting for him. "Sergeant, let's go back to the foxhole I'm sharing with the RTO. We can talk there."

The two men scurried down the pathway and moved as quickly and quietly as possible through the pitch-blackness.

"L-T, is that you?" A voice inquired from below.

"Yes, Spencer, Sergeant Kowalski is with me."

They reached the two-man hole and joined the RTO who sat on the back ledge of his foxhole, letting his feet dangle into the blackness of the hole. Spencer held the handset to his ear.

"Anything change, Spencer?"

"No sir, still the same."

"Sergeant, something's not quite right. Earlier when I tried to contact the battalion FO in the CP to coordinate the fire mission against the rocket launchers, I couldn't reach Fuzzy and had to call the firebase directly."

"Did you try contacting the captain?"

"Yeah, there's no answer there either."

"I've been able to speak with Second and Third Platoons, but haven't had any luck contacting the Fourth or the CP," Spencer volunteered.

"Who was on the hill that just got rocketed?"

"Nobody knows."

"Spencer, switch to the battalion net and see if there's any traffic there."

The RTO dialed in the frequency and listened intently. "Sounds like Fourth Platoon is on the horn with battalion."

"Let me have the handset, Spencer."

Somebody from the Fourth Platoon spoke directly to the colonel, but John did not recognize the voice. When he heard the call sign, he knew then that it was the platoon sergeant. Four rockets had landed on the hilltop; there were many injured and dead. Only the one radio survived, leaving the sergeant to try to coordinate everything at the same time. The colonel responded that he would direct all support units to use the company frequency, making it easier for the sergeant and everyone else.

Flares started popping over the glowing hilltop, hanging in the air and providing much needed light to those below. A number of gunships came on station and circled overhead; only their running lights were on, the red beacons moving about like fireflies. There was no need for them to fire yet, but their presence allowed the pilots of the Medevac helicopters to feel more secure during the evacuations. In fact, several red flashing lights were aligned in the sky and moving toward the hilltop at that very moment. One by one, they dropped out of sight as they landed, then reappeared in the sky seconds later, executing tight turns and heading back the way they came.

"Looks like the Medevacs are extracting the wounded. Is there any word on the casualties or the CP?"

"Not yet L-T. The sergeant has his hands full coordinating the artillery, gunships, and Medevac pilots during all this chaos. Even the colonel is keeping quiet."

The men continued to watch the activity to their front and saw the string of flashing red lights of the Medevac Choppers heading back to the hilltop fifteen minutes later. Meanwhile, the L-T passed around a message that rockets had landed on the hill where Fourth Platoon had their NDP - the same hill where all the activity was taking place. His neighbor to the right acknowledged and passed it on to the next foxhole. John wondered what would happen when the message got to his vacant hole. Somehow, two minutes later, the message completed the circuit.

"I'm really concerned about what's happening on that hilltop. Wasn't the CP supposed to be attached to the Fourth Platoon tonight?"

"I believe you're right, sergeant. Maybe that's why we can't reach them on any of the frequencies; maybe the radios are just damaged."

"Hopefully, you're right. It does bother me, though, to see so many Medevac choppers landing. A shitload of people got hurt on that hilltop, L-T."

John handed the receiver back to Spencer. "Let us know when the platoon sergeant starts to brief the colonel about his situation."

"No problem!"

John was anxious to find out about Cotton Top, Stud, Fuzzy, and Cap. From what he had heard so far, it did not look good. It seemed that even if they sustained damage to the radios, one of the CP members would be communicating with the colonel instead of the platoon sergeant.

At five in the morning, the sky to their east began to lighten, signaling the approaching dawn of a new day.

"L-T, the colonel's on the horn with the sergeant."

This time the L-T took the handset.

"Four 122mm rockets hit the hilltop. The first one landed in the midst of the CP, killing everyone and destroying the radios. All in all, nine killed, thirty-one wounded; platoon strength is less than twenty. Some of the troops have minor wounds and are still with the platoon. Survivors will be pulled from the hill at first light and brought back to the rear area."

"L-T, if it's okay with you, I want to head back to my foxhole. We've got another hour before daylight and we still need to keep our guard up until we're pulled off this hill."

He nodded his head in agreement. John returned uphill and then back down into his own foxhole. Once there, he informed his neighbors of his return.

John was overwrought with grief. The CP took a direct hit and they were all dead. He thought back to that last day they spent together. It was the day of his promotion, and John remembered the mock ceremony and homemade paper stripes. The smiling faces of Cotton Top, Stud, Fuzzy, and even the captain burned fresh into his memory.

Did fate put him in the First Platoon? The 'Man' upstairs must have had other plans for him. He shuddered to think that if he had not received the promotion, he would most likely have been on that hilltop and had his life snuffed out along with the other members of the CP. He was devastated by their losses, but so very thankful that he survived.

John tried to shake the visions from his head and knew he must put aside his emotions for the time being and focus on the situation at hand. He was not out of the woods yet, and still had to survive until he was on the plane leaving for home. By this time in his tour of duty, he had been forced to learn to compartmentalize his feelings. There would be time to grieve later.

In the morning, a gaggle of choppers picked up the First Platoon and transported them to another hilltop on the outskirts of the A Shau Valley. As the men jumped off the chopper, John thanked them and wished them well. He remained on board and waved to the men as they deployed around the hilltop to secure the new perimeter.

He would never forget the looks on their faces as he left the bush for the last time, finally returning to Phu Bai for out-processing.

By eleven-thirty in the morning, John had returned all his supplies and weapon, received his travel orders, and said his final goodbyes. John and the First Sergeant shared a sincere and deep hug before boarding a truck in the convoy heading for Cam Rahn Bay.

At eight-thirty the next morning - August 4, 1971 – two hundred and twenty soldiers boarded a Pan American jet, bound for the United States. Chronologically, they were all very young, many not even old enough to legally buy beer to celebrate when getting home. Every one of them, however, looked ten years older than when they had arrived. The pain, suffering, and horror they had experienced during the past year were evident - especially in their eyes, which appeared distant and hollow. Faces were drawn tight, ravaged by stress and fear. Some of the men who boarded had eyes wide in disbelief, unable to believe that the war was finally over for them. They followed those in front of them on 'automatic pilot'.

It was very quiet onboard as the jet taxied to the far side of the airfield and then turned onto the main runway. The turbines whined loudly, pushing everyone back into their seats when the plane accelerated. All on board held their breath at the sound and mechanically waited for the mortars and rockets to land. As soon as the wheels of the aircraft left the ground, there was one huge cheer. Everyone clapped. Many finally smiled; others sat silently and wept.

"Polack" sat back in his seat, thankful that he had somehow survived this war; it was truly a miracle after all he had been through. Zeke had called it 'luck' and said that a person either had it or he did not. John thought about it and agreed that he had his share of luck during his tour of duty. He should have died or have been seriously injured on several occasions, but luck allowed him to make it. He clasped his hands behind his head, and looked up at the ceiling overhead. He noticed a tiny inscription scrawled next to one of the air nozzles and had to get out of his seat to read it: 'When I die, I'm going straight to Heaven – because I've already served my time in Hell.'

He sat back down and smiled broadly, knowing that he would never experience anything like this ever again. The rest of his life would be charmed.

# EPILOGUE

The return flight took them across the northern route over Japan and Alaska to their destination in Ft. Lewis, Washington.

There, they were shepherded off the plane and moved across the landing field to a large building. On the way, many signs were posted along the sides of buildings and fences. Some said the country was proud of them. Some offered thanks. Others simply read 'Welcome Home'. There was no military band to greet the returning warriors, and not a single person stood to the side to cheer their return, to applaud or wave to show that they were happy that the young men were finally home, safe and sound. Instead, it was a silent and dreary arrival, with only one column of men wordlessly marching across the tarmac.

Once inside the building, everyone stripped, showered, endured another physical examination, and then requisitioned new uniforms, much smaller than what they wore a year earlier. John was surprised at how much he had changed physically, rarely noticing it while in Vietnam. He remembered that upon leaving for war, he weighed 196 pounds and had a thirty-six inch waist. That day, he weighed 155 pounds and had a twenty-nine inch waist.

When the veterans were all fully dressed with their appropriate ribbons and campaign medals in place, the soldiers were escorted to yet another building where they were served a steak dinner.

There were no speeches or parades. When they finished eating, a bus drove them to the airport to make their own connection home.

The whole process had repeated itself thousands of times since the war started. To many of the returning veterans, it all just happened too quickly. On one night the enemy was shooting at you and the bodies of your dead friends lay nearby - then, four days later, John Kowalski was sitting on his front porch in Detroit, watching cars drive by and kids playing in the street. There was no transition period for him to adjust to life back "in the world".

John did not regret anything he did during his time in Vietnam, but found life difficult upon his return. He was the only person from his high school graduating class and group of friends that went to Vietnam; there was nobody to share his experiences with, or anyone who had any understanding whatsoever of what he had endured during those last twelve months.

Friends and family tried to understand, but had no ability to comprehend or even imagine what he was telling them. He only got so far before their eyes glazed over. In their minds, it was just a bunch of exaggerated war stories, blown out of proportion. After all, it would be impossible for somebody to actually endure all of that.

Most of these conversations ended with John apologizing, saying, "Sorry, I guess you would have had to have been there to fully understand."

John never heard from his former friends in Vietnam, and was not sure if they even survived the war. Most had only used first names and nicknames, and trying to find them afterwards was an exercise in futility.

At the time, he could never have imagined breaking the powerful bonds he had formed with other young soldiers from across the country as they withstood matters of life and death together, but sadly, once back in the world, he was never to have contact with his "brothers" again.

#####

I hope you enjoyed my story, and I would appreciate if you could take few moments to leave a review at your favorite retailer. This is the only way for authors to get feedback regarding their work, and without it, improvements are difficult to make. Thank you for your continued support!

You might also be interested in visiting my website for more articles, pictures, videos, music and reader comments about my books and the Vietnam War. Check it out here:

*https://cherrieswriter.com*

## More books by this author:

***When Can I Stop Running? A Vietnam War Story:*** Outstanding read that paints a dramatic picture of what it was like to man an LP (listening post) in enemy territory on a night that never seems to end. Interwoven with the story is flashbacks from the author's youth when terrifying events scared him into running for his life. But now, in the darkness, a short distance from the enemy, he cannot run. He must stay at his assigned station, maintain total silence, and report enemy activities to his headquarters.

It is one thing to read that our soldiers were sent from their outposts, in teams of two, to maintain reconnaissance of the enemy territory. It is quite another to learn the intimate details of what that entailed. This book paints a graphic picture of everything involved in LP duty - constant mosquito bites, sitting in a mud hole being pelted by rain, hearing (and smelling) enemy soldiers taking their latrine breaks mere feet away.

The descriptions are extremely well-crafted and vivid, and the flashbacks might evoke memories from your own reckless youth.

Find it here:

https://www.amazon.com/When-Can-I-Stop-Running-ebook/dp/B01H9BESNC

***Unhinged – A Micro Read:*** Two fourteen-year-old boys are offered a great first-time opportunity to watch a movie by themselves at a local drive-in theater. Little did they realize that the movie would affect them in ways neither imagined nor will ever forget.

Find it here:

https://www.amazon.com/Unhinged-Micro-Read-John-Podlaski-ebook/dp/B089LGHPZJ

***Unwelcomed: A Short Story*** - John Kowalski makes it home from the Vietnam War in one piece, and his battles are finally over.

Or so he thought. Home for less than a week, John must defend his family from a pair of unwelcomed thugs hell-bent on revenge.

Find it here: https://www.amazon.com/Unwelcomed-Short-Story-John-Podlaski-ebook/dp/B08GY46XGZ

*Death in the Triangle* is a sequel to "When Can I Stop Running?". That was one hell of a night!

Only a couple of hours passed since returning to the firebase, now, the sleep deprived, and weary First Platoon soldiers must go back out on another patrol. Last night, an enemy mortar team fired several rounds into the base and was soon silenced by return artillery fire. The Third Squad also ambushed a group of enemy soldiers leaving nine dead bodies on the trail before moving out to a new location. A thorough search of both areas may locate items overlooked in the dark. It was thought to be an easy patrol – two clicks out and two clicks back, so the brass expected their return before lunch. At least, that was the plan.

Many patrols during the Vietnam War did not quite go as planned and this was one of them. These soldiers soon found themselves in dire straits to satisfy their battalion commander's thirst for body counts and fame. Will they all survive?

Sixpack, Polack, LG, and the bunch are back in this new installment from the award-winning author of "Cherries: A Vietnam War Novel."

Find it here:

https://www.amazon.com/Death-Triangle-Vietnam-War-Story-ebook/dp/B096R3TTMD

**2-27-70 – A Short Story:** I grew up in the city of Detroit and was taught that my heritage and strong family values were important. Every year, our birthdays were a cherished event within the family –

especially when it was dad's special day – we always celebrated his with great fanfare, a special family dinner and dessert.

However, on February 27, 1970, my dad's birthday, that annual tradition was broken when I was forced into a situation beyond my control. I had to leave home and the family gave me an emotional send off, but the thought and possibility of my never returning devastated them.

This short story follows me on this one special day. Thousands of young men preceded me on this path, and tens of thousands never made it home. Find out where I was heading and why I had to go.

Here's the link:

https://www.amazon.com/2-27-70-John-Podlaski-ebook/dp/B0B4TVSBSN

## About the author:

John Podlaski served in Vietnam during 1970 and 1971 as an infantryman with both the Wolfhounds of the 25th Division and the 501st Infantry Brigade of the 101st Airborne Division. His awards include the Combat Infantry Badge, Bronze Star, two Air Medals, and a Vietnamese Cross of Gallantry. He has spent the years since Vietnam working in various management positions within the automotive industry, and recently received his Bachelor of Science degree in Business Administration. John is a member of both the Vietnam Veterans of America Chapter 154 and The Great Lakes South East Michigan Chapter of Harley Owners Group (HOG) and lives with his wife of thirty-eight years, Janice, in Sterling Heights, Michigan. This is his first novel.

## Cast of main characters
## In order of appearance

**John Kowalski** – Lead character from Detroit and protagonist – also called "**Polack**".
**Bill Sayers** – Best friend of John Kowalski, Bill is from Tennessee. Buds since their first day in the Army.
**Junior Brown** – African American soldier from Detroit who takes John under his wing, helping him prepare for the field. John spends his first night at the firebase pulling guard duty with Junior and gets his first indoctrination to war. Junior also teaches him many valuable lessons during their time together.
**Captain Fowler** – Company commander of Alpha Company.
**Lieutenant Ramsey** - Leader of the First Platoon, also called "**L-T**". He eventually develops pneumonia and is forced by the captain to leave the field.
**Larry Nickels** – Trained with both John and Bill during Basic and AIT, joining them in VN. This Cherry felt comfortable carrying the M60 machine gun and was eventually Medevac'd with malaria.
**Sergeant Holmes** – Training NCO of the AIT platoon which Larry, Bill and John were assigned to in Fort Polk. This is his second tour forced to volunteer because of stateside fights with pacifists about the war; also called "**Sixpack**". He rotates between squad leader and platoon leader in the absence of officers and ends up going to the 101st with John.
**Zeke** – Most seasoned soldier in the First Squad, he only has thirty days left on his tour and is anxious to get back home. Zeke was awarded the Bronze Star with a "V" device for bravery when he rescued wounded soldiers during a firefight. He is also an explosive expert and solely responsible for setting up mechanical ambushes.
**Frenchie** – Seasoned squad member in First Platoon, who carries the M79 grenade launcher and is the other explosive experts in the squad. He, Wild Bill and Scout all arrived at the same time and plan to go home in February. Frenchie remains in the background and just does his job.
**Scout** – Cherokee Indian and fellow squad member who spent much of his time walking point during many of the patrols. Scout woke

John for his first night of guard duty in the jungle NDP and stayed with him until he was accustomed to the dark. Scout is the most outspoken of the squad members and comments on everything.
**Doc** – African American medic for the platoon. He and John are normally in close proximity of one another and often spend their breaks and free time together. Doc is scheduled to leave at the end of January and is second to Zeke with time spent in country.
**Wild Bill** – aka Bill Hickock, a former rodeo star and cowboy from Texas, who befriends John while building bunkers in a new firebase. Wild Bill is scheduled to go home in February with Scout and Frenchie, he is second to Scout in voicing his opinions.
**Nung** – Former VC soldier, who surrendered to the Americans early in the war, was retrained and assigned as the First Platoon's "Kit Carson" Scout. He was a valuable resource to the men in the First Platoon and watched over his allied American friends. Nung was a good teacher and shared his skills with the rest of the squad members.
**Bob, the L-T's RTO** – Not actually part of the First Squad, but participates in patrols with them at times.
**Billie Joe Johnson** – New replacement, who joined the squad in FSB Lynch and was quickly nicknamed "**BJ**" and assigned as Larry's ammo bearer. He is from Alabama and full of questions.John takes him under his wing and teaches him about the bush, just as Junior Brown did for him during his first few days in the field.
**Lieutenant Stryker** - New 2nd Lieutenant for the First Platoon. He wasn't too sharp and was nicknamed "**Rubber Duckie**". During his first mission in the field, he makes a critical error that results in the injuries of two First Platoon soldiers.
**Lieutenant Alphonso Rodriguez** – New First Lieutenant assigned to lead the First Platoon after Rubber Ducky leaves. He had been in country for many months and was reassigned from the First Cavalry, which recently pulled out of the country. He preferred that the men call him "**Rod**". The L-T is from Hollywood and shares much of his personal life with John, who soon becomes his RTO.
**Danny Jigelewski** – New Cherry and former gang member from New Jersey. He is quickly nicknamed "**Ski**". Danny finds himself

at home and very comfortable with his new squad members, aka "new gang members". He is gung ho and ready to contribute in any situation. He later volunteers to be the slackman whenever John walks point.

**Malcolm Dupree** – African American Cherry from Jackson, Mississippi. Top outfitted him with the M79 grenade launcher and vest prior to coming out to the bush. He, too, remains in the background.

**First Sergeant Trombley** – Head NCO for Alpha Company 1/501st Airborne, who took a liking to John and agreed to help him get a job in the company CP carrying a radio for **Captain Robertson** – Leader of Alpha Company 1/501, who accepts John as a new member of the company CP. As with most officers of this rank, he preferred to be called "**Cap**" and is later instrumental in helping John get a promotion to sergeant.

**Cotton Top** – Company CP member carrying the battalion radio, he looks to be fifteen years old and is so nicknamed because of his light blond nubby hair.

**Fuzzy** – Eldest member of the CP and is the Forward Observer for the firebase artillery unit. In the field, it was his responsibility to pre-determine defensive targets around NDP's, and assist with radio watch. He was also the direct liaison between the grunts and the support units.

**Stud** – final member of the CP. Works in tandem with Fuzzy on the artillery and controls the fast movers whenever they are in the area.

**Lieutenant Bozolynsky** – Cherry ROTC Lieutenant assigned to the First Platoon. After receiving his promotion, John was assigned to the First Platoon to help train and mentor the new officer. Initially, they butt heads, and a feud develops, which disrupts the platoon during a precarious time in the mission.

# Glossary of Terms
## Taken in part from Viet Nam Generation, Inc Sixties Project, copyright (c) 1996

**Actual**: The unit commander. Used to distinguish the commander from the radioman when the call sign is used over the radio.
**Advanced Individual Training**: Specialized training taken after Basic Training, also referred to as AIT, i.e. infantry, cook school, armor, helicopters, artillery, etc.
Airborne: Refers to soldiers who are qualified to jump out of planes with chutes.
**AK-47**: Soviet combat assault rifle that fires a 7.62-mm round - primary weapon of VC / NVA
**Ammo dump**: Location where live or expended ammunition is stored in any compound
**AO**: Area of operations – designated area where an infantry unit will patrol through
**APC**: Armored personnel carrier. A tracked vehicle used to transport Army troops or supplies ARVN: Army of the Republic of Vietnam; the South Vietnamese Regular Army and US ally
**Azimuth**: A compass bearing to a set location or point of travel
**B-40 rocket**: A shoulder-held rocket-propelled grenade launcher also called RPG
**B-52**: U.S. Air Force high-altitude bomber – dropped 500# bombs leaving hundreds of craters.
**Bandolier**: A cloth cummerbund filled with two-hundred rounds of .223 caliber ammunition for the M16. Soldiers usually refill their magazines with these rounds and then store the filled magazines in the five pouches of the bandolier; laces on both ends allow the rifleman to secure it almost anywhere.
**Basecamp**: A large, permanent base in the "rear area" that supports brigade or division size units, artillery batteries and airfields. It is here where all new recruit training and standown occur, and where headquarters, mail, supplies, aircraft and ammo are stored.
**Basic: Basic training** – first eight weeks of military training when one enters the service.

**Battalion:** A military unit composed of a headquarters and two or more companies, batteries, or similar units comprised of 400 + personnel.

**Beehive round:** An artillery shell, containing thousands of small flechettes (nails with fins) that exit the barrel when the weapon fires. This mimics a shotgun. A 40mm version is also available for M79's.

**Berm:** Perimeter fortification comprised of bulldozed earth raised higher than the surrounding area - usually found surrounding smaller firebases.

**Bird:** Any aircraft, but usually refers to helicopters

**Blasting cap:** An electronic detonator similar in size to a short silver pencil - two-fifty foot long attached thin wires send an electrical charge to the cap – either by battery or manually via a detonation clacker. When exploding by itself, it sounds like a small firecracker.

**Blood trail:** A trail of blood left on the ground or vegetation by a wounded man, who is trying to get away. The amounts vary from periodic droplets to puddles.

**Body bag:** Thick, plastic, zippered bag used to transport dead bodies from the field.

**Body count:** The number of enemy killed, wounded, or captured during an operation. The term was used by Washington and Saigon as a means of measuring the progress of the war.

**Boony hat:** Soft cloth hat with a brim, similar to a fishing hat, worn by infantry soldiers in the boonies.

**Boonies:** Infantry term for the field; jungles or swampy areas far from the comforts of civilization.

**Bouncing Betty:** Antipersonnel mine with two charges: the first propels the explosive charge upward, and the other is set to explode at about waist level.

**Breaking squelch:** Disrupting the natural static of a radio by depressing the transmit bar on another radio set to the same frequency, also called keying the mike.

**Bro / Brother:** A black soldier; also, at times, referencing fellow soldiers from the same unit

**Bronze Star:** U.S. military decoration awarded for heroic or meritorious service in combat

**BS**: Bullshit, as in chewing the fat, telling tall tales, or telling lies
**Bummer**: Bad luck, a real drag
**Bush**: Infantry term for the field

**C-4**: Plastic, putty textured explosive carried by infantry soldiers to blow up bunkers and weapon caches. When not compressed, it burns like sterno and was sometimes used to heat C-rations in the field.
**Cache**: Hidden supplies
**C&C**: Command and control helicopter used by reconnaissance or unit commanders
**Cav**: Cavalry; the 1st Cavalry Division (Airmobile)
**Charlie**: Viet Cong; the enemy
**Cherry**: Slang term for youth and inexperience; a virgin
**Chinook**: Twin bladed CH-47 cargo helicopter used to transport troops and equipment
**Chop chop**: Vietnamese slang for food
**Chopper**: Any helicopter
**Chuck**: Term used by black soldiers to identify white individuals; often derogatory
**CIB**: Combat infantry badge. An Army award received after coming under enemy fire in a combat zone.
**Clacker**: A small hand-held firing device for a claymore mine
**Claymore**: An antipersonnel mine carried by the infantry which, when detonated, propels small 25mm steel balls in a 60-degree fan-shaped pattern to a maximum distance of 100 meters.
**Clearance**: Permission from both military and political authorities to engage the enemy in a particular area – usually near populated areas.
**Cobra**: Narrow, two-man AH-1G attack helicopter / gunship, armed with rockets and machine guns.
**Commo**: Short for "communications"
**Commo bunker**: Bunker containing vital communications equipment normally within a battalion-sized firebase, where communications is maintained with all the battalion elements outside of the camp. Usually houses the Colonel and Executive Officer.
**Commo wire**: Communications wire similar to phone wire

**Company**: Military unit usually consisting of a headquarters and two or more platoons usually comprised of 150 + personnel.
**Compound**: Any fortified military installation
**Concertina wire**: Coiled barbed wire used as an obstacle and normally surrounding compounds
**Contact**: Engaged with the enemy in a firefight
**C-rations**: Combat rations. Canned meals for use in the field; each consisting of a basic course, a can of fruit, a packet of some type of dessert, a packet of powdered coca, a four-pack of cigarettes, and two pieces of chewing gum.
**CS**: Riot-control gas which burns the eyes and mucus membranes

**Dai uy**: Vietnamese for captain
**Dap**: Handshake and greeting which may last up to ten minutes and is characterized by the use of both hands and often comprised of slaps and snaps of the fingers. Used by black soldiers, highly ritualized and unit specific.
**Det-cord**: White, rope like cord used with explosives or as a stand along
**Deuce-and-a-half**: Two-and-a-half ton truck – ten wheeler with cab and large bed used for transporting equipment and personnel; usually covered with a canvas roof.
**DMZ**: Demilitarized zone. The dividing line between North and South Vietnam established in 1954 at the Geneva Convention.
**Doc**: Any medic or corpsman
**Dust-off:** Medical evacuation by helicopter

**Elephant grass**: Tall, razor-edged tropical plant that grows in dense clumps up to ten feet high. The grass is the favorite meal for elephants and also for feeding livestock and wildlife.
Eleven Bravo: The military occupation specialty description for an infantryman
**E-tool**: Entrenching tool. Folding shovel carried by infantrymen.
**Evac'd**: Evacuated
**F-4**: Phantom jet fighter-bombers. Range: 1,000 miles. Speed: 1400 mph. Payload: 16,000 lbs. The workhorse of the tactical air support fleet.

**Fast mover**: An F-4 jet
**Fatigues:** Standard combat uniform, green in color
**FSB**: Fire support base
**Firebase**: Temporary artillery encampment used for fire support of forward ground operations
**Firefight**: A battle or exchange of fire with the enemy
**Flak jacket**: Heavy fiberglass-filled vest worn for protection against shrapnel
**Flare:** Illumination projectile; hand-fired or shot from artillery, mortars, or dropped by aircraft. They float on parachutes and depending upon size, could last several minutes.
**Flechette:** A small dart-shaped projectile clustered in an explosive warhead. A mine without great explosive power containing small pieces of shrapnel intended to wound and kill.
**FNG**: Acronym for fucking new guy or cherry
**Frag:** Fragmentation grenade
**Fragging**: The assassination of an officer by his own troops, usually by a grenade
**Freak**: Radio frequency, also, a junkie or doper.
**Freedom Bird**: The plane taking soldiers from Vietnam back to the World after their tours end
**Free fire zone**: Designated zone where soldiers are free to fire upon suspected targets without having to await permission - area where everyone was deemed hostile and can be fired upon.
**Friendly fire**: Accidental attacks on U.S. or allied soldiers by other U.S. or allied soldiers
**Fucked up**: Wounded or killed, also, stoned, drunk, foolish or doing something stupid.

**GI:** Government issue. Usually refers to an American soldier or supplies owned by the military.
**Gook:** Derogatory term for an Asian, most often-used name for enemy soldiers
**Grunt**: Infantryman in Vietnam
**Gung ho**: Enthusiastic and ready to go
**Gunship:** Armed helicopter with rocket pods and side mounted mini-guns.

**H&I** : Harassment and Intimidation - random artillery fire into suspected hostile areas to keep the enemy off balance.
**Hard-stripe sergeant**: Rank indicated by three chevron insignia, equivalent to an E5 – lowest grade of a non-commissioned officer.
**Heart**: Purple Heart award for a wound; the wound itself
**Heat tabs**: Flammable tablet used to heat C-rations that were always in short supply. These tabs were not a hot as C4 and took longer to cook a meal that wasn't as hot.
**Ho Chi Minh sandals**: Sandals made from tires. The soles are made from the tread and the straps from inner tubes. All VC and many local villagers wore these.
**Hooch / Hootch**: A hut or simple dwelling, either military or civilian where people can sleep.
**Hoochgirl:** Vietnamese woman employed by American military as maid or laundress
**Horn:** Radio microphone
**Hot LZ**: Landing zone under enemy fire
**HQ:** Headquarters
**Huey:** Nickname for the UH-1 series helicopters
**Hump:** March or hike carrying a rucksack and full supplies

**Illum**: Illumination flare, usually fired by a mortar or artillery weapon
**Immersion foot**: Condition resulting from feet being submerged in water for a prolonged period of time, causing cracking and bleeding. Also called jungle rot or trench foot.
**In-country**: Within the country of Vietnam
**Iron Triangle**: Viet Cong dominated area between the Thi-Tinh and Saigon rivers, next to Cu Chi district; an area laced with enemy supply trails, which transport goods into South Vietnam from the Ho Chi Minh trail in Cambodia.

**Jungle boots**: Footwear that looks like a combination of combat boot and canvas sneaker used by the U.S. military in a tropical climate, where leather rots because of the dampness. The canvas structure also speeds drying after crossing streams, rice paddies, etc

**Jungle penetrator**: Winch and cable device used by Medevac helicopters to extract wounded soldiers from dense jungle locations where an LZ is not available. They are usually used in conjunction with either a seat or a flat platform where the patient is tied in and pulled up through the thick, overhead canopy and into the helicopter.
**Jungle rot**: Skin disease common in tropical climates. Symptoms are similar to trench foot and immersion foot where the skin cracks, itches, and blisters may form, followed by skin and tissue dying and falling off. This was difficult to treat because of the harsh tropical environment.

**KIA**: Killed in action
**Kill zone**: The radius of a circle around an explosive device within which it is predicted that 95 percent of all occupants will be killed should the device explode
**Kit Carson scout**: Former Viet Cong who act as guides for U.S. military units
**Klick**: Kilometer – one-thousand meters or six-tenths of a mile
**KP**: Kitchen police; mess hall duty
**LAW**: Shoulder-fired, 66-millimeter rocket, similar in effect to a 3.5-inch rocket, except that the launcher is made of Fiberglass, and is disposable after one shot
**LBJ**: Long Binh Jail, a military stockade on the Long Binh post
**Lifer**: Career military man. The term is often used in a derogatory manner.
**Litters**: Stretchers to carry dead and wounded
**Loach**: Small two passenger LOH helicopter used by military as decoys to lure the enemy into firing upon this small craft. Usually, they are part of a hunter-killer team, and after identifying the enemy, gunships attack the suspect area
**LP**: Listening post. A two or three-man position set up at night outside the perimeter away from the main body of troops, which acts as an early warning system against attack.
**LRRP**: Long Range Reconnaissance Patrol. An elite team usually composed of five to seven men who go deep into the jungle to observe enemy activity without initiating contact.

**L-T**: Acronym for lieutenant and used primarily in the field**LZ**: Landing zone. A clearing designated for the landing of helicopters. Used for combat assaults, resupply and medical evacuation.

**M-16**: Standard U.S. military rifle used in Vietnam from 1966 onward
**M-60**: Standard lightweight machine gun used by U.S. forces in Vietnam. It weighs twenty-three pounds and fires 7.62mm ammunitions – same as an AK-47.
**M-79**: U.S. military hand-held 40mm grenade launcher sometimes called a blooper
**MA**: Mechanical ambush - an American set booby trap using claymore mines.
**Mad minute**: An all-out weapons free-fire, used for testing weapons or firing into suspected enemy locations prior to an element sweeping through the area.
**MARS**: Military Affiliate Radio Station. Used by soldiers to call home via Signal Corps and ham radio equipment.
**Marker round**: First round fired by mortars or artillery, used for confirming a location on a map or an adjustment point when firing upon the enemy.
**Mechanized platoon**: A platoon operating with tanks and/or armored personnel carriers
**Medevac**: Medical evacuation from the field by helicopter
**MIA**: Missing in action
**Minigun**: Electronically controlled, extremely rapidly firing machine gun. Most often mounted on aircraft to be used against targets on the ground – similar to a Gatling gun.
**Mortar**: A muzzle-loading cannon with a short tube in relation to its caliber that throws projectiles with low muzzle velocity at high angles.
**MOS**: Military occupational specialty
**MP**: Military police
**MPC**: Military payment currency. The scrip U.S. soldiers were paid in.
**Nam**: Vietnam

**Napalm**: A jellied petroleum substance which burns fiercely, and is used as a weapon against personnel. The burst is so hot that the oxygen is literally removed from the air and some enemy soldiers had died from suffocation instead of the flames.
**NCO**: Noncommissioned officer, usually a squad leader or platoon sergeant.
**NDP**: Night defensive position where platoon-sized or larger units set-up sleeping and defensive positions in a circle. Claymore mines and trip flares are used outside of the perimeter and a guard position routinely positioned in the center where individuals rotate on hourly watches.
**Net**: Radio frequency setting, from "network."
**No sweat**: Slang for easy or simple
**NVA**: North Vietnamese Army – these soldiers complete formal training just like the Americans

**Observation post**: Similar to a listening post but implemented during the day

**Papa san**: Used by U.S. servicemen for any older Vietnamese man
**Perimeter**: Outer boundaries of a military position. The area beyond the perimeter belongs to the enemy.
**PFC**: Private first class – enlisted rank achieved usually after completing AIT
**Platoon**: A subdivision of a company-sized military unit, normally consisting of two or more squads or sections containing 40 + personnel
**Point**: The forward man or element on a combat patrol
**Poncho**: Five-foot square, plastic coated nylon poncho had a permanently attached hood in the center, and snap fasteners down both sides. Used as a rain cape, blanket, sleeping bag cover, ground cover for sleeping, tent half and litter to carry wounded soldiers.
**Poncho liner**: Thin, lightweight, nylon comforter used as a blanket or insert for a poncho.
**Pop smoke**: Request to ignite a smoke grenade to signal an aircraft.

**PRC-25**: Portable Radio Communications, Model 25. A backpacked FM receiver-transmitter used for short-distance communications. The range of the radio was 5-10 kilometers.
**Prick 25**: Slang for the PRC-25 radio
**R&R**: Short for rest and recreation, this is usually a three to seven-day vacation from the war for a soldier.
**Red alert: The most urgent form of warning, this signals an imminent enemy attack.**
**REMF**: Acronym for rear area support soldiers; infantry soldiers refer to them as (rear-echelon motherfuckers)
**RIF**: Reconnaissance in force.
**Rome plow**: Mammoth bulldozer used to flatten dense jungle and create berms on **perimeters**
**ROTC**: Reserve Officer's Training Corps. Program offered in many high schools and colleges, geared to prepare students to become military officers.
**RPG**: Rocket-propelled grenade, a Russian-made portable antitank grenade launcher.
**RTO**: Radio telephone operator, carries his unit's radio on his back in the field.
**Ruck/rucksack**: Backpack issued to infantry in Vietnam to carry rations and other supplies

**Saddle up**: Command given to put on one's pack and get ready to march
**Sapper**: A Viet Cong or NVA commando armed with explosives, his goal is to infiltrate defensive perimeters prior to a planned ground attack, opening lanes of attack for the enemy.
**Satchel charges**: Pack used by the enemy containing fused explosives that is dropped or thrown; they are powerful and can destroy bunkers and other equipment.
**Search and destroy**: An operation in which Americans searched an area and destroyed anything which the enemy might find useful
Shit burning: The burning of waste at remote firebase locations using kerosene and diesel fuel, this duty, considered the worst overall, was dreaded and looked upon as punishment.

**Short**: A term used by soldiers in Vietnam to signify that his tour was almost over
**Short-timer**: Soldier nearing the end of his tour in Vietnam
**Shrapnel**: Pieces of metal sent flying by an explosion, i.e. bomb, grenade, mortar, artillery.
**Sit-rep**: Short for a situation report, command personnel routinely contacted units in the field hourly for these updates
**SKS**: A Russian 7.62 mm semi-automatic carbine – not too many were used by the enemy.
**Slackman**: The second man on a patrol, following behind the point man to cover his back. He usually scans the treetops and flank areas; takes compass readings and counts steps.
**Slick**: UH-1 helicopter used for transporting troops in tactical air assault operations. The helicopter did not have protruding armaments and was, therefore, "slick".
Smoke grenade: A canister, armed similar to a grenade, emits brightly colored smoke after the contents are ignited by the blasting cap. They are available in various colors and used for signaling.
**Spec-4**: Specialist 4th Class. An Army rank immediately above Private First Class. Most enlisted men who had completed their individual training and had been on duty for a few months were Spec-4s, the most common rank in the Vietnam-era Army.
**Spider hole**: Camouflaged enemy foxhole with an overhead cover that raises and lowers after firing – sniper is well hidden and hard to find. Sometimes these holes are connected to small escape tunnels.
**Squad**: Small military unit consisting of less than ten men
**Staff sergeant**: E-6, the second lowest noncommissioned officer rank
**Stand-down**: An infantry unit's return from the boonies to the base camp for refitting, training and resting.
**Starlight scope**: An image intensifier using reflected light to identify targets at night
**Steel pot**: The standard U.S. Army helmet. The steel pot is the outer metal cover that is sometimes used as a sink.
**Steel Helmet insert**: Fiberglass insert with straps and cushions that rest on a soldier's head – similar to a football helmet's inside. The steel pot fits over the top of this insert.

**Strobe:** Hand held strobe light for marking landing zones at night or identifying friendlies to overhead aircraft

**Ti-ti:** Vietnamese slang for a small amount or a little bit
**Top:** Nickname for a First Sergeant, the second highest non-commissioned officer rank
**Tracer**: A round of ammunition chemically treated to glow or give off smoke so that its flight can be followed. Belts of ammunitions for machine guns normally have every fifth round in the belt a tracer. When firing long bursts, the lighted round helps in adjusting the aim toward targets. Infantry soldiers usually load a couple of tracer rounds in their magazines; some only use them as a last round to signify an empty magazine. VC and NVA tracers are mostly green and USA is red.
**Tracks:** Any vehicles which move on tracks rather than wheels
**Tree line**: Row of trees at the edge of a field or rice paddy
**Trip flare:** A ground flare triggered by a trip wire used to signal and illuminate the approach of an enemy at night.
**Tropic Lighting**: The U.S. 25th Infantry Division

**USO:** United Service Organization. Provided entertainment to the troops, and was intended to raise morale.

**VC**: Viet Cong, the National Liberation Front
**Victor Charlie**: Military phonetic spelling for Viet Cong; the enemy.
**Viet Cong**: The Communist-led forces fighting the South Vietnamese government.

**Wake-up**: As in "13 and a wake-up" -- the last day of a soldier's Vietnam tour.
**Walking wounded**: Soldiers injured but still able to walk without assistance.
**Web gear**: Canvas belt and shoulder straps for packing equipment and ammunition on infantry operations – similar to a belt and suspenders.
**Weed:** Marijuana

**White phosphorus**: A type of explosive round from artillery, mortars, or rockets. The rounds exploded with a huge puff of white smoke from the hotly burning phosphorus, and were used as marking rounds or incendiary rounds. When white phosphorus hit the skin of a living creature it continued to burn until it had burned through the body. Water would not extinguish it.
**WIA**: Wounded in action
**Willy Pete**: Slang for white phosphorus
**World, the**: How soldiers referenced the United States and back home.
**XO**: Executive officer; the second in command of a military unit

**Zapped**: Killed

Made in the USA
Middletown, DE
26 June 2023